# Literature by and about the American Indian

## On Native American Literature

*Background:* The National Council of Teachers of English has supported Resolutions 698, 726, and 755 promoting an awareness of and support for the study of the literature of diverse cultural groups. However, Native American literature, both oral and written, largely has been ignored in language arts curricula. Be it therefore

*Resolved,* That Native American literature and culture be taught kindergarten through college, and be it further

*Resolved,* That programs in teacher preparation be encouraged to include resources, materials, and methods of presenting Native American literature and culture.

Resolution passed by the National Council of Teachers and English at its Sixty-Eighth Annual Meeting, 1978.

# Literature by and about the American Indian

An Annotated Bibliography

Second Edition

Anna Lee Stensland
University of Minnesota, Duluth

With contributions by
Aune M. Fadum
University of Minnesota, Duluth

National Council of Teachers of English
1111 Kenyon Road, Urbana, Illinois 61801

Book Design: Tom Kovacs, interior; V. Martin, cover

NCTE Stock Number 29846

Library of Congress Cataloging in Publication Data

Stensland, Anna Lee.
    Literature by and about the American Indian.

    Bibliography: p.
    Includes index.
    1. Indians of North America—Juvenile literature—Bibliography.   2. Indians of North America—Bibliography.
I. Title.
Z1209.S73  1979  [E77.4]    016.97′0004′97    79-18073
ISBN 0-8141-2984-6 pbk.

Such are our antiquities. These were our predecessors. Why, then, make so great ado about the Roman and the Greek, and neglect the Indian? We [need] not wander off with boys in our imagination to Juan Fernandez, to wonder at footprints in the sand there. Here is a print still more significant at our doors, the print of a race that has preceded us, and this is the little symbol that Nature has transmitted to us. Yes, *this* arrowheaded character is probably more ancient than any other, and to my mind it has not been deciphered. Man should not go to New Zealand to write or think of Greece and Rome, nor more to New England. New earths, new themes expect us. Celebrate not the Garden of Eden, but your own.

> Henry David Thoreau
> *Journals*, 1852

# Contents

*Foreword*                                                          ix

*Preface*                                                           xi


I. Teaching the Literature of the American Indian

Introduction                                                         3
   Important Themes in Indian Literature               3
   Indian Stereotypes in Literature                   11
   Indian Literature of the Mid-Seventies             20
   References                                         24

Aids for the Teacher                                                26
   Guides to Curriculum Planning                      26
   A Basic Library of Indian Literature               35
   Sources of Additional Materials                    42

Biographies of Selected American Indian Authors                    45


II. Bibliography

Introduction to the Bibliography                                   67
   Criteria for Selection                             67
   How to Use This Bibliography                       75

Myth, Legend, Oratory, and Poetry                                  77

Fiction                                                           114

Biography and Autobiography                                       187

History                                                           239

Traditional Life and Culture                                      279

Modern Life and Problems                                          320

Music, Arts, and Crafts                                           337

*Directory of Publishers*                                        355

*Author Index*                                                   363

*Title Index*                                                    370

# Foreword

Nearly four hundred years have passed since Jamestown was settled in 1607, but Americans are still intrigued with the stories, legends, poetry, songs, philosophy, history, art, and lifestyles of the peoples who are native to this country. Euro-Americans still write extensively about the "American Indian," and continue to be fascinated with the complexities of the various Indian cultures. Beyond initial fascination with a native people, the interest in the American Indian has become an absorbing study for scholars.

The fact is, this is the land of the American Indian. This is the land that was specially given to the American Indian by the Great Spirit. The American Indian has achieved self-recognition. Peoples from other countries came to this land seeking to claim it, seeking to settle, seeking to exploit it. After hundreds of years of struggle among major European nations for control over the "new land," England gained the upper hand, but not before Spain had left a most impressive mark in Florida, in Texas, and in the entire Southwest. France was active in trading, and England in settlement for homes. As these Europeans traveled across the country, they sought to rename the natives, and the names are still with us— Spanish names in the Southwest, English and Scottish in the Northeast, and French for the Lakotas of the Plains.

The colonists fought the British for their freedom, and Indian nations were split as to their allegiance. After the new nation was formed on the Atlantic Seaboard, there were bitter feelings. Foreigners dared to call this land their own. They formed a government and began to tell the Indian nations what to do. They began to make treaties, always at the protest of the Indian. They began to take the land which traditionally belonged to Indian groups and to move the native people westward. The trend continued until nearly all the land was taken. Wars were fought to keep the land and to maintain the native rights in treaties. Finally, Indians were placed on reservations in the West. After that came the Dawes Allotment Act, which took away more land on the reservation, and finally there was the lease arrangement (still in effect today) which all but robs Indians of their last remaining land. Railroads and timber interests pushed the Indian off the land and moved tribe after tribe to Indian Territory and Oklahoma after it became a state. Even there, white inroads were made. Mineral interests and water and fishing rights are so controversial that some would advocate the abolition of all Indian treaties. This is where we stand today.

There are all sorts of philosophical questions that can be discussed in relation to the American Indian on the Indian's own land and the white aggressor's interest in owning everything the Indian has, and these questions can be found in the literature by and about the American Indian. Varying points of view are held according to the experience and knowledge of the writer and, of course, the writer's attitudes towards the American Indian. Stereotypes are found in some of the writings of non-Indian authors, and some of these are biased and derogatory. We would hope for literature free of bias, but this may be a long time in coming. Ignorance is evident in some of the literature, and there are reasons for this ignorance, largely a lack of education. American Indian literature and history have been notably missing from the reading fare of American children and youth. There has been an attempt to ignore the people of the land.

We can see a change. The National Council of Teachers of English at its annual conference in Kansas City in 1978 passed a resolution to promote Native American literature and culture from kindergarten through college, urging that teacher training institutions provide adequate preparation for teachers of Native American literature and culture.

This new edition contains an abundance of new materials and a new format, making it a highly useful reference for teachers, librarians, and general readers. There are still many works *about* the American Indian. As time goes on, and as other revisions are made, more works *by* the American Indian can be added. I am glad for the effort that Anna Lee Stensland continues to make to aid teachers, and I commend the National Council of Teachers of English for supporting this effort.

Montana H. R. Walking Bull
Monmouth, Oregon
February 1979

# Preface

Since 1973 when this bibliography made its first appearance, the number of books published on the American Indian has increased significantly. Works for readers of all ages abound. The popularity of the first edition indicated that teachers, librarians, and general readers feel the need for guidance in finding books that accurately portray Native Americans. It is hoped that with so much material to choose from, this new and more comprehensive bibliography will be even more effective in meeting that need.

Nearly 800 titles have been annotated in this second edition. As many as possible of the worthwhile books published since 1973 have been added, and the number of titles published prior to that has been enlarged. Again the primary emphasis is on literature—myth, legend, poetry, fiction, and biography. But because literature cannot be considered apart from history, anthropology, the arts, and current political and social issues, selected new and older books in these fields are included.

No effort was made in the earlier edition to single out books for children of elementary school age. This shortcoming was remedied by inviting Aune M. Fadum, Assistant Professor of Elementary Education, University of Minnesota, Duluth, to select and evaluate titles for children in the primary and intermediate grades. The bibliography now gives ample proof that for this age group, too, there are many good books about the Native American. Likewise, the scope has been extended to include some Canadian, Alaskan, and Mexican Indian literature, whereas the first edition was limited mainly to literature about Native Americans living within the contiguous United States.

The idea for this book came from recurring requests for help from teachers who were looking for books to use in their classes. The Indian voice was attracting attention everywhere, and they wanted to give their students an exposure to writings that deal honestly with Indian life. I had known Indians as playmates and as high school classmates in the northern Wisconsin town where I grew up, but I soon realized that I was of little help to these teachers because I knew very little about Indian literature. Then a sabbatical leave provided the necessary free time from teaching, and I set about to correct the situation.

What began as an obligation soon became an adventure as one discovery after another revealed a valuable new item to add to the collection. Although Indians have always had a place in the study of American history, it became increasingly apparent that their literature had indeed been neglected. As the scope and significance of Indian writings enlarged in my mind, I felt more keenly the need to share information about the precious heritage of the first Americans.

The sense of purpose was intensified in the preparation of the second edition. Much has happened in the intervening years to create an ever widening public for the literature of the American Indian. Contemporary America—and indeed the world—has heard about Wounded Knee and what happened there in 1973. Now it wants to know more about events at Wounded Knee in 1890 and about other places and times that are important in Indian affairs. This amplified and updated bibliography should help to fulfill that wish. There are no pretensions that the list is all-inclusive, and readers with special favorites may not find them here. It is, however, a bountiful and representative collection that will inform its users of the many resources at their command and lead them to make other discoveries of their own. As such, this volume becomes another step in a pioneering effort to survey some of the riches of Indian writing and give them their rightful place in the body of American literature.

To Aune Fadum I express my deepest appreciation and thanks for her many hours of work in searching out the books that have been added for readers of elementary school age. I am indebted to Diane Allen and Paige Reynolds of the National Council of Teachers of English for their work with this edition in its formative stages. Special thanks go to Lorrie Bissonett, librarian of the Children's Library, University of Minnesota, Duluth, for her aid and encouragement and also, once again, to those who assisted in various ways with the first edition.

Anna Lee Stensland
Duluth, Minnesota
August 1979

# I Teaching the Literature of the American Indian

# Introduction

There are at least three good reasons for the study of Indian authors and themes in the English classroom. First, the Indian is an essential part of our American history and literature. When the Pilgrims arrived in the New World, the Indians already had an oral tradition of storytelling and ceremony which integrated all of life. Only recently have others begun to realize the richness of this literature. Second, the Indian has always furnished inspiration and characters for the classic writers and works from American literature—from Freneau to Faulkner. Unfortunately, some of these writers have helped to create generalizations and stereotypes of the Native American which need to be dispelled. Third, American Indians—with their spiritual oneness, their concept of the sacred hoop—have much to teach modern youth, many of whom find their own world dreary and materialistic. The Indian's problem of trying to live in two worlds also strikes a responsive chord in teenagers who are in search of self-realization.

In 1927 the Grand Council Fire of American Indians made these recommendations to the mayor of Chicago: "We ask only that our story be told in fairness. We do not ask you to overlook what we did, but we do ask you to understand it. A true program of America First will give a generous place to the culture and history of the American Indian." This can hardly be called an unreasonable request. Yet, in order to understand what the Indians did, it is also necessary to understand the actions of white people at the time.

### Important Themes in Indian Literature

The tragic results of the whites' betrayal and violence are themes in many biographies and novels about the Indian. Histories have now been written that are sympathetic to the Indian—notably Ralph Andrist's *Long Death: The Last Days of the Plains Indians* and Dee Brown's *Bury My Heart at Wounded Knee*—but literature adds a more personal dimension to history.

3

How the dominant culture sought to destroy a minority culture often can be understood most clearly when the reader suffers vicariously with a character in a book. In Theodora Kroeber's *Ishi*, the last surviving member of the Yahi tribe stumbles into the corral of a California ranch. Only the concern and interest of anthropologist A. L. Kroeber save Ishi from imprisonment as the dangerous "last wild Indian in North America." It was not starvation but excruciating loneliness that drove Ishi to seek aid from the race that had set out to exterminate his tribe.

## Betrayal by Whites

The whites' desire to imprison, kill, or starve an entire tribe is the theme of *A Navajo Saga*. Kay Bennett, a Navajo and co-author of the book, tells of her grandfather's family, first as they were determined to remain free in the mountains of the Southwest, then as they were hunted, and finally as they gave in to the whites' demands and joined the march to Bosque Redondo Reservation where crowded conditions, a smallpox epidemic, and tremendous suffering awaited them.

How often in American history have Indian leaders in good faith followed the whites' orders, only to be betrayed. Osceola, the Seminole chief, was captured and betrayed by General Thomas Sidney Jesup as he was brought in under the flag of truce as related in *Hunted Like a Wolf* by Milton Meltzer. Sitting Bull was living peacefully at the Standing Rock Reservation following the Indian agent's orders, when he was killed in an attempted capture to satisfy white settlers and Indian agents made nervous by the Indians' Ghost Dance (Stanley Vestal, *Sitting Bull: Champion of the Sioux* and Shannon Garst, *Sitting Bull: Champion of His People*). The massacre of Black Kettle's Cheyennes by the fanatical Colonel Chivington on Sand Creek, where they had been instructed to settle, is told in Michael Straight's novel, *A Very Small Remnant.*

In some ways among the most repressive and cruel of the white people's policies were those in the schools, because the victims were the very young. Although some of these schools may have been founded by people of good will, they nevertheless compounded the fear and loneliness brought on by life in two very different worlds. In *The Middle Five*, Francis LaFlesche, well-known Omaha Indian anthropologist, tells of the misdirected policies typical of many mission schools of the last century. For instance, three of the boys were severely punished because they ran off to join their tribe in the spring buffalo hunt. Francis was placed in a hot, stuffy dining room with his back to a post, arms tied so he could not fend off the flies that attacked his bare feet. A more severe tragedy is that of Slim Girl, in Oliver La Farge's *Laughing Boy*, whose missionary school experience taught her nothing but prostitution and the corrupt nature of white men.

Obviously the Indian way of life appeals greatly to modern young people, disillusioned by the materialism of their lives, as evidenced by the Indian headband and pseudo-Indian dress some of them have worn. A full understanding of the nature of that appeal requires the experience of a social worker and the knowledge of a psychologist, but there is no doubt that many youths have wanted to proclaim themselves the spiritual descendants of the Indians whose value system offers some attractive alternatives to their own.

## The Spirituality of Life

The oneness and spiritual nature of all life in the original tribal society is a constantly recurring theme among authors who write about Indians. Religion, food gathering, songs, poetry, ceremony—all are one. All Indians are poets and singers. They sing to capture the universal spirit and mystery, and for health in time of illness. A glance at the contents of a collection of Indian poetry (William Brandon's *The Magic World*) shows love-charm songs, a hymn for fasting, many medicine songs, a hunting song, war songs, a song for child-naming rites, a lullaby, and a mourning song.

All life to the Indian is an integrated whole, a roundness. In Hal Borland's *When the Legends Die*, Bessie prepares to take her son back to the mountains where his father has retreated following the murder of Frank No Deer, and she thinks how good it will be to know the roundness and completeness again and to be away from the rigid squareness of houses and streets. Few express this as eloquently as Eagle Voice in John Neihardt's *When the Tree Flowered* (pp. 7–8):

> The sacred hoop of our people would be broken by the evil power of the strangers, and in that time we would live in little square gray houses, and in those houses we would starve. . . . I will not live in them, for the Great Mysterious One meant all things to be round—the sky and the prairie, the sun and the moon, the bodies of men and animals, trees and the nests of birds, and the hoop of the people. The days and the seasons come back in a circle, and so do the generations. . . . It is the sacred way.

Nothing demonstrates the spiritual nature of life so much as the significance attached to a young man's having a vision to show him the way. This is the theme of *Conquering Horse* by Frederick Manfred. Young No Name has tried three times to have a vision. He has gone to the mountain; he has starved—but to no avail. Because he has not had a vision he has no name, his deeds go unrecognized, he cannot ask for the woman he loves, and he must bear the disappointment of his family. Life holds only barrenness and torment.

The stories of the great chief Crazy Horse and his dreams and visions are part of the history and legend of the Sioux. Mari Sandoz in her fine adult biography, *Crazy Horse: The Strange Man of the Oglalas*, and Shannon Garst in his elementary biography, *Crazy Horse: Great Warrior of the Sioux*, give details of his life. But it is in Vinson Brown's small biography, *Great upon the Mountain*, that we find emphasis on the chief's spiritual crises and his visionary life. The change that came over the young Crazy Horse upon witnessing the death of the great chief Conquering Bear, killed by whites because of a quarrel over a cow; the troubled days when the youth sang his dawn song, his song to the twilight, and songs of roundness; his solitary experience on Bear Butte, going for days without food and water, trying to determine what he and his people should do about the whites; and finally his vision—all are experiences that surely bring the young reader closer to understanding what it was to be Indian.

One of the most moving of all stories of a vision is that of Black Elk (John Neihardt, *Black Elk Speaks*). Although the story of Crazy Horse is a tragedy because a gifted leader died too young, nevertheless his vision was fulfilled. He did lead his people in victory over the white army at the Little Bighorn. The tragedy of Black Elk, as expressed in the opening pages of Neihardt's book, is that of a vision unfulfilled: "I know it was the story of a mighty vision given to a man too weak to use it; of a holy tree that should have flourished in a people's heart with flowers and singing birds, and now is withered; and of a people's dream that died in a bloody snow."

*Loyalty to the Tribe*

Indian boys, and often girls too, had no problem in deciding where their loyalties lay, as do so many modern youths. Their only question was how they could adequately demonstrate that loyalty.

In some tribes, for the boys this meant having a vision, but show-ing one's bravery was important also. This was not, however, simply an ego-satisfying thing, proving that the boy had courage and therefore was entitled to take his place among the men of the tribe. The vision was supposed to reveal to the boy what his future role in the tribe would be.

Mari Sandoz has written two junior novels with this theme. In *The Horsecatcher*, Young Elk, a Cheyenne youth, does not want to kill and would rather catch and tame wild horses. But he lives in a warrior society. He must prove that he is brave and can contribute to his tribe without killing. In *The Story Catcher*, Young Lance, a Sioux, wants to be a storyteller and historian of his tribe, but such a person is equal to a warrior so he must first prove his bravery. The story of Wakan, a boy who dreams too much, is told by Harold McCracken in *The Great White Buffalo*. His problem is to prove the truth of his story of living with a white buffalo, which is sacred to his tribe. He must demonstrate that he is a hero and a man of action, not just a dreamer. Another story, Grace Jackson Penney's *Moki*, gives the girl's side of this theme. Moki watches her older brother doing brave deeds for his people, and wonders what she might do to prove her loyalty and worth to the tribe besides caring for her rabbit and looking after her younger brother. Needless to say, she too finds a way to prove herself.

Another common theme dealt with the fear which often accom-panied the testing of a boy who was, after all, still a child, and yet the question of whether it was worthwhile was never raised. Surely at least a peace of mind must have resulted from such loyalty and fulfillment of common goals. A memorable picture of such fear occurs in Frank Waters's *The Man Who Killed the Deer* when the boy Napaita is wrenched from his mother's protection and tested, to prove his readiness to join the kiva. From the experience a man is born. In D'Arcy McNickle's *Runner in the Sun*, Salt under-goes a number of terrifying experiences, caused by the intrigue among the clans of his tribe, before he is finally chosen by the Holy One to go to the Land of Fable on a dangerous journey which is to save his people.

## Women of Bravery

During recent years more books have been written about women who, in one way or another, demonstrate courage and loyalty. Such a real-life woman was Susette La Flesche Tibbles, an Omaha, who overcame great shyness in order to spend two years lecturing throughout the East, crusading for citizenship for her people (Margaret Crary, *Susette La Flesche: Voice of the Omaha Indians*). Among elementary books, Rose Sobol's *Woman Chief* tells of a girl, born a Gros Ventre but captured by Crows, who is raised and trained as a warrior and eventually performs so valiantly that she is named chief of her tribe. *Nancy Ward, Cherokee*, by Harold Felton, tells of a woman who fights bravely beside her husband during battle, and who introduces the raising of cattle among her people, earning her the title "Beloved Woman."

## The Sacredness of Nature

In time of trouble or triumph the sacred attachment for earth and nature is ever present. Unlike the white people who are determined to have dominion over natural things, the Indians believe that they are brothers to all living things. In Hal Borland's *When the Legends Die*, when Young Bear's Brother is left alone in the mountains by the death of both parents, he talks to the animals and they answer him. When he returns to the mountains after years in the white world, he experiences stomach cramps because he has not sung the deer chant nor prepared and used all of the deer meat. In a humorous episode in Edwin Corle's *Fig Tree John*, Agocho is delighted when the River Spirit floods the Colorado River and the white settlers' irrigation ditches. The foolish people were justly punished for interfering with a Great Spirit, and so the Salton Sea, a dead sea caused by the flood, becomes his home.

Spiritual relationships between Indians and their animals are common. A book for elementary children, *Dog Story* by Oren Lyons, tells of a strange attraction between a boy and a dog, even though the dog has bitten the boy. The boy only knows that he wants the dog, which proves to be a great hunter, loyal to his master until death. In *Spotted Flower and the Ponokomita*, K. Follis Cheatham tells how the Blackfeet might have obtained their first horse around 1730. After capture by the Shoshones, Spotted Flower, a young girl, eludes the enemy and finds a strange, injured animal which she nurses. Ponokomita or "elk-dog," which is the term the early Blackfeet used for the horse, becomes Spotted Flower's friend, and she then teaches other Indians how to ride him.

## The Search for Self

The "Who am I?" theme, common to adolescent literature, becomes especially significant and crucial when Indian and white cultures clash. On one side there are the Indians, who find they must adjust to the white world; on the other side there is the white child who is captured by Indians, grows up among them, and either is forced back into white society or must decide whether to return to it. Often the change of name is symbolic of the Indian child's moving from one society into another. In Thomas Fall's *The Ordeal of Running Standing* the hero changes his name from Running Standing to Joe Standing and his sweetheart, Crosses the River, becomes Sara Cross. Bear's Brother in *When the Legends Die* becomes Thomas Black Bull and finally Tom Black, and in *Fig Tree John*, N'Chai Chidn becomes Juanito and then Johnny, while Agocho, his father, remains Agocho until the end, although the whites call him Fig Tree John.

In real life, too, a new name signified change. Francis LaFlesche, in *The Middle Five*, tells of the naming process that took place as the boys entered school: Wa-pah-dae became Ulysses S. Grant and Koo-we-he-ge-ra became Alexander, names which the boys carried into adult life. Polingaysi Qoyawayma, in *No Turning Back*, recalls her family's distress when she returned from school with the name "Bessie" on a cardboard around her neck, and she remembers her mother's words: "It is I who named you Polingaysi. It is a beautiful name. It fits you well. You are a daughter of the Kachinas, as any Hopi will know by your name."

The change of name, however, was only symbolic. The real tragedy occurred in the conflict of values. The tragedy comes to Abel in N. Scott Momaday's *House Made of Dawn*, in the clash between the white people's court, which convicts a man for murder, and the Indian system which says (p. 95), "They must know that he would kill the white man again, if he had the chance, that there would be no hesitation whatsoever. For he would know what the white man was, and he would kill him if he could. A man kills such an enemy if he can." The tragedy is there in Martiniano, in *The Man Who Killed the Deer* by Frank Waters (p. 10), when he pleads before the Indian Council after killing a deer out of season.

> The Council does not give me the privileges of others since I have come back from away-school. It would not give me my turn at the thresher for my oats, my wheat. . . . Should I go without my rights for two days of white man's law? The white man's Government that took me away to school, for which you do not give me the privileges of others? What is the difference between killing a deer on Tuesday or Thursday? Would I not have killed it anyway?

And it is there in Slim Girl who feels that one sure way of securing

her place among Laughing Boy's family and the Navajos is to
return to them with a sufficient amount of material goods.

In Arthur G. Kerle's novel, *Whispering Trees*, Johnny Shawano
realizes on the one hand that the lumber industry and its western
movement is important, but on the other, he longs to grow to
manhood as his father did, as a hunter and builder of canoes.
A book for junior high students, Elizabeth Witheridge's *Just One
Indian Boy*, develops the story of a young Chippewa boy in
northern Minnesota, who tries to find acceptance in high school
but leaves when white students taunt him and make life miserable.
A similar situation exists in Janet Campbell Hale's junior high
school book, *The Owl's Song*, when Billy White Hawk leaves the
Coeur d'Alene reservation in Idaho for a California high school
which has mainly black students, and finds that he cannot accept
the students' intolerance.

### White Child in Captivity

A theme that has captured the imagination of many white writers
is that of the white child captured by Indians. In the junior novels
the white child is usually treated quite well, and in fact is often
adopted by Indian parents to replace an Indian son or daughter
who has died. In these books the white child grows to love the
foster Indian parents and wants to stay with them. This is the
situation in Conrad Richter's two novels, *The Light in the Forest*
and *A Country of Strangers*, and in Lois Lenski's *Indian Captive:
The Story of Mary Jemison*, Alice Marriott's *Indian Annie: Kiowa
Captive*, and Benjamin Capps' *A Woman of the People*. These
young characters either decide to remain with the Indian tribe or
are returned to their white parents against their will. In Harold
Keith's adult novel, *Komantcia*, fifteen-year-old Pedro Pavon
suffers great humiliation at the hands of his captors, but he is
finally adopted by a Comanche chief because of his ability and
stamina, and marries an Indian wife. Seth Hubbard, in *Sword of
the Wilderness*, escapes his Indian tribe to return home, but only
after finding an Indian brother in the tribe and learning respect
for the Indian way of life.

Walter O'Meara's *Last Portage* is the fictionalized biography of
John Tanner, a white child captured by Indians and eventually
adopted by Netnokwa, Ottawa queen. He apparently remained his
Indian mother's most loyal son, but after her death he felt ob-
ligated to return to the white community. His is the tragedy of a
man who felt, thought, and acted like an Indian but had to be

judged as a white man. A highly romanticized version of Tanner's story, with hardly a hint of the real terror which his life became, is Elliot Arnold's *White Falcon.*

Recently publishers have reissued several old manuscripts by former captives: Derek G. Smith's *The Adventures and Sufferings of John R. Jewitt, Captive among the Nootka, 1803-1805;* James Smith's *Scoouwa;* and Fanny Kelly's *My Captivity among the Sioux Indians.*

In summary, books by and about the Indian clearly deserve a place in the English classroom. The Indian's was the first known culture in North America and became an essential part of our American heritage. The whites and their writers have created erroneous impressions of a group of American citizens which can and should be dispelled through knowledge and understanding gained from accurate sources. Finally, and probably most important, the Indian life and values have a spiritual and moral appeal, an integration and wholeness, that are so needed in the fragmented twentieth century.

## Indian Stereotypes in Literature

If we were to ask most young people and many adults "What are Indians?" we could predict the answers. They were early inhabitants of America who rode horseback, hunted buffalo, wore feathered headdresses and beaded buckskin, and lived in tepees. This is the picture of Indians perpetuated by Buffalo Bill and his original Wild West Show during the latter part of the nineteenth century, and kept alive by television, museum displays, and summer ceremonials planned especially for tourists. The row of Indian braves, wearing eagle-feather headdresses and riding horseback along the brow of a hill, is a threatening sight for the hero of many a television western. Paintings of the Pilgrims landing at Plymouth Rock show them being greeted by Indians wearing the Sioux costume. Television westerns set in the Southwest picture wagon trains being chased by Indians on horseback and wearing the feathers of the Plains Indians.

The Southwest Pueblo Indians are one of the few major tribes to escape this stereotype. They are neither hunters nor wanderers, but farmers and cultivators who have lived for centuries in villages. Today this pueblo way of life is probably most. representative of

Indians of the past. The stereotyped lifestyle of the Plains Indians with their tepees, buffaloes, and eagle-feather war bonnets has vanished, but the Pueblo Indians, the Hopi for example—with their desert homes, their fields of maize, their pottery and kachina dolls—are living very much as their ancestors did.

## The Noble Red Man

Historically, the first stereotype of the Indian was that of the Noble Red Man or the child of nature. As early stories of the New World found their way back to Europe, the nobility and freedom of the natives captured the imaginations of men like Montaigne, Erasmus, and Rousseau. For those convinced of the perfectibility of humanity in a simpler society, here was proof of their belief. The first settlers found Indians living in an equality unknown in stratified European societies. Among early American writers, the picture of the Noble Red Man was evoked in words such as those of the poet Philip Freneau: "All, all are free;—here God and nature reign." Emerson, Margaret Fuller, and Thoreau, who during his last ten years of life filled some twenty-eight hundred pages with notes on the Indian, all wanted, as Roy Harvey Pearce says in *Savagism and Civilization*, "to demonstrate the perfectibility of civilized man in America." Cooper's young Chingachgook and Longfellow's Hiawatha fit the stereotype as free, independent natives who were as yet uncorrupted by white civilization. Helen Hunt Jackson's Alessandro and Faulkner's Sam Fathers carry echoes of the Noble Red Man stereotype, but by the time they were created, the country had been so corrupted by white civilization that there no longer was room for such nobility.

A teacher who is concerned about the overly romanticized picture of the Indian found in *Hiawatha* can perhaps provide balance with the supplementary reading of the legends of Manabozho, the creator-trickster after whom Longfellow fashioned his hero. Vizenor's collection of Chippewa tales, *Anishinabe Adisokan: Tales of the People*, devotes a section to these stories. In fact, a study of Indian legends through a general collection such as Susan Feldman's *The Storytelling Stone* or Stith Thompson's *Tales of the North American Indians* would do much to dispel many of the stereotypes created by non-Indians.

## The Heathen Savage

While Europeans and East Coast Americans could revel in the idea of an idealized Indian society, the settlers on the frontier had to find reasons for seizing Indian lands and wealth. So the pioneer encroaching ever westward created a stereotype of an ignoble heathen savage. The Puritans with their Christian imperialism contended that God meant the civilized English to win the land from the so-called heathen Indian. They theorized that the Indians were descendants of Adam through the Asiatic Tartars who had come to America by a land bridge from northern Asia. Because they had wandered so far, the Indians were far from God and had lost their civilization and adherence to laws. They were in the power of Satan. Thus the whites concluded that the Indians' lives as hunters and wanderers were what made them savages.

Because the early settlers never tried to understand the religions of the Indians, or never even recognized that they had religions, they labeled them as heathens. Only in the mid-1800s when ethnographers decided that Indian cultures might be vanishing did a few white people begin to realize that the Indians' religion integrated their entire lives.

Another aspect of this stereotype is scalping, a practice that was actually unknown among New England Indians until 1637, when the Puritans began to offer cash for the heads of their enemies and later accepted scalps if both ears were attached. The French in Canada offered bounties for scalps and the English soon followed suit.

## Murderous Thieves

Although Chingachgook and Uncas are close to the Noble Red Man stereotype, Cooper was sufficiently near the frontier to be aware of the contradictory Indian image, so he also created murderous, villainous thieves among his Indians. Such a character is Magua, the Huron, made treacherous by his lust and love of liquor. In modern books the stereotype persists. In Ralph Moody's *Geronimo: Wolf of the Warpath* (p. 32), we read about Geronimo's people:

> As if in answer, the Apache war whoop filled the canyon like the howl of a thousand wolves. From behind every boulder and tree leaped a red-brown, shrieking Apache, naked except for his loincloth. With spears high and knives flashing they circled the little camp in a screeching, writhing dance of death.

Expressions such as "war whoop," "howl of a thousand wolves," "naked except for his loincloth," and "screeching, writhing dance of death" are terms that suggest to a young child a savage Indian. Many of the Indians in primarily white novels, such as Walter

Edmonds's *Drums along the Mohawk*, are pictured with scalps
hanging from their belts. In the popular captive narrative a white
child or youth is kidnapped by an Indian tribe and sometimes
submitted to brutal treatment. Harold Keith's *Komantcia* and
Carter Vaughan's *Seneca Hostage* are two such novels. Fortunately,
some of the captive narratives, such as Richter's *Light in the
Forest* and Alice Marriott's *Indian Annie*, tell a different story in
which the white child becomes a beloved member of an Indian
family.

One cannot read the biographies of the great chiefs such as
Chief Joseph, Black Hawk, and Tecumseh without acknowledging
that these were men of religion and of peace who fought only to
try to save their lands. The Apache chief Cochise—whose name
strikes terror in the hero's heart on too many television programs—
was really a gentle man, who became an enemy of the United
States troops only after being tricked and wrongly accused of
kidnapping a child and stealing cattle. But the fighting, raiding,
war-whooping Indian still dominates movies, television, and even
textbooks. Words such as *savage*, *warlike*, and *thievery*, which are
all too common, are especially degrading and misleading.

## Idlers and Drunkards

In the seventeenth and eighteenth centuries the Indian attitude
toward land encouraged the idea of the Noble Red Man and an
egalitarian, classless society. By the nineteenth century that same
characteristic led the United States government, which was trying
to move Indians onto reservations, to the conclusion that as a
people, Indians were lazy and did not want to progress. Since
settling and working the land were alien ideas to some tribes,
they earned the reputation of being shiftless. Because to the
whites hunting was most often a sport, they did not recognize
the Indians' hunting as work to support their families and tribes.
People who were grounded in Jefferson's creed, "Those who labor
in the earth are the chosen people of God," and Ben Franklin's
"Time is money," could not comprehend a hunter's culture. As
William Brandon puts it (*American Heritage Book of Indians*,
p. 243), "In a word the Indian world was devoted to living, the
European world to getting."

Another aspect of this stereotype is the drunken Indian. The
liquor which the whites provided was regarded as a way of getting
the Indians' wealth—their pelts, food, or land. Cooper's Magua
has already been mentioned as an Indian character who was

corrupted by liquor. Even the noble Chingachgook in his later years fell victim to the evil.

A modern book which seems to overdo the idle, drinking Indian is Huffaker's *Flap*, or *Nobody Loves a Drunken Indian*, as it was originally titled. In the midst of a series of drinking sprees, a group of young Paiutes embarks on a series of unbelievable escapades in which they stop a road gang from running over a Paiute grave, kidnap a circus train, and finally take over the city of Phoenix. This book also has been made into a movie which the *Indian Historian* calls "a revealing mixture of slapstick and misplaced caricature." The drunken old Indian, harmless except to himself, is a common picture on television westerns. As Matt Dillon, or some other noble white sheriff, goes after a really dangerous criminal, he is reminded by his assistant that old Injun Joe has been picked up again and is sleeping it off. Who can judge the effect of the repetition of such needless statements on the Indian, or non-Indian, child who is viewing or reading these works?

An antidote to this stereotype might well be Charles Eastman's *Indian Boyhood* or *Soul of an Indian*, books that describe true Indian life and values in the Sioux tribe, a hunter's culture. Other possibilities are the biographies of Sequoyah, Jim Thorpe, or Emerson Blackhorse Mitchell—men who, through hard work, overcame great odds.

## The Beautiful Indian Maiden

Nothing has yet been said about stereotypes of Indian women. Vine Deloria, Jr., in *Custer Died for Your Sins*, tells that while he was executive director of the National Congress of American Indians, few days passed that a white person did not visit his office, proclaiming Indian ancestry through a grandmother. Why so often an Indian grandmother? Deloria's explanation is that Indian males were thought of as too cruel and savage, but a beautiful Indian princess in one's background is an ancestor to be proud of. This most common stereotype of the Indian woman grew out of the Pocahontas legend. The image of the noble maiden, helping the white settler, was further enhanced by tales, real and romantic, of Sacajawea, the girl guide for Lewis and Clark. It is said that more statues have been erected of her than of any other woman in American history.

Hiawatha's Minnehaha added to the romance. Then in 1884 Helen Hunt Jackson gave the world Ramona, the half-Indian maiden who played out her sad story with her tragic lover, the noble Indian, Alessandro. By the time this story took place the Indians had been defrauded, harassed, and routed from their land until they no longer had any place to go. Although the romanticized Ramona was no true California Indian, her sad story aroused the sympathy of millions of Americans. Lover's Leaps—where a beautiful Indian maiden, unrequited in love, supposedly leaped to her death—abound in all parts of the United States, and "Indian Love Call" is sung at Indian ceremonials that are produced for tourists.

Although beauty, loyalty, and nobility are generally good qualities, there are more realistic, well-developed pictures of Indian women to be found in a number of biographies. Alice Marriott's *Maria: The Potter of San Ildefonso* gives us a woman's modern success story but also the human tragedy of her Pueblo family. Two biographies of Hopi women—Polingaysi Qoyawayma's *No Turning Back* and Helen Sekaquaptewa's *Me and Mine*—and Kay Bennett's junior biography, *Kaibah*, describe a woman's struggle to find a place between two worlds. Alice Marriott, in *The Ten Grandmothers*, tells of the Kiowa, Spear Woman, and her sister, both married to a man who becomes a Christian and feels that he must give up one wife. Two intermediate books—*Annie Wauneka* by Mary Carroll Nelson, which tells of a Navajo woman who worked to improve the health and welfare of her people, and *Maria Tallchief* by Adèle de Leeuw, which is a biography of the famous Osage ballerina—are stories of Indian women who worked against great odds to make significant contributions.

### The Vanishing Race

By the mid-1800s, white Americans, like white Englishmen, had taken up the White Man's Burden. Many people—including the Great Emancipator, who opened ten million acres of Indian land to homesteaders in 1862—came to the conclusion that the Indian must either be "civilized" or eliminated. At the same time ethnographers were worrying that a culture was disappearing and therefore must be studied while it lasted. Missionaries and would-be humanitarians worried about the poverty of remnants of tribes who had seen their numbers depleted. The image that grew out of this was that of a vanishing race. Cooper's Uncas was the last of his race, and even Hiawatha, who lived before the whites arrived, saw the vision of his people "sweeping westward, wild and woeful . . . ." Poets as far back as Freneau and Bryant were overwhelmed by a sentimentalized picture of a vanishing race. Perhaps the most insidious stereotypes of this sort are found in novels like Zane Grey's *The Vanishing American,* where we find not only Nophaie the vanishing Indian, but also two-dimensional, evil missionaries and disloyal government agents, and a sentimentalized resolution of their conflicts. Even in contemporary fiction, Faulkner pictures Sam Fathers as "childless, kinless, peopleless," the last of his race.

But is the Indian vanishing? Hardly. Wendell Oswalt reports, for example, that estimates placed the aboriginal Hopi at about 2,800—a number that dropped to 2,000 in 1907, but is currently at about 5,000 (*This Land Was Theirs,* p. 348). McNickle reports that since the Indian population in the United States reached a low of 250,000 in 1850, the census has shown a steady increase to more than 700,000 in the 1970s, approaching the estimated 850,000 here when the whites first arrived (*Native American Tribalism,* pp. 4-5). Fey and McNickle report that of an estimated 300 Indian languages spoken in the area north of Mexico at the time of discovery, at least half are still in use. Indian kinship systems still function, and Indians still have roles as clansmen and heads of Indian societies (*Indians and Other Americans,* p. 12). In addition, there is a resurgence of Indian values, religion, and ceremonies. The Native American Church, whose rites combine evangelical Protestantism with the use of peyote and the beating of the drum, has doubled its membership in recent years (Deloria, *Custer Died for Your Sins,* p. 116).

Perhaps nothing can do so much to convince both Indians and non-Indians that the Native American is not a vanishing race as reading from the works of talented young Indian writers such as Vine Deloria, Jr., N. Scott Momaday, James Welch, and Emerson Blackhorse Mitchell, or from the *Indian Historian* and the *Weewish Tree,* two magazines published by the Indian Historian Press, or from Natachee Scott Momaday's *American Indian Authors.*

As the white settlers' empire moved westward, some people concluded that if the Indians were not vanishing, they at least were self-effacing and inarticulate. The silent, humorless, granite-faced cigar store Indian is the image that has been reflected on the nickel. The "ugh-ugh" of the Hollywood and television Indian and the broken English of some Indian characters in the fiction of white writers also are part of the image. Some of this may have come from the missionary and Bureau of Indian Affairs schools of the past, which forbade Indian children to speak their native language, so that until they learned English they had to remain silent (see Francis LaFlesche's *The Middle Five*). In some fiction the language which the Indian speaks, communicating in a second tongue, takes on all sorts of artificial dialects. In Howard Fast's *The Last Frontier*, the Indians sometimes speak something that resembles a false black dialect: "Dey already dead, dey say." Even in a biography, *Karnee: A Paiute Narrative* by Lalla Scott, in which an old man is speaking Paiute, we find the following: "'Bungey Jim, he heap good boy,' cried the trembling old man. 'He my good son, he no harm nobody.' He was talking Paiute but he made himself understood with pitiful motions." Why does an author translate Paiute into substandard English dialect?

To prove the falseness of the portrait of Indians as humorless, silent, or halting in speech, one need only read Deloria's chapter on Indian humor in *Custer Died for Your Sins*. Recent collections of Indian oratory give ample evidence of the greatness of the oratory of Indian leaders, especially of such men as Chief Joseph, Tecumseh, and Black Hawk (see especially *The Way* by Shirley H. Witt and *I Have Spoken* by Virginia Armstrong). Who can forget the Priest of the Sun in Momaday's *House Made of Dawn* as he describes his grandmother's feeling about language: "You see, for her words were medicine; they were magic and invisible. They came from nothing into sound and meaning. They were beyond price; they could neither be bought or sold. And she never threw words away."

## Faithful Friend and Servant

If the Indians were not vanishing or self-effacing, as portrayed by white writers, they were made to appear subservient. This is best illustrated in a common Indian character, the loyal friend to a white person. In Cooper's novels, Chingachgook, the Indian friend, is a chieftain. Leatherstocking is proud to be considered one of the Delaware Nation. Their relationship is one of friendship based upon equality and mutual respect. In more recent fiction, however, Indian-white friendships have changed considerably. The Lone Ranger rides his magnificent white stallion, Silver, while Tonto rides his modest pinto named Scout. Tonto's name means *silly* or *foolish*. He has no particular face and is really one of the invisible ones, clearly inferior to the Lone Ranger. In some ways these characters in modern fiction and film are little different from the faithful black servant. Such Indian characters often have a high moral purpose—as defined by the whites, of course. They want to help their people by defeating those elements in the tribe who want to keep the Indian way of life. They never question the decisions of their white friends. So, as the Noble Red Man stereotype had given way to the White Man's Burden, Chingachgook became Tonto.

There are a number of Indian-white friendships in junior novels. In *Never Step on an Indian's Shadow* by Diana Walker, a friendship between a white Canadian girl and a Cree Indian boy dissolves into hopelessness when the girl turns to a presumably happy friendship with an older white man and the Indian boy leaves his community for what apparently will be a life of discouragement and discrimination, possibly ending in suicide. The message is that a friendship between a white girl and an Indian boy can lead only to unhappiness and tragedy. The friendship of True Son and his Indian cousin, Half Arrow, in Richter's *Light in the Forest* is less one-sided because during most of the book the hero, True Son, believes his Indian life is better and more desirable than his white life. In Charles McNichols's *Crazy Weather*, South Boy, a white fourteen year old, finds his life so boring that he goes name-traveling with his Mojave friend, Havek—a situation in which the Indian friend is clearly superior in knowledge and understanding. A well-known historical friendship, that of Chief Cochise and Tom Jeffords, appears in biographies of Cochise and in Elliott Arnold's junior novel, *Broken Arrow*.

Whether they are working with Indians or non-Indians, it is most important that teachers and others involved with book selection recognize the vast diversity of Indian lifestyles and cultures. Indians are not just Indians. They are Navajo, or Sioux, or Cherokee. Which tribe they belong to or which combination of Indian backgrounds they come from makes all the difference in the way they think, their attitudes toward life, and the way they dress for tribal celebrations. As Gerald Vizenor, a Minnesota Chippewa, explains in *The Everlasting Sky* (p. 15), "The dominant society has created a homogenized history of tribal people for a television culture. Being an *indian* is a heavy burden to the *oshki anishinabe* [new people of the woodland] because white people know more about the indian they invented than anyone." Apart from the diversity of tribes, within a single tribe Indians, like everyone else, are unique human beings with their own loves, hates, and yearnings. It is not the Indians that whites created whom we need to know and understand; it is the real, complex Indians. Teachers, librarians, and readers in general need to make that distinction.

Indian Literature of the Mid-Seventies

Some truly notable books about Indians have been published in
the six years since the first edition of this bibliography appeared.
Among the very best mature novels are two by Native Americans:
James Welch's *Winter in the Blood* and Leslie Marmon Silko's
*Ceremony*. Silko's hero, Tayo, is a World War II prisoner of the
Japanese who is released and returns home, first to a veteran's
hospital, where in his delirium he relives his experiences in the
jungles of the South Pacific, and then to his home on the Laguna
Reservation, where his family finds it difficult to understand what
he has been through and to accept his illness. Welch's young,
nameless hero is the embodiment of loneliness, aimlessness, and
frustration. These two young characters have things in common
with each other and also with Momaday's Abel in *House Made of
Dawn*. All three are caught between the modern white world and
the older culture of their ancestors, and find comfort one way or
another in their ancient cultures and traditions. Another book
that ranks among the fine mature novels is Rudy Wiebe's *The
Temptations of Big Bear*, a historical novel which won the Canadian Governor General's Award for 1973. Wiebe has chosen to
stay with historical data as much as possible in telling the story of
Big Bear, the resistance Cree chief, and his family from 1876 to
1888. His novel is a remarkable example of the craft of historical
fiction.

Some other adult novels are of more than passing interest—
good but not great. Dorothy Johnson's *Buffalo Woman* is the
life story of Whirlwind, an Oglala Sioux woman who lived from
1820 when life was good and complete, through the Battle of the
Little Bighorn. This is one of the few attempts to give a woman's
perspective of nineteenth century tribal life and the effects of the
struggle to survive. Another adult novel, Byrd Baylor's *Yes Is
Better Than No*, is an unusual chronicle of the Papago Indians in
Tucson, who are at odds with both the dominant Anglo society
and the organizers of a Red Power movement. Elliott Arnold, in
*The Camp Grant Massacre*, and Jessamyn West in *The Massacre at
Fall Creek*, use historical materials for novels that are commend-
able, though less impressive than Wiebe's.

Some of the best junior high school novels published since 1973
are those based soundly on history or anthropological research.
Joyce Rockwood, an anthropologist, has written *Long Man's
Song* and *To Spoil the Sun*, both set in a time before whites had
really colonized the region of the ancient Cherokees. The first

novel tells of Soaring Hawk, a young Cherokee apprentice medicine man, as he struggles to save his only sister during her illness
because only she can carry on his clan. *To Spoil the Sun* is the
story of Rain Dove, a young Cherokee girl, in her two marriages,
and the tragedy of a smallpox epidemic brought on by the first
white explorers. We hope that other writers will engage in the
kind of research required for writing about a time and place
untouched by white cultures. Another good novel, also based
on historical fact, is Eileen Thompson's *White Falcon*, not to
be confused with Elliott Arnold's novel with the same title.
Thompson used a brief statement about "the lad from Petatlan,"
who accompanied Coronado's expedition from Mexico City to
Cibola, as the basis for her novel.

Two young Native American writers have written novels for
junior high school students. Janet Hale, a member of the Idaho
Coeur d'Alene tribe, is the author of *The Owl's Song*, a sensitively
written story of a young boy who thinks he wants to leave the
reservation, only to discover through persecution and misunderstanding in a California high school that he really belongs back
home in Idaho. Jamake Highwater has combined many legends,
especially from the northern plains, into a novel, *Anpao: An
American Odyssey*, about a young man who must go on a long and
dangerous journey to prove to his sweetheart that he has the
Sun's permission to marry her.

## The Pitfalls of Popularity

Native Americans are a popular subject for authors, and, predict-
ably, some shallow works are being written in response to that
interest. Not all of these are fiction. Some books on anthropology
and history try to cover so much material that they must do it
very superficially. In fact, some try to cover the anthropology *and*
the history of all United States tribes in one volume. The result
is most unsatisfactory.

Fiction also often seems to be written to exploit current interest in Indians. Even though some of these novels inadequately
portray Native Americans, some may be appealing stories for
other reasons. Evelyn Sibley Lampman, who has written some
good junior high school books—such as *Cayuse Courage*, the story
of the Whitman Massacre in Oregon, and *Half-Breed*, about a boy
whose father was a friend of mountain man Joe Meek—now seems
to treat her subject matter more superficially. The Chinook family
in *The Potlatch Family* are basically white in their interests,
concerns, and way of life, and the introduction of a dying brother,

who tries to persuade them to show pride in their Indian heritage, results in a fairly unimaginative plot. In *Bargain Bride*, which merely pictures prejudice and bigotry on the frontier, the distinguishing feature of the one Indian character, Nona, is that she rarely speaks and when she does, she uses broken English that tends to perpetuate the stereotype of the halting, illiterate Native American. *White Captives*, perhaps the best of Lampman's recent works, is based on the historical capture of Olive and Mary Oatman and is more accurate in picturing the conflict between Indians and white settlers along the frontier.

Don Schellie's book, *Me, Cholay & Company*, is another novel that capitalizes on a theme but does not do it very well. The setting is Arizona in the aftermath of the 1870 massacre at Camp Grant. Joshua Thane and the Apache, Cholay, are both a bit too clever and good to be believable. Moreover, Joshua, who hails from Chicago, tells the story in what seems to be a backwoods dialect, which does not ring true. Elliott Arnold did a much better job with the same historical material in his recent adult novel, *The Camp Grant Massacre*.

Possibly another victim of the rush to print is Diana Walker's Canadian novel, *Never Step on an Indian's Shadow*. If more care had been taken in the writing, the characters—Teresa Denys, the white fifteen year old from Montreal, and Michael Big Canoe, a Cree teenager from the James Bay area—might have emerged as real people. The actual result is a book that says to whites, "Be nice to Native Americans, but you must not marry one because we're really very different from them."

The popularity of books on Native Americans has resulted in the publication of many accounts of personal experience, some reprinted and others just recently discovered or written. The most valuable of these is Momaday's *The Names: A Memoir*, a book that combines the author's genealogy and a memoir of his childhood. A recent autobiography which has been very popular with teenagers is *The Education of Little Tree* by Forrest Carter, the Cherokee author of *Gone to Texas* and *The Vengeance Trail of Josey Wales*. Elaine Goodale Eastman's manuscript, *Sister to the Sioux*, has recently been published. It is the work of "a properly brought-up New England girl" who in 1885 responded to the request of Chief Medicine Bull to open a day school in his Brulé Sioux village. Although some of her goals—the elimination of Indian languages and culture and the forced assimilation of Indian children into white culture—seem wrong today, we must admire her for her eagerness to share the life of her charges and their families.

Because they may perpetuate the misconceptions of their time or because they may be lacking in value, some of these earlier writings probably should have remained unpublished. Younger students who read them must be helped to look at them within the context of their times or to consider the writers' limitations. Whether or not the modern reader accepts what the recorder of the experience says depends greatly on the writer's perspective. Some eighteenth and nineteenth century narrators constantly make moral judgments about their observations and experiences. Those who seem to record events objectively remain the most believable today.

Fanny Kelly, for example, wrote *My Captivity among the Sioux Indians* in 1872. Nineteen years old and newly married when her experience occurred, she emerges as a typical female adolescent of her day. Accepting the concept of the Indian as savage and of whites as the superior race, she is unaware of national policies which force the Sioux to use every means possible to protect their homeland. George Boyce, a teacher among the Navajo for thirty years, wrote a series of short stories growing out of his experiences, but in spite of long experience with the Navajo, he did not anticipate the effects of some badly misplaced humor about Navajo customs. Other such publications are more acceptable, primarily because they mainly record instead of judging Indian cultures by the white culture of the time. Although it describes a massacre by Nootka Indians, John Jewitt's manuscript, edited by Derek Smith and republished in 1974 from an 1824 publication, is fairly objective. In *Two Great Scouts and Their Pawnee Battalion*, George Bird Grinnell, although biased in favor of the Pawnees and his friends the Norths, does contribute significantly to our knowledge about Plains Indians in the nineteenth century.

## Books of Special Interest

In the areas of art and photography, really beautiful books are appearing. The University of New Mexico Press has a number of publications on Indian pottery, weaving, silver, and architecture, and the New York Graphic Society has published the first history of American Indian painting—Jamake Highwater's *Song from the Earth*—as well as *Fritz Scholder Lithographs* and Frank and Harlow's *Historic Pottery of the Pueblo Indians*. Growing appreciation for the work of photographer and writer Edward S. Curtis has led to the publication of several books. Especially interesting are a biography by Victor Boesen and Florence Curtis Graybill and a collection of Curtis's writings and photographs, edited by a British scholar, Mick Gidley. Both books are profusely illustrated with Curtis's photographs.

One more book should be mentioned because it seems to be the only one of its kind: John R. Maestas's collection, *Contemporary Native American Address*, published by Brigham Young University Press. For many years, little notice was taken of Indian oratory outside the tribes. When it was finally recognized, attention focused on the oratory of the resistance leaders of the last century. Now the Maestas collection gives us examples of modern Indian oratory, both activist and conservative.

Teachers and librarians must exercise careful discrimination in choosing books that will influence others' conceptions of Native Americans. Several kinds are especially troublesome: history or anthropology books that try to cover too much material and do it superficially, novels that purport to be Indian but are really white books with Indian characters, and books that recount the experiences of whites who lived among the Indians without really knowing or understanding them. On the brighter side, however, there are books by an increasing number of fine Native American authors—James Welch, Leslie Marmon Silko, Janet Campbell Hale, and Jamake Highwater, to mention only a few. In addition, a growing number of non-Indian writers, notably Rudy Wiebe, Elliott Arnold, Dorothy Johnson, and Joyce Rockwood, have turned to serious Native American themes, treating them with accuracy and dignity.

### References

Armstrong, Virginia, ed. *I Have Spoken: American History Through the Voices of the Indians.* Chicago: Swallow, 1971.

Bigelow, John, ed. *The Complete Works of Benjamin Franklin.* New York: G. P. Putnam, 1877.

Brandon, William. *American Heritage Book of Indians.* New York: Dell, 1961.

Costo, Rupert, ed. *Textbooks and the American Indian.* San Francisco: Indian Historian Press, 1970.

Deloria, Vine, Jr. *Custer Died for Your Sins.* New York: Avon, 1969.

Fast, Howard. *The Last Frontier.* New York: New American Library, 1971.

Fey, Harold E., and D'Arcy McNickle. *Indians and Other Americans.* New York: Harper and Row, 1959.

Ford, Paul Leicester, ed. *The Works of Thomas Jefferson.* New York: G. P. Putnam, 1904-05.

McNickle, D'Arcy. *Native American Tribalism: Indian Survivals and Renewals.* New York: Oxford University Press, 1973.

Momaday, N. Scott. *House Made of Dawn.* New York: New American Library, 1968.

Moody, Ralph. *Geronimo: Wolf of the Warpath.* New York: Random House, 1958.

"Movies: 'Flap' Is Flop." *Indian Historian* 4 (1971): 44.

Neihardt, John. *Black Elk Speaks.* New York: Pocket Books, 1961.

Neihardt, John. *When the Tree Flowered.* Lincoln: University of Nebraska, 1970.

"1977 Books for Young Adult Book Poll." *English Journal* 67 (1978): 90-95.

Oswalt, Wendell. *This Land Was Theirs.* New York: John Wiley, 1966.

Pearce, Roy Harvey. *Savagism and Civilization.* Baltimore: Johns Hopkins, 1965.

Qoyawayma, Polingaysi. *No Turning Back.* Albuquerque: University of New Mexico, 1964.

Scott, Lalla. *Karnee: A Paiute Narrative.* Greenwich: Fawcett, 1966.

Steiner, Stan, and Shirley Witt. *The Way: An Anthropology of American Indian Literature.* New York: Knopf, 1972.

Torrey, Bradford, ed. *The Writings of Henry David Thoreau.* Boston: Houghton Mifflin, 1906.

Vizenor, Gerald. *The Everlasting Sky.* New York: Crowell-Collier, 1972.

Waters, Frank. *The Man Who Killed the Deer.* Chicago: Swallow, 1942.

# Aids for the Teacher

This chapter is designed to help teachers find materials for planning units or working with specific groups, and for establishing a library of quality books by and about American Indians. For those whose interest goes beyond the local library offerings, there is a list of less accessible sources of information.

## Guides to Curriculum Planning

This section contains an annotated list of various materials that will help teachers in working with specific ages or groups of students, or in planning specific courses or units of study. Four of the selections are especially useful in developing an understanding of the kinds of Indian characters created by non-Indian writers: *The Return of the Vanishing American* (Fiedler), *The Indian in American Literature* (Keiser), *Savagism and Civilization* (Pearce), and *The Writer and the Shaman* (Zolla). During the last few years we have witnessed an increase in Indian reference works. Notable examples are *Contemporary American Indian Leaders* (Gridley), *The Newberry Library American Indian Bibliographical Series* (Jennings, ed.), *The American Indian: Language and Literature* (Marken), *Bibliography of Nonprint Instructional Materials on the American Indian* (Brigham Young University), *About Indians* (Department of Indian and Northern Affairs, Canada), and *Great North American Indians* (Dockstader). Teachers of Indian students will find several invaluable works about Indian students and Indian education, including *The American Indian Reader: Education* (Henry), and *The Education of the American Indians* (Berry). Two works will help in choosing texts: for elementary and secondary teachers, *Textbooks and the American Indian* (Costo); for college teachers, *Searching for America* (Kelly).

American Indian Historical Society. **Index to Literature on the American Indian: 1970.** Indian Hist Pr 1972.

More than 250 periodicals, books, and dissertations have been searched, and their articles on American Indians have been indexed according to sixty-three subject areas. Of greatest interest to the English teacher are the sections on arts, biography, fiction, folklore, literature, music, and poetry. Entries are not annotated. This publication will appear annually.

Berry, Brewton. **The Education of the American Indians: A Survey of the Literature.** US HEW 1968.

This is a summary of the published literature on American Indian education—studies on topics such as the intelligence of American Indian students, how they are affected by teachers and parents, cultural and language barriers, kinds of schools Indian students attend, and self-concepts of Indian children. There is an extensive bibliography of published and unpublished materials.

Beuf, Ann H. **Red Children in White America.** U of Pa Pr 1977.

The author, a sociologist, says that her aim is "to investigate whether the Native American children's [racial] attitudes are different from those of a control group of white children, and, if so, what may be the sources of such differences." She studied the perceptions and values of 229 preschool children—more than half of them Native Americans and the remainder whites. The Native Americans came from three tribal groups—one south of Phoenix, Arizona, another from a Dakota plains tribe, and a third from a plains group of the upper Missouri.

Black, Nancy B., and Bette S. Weidman, editors. **White on Red: Images of the American Indian.** Kennikat 1976.

The purpose of this collection is to "draw together literary treatments of the North American Indian, written by whites in the course of a three-hundred-year period, roughly from the settlement of Virginia in 1607 to the Battle of Wounded Knee in 1890." Excerpts in the first part of the book are mainly nonfiction; the remainder are mostly from drama, poetry, and fiction of authors such as Charles Brockden Brown, Washington Irving, Nathaniel Hawthorne, Melville, Longfellow, and Whitman. The editors believe that whites bear a burden of guilt that amounts to a "national obsession."

Brigham Young University, Instructional Development Program for the Institute of Indian Services and Research. **Bibliography of Nonprint Instructional Materials on the American Indian.** Brigham 1972.

A much-needed bibliography of 16mm motion pictures, 8mm

film loops, film strips, 35mm slides, overhead transparencies, study prints, maps, charts, audio recordings, and multimedia kits on the American Indian. Hard copy and microfilm print materials are not included. Information was gathered by publishing requests in national media magazines, by corresponding with instructional materials producers, and by checking the lists in various media directories. The bibliography is arranged according to title and is indexed by subject and by distributor. Items that are especially appropriate for particular grade levels are indicated. Any school using Indian materials in its curriculum should have this inexpensive resource.

Cashman, Marc, editor. **Bibliography of American Ethnology.** Todd Pubns 1976.

This is a partially annotated bibliography of about forty-five hundred books on ethnology and race relations, divided into four categories: General Ethnology, American Indians, Black Americans, and Other Minority Groups. The American Indian books are arranged by tribes, and by topics such as arts and crafts, assimilation, civil rights, education, folklore and mythology, and literature. The bibliography lacks author and title indexes and is inconsistent in its use of tribal names—for instance, *Dakota* and *Sioux* are used synonymously, as are *Chippewa* and *Ojibwa*.

Costo, Rupert, editor. **Textbooks and the American Indian.** Indian Hist Pr 1970.

Concern about omissions, distortions, and inaccuracies in the information presented to elementary and secondary students about the American Indian led the American Indian Historical Society to undertake a study of history, geography, and civics texts and what they say about the Indian. This is a report of the study, including recommendations for choosing texts. Despite the fact that the study is more than ten years old, it is still perhaps the most useful guide to books that give a reasonably accurate picture of the Indian, and a necessary reference for teaching a unit or course in Indian literature or culture.

Department of Indian and Northern Affairs. **About Indians: A Listing of Books.** Dept Ind NA Canada 1975.

The third and considerably expanded edition of a bibliography in two languages, English and French, compiled "to provide information to the many teachers, librarians and other people interested in books written by or about Indians." It covers books about the native peoples of all of North America, with asterisks denoting works by Canadian authors or of special interest for Canadians. The bibliography is arranged by reading level, from kindergarten through grade 6 and beyond, including adult books. Canadian university students, among them Indians, read and annotated more than six hundred of the books, but not all books are annotated.

Dockstader, Frederick J. **Great North American Indians: Profiles in Life and Leadership.** Van Nos Reinhold 1977.

To help solve the problem of finding accurate information on many Indian leaders, Dockstader has collected short biographies of three hundred outstanding people of Indian ancestry who are no longer living. All were important to the Indians, not to white history, even though some were betrayers of their people. Portraits of individuals have been included where possible and there are other illustrations of Indian scenes, paintings, and artifacts.

Fiedler, Leslie A. **The Return of the Vanishing American.** Stein & Day 1969.

In a scholarly and provocative book, Leslie Fiedler discusses what he feels to be the uniquely American experience—the encounter between the mythical white person and the mythical nonwhite, primarily the Indian, but by extension the Negro and the Jew. He is concerned with four basic myths in the Western novel: love in the woods, or the Pocahontas legend; the white woman with the tomahawk, or the Indian captive; the good companions, such as Natty Bumppo and Chingachgook; and the runaway male who tries to escape home and civilization.

Grant, Bruce. **American Indians Yesterday and Today.** Illus. Lorence F. Bjorklund. Dutton 1960.

Exhaustive research has resulted in this comprehensive, alphabetically arranged encyclopedia on the American Indians. The carefully cross-indexed entries cover the legends, lore, beliefs, customs, and characteristics of all known tribes. There are more than eight hundred items, including biographies of great leaders, Indian wars, and American place names that have Indian origins. More than two hundred line drawings enhance this valuable resource for quick reference and study.

"An encyclopedia about Indians with over 800 entries touching on the lives of great Indian leaders, the influence of the Indian language on the white man's language, Indian wars and weapons and Indian peace aims, covering the time of historical contact to present day" (*About Indians*, p. 177).

Gridley, Marion E. American Indian Tribes. Dodd 1974.

A short book—such as this—which covers all Indian tribes in eleven geographical sections of the United States and Canada must be a somewhat superficial treatment. It could be a useful handbook for a high school classroom, however, because it gives information on linguistic stocks, outstanding individuals in various tribes, the locations of reservations, and a bit of the history and culture of each area.

Gridley, Marion E. Contemporary American Indian Leaders. Dodd 1972.

This is a collection of biographies of twenty-six modern Indian leaders, ranging from activists to conservatives and from young to old. Each biography includes a statement of the subject's attitudes toward Indian-white relationships. The leaders are from several different tribes and various vocations: government, science, literature, art, music, and public service. Biographies range in length from five to nine pages. A useful classroom reference.

Henry, Jeannette, editor. The American Indian Reader: Anthropology. Indian Hist Pr 1972.

The first of a series of readers intended especially for classroom use and teacher preparation. The collections contain the most important articles published in the *Indian Historian* during the preceding seven years and introduce new materials that were prepared for the series. The articles are divided into topics such as the man and the discipline, archaeology, and early agriculture and economy, and Indian criticisms of several anthropological articles are included. Four other collections in this series are: *Education* (annotated below), *Literature*, *History*, and *Current Affairs*.

Henry, Jeannette, editor. The American Indian Reader: Education. Indian Hist Pr 1972.

The second book in a series designed for classroom use, teacher preparation, and general reading for those with a special interest in the Native American. The articles, which are intended to inform the reader about Indians and problems of the education of the Indian, are divided into these categories: approach and philosophy, lessons of history, problems of today, critique and evaluation, a sampling of film and book reviews, "relevant" education, and a sampling of curriculum. Four other collections in this series are: *Anthropology* (see preceding annotation), *Literature, History,* and *Current Affairs.*

Jennings, Francis, editor. The Newberry Library American Indian Bibliographical Series. Ind U Pr 1976.
Dobyns, Henry F. Native American Historical Demography: A Critical Bibliography.
Heizer, Robert F. The Indians of California: A Critical Bibliography.
Helm, June. The Indians of the Subarctic: A Critical Bibliography.
Iverson, Peter. The Navajos: A Critical Bibliography.
Tanner, Helen Hornbeck. The Ojibwas: A Critical Bibliography.

As the Newberry bibliographies say in their introductions, because so much of the existing literature on the American Indian is "very uneven," the purpose of the series is "to put Indians properly back into the central role in their own history and into the history of the United States of America as well—as participants in, rather than obstacles to, the creation of American society and culture." Each bibliography has an introductory essay, followed by book lists for beginners and for a basic library collection. The complete bibliographical list includes journal articles and books, with asterisks to indicate those that are suitable for secondary students.

"This is a most ambitious undertaking, and certainly few other institutions could have put the funds together and the scholars as well, in order to perform such a monumental task" (*Indian Historian* 10: 46, Summer 1977).

Keiser, Albert. The Indian in American Literature. Octagon 1970.

This book traces the concept of the Indian in American literature, from the creation of the Pocahontas legend by Captain John Smith to John Neihardt. It includes useful discussions of American writers such as Longfellow, Cooper, Thoreau, and Garland. A documented and scholarly work on the part the Indian has played in American literature.

Kelly, Ernece B., editor. Searching for America. NCTE 1972.

In keeping with a policy statement by the NCTE Board of Directors at its 1970 annual meeting, the NCTE Task Force on Racism and Bias in the Teaching of English sponsored a study of twelve books widely used as college-level American literature texts. This is the report of their findings. In addition, members of the committee, all of whom represented minorities, contributed essays commenting on the literature, culture, or history of their particular racial or ethnic group. The reviews are mainly intended for college teachers, but they are also helpful for high school teachers in promoting sensitivity to stereotypes and racism in American literature. Especially helpful is the essay "Native American Literature" by Montana H. Rickards. Now out of print, the book may be ordered through the ERIC system (ED 058 213).

Klein, Barry T., editor. Reference Encyclopedia of the American Indian. Vol. I. Todd Pubns 1973.

This is the second edition of a useful guide to resources such as museums, libraries, Indian associations, monuments, parks, reservations, tribal councils, schools, Indian courses, arts and crafts shops, visual aids, government publications, magazines, and periodicals. Includes a bibliography.

Lass-Woodfin, Mary Jo, editor. Books on American Indians and Eskimos: A Selection Guide for Children and Young Adults. ALA 1978.

This annotated bibliography is designed to aid educators in selecting books for children and young adults that accurately portray American Indians and Eskimos. Over 800 fiction and nonfiction books, arranged alphabetically by author, are critically reviewed. Each annotation gives the approximate grade level of the book and discusses in some detail the book's plot, illustrations, writing style, and portrayal of Indian life. Books are assigned ratings of good, adequate, or poor based on the above criteria. The thought-provoking introductory essay offers suggestions for selecting accurate children's books on American Indians and examines common problems and misconceptions in the existing literature. A subject index is included.

Marken, Jack W., compiler. The American Indian: Language and Literature. AHM Pub 1978.

This is the most nearly complete bibliography available on the languages and literature of the American Indian. Except for

some critical works about non-Indian authors such as James
Fenimore Cooper, the emphasis is on literature about Indians
by Indian writers. Articles from books and from more than
three hundred journals are organized geographically from west
to east, with four major nongeographical sections covering
bibliography, autobiography, general literature, and general
language. Although the entries are not annotated, this is a
valuable and comprehensive work for anyone doing scholarship
in the field.

Morey, Sylvester M. American Indians and Our Way of Life. Myrin
Institute 1961.

An address delivered in 1961 at the Waldorf School of Adelphi
College under the auspices of the Myrin Institute for Adult
Education, summarizing some of the ways in which the Indian,
particularly the Iroquois, has affected American life in the past
and the "opportunity which he points out to us for the future."
Morey emphasizes the political influence of the League of the
Iroquois upon Franklin, Jefferson, and Paine, and expresses his
belief that the Indians' intuitive ideas and their openness to
spiritual reality and nature can help solve the problems of
modern society.

Pearce, Roy H., and J. Hillis Miller, editors. Savagism and Civilization: A Study of the Indian and the American Mind. Johns
Hopkins 1967.

In this reissue of a primarily historical study, the authors explore the eighteenth century belief that the Indian was savage—
everything which white Americans believed they had put behind
them and therefore could not tolerate in others. Thus the
Indian either had to conform to what white America called
civilization or be destroyed. Of special interest to the teacher
of literature are Chapters VI and VII, which examine the idea
in drama and poetry, and the image in fiction, respectively.

Rose, Alan Henry. Demonic Vision: Racial Fantasy and Southern
Fiction. Archon. Shoe String 1976.

A scholar of English literature examines the use of black and
Indian characters in southern fiction as symbols of evil, irra-
tionality, and bestiality. He contends that from the beginning,
the British settler in both the North and the South saw the
Indian as having characteristics attributed to the devil. In the
South there was "a consequent blurring together of Negro and

Indian as both agents of the devil. . . ." Although the emphasis
is on blacks, some Indian characters are discussed, especially
those in the literature of William Gilmore Simms, Mark Twain,
and William Faulkner.

Snodgrass, Jeanne O., compiler. American Indian Painters: A Biographical Directory. Mus Am Ind 1968.

This directory contains the biographies of more than eleven
hundred American Indian artists with statistics about their lives
and works, famous Indian ancestors, and lists of exhibitions
of their art.

Ullom, Judith, compiler. Folklore of the North American Indians:
An Annotated Bibliography. LC 1969.

A bibliography of folklore collections, compiled especially for
"the storyteller or librarian serving children and for the child's
own reading." The eleven culture areas used by Stith Thompson
in his *Tales of the North American Indians*, including the
Eskimo, are employed in this volume. Each section is followed
by a list of special editions for children. The annotations
contain information about the collector, the kinds of tales in
the volume, and sometimes a review statement about the book.
Illustrations in black and white are from various books annotated in the bibliography.

Zolla, Elémire (translator Raymond Rosenthal). The Writer and
the Shaman: A Morphology of the American Indian. HarBraceJ
1973.

Zolla, a professor of American literature at the University of
Genoa, has undertaken the difficult task of tracing the image
and the myths about the American Indian throughout the
breadth of literature. Beginning with the literature of the
Renaissance and Enlightenment, with its longing for innocence
on the one hand and its view of Indian savagery and demonol-
ogy on the other, the study is well done where it concerns
white literature through the nineteenth century. But when the
author discusses Indian literature and what he calls "poetic
ethnography," he is dealing with such a massive amount of
material that he omits important writers, mixes purely literary
works with ostensibly anthropological works, and makes gross
errors of fact. He sloughs off Momaday as "the author of
paintings in prose" in little more than half a page and uses

student poems, moving though they may be, as signs of the future, instead of using works by established Indian poets.

"I myself do not find convincing Professor Zolla's celebration of currently chic popular mysticism as the final revelation of the 'truth about the Indians.' As a matter of fact, it mars an otherwise immensely learned and carefully researched book" (*American Indian Quarterly* 1: 122, Summer 1974).

## A Basic Library of Indian Literature

The following are suggestions for schools that would like to start or add to a basic collection of works by and about the American Indian. Effort has been made to select representative, quality books that are available at reasonable cost, but a number of more expensive editions have been included because they are written by Indians or are Newbery Award-winning books.

*Primary Grades*

Aliki. Corn Is Maize: The Gift of the Indians. T Y Crowell, 1976.

Baylor, Byrd, ed. And It Is Still That Way. Scribner, 1976.

Baylor, Byrd, ed. Before You Came This Way. Dutton, 1969.

Baylor, Byrd, ed. The Desert Is Theirs. Scribner, 1975.

Baylor, Byrd, ed. Hawk, I'm Your Brother. Scribner, 1976.

Baylor, Byrd, ed. They Put on Masks. Scribner, 1974.

Baylor, Byrd, ed. When Clay Sings. Scribner, 1972.

Benchley, Nathaniel. Small Wolf. Har-Row, 1972.

Bierhorst, John, ed. The Ring in the Prairie. Dial, 1976.

Biesterveld, Betty. Six Days from Sunday. Rand, 1973.

Blades, Ann. A Boy of Taché. Tundra Bks, 1976.

Blood, Charles L., and Martin A. Link. The Goat in the Rug. Parents, 1976.

Buff, Mary, and Conrad Buff. Hah-Nee of the Cliff Dwellers. HM, 1956.

Bulla, Clyde Robert. Indian Hill. T Y Crowell, 1963.

Clark, Ann Nolan. Along Sandy Trails. Viking Pr, 1969.

Clark, Ann Nolan. In My Mother's House. Viking Pr, 1941.

Conklin, Paul. Choctaw Boy. Dodd, 1975.

Dodge, Nanabah Chee. Morning Arrow. Lothrop, 1975.

Fall, Thomas. Jim Thorpe. T Y Crowell, 1970.

Hodges, Margaret. The Fire Bringer: A Paiute Indian Legend. Little, 1972.

Keegan, Marcia. The Taos Indians and Their Sacred Blue Lake. Messner, 1972.

McDermott, Gerald. Arrow to the Sun. Viking Pr, 1974.

Maher, Ramona. Alice Yazzie's Year. Coward, 1977.

Miles, Miska. Annie and the Old One. Little, 1971.

Moyers, William, and David C. Cooke. Famous Indian Tribes. Random, 1954.

Perrine, Mary. Nannabah's Friend. HM, 1970.

Pine, Tillie S., and Joseph Levine. The Indians Knew. McGraw, 1957.

Rockwell, Anne. The Dancing Stars: An Iroquois Legend. T Y Crowell, 1972.

Schweitzer, Byrd Baylor. One Small Blue Bead. Macmillan, 1965.

Showers, Paul. Indian Festivals. T Y Crowell, 1969.

Sleator, William. The Angry Moon. Little, 1970.

Tobias, Tobi. Maria Tallchief. T Y Crowell, 1970.

Toye, William. The Loon's Necklace. Oxford U Pr, 1977.

Witter, Evelyn. Claw Foot. Lerner Pubns, 1976.

Young, Biloine, and Mary Wilson. How Carla Saw the Shalako God. Independence Pr, 1972.

Young, Biloine, and Mary Wilson. Jennie Redbird Finds Her Friends. Independence Pr, 1972.

Young, Biloine, and Mary Wilson. The Medicine Man Who Went to School. Independence Pr, 1972.

*Intermediate Grades*

American Indian Historical Society. The Weewish Tree. Am Ind Hist Soc, seven times each year.

Barnouw, Victor. Dream of the Blue Heron. Dell, 1969.

Bealer, Alex W. Only the Names Remain: The Cherokees and the Trail of Tears. Little, 1972.

Bierhorst, John. Songs of the Chippewa. FS&G, 1974.

Bleeker, Sonia. The Apache Indians: Raiders of the Southwest. Morrow, 1951.

Bleeker, Sonia. The Cherokee: Indians of the Mountains. Morrow, 1952.

Bleeker, Sonia. The Chippewa Indians: Rice Gatherers of the Great Lakes. Morrow, 1955.

Bleeker, Sonia. The Delaware Indians: Eastern Fishermen and Farmers. Morrow, 1953.

Bleeker, Sonia. Horsemen of the Western Plateaus: The Nez Perce Indians. Morrow, 1957.

Bleeker, Sonia. Indians of the Longhouse: The Story of the Iroquois. Morrow, 1950.

Bleeker, Sonia. The Navajo: Herders, Weavers, and Silversmiths. Morrow, 1958.

Bleeker, Sonia. The Sea Hunters: Indians of the Northwest Coast. Morrow, 1951.

Bleeker, Sonia. The Seminole Indians. Morrow, 1954.

Bleeker, Sonia. The Sioux Indians: Hunters and Warriors of the Plains. Morrow, 1962.

Cheatham, K. Follis. Spotted Flower and the Ponokomita. Westminster, 1977.

Clifford, Eth. The Year of the Three-Legged Deer. HM, 1972.

Clymer, Theodore. Four Corners of the Sky. Little, 1975.

Coen, Rena Neumann. The Red Man in Art. Lerner Pubns, 1972.

Crompton, Anne Eliot. The Winter Wife: An Abenaki Folktale. Little, 1975.

Davis, Russell, and Brent Ashabranner. Chief Joseph: War Chief of the Nez Perce. McGraw, 1962.

de Leew, Adèle. Maria Tallchief. Dell, 1975.

Epstein, Anne Merrick. Good Stones. HM, 1977.

Felton, Harold W. Nancy Ward, Cherokee. Dodd, 1975.

Garst, Shannon. Crazy Horse: Great Warrior of the Sioux. HM, 1950.

Goble, Paul, and Dorothy Goble. Red Hawk's Account of Custer's Last Battle. Pantheon, 1969.

Goble, Paul, and Dorothy Goble. Brave Eagle's Account of the Fetterman Fight. Pantheon, 1972.

Goble, Paul, and Dorothy Goble. Lone Bull's Horse Raid. Bradbury Pr, 1973.

Grimm, William C. Indian Harvests. McGraw, 1973.

Harnishfeger, Lloyd. The Collector's Guide to American Indian Artifacts. Lerner Pubns, 1976.

Hofsinde, Robert. The Indian and His Horse. Morrow, 1960.

Hofsinde, Robert. The Indian and the Buffalo. Morrow, 1961.

Hofsinde, Robert. Indian Arts. Morrow, 1971.

Hofsinde, Robert. Indian Costumes. Morrow, 1968.

Hofsinde, Robert. Indian Hunting. Morrow, 1962.

Hofsinde, Robert. The Indian Medicine Man. Morrow, 1966.

Hofsinde, Robert. Indian Music Makers. Morrow, 1967.

Hofsinde, Robert. Indian Picture Writing. Morrow, 1959.

Hofsinde, Robert. Indian Sign Language. Morrow, 1956.

Hunt, W. Ben. The Complete Book of Indian Crafts and Lore. Golden Pr. Western Pub, 1954.

Jones, Hettie, ed. The Trees Stand Shining. Dial, 1971.

Lavine, Sigmund A. The Games the Indians Played. Dodd, 1974.

Lavine, Sigmund A. Indian Corn and Other Gifts. Dodd, 1974.

Lyons, Oren. Dog Story. Holiday, 1973.

McGaa, Ed. Red Cloud. Dillon, 1971.

Marriott, Alice. Sequoyah: Leader of the Cherokees. Random, 1956.

Moyer, John W. Famous Indian Chiefs. Rand, 1957.

Nelson, Mary Carroll. Annie Wauneka. Dillon, 1972.

Nelson, Mary Carroll. Michael Naranjo. Dillon, 1975.

O'Dell, Scott. Island of the Blue Dolphins. Dell, 1971.

O'Dell, Scott. Sing Down the Moon. HM, 1970.

O'Dell, Scott. Zia. HM, 1976.

Sneve, Virginia Driving Hawk. The Chichi Hoohoo Bogeyman. Holiday, 1975.

Sneve, Virginia Driving Hawk. High Elk's Treasure. Holiday, 1972.

Sneve, Virginia Driving Hawk. Jimmy Yellow Hawk. Holiday, 1972.

Sneve, Virginia Driving Hawk. When Thunders Spoke. Holiday, 1974.

Sobol, Rose. Woman Chief. Dial, 1976.

Supree, Burton, and Ann Ross. Bear's Heart. Lippincott, 1977.

Williams, Neva. Patrick des Jarlait: The Story of an American Indian Artist. Lerner Pubns, 1975.

Wolf, Bernard. Tinker and the Medicine Men. Random, 1973.

Wood, Nancy. Many Winters. Doubleday, 1974.

*Junior High School*

Allen, Terry, ed. The Whispering Wind: Poetry by Young American Indians. Doubleday, 1972.

Armer, Laura Adams. Waterless Mountain. McKay, 1931.

Armstrong, Virginia I., ed. I Have Spoken: American History through the Voices of the Indians. Swallow, 1971.

Borland, Hal. When the Legends Die. Bantam, 1972.

Brandon, William, ed. The American Heritage Book of Indians. Dell, 1964.

Brandon, William, ed. The Magic World: American Indian Songs and Poems. Morrow, 1972.

Brown, Dee. Wounded Knee: An Indian History of the American West. Adapted for young readers by Amy Ehrlich. HR&W, 1974.

Burt, Jesse, and Robert B. Ferguson. Indians of the Southeast: Then and Now. Abingdon, 1973.

Carter, Forrest. The Education of Little Tree. Delacorte, 1976.

Cody, Iron Eyes. Indian Talk: Hand Signals of the North American Indian. Naturegraph, 1970.

Day, A. Grove, ed. The Sky Clears: Poetry of the American Indians. U of Nebr Pr, 1964.

Doughty, Wayne Dyre. Crimson Moccasins. Har-Row, 1972.

Eastman, Charles Alexander. Indian Boyhood. Dover, 1971.

Ellis, Mel. Sidewalk Indian. HR&W, 1974.

Erdoes, Richard. The Rain Dance People: The Pueblo Indians, Their Past and Present. Knopf, 1976.

Erdoes, Richard. The Sun Dance People: The Plains Indians, Their Past and Present. Knopf, 1972.

Forman, James. People of the Dream. Dell, 1974.

Fuller, Iola. The Loon Feather. HarBraceJ, 1940.

Hagan, William T. American Indians. U of Chicago Pr, 1961.

Hale, Janet Campbell. The Owl's Song. Avon, 1976.

Highwater, Jamake. Anpao: An American Indian Odyssey. Lippincott, 1977.

Keith, Harold. Rifles for Watie. T Y Crowell, 1957.

Kroeber, Theodora. The Inland Whale: Nine Stories Retold from
California Indian Legends. U of Cal Pr, 1959.

Kroeber, Theodora. Ishi, Last of His Tribe. Bantam, 1973.

McNichols, Charles. Crazy Weather. U of Nebr Pr, 1967.

Marriott, Alice, and Carol Rachlin. American Indian Mythology.
NAL, 1972.

Meyer, William. Native Americans: The New Indian Resistance.
Int Pub Co, 1971.

Momaday, N. Scott. The Way to Rainy Mountain. Ballantine,
1972.

Richter, Conrad. The Light in the Forest. Knopf, 1966.

Rockwood, Joyce. Long Man's Song. HR&W, 1975.

Rockwood, Joyce. To Spoil the Sun. HR&W, 1976.

Sandoz, Mari. The Story Catcher. G&D, n.d.

Schoor, Gene. The Jim Thorpe Story: America's Greatest Athlete.
Messner, 1951.

Stump, Sarain. There Is My People Sleeping. Gray, 1970.

Witheridge, Elizabeth. Just One Indian Boy. Atheneum, 1974.

Witt, Shirley Hill, and Stan Steiner, eds. The Way: An Indian
Anthology of American Indian Literature. Vin. Random, 1972.


*Senior High School*

American Indian Historical Society. Indian Historian. Am Ind Hist
Soc, quarterly.

Ball, Eve. In the Days of Victorio: Recollections of a Warm
Springs Apache. U of Ariz Pr, 1970.

Berger, Thomas. Little Big Man. Fawcett, 1977.

Borland, Hal. When the Legends Die. Bantam, 1972.

Brandon, William, ed. The American Heritage Book of Indians.
Dell, 1964.

Brandon, William, ed. The Magic World: American Indian Songs and Poems. Morrow, 1972.

Brown, Dee. Bury My Heart at Wounded Knee: An Indian History of the American West. Bantam, 1972.

Corle, Edwin. Fig Tree John. Liveright, 1971.

Day, A. Grove, ed. The Sky Clears: Poetry of the American Indians. U of Nebr Pr, 1964.

Deloria, Vine, Jr. Custer Died for Your Sins: An Indian Manifesto. Avon, 1970.

Deloria, Vine, Jr., ed. Of Utmost Good Faith. S&S, 1971.

Dodge, Robert K., and Joseph B. McCullough, eds. Voices from Wah'Kon-Tah: Contemporary Poetry of Native Americans. Intl Pub Co, 1974.

Hagan, William T. American Indians. U of Chicago Pr, 1961.

Herbert, Frank. Soul Catcher. Bantam, 1973.

Highwater, Jamake. Song from the Earth: American Indian Painting. NYGS, 1976.

Katz, Jane, ed. I Am the Fire of Time: The Voices of Native American Women. Dutton, 1977.

Kopit, Arthur. Indians: A Play. Hill & Wang, 1969.

Kroeber, Theodora. Ishi in Two Worlds: A Biography of the Last Wild Indian in America. U of Cal Pr, 1961.

La Farge, Oliver. Laughing Boy. HM, 1929.

Lame Deer, John, and Richard Erdoes. Lame Deer: Seeker of Visions: The Life of a Sioux Medicine Man. S&S, 1972.

Lurie, Nancy Oestreich, ed. Mountain Wolf Woman, Sister of Crashing Thunder: The Autobiography of a Winnebago Indian. U of Mich Pr, 1961.

McNickle, D'Arcy. Native American Tribalism: Indian Survivals and Renewals. Oxford U Pr, 1973.

McNickle, D'Arcy. The Surrounded. U of NM Pr, 1978.

Maestas, John, ed. Contemporary Native American Address. Brigham, 1976.

Marriott, Alice, and Carol Rachlin. American Indian Mythology. NAL, 1972.

Milton, John R., ed. The American Indian Speaks: Poetry, Fiction and Art by the American Indian. Dakota Pr, 1974.

Momaday, N. Scott. House Made of Dawn. Har-Row, 1968.

Momaday, N. Scott. The Names: A Memoir. Har-Row, 1976.

Neihardt, John G. Black Elk Speaks: Being the Life Story of a Holy Man of the Oglala Sioux. PB, 1961.

Rosen, Kenneth, ed. The Man to Send Rain Clouds: Contemporary Stories by American Indians. Vin. Random, 1974.

Silko, Leslie Marmon. Ceremony. Viking Pr, 1977.

Steiner, Stan. The New Indians. Delta. Dell, 1969.

Thompson, Stith, ed. Tales of the North American Indians. Ind U Pr, 1966.

Underhill, Ruth Murray. Red Man's America: A History of the Indians in the United States. U of Chicago Pr, 1971.

Vanderwerth, W. C., ed. Indian Oratory: Famous Speeches by Noted Indian Chieftains. Ballantine, 1975.

Washburn, Wilcomb E. The Indian in America. Har-Row, 1975.

Waters, Frank. The Man Who Killed the Deer. PB, 1971.

Welch, James. Winter in the Blood. Har-Row, 1974.

Wiebe, Rudy. The Temptations of Big Bear. McClelland, 1973.

Witt, Shirley Hill, and Stan Steiner, eds. The Way: An Indian Anthology of American Indian Literature. Vin. Random, 1972.

## Sources of Additional Materials

Most of the books in this bibliography are readily available from public or university libraries. However, for the serious student of the American Indian there is a wealth of material from other sources that are less accessible. The following list of addresses is intended to direct researchers, teachers of Indian students, and other interested persons to a few basic sources of information.

*Akwesasne Notes*, Rooseveltown, NY 13683

Many outstanding books on the American Indian are available for purchase from this newspaper.

American Indian Historical Society, 1451 Masonic Avenue, San Francisco, CA 94117

Publisher of monographs by and about Indians, as well as the journal *Indian Historian*, the newspaper *Wassaja*, and *The Weewish Tree*, a magazine for young Indians.

American Museum of Natural History, Central Park West at 79th Street, New York, NY 10024

Publisher of *Natural History* and *Curator.* The museum has a library and reading room.

Association on American Indian Affairs, 432 Park Avenue South, New York, NY 10016

Publishers of booklists and the bulletin *Indian Affairs.*

Indian Arts and Crafts Board Library, Room 4004, U.S. Department of the Interior, 18th and C Streets N.W., Washington, DC 20240

A source of many books on Indian arts and crafts.

*Journal of American Indian Education,* Bureau of Educational Research and Services, College of Education, Arizona State University, Tempe, AZ 85281

Published triannually, this journal includes materials about Indian education and Indian affairs.

Library of Congress, General Reference and Bibliography Division, Washington, DC 20540

In addition to research materials, the library has children's books.

Library of Congress, Music Division, Archive of Folksong, Washington, DC 20540

Holdings include more than 10,000 recorded items of American Indian music, lore, language, and oral history.

Museum of the American Indian, Heye Foundation, Broadway at 155th Street, New York, NY 10032

A library, photographic archives, and publications department are located at this museum.

Navajo Curriculum Center, Rough Rock Demonstration School, Chinle, AZ 86503

The center publishes Navajo biographies, histories, legends, and curriculum materials especially for use by elementary and secondary schools.

Publications Service, Haskell Indian Junior College, Lawrence, KS 66044

Many Indian titles, including bilingual curriculum materials, are available from this source.

Superintendent of Documents, U.S. Government Printing Office, Washington, DC 20402

Publications of the Bureau of Indian Affairs and reports of government agencies and committees about Indian affairs may be ordered from the above address. Many other pamphlets and books on the American Indian are available at little or no cost.

The following sources provide copies of photographs from their collections for a nominal fee. Write for information.

Office of Anthropology, Smithsonian Institution, Washington, DC 20560

Still Pictures Section, National Archives, Washington, DC 20408

# Biographies of Selected
# American Indian Authors

In this section are capsule biographies of fifty-four of the more prolific or better known American Indian scholars and writers—novelists, poets, editors, compilers, historians, and anthropologists. Authors whose only works are autobiographies are not included, even though those autobiographies may be valuable and well written. A number of young Indian short story writers and poets, not listed here, are publishing individual works in magazines and collections.

### Edward Ahenakew, 1885-1961

Part French and part Cree, Ahenakew, who claimed Chief Pound-maker among his ancestors, was born on the Sandy Lake Reserve in Canada. He attended Wycliffe College in Toronto, was ordained an Anglican priest in 1912, and was sent to the Mission at Onion Lake. When the influenza epidemic swept his reserve in 1918-19, the suffering of his people caused him to begin the study of medicine. A serious illness interrupted his career, however, and he was sent to Chief Thunderchild's reserve to recover his health under a medical mission worker there. It was suggested to Ahena-kew that he collect the stories of the old days of his tribe, which proved to be good therapy for him. He went on to write stories about Old Keyam, a fictional character, and eventually continued his mission work. The notes that he made during his illness were edited by Ruth Buck for publication in *Voices of the Plains Cree.*

### Will Antell, 1935-

A member of the Chippewa tribe, Mississippi band, Antell is the author of the children's biography of his fellow tribesman *William Warren,* and a director of Indian education with the state of Minnesota. He was born on the White Earth Reservation in Minnesota, and has been a visiting professor at Harvard University. He has par-

ticipated in many community and professional organizations and
is a past president of the National Indian Education Association.


Kay Bennett, 1922–

Kay Bennett, Navajo author, artist, and doll maker, was born in
a hogan at Sheepsprings Trading Post, New Mexico. Her Indian
name was Kaibah. She attended boarding school at Toadlena, New
Mexico, and served as a teacher-interpreter at Phoenix Indian
School for seven years. She lived in Afghanistan during 1958–1960
and has traveled in the Far East, Middle East, and Europe. Her
autobiography, *Kaibah*, is the story of her childhood on the
reservation and her going away to school. Her second book,
*Navajo Saga*—written with her husband, Russ Bennett, a retired
engineer—covers the early history of her family, including the
period of the Navajos' attempted resistance as they faced removal
to the Bosque Redondo Reservation. Kay Bennett illustrates her
own books and lives with her husband in Gallup, New Mexico,
where she was chosen as New Mexico's Mother of the Year in
1968.


Black Elk, 1862–1950

Black Elk was a holy man of the Oglala Sioux, a visionary and
medicine man. He was a cousin of Crazy Horse and knew Sitting
Bull, Red Cloud, American Horse, and Spotted Tail. During his
youth he had many visions, and since he had been instructed in
the sacred lore of his people by famous medicine men such as
Whirlwind Chaser, Black Road, and Elk Head, the Keeper of the
Pipe, these visions imposed a heavy burden to help his people and
to keep whole the sacred hoop of his nation. Black Elk fought at
the Little Bighorn and was present at Wounded Knee in 1890.
In later years he traveled with Buffalo Bill to Italy, France, and
England, where he danced for Queen Victoria. In 1930 he told his
life story to the Nebraska poet John G. Neihardt and it was published in 1932 as *Black Elk Speaks*. He lived for many years in a
log house near Manderson, South Dakota. When he was over
ninety, Black Elk gave an interview with anthropologist Joseph
Epes Brown (published in *The Sacred Pipe*), in which he expressed
his fear that the religion of his people would die.

## Michael Borich, 1949–

Michael Borich is a native of Waterloo, Iowa, where he teaches high school and where he has spent considerable time at the nearby Tama Indian settlement. His maternal great-grandmother was a full-blooded Sac and Fox. "Swimming in the Rock," his first submitted poem, was published in *The New Yorker*. *The Black Hawk Songs*, a collection of his poems, has been published by the University of Illinois Press.

## Maria Campbell, 1940–

Daughter of Scottish and Cree parents, Maria Campbell represents the Metis or mixed bloods of Canada. She was born while her parents were on the trap-line in northern Saskatchewan. Her great-grandfather emigrated from Scotland and married the niece of Gabriel Dumont, president of the provisional government which the half-breeds of Canada set up before the Riel Rebellion in 1884. Other members of her family were either half-breeds or Cree Indians from the Sandy Lake Reserve. She is active in the Alberta Native Movement and has written an autobiography, *Halfbreed*.

## Forrest Carter, 1925–

As a boy of five, Carter went to live in the mountains of Tennessee with his Cherokee grandparents, who taught him the history and values of the Cherokees. Following their death, he became a cowhand and worked throughout the South and Southwest, but his main interest is in the history of his people. In addition to his autobiography, *The Education of Little Tree*, Carter has also written two novels, *Gone to Texas* and *The Vengeance Trail of Josey Wales*. The first of these was made into a motion picture, *The Outlaw Josey Wales*.

## K. Follis Cheatham, 1943–

Cheatham is a free-lance writer and photographer living in Raleigh, North Carolina. She has given programs on Native American culture and history to groups of all ages in Michigan, Tennessee, and North Carolina. She is the author of a children's book, *Spotted Flower and the Ponokomita*.

## Vine Deloria, Jr., 1933–

Deloria is a Standing Rock Sioux and was born at Martin, South Dakota, on the Pine Ridge Reservation. He comes from a distinguished family of scholars, churchmen, warriors, and chiefs. He has degrees from Iowa State University, Lutheran School of Theology at Rock Island, Illinois, and the University of Colorado. He was a member of the Board of Inquiry on Hunger and Malnutrition and of the National Office for the Rights of the Indigent, and was executive director of the National Congress of American Indians. His publications include *Custer Died for Your Sins: An Indian Manifesto* (1969); *We Talk, You Listen* (1970); *Of Utmost Good Faith* (1971), an anthology of documents pertaining to Indian affairs, which he edited; and *God Is Red* (1973), a discussion of Indian religion. He is presently teaching in the College of Ethnic Studies, Western Washington State College.

## Adolph L. Dial, 1922–

A Lumbee Indian, Dial is a professor of history at Pembroke State University in North Carolina. He was born near Pembroke and educated in the Indian public schools of Robeson County. After receiving his bachelor's degree in history, he served in the United States Army in Europe during World War II. He received his M.A. and Certificate of Advanced Graduate Studies at Boston University and was a teacher in the Lumbee Indian schools, and presently heads the department of American Indian Studies at Pembroke State University. He is the author of several publications on Lumbee history, including *The Only Land I Know: A History of the Lumbee Indians.*

## Frederick J. Dockstader, 1919–

An Oneida-Navaho Indian, Dockstader was born in Los Angeles. He received a B.A. in 1940 and an M.A. in 1941 from Arizona State College and a Ph.D. from Western Reserve University in 1951. He taught school in Flagstaff, Arizona, and Cranbrook, Michigan, and was staff ethnologist at Cranbrook Institute of Sciences, 1949–1952. From 1952 to 1955 he was a faculty member and curator of anthropology at Dartmouth College. In 1955 he became assistant director of the Museum of the American

Indian, Heye Foundation, New York, and was made director in 1960. He is a practicing artist and silversmith and the author of *The Kachina and the White Man* (1954), *The American Indian in Graduate Studies* (1955), *Indian Art in America* (1962), *Indian Art in Middle America* (1964), and *Indian Art in South America* (1966).

## Nanabah Chee Dodge, 1946–

A young Navaho, Dodge has written a book for children, *Morning Arrow*, which received first prize in the annual contest of the Council on Interracial Books for Children. She lives in Phoenix, Arizona, where her interests, in addition to writing, are gardening, horseback riding, music, and drama.

## Michael Dorris, 1945–

Dorris, a Modoc, is founder and chair of the department of Native American studies at Dartmouth College. An anthropologist who has worked in Alaska and Montana, he has taught Native American studies and anthropology at several colleges. He is a member of the Minority Commission of the Modern Language Association and the American Association for the Advancement of Science. He wrote the introduction to Joseph Farber's collection of photographs, *Native Americans: 500 Years After*.

## Charles Alexander Eastman, 1858–1939

Eastman, whose Indian name was Ohiyesa, was born near Redwood Falls, Minnesota, but fled into Canada with his uncle following the Minnesota Uprising of 1862. He was living among the Santee Sioux when he began his education in 1882 at Santee, Nebraska. He attended Dartmouth College and received his M.D. from Boston University. After a disillusioning experience as government physician on the Pine Ridge Reservation, where he treated captives from the Wounded Knee Massacre, he began a private practice. He spent considerable time in Washington, D.C., where he sought reparations for Indians whose land was taken. He was the author of four books: *Indian Boyhood* (1902), *Soul of an Indian* (1911), *From the Deep Woods to Civilization* (1916), and *Indian Heroes and Great Chieftains* (1918).

Dan George, 1899–

Dan George is chief of the Capilano tribe of British Columbia, a movie and television actor, and the author of a book of prose poems, *My Heart Soars*. He was nominated for an award for his role in the film *Little Big Man*, and he also starred in the Canadian National Film Board movie *Cold Journey* and in the television version of *The Ecstasy of Rita Joe*.

Janet Campbell Hale, 1946–

Born in Riverside, California, Janet Campbell Hale lived on the Coeur d'Alene Reservation in northern Idaho until she was ten and for a short time on the Colville Reservation in Washington, before settling on the Yakima Reservation. She attended Wapato High School in Washington, but as a junior she transferred to the Institute of American Indian Arts. She was awarded a scholarship to the University of California Writing Workshop and attended City College in San Francisco and the University of California in Berkeley. Her poetry has appeared in many publications and in Terry Allen's anthology, *The Whispering Wind*. She is the author of a junior novel, *The Owl's Song*.

Jamake Highwater, 1942–

Of Blackfoot and Cherokee parentage, Jamake Highwater has earned B.A., M.A., and Ph.D. degrees and writes widely on Indian affairs, travel, art, myths, dances, and ceremonies. He has recently been appointed American Indian consultant for special programs of the New York State Council on the Arts, to inaugurate activities in the arts among New York State's Indian population. Writing under the name of J. Marks Highwater, he has published a controversial best-seller, *Mick Jagger*, and with Eugene Fodor is coeditor of *Europe under 25: The Young Person's Guide*. He is the author of *Rock and Other Four Letter Words; Song from the Earth*, the first history of American Indian art; *Anpao*, a junior novel which was a Newbery Honor Book; and Fodor's *Indian America*. His by-line has appeared in *The New York Times*, *Esquire*, *Cosmopolitan*, *Vogue*, *Penthouse*, *Playgirl*, *Gallery*, *Stereo Review*, *Harper's Bazaar*, *Los Angeles Free Press*, *Look*, and *The Chicago Tribune*.

## Adolf Hungry Wolf, 1944–

Hungry Wolf and his family have issued a series of books about Indian life from their home, Good Medicine Ranch, in a valley in the Rocky Mountains of Canada. Their titles are: *Good Medicine: Companion Issue* (1971); *Good Medicine in Glacier National Park: Inspirational Photos and Stories from the Blackfoot People* (1971); *Good Medicine: Life in Harmony with Nature* (1971); *Good Medicine Traditional Dress Issue: Knowledge and Methods of Old-Time Clothing; Legends Told by the Old People* (1972); *Charlo's People: The Flathead Tribe of Montana* (1974); and *Indian Summer* (1975).

## E. Pauline Johnson, 1861–1913

Emily Pauline Johnson, the daughter of a Mohawk chief, was born on the Six Nations Reservation at Brantford, Ontario. Her father's family could be traced to Hiawatha; on her mother's side she was related to the novelist William Dean Howells. Johnson began writing poems at an early age and later lectured and gave poetry readings in both England and the United States. Her volume *Legends of Vancouver* is based on stories told to her by Chief Jo Capilano, a Siwash. In 1961 the Canadian government issued a stamp with her picture on it, to celebrate the centenary of the year of her birth. She was the first author and the first Indian to be so recognized by Canada.

## Basil Johnston, 1929–

Johnston was born on the Parry Island Reserve and is a member of the Ojibway tribe of the Cape Coker Indian Reserve in Ontario. He was educated in reserve schools in Ontario and at Loyola College in Montreal, where he took his degree in 1954. At the Ontario College of Education he received his certification as a secondary-level history teacher. Johnston is currently with the department of ethnology at the Royal Ontario Museum in Toronto where he is a teacher of Ojibway language and mythology and a lecturer in North, Central, and South American history. He is the author of *Ojibway Heritage* and a contributor to the *Dictionary of Canadian Biography*.

## Jack Frederick Kilpatrick, 1915-1967

Kilpatrick, a Cherokee whose formal education was in music, was born in Stillwater, Oklahoma. He attended Bacone College and Northeastern State College of Oklahoma, and received his Bachelor of Music degree from the University of Redlands in 1938. He earned the Master of Music degree from Catholic University of America in 1946, and the Doctor of Music degree in 1950 from the University of Redlands. He composed 168 symphonies, an opera, and music for six historical dramas and was on the music faculty at Southern Methodist University during 1946-1967. His writing was in the area of Cherokee legend and religion: *Friends of Thunder* (1964), *Walk in Your Soul* (1965), *The Shadow of Sequoyah* (1965), *Sequoyah: Of Earth and Intellect* (1965), and *Run Toward the Nightland* (1967), which he coauthored with his wife, Anna Gritts Kilpatrick. In 1959 he was presented the second citation ever given by the Cherokee Nation (the first was given in 1824 to Sequoyah for his syllabary). The award was given to Kilpatrick "for exceptional contribution and achievement in music and in the drama and exemplary service to the cultural welfare of the Cherokee Nation." The chief of the Cherokee called him "another Sequoyah."

## Francis LaFlesche, 1857-1932

Francis LaFlesche, son of a famous Omaha family, began his education in the Presbyterian Mission School on the Omaha Reservation in Nebraska. When he was in his twenties he attracted the attention of Senator Samuel J. Kirkwood of Iowa for his ability as an interpreter. When Kirkwood later became Secretary of the Interior he remembered the young Omaha and had him appointed as a copyist in the Office of Indian Affairs. LaFlesche's early ethnological work was as an interpreter and aide for well-known ethnologist Alice Fletcher. During the years in Washington, D.C., he studied law. While working for the Bureau of American Ethnology, he became known for preserving the ceremonials and ancient songs of the Plains Indians, especially those of the Osage. He was author of *The Middle Five: Indian Schoolboys of the Omaha Tribe; The Omaha Tribe*, with Alice Fletcher; *The Osage Tribe: Rite of the Chiefs* (1914-15); *The Osage Tribe: The Rite of Vigil* (1917-18); *The Osage Tribe, Two Versions of the Child-Naming Rite* (1925-26); and *The Osage Tribe, Rite of the Wa-xo-*

*be* (1927–28). In 1929 the University of Nebraska awarded him the honorary Doctor of Letters degree.

## Frank LaPointe

A member of the Rosebud Sioux, LaPointe was formerly editor of *Eyahapa—The Rosebud Sioux Herald.* He is now an assistant school superintendent at St. Francis, South Dakota, and executive director of Sicangu Oyate Ho, Inc., a Sioux parent group which has assumed greater control of school operations. He spent four years at Rockhurst College in Kansas City, Missouri, and four years in the United States Navy as an enlisted journalist. For one year he was a reporter with the *Littleton Independent* and the *Arapahoe Herald* in Littleton, Colorado. He is the author of *The Sioux Today.*

## Robert Franklin Leslie, 1911–

Leslie was born in Texas of Scottish and Cherokee ancestry. Since boyhood he has explored the wilderness of western Canada, the United States, and Mexico. He received his B.A. degree from Santa Barbara State College and his M.A. in botanical ecology from the University of Southern California. He has been a teacher of French and Spanish at various schools in California since 1940. As an ecologist and photographer, he has lectured widely and conducted photography tours of southwestern Indian reservations, Mexico, Canada, and Europe. He is the author of *The Bears and I*—which has been translated into five European languages and fictionalized as a Disney production—and *Read the Wild Water, High Trails West, Wild Courage,* and *In the Shadow of a Rainbow.*

## Oren Lyons

Chief of the Turtle Clan of the Onondaga Nation, Lyons has the Indian name of Jo-ag-quis-ho, which means "bright sun rays making a path in the snow." He received a Bachelor of Fine Arts degree from Syracuse University and is now an assistant professor of American studies, teaching Indian history, at the State University of New York in Buffalo. He is the illustrator of two children's books by Virginia Driving Hawk Sneve, *Jimmy Yellow Hawk* and *High Elk's Treasure,* and the author and illustrator of a children's book, *Dog Story.*

## Ed McGaa, 1936–

Born on the Pine Ridge Reservation in South Dakota, McGaa is a member of the Oglala Sioux tribe and a fifth-generation descendant of Red Cloud. He is a graduate of St. John's University, Collegeville, Minnesota, and the law school at the University of South Dakota. As a marine fighter pilot he flew 110 combat missions over Vietnam, for which he was awarded eight Air Medals and the Vietnamese Cross of Gallantry. He was deputy director of human rights for St. Paul, Minnesota, and assistant director of Indian education for the Minnesota State Department of Education. He is author of a children's biography, *Red Cloud*.

## D'Arcy McNickle, 1904–1977

McNickle, a member of the confederated Salish and Kootenai tribes of the Flathead Indian Reservation, was born in St. Ignatius, Montana. He was educated in mission and public schools and at the University of Montana (1921–25), Oxford University (1925–26), and the University of Grenoble (1931). He was co-founder of the National Congress of American Indians and from 1936 to 1952 was director of the Branch of Tribal Relations for the Bureau of Indian Affairs. He also was executive director of American Indian Development, Inc., a privately financed project for leadership training and group development in Indian communities; professor of anthropology at the University of Saskatchewan; program director of the Center for American Indian History, Newberry Library, Chicago; and member of the Smithsonian Institution's editorial advisory board for revision of the *Handbook of North American Indians*. McNickle was the author of several works of history and anthropology: *The Indian Tribes of the United States: Ethnic and Cultural Survival* (1962), *They Came Here First* (1949), *Indians and Other Americans*, with Harold E. Fey (1959), and *Native American Tribalism: Indian Survivals and Renewals* (1973). He wrote two novels, *The Surrounded* (1936) and *Runner in the Sun* (1954), and a biography of Oliver La Farge, *Indian Man* (1971).

## George Manuel, 1921–

Born in Chase, British Columbia, George Manuel, a member of the Shuswap tribe, coauthored *The Fourth World* (1974). He grew up with his grandparents on the Shuswap Reserve, where his grandfather was an Indian doctor or shaman. As a young man, Manuel suffered tuberculosis of the hip, and following three years in hospitals and sanitariums, he worked in a sanitarium until the end of World War II. Later he farmed and worked in a lumber mill. He turned to politics when he realized that the Department of Indian Affairs would no longer help to pay the medical bills for his son's tonsillectomy. He has since served as president of the National Indian Brotherhood of Canada.

## John Joseph Mathews, 1895–

Mathews was born in Pawhuska, Oklahoma, on the Osage Reservation. He is the great-grandson of William Shirley Williams, known in western history as Old Bill Williams, and his Osage wife. After a tour of duty in the U.S. Flying Service during World War I, Mathews earned a B.A. degree from the University of Oklahoma in 1920. He then studied natural science at Merton College, Oxford University, taking a B.A. degree in 1923. After spending three years in business in Los Angeles, Mathews returned to the Osage Reservation, where he has engaged in ranching and writing. In 1932 his *Wah' Kon-Tah: The Osage and the White Man's Road* received a Book-of-the-Month Club award. Mathews's other books include *Sundown* (1934), *Talking to the Moon* (1945), *Life and Death of an Oilman: The Career of E. W. Marland* (1951), and *The Osages: Children of the Middle Waters* (1961).

## William Meyer, 1938–

Meyer is an Eastern Cherokee and was born in Georgia. He studied at Colorado College, Cooper Union, and the Art Students' League, majoring in engineering and art. He has exhibited his paintings and sculptures extensively. He also has worked as a theatrical engineer and taught or lectured on the American Indian heritage at New York University, Brooklyn College, Hunter College, Columbia University, and Bucknell University. In addition to his membership in numerous Indian organizations, Meyer has been an officer of the Young American Indian Council and the American Indians United. As a journalist he has worked on two reports—*Hunger and Malnutrition USA*, and the Citizens' Advocate Center's *Our Brother's Keeper*. He is the author of *Native Americans: The New Indian Resistance*.

## Emerson Blackhorse Mitchell, 1945–

Mitchell, a Navajo, was born near Shiprock, New Mexico, where he looked after his grandmother's sheep as a boy. He attended public school, and in 1962 was admitted to the Institute of American Indian Arts in Santa Fe, New Mexico. There he had Terry Allen as a teacher of creative writing. As an assignment she encouraged him to write about his boyhood on the reservation. This developed into *Miracle Hill: The Story of a Navaho Boy*, published in 1967. He later attended Fort Lewis College. He is winner of the National Poetry Day Award, the Vincent Price Award for Creative Writing, and the Scottsdale Short Story Award. He currently is the community development supervisor for the Office of Navajo Economic Opportunity in Chinle, Arizona.

## Natachee Scott Momaday, 1913–

Natachee Scott Momaday is the mother of novelist and poet N. Scott Momaday and the wife of Kiowa artist Al Momaday. She was born in Fairview, Kentucky, of Cherokee, French, and English descent. She attended Haskell Junior College, Crescent College, and the University of New Mexico, and received a B.A. from the University of California, Los Angeles, in 1954. She has been a newspaper reporter and, since 1936, has taught in reservation schools for the Bureau of Indian Affairs. She is also an artist, having exhibited and won awards for her works in oil, pastel, pen and ink, and charcoal. She is the author of a number of works for children: *Woodlawn Princess, Velvet Ribbons*, and *Owl in the Cedar Tree*. Her latest book is the collection of short works by Indian authors, *American Indian Authors* (1972).

## N. Scott Momaday, 1934–

Momaday is the winner of the 1969 Pulitzer Prize in fiction for his novel, *House Made of Dawn*. Born in Lawton, Oklahoma, son of Kiowa artist Al Momaday and Cherokee author Natachee Scott Momaday, he grew up on Navajo, Apache, and Pueblo reservations in the Southwest. He received his A.B. degree from the University of New Mexico in 1958, his M.A. in 1960, and his Ph.D. in 1963 from Stanford University. He has been professor of English and comparative literature at the University of California at Berkeley, and is currently on the staff at Stanford University. He edited *The Complete Poems of Frederick Goddard Tuckerman* (1965) and is the author of *The Way to Rainy Mountain* (1969), in which the migration of the Kiowa tribe is retraced in a blend of tribal legend, history, and family memoirs. His latest books are a collection of poems, *The Gourd Dancer* (1976), and *The Names: A Memoir* (1976). He has received the Stanford University Creative Writing Fellowship in Poetry, a John Jay Whitney Foundation Fellowship, and a Guggenheim Fellowship, among other honors.

## Nasnaga, 1941–

A member of the United Remnant Band of the Shawnee Nation, Nasnaga has written his first book, *Indians' Summer.*

## Duane Niatum, 1938–

A poet and editor of poetry collections, Duane Niatum—better known to some readers as Duane McGinnis—was born in Seattle, Washington, as a member of the Klallam tribe. After serving in the United States Navy he graduated from the University of Washington and received his M.A. from Johns Hopkins University. After two years of naval service in Japan, Niatum feels that his poetry has been influenced by Oriental culture. He has published four volumes of poetry: *After the Death of an Elder Klallam, Ascending Red Moon, Carriers of the Dream Wheel,* and *Digging out the Roots.* He has given poetry readings at many colleges and universities and was awarded first prize in poetry by the Pacific Northwest Writers' Conference in 1966 and 1970.

## John Milton Oskison, 1874–1947

Oskison, a Cherokee, had many Oklahoma Shawnees as friends in his boyhood. These contacts and his admiration for Tecumseh caused him to write the biography *Tecumseh and His Times.* He also is the author of *Brothers Three,* a novel of an Oklahoma farm family, and *A Texas Titan: The Story of Sam Houston,* a biography that features Houston's numerous contacts and friendships with Indians.

## Arthur Caswell Parker, 1881–1955

Arthur Parker was a folklorist, archaeologist, museologist (a word he coined), defender of Indian rights, writer of children's books, historian, and museum director. His father, a graduate of Fredonia State Normal School in New York, was of Seneca Iroquois ancestry. His mother, who was of Scottish-English descent, was a teacher among the Senecas for a number of years. As an ethnologist, Parker pioneered in describing the subsistence patterns and food resources of the American Indians. His study of maize and its uses was a model for similar work on the Plains Indians. His recovery of the Code of Handsome Lake contributed to the revitalization of interest in Native American culture. He is the author of *A History of the Seneca Indian, The Life of General Ely S. Parker, Seneca Myths and Folk Tales, Red Jacket: Last of the Senecas,* and *Parker on the Iroquois.*

## Wilfred Pelletier

An Ojibway, Pelletier was born in Wikwemikong on Manitoulin Island in Lake Huron. He left school at age nine, became a guide for campers in the forests of Ontario, and later a successful businessman in the white world. Finding the experience dehumanizing, he returned to his reserve to become a political Indian—attending conferences, making speeches, and trying to help the poor. He is now co-director of the Nishnawbe Institute in Toronto, an Indian educational and cultural project. In addition to *No Foreign Land: The Biography of a North American Indian,* which he wrote with Ted Poole, a white friend, he also has written *For Every North American Indian Who Begins to Disappear I Also Begin to Disappear* and *Who Is Chairman of This Meeting?*

## James Redsky, 1899–

Redsky was born at Rice Bay on Lake of the Woods, Ontario. In 1915 he joined the 52nd Canadian Light Infantry Regiment and was trained as a machine-gunner. At the end of World War I he returned to his home in Shoal Lake, where he lived from the land and worked as a carpenter and tourist guide. He is a holy man of the Ojibway Mide-wi-win religion and has recorded tales of the Ojibway in his book *Great Leader of the Ojibway: Mis-quona-queb,* edited by James R. Stevens.

## John Rogers, 1890–

John Rogers, whose Chippewa name is Way Quauh Gishig, was born near Mahnomen, Minnesota. He attended the Indian school at Flandreau, South Dakota, for six years and then returned to his mother's home in Minnesota where he found that he had to relearn Indian ways. Later he went to live with his father at Cass Lake, Minnesota. He is the author of *Red World and White: Memories of a Chippewa Boyhood.*

## Joe Sando, 1923–

Sando was born at Jemez Pueblo in New Mexico and was raised in the traditional way. He was educated at Indian and mission schools and later at Eastern New Mexico College at Portales and at Vanderbilt University in Nashville, Tennessee. An educator, lecturer, and participant in many Indian organizations, he is author of the book *The Pueblo Indians* and articles on Indian education and economy.

## Anna Moore Shaw, 1898–

Shaw, a Pima, began collecting legends when she realized those of the Pima tribe might be lost. She first heard the legends in the Piman language in the early 1900s and began recording them thirty years later. The youngest of ten brothers and sisters, she was born on the reservation and attended reservation schools. She graduated from Phoenix Technical School and now teaches the Pima tongue to children in kindergarten. She has served on the board of trustees of the C. H. Cook Christian Training School, Tempe, Arizona, and on the Salt River Reservation Mutual Self-Help Housing Commission. She has edited the Salt River Pima monthly *Tribal Newsletter* and is the author of *Pima Indian Legends* (1968).

## Leslie Marmon Silko, 1948–

A writer of poetry and short stories, Silko is of mixed ancestry—Laguna Pueblo, Mexican, and white. She grew up on the Laguna Pueblo. Her stories have appeared in magazines and in anthologies, including Kenneth Rosen's *The Man to Send Rain Clouds*, Martha

Foley's *Best Short Stories of 1975*, and *Two Hundred Years of Great American Short Stories*. She is also the author of a novel, *Ceremony*.

### Allen P. Slickpoo, Sr., 1929–

Director of the Nez Perce History and Culture Projects, Slickpoo graduated from the Chemawa Indian School in Oregon and attended the University of Idaho for two years. He served on the Nez Perce Executive Committee and was recording secretary of the National Congress of American Indians, 1960–61. He wrote the first Overall Economic Development Program report for the Nez Perce tribe, was the director and principal informant in the Lewis and Clark College of Education housing and resource development survey for the Nez Perce Reservation, and assisted in solving employment problems among the Nez Perce people in cooperation with the Bureau of Indian Affairs and the state of Oregon. The Nez Perce legends in the book *Nu Mee Poom Tit Wah Tit* were collected under his direction.

### Virginia Driving Hawk Sneve, 1933–

Born in Rosebud, South Dakota, Sneve is the daughter of an Episcopalian priest. She holds B.S. and M.S. degrees from South Dakota State University and lives in Flandreau, South Dakota, where she has been a counselor and teacher of English. She is married to Vance M. Sneve, an industrial arts teacher, and is the mother of three children. Sneve is the author of several junior novels: *Jimmy Yellow Hawk, High Elk's Treasure, When Thunders Spoke, The Chichi Hoohoo Bogeyman,* and *Betrayed*. In 1971 her book *Jimmy Yellow Hawk* won the Council on Interracial Books for Children award for the best manuscript by an American Indian author.

### Luther Standing Bear, 1868–?

Luther Standing Bear, hereditary chief of the Dakotas, spent his boyhood on the plains of Nebraska and South Dakota. He spent four years at Carlisle Indian School and worked for a time at John Wanamaker's in Philadelphia, but then returned to the Rosebud agency in South Dakota, where he became a tinsmith and teacher in the Indian school. In 1898 he joined Buffalo Bill's Wild

West Show as an interpreter. In later years he acted in motion pictures, lectured, and wrote books. During the 1920s and '30s he worked to get the best possible conditions for his people on the reservation. He is the author of *My People, the Sioux, My Indian Boyhood,* and *Land of the Spotted Eagle.*

## John Stands In Timber, 1882-1967

Stands In Timber was a Northern Cheyenne and the official historian of his tribe. He was a founding member of the American Indian Historical Society and in 1965 received its annual award of Honored Indian Historian. Up until his death he wrote a column entitled "A Cheyenne Man" for the *Indian Historian.* In 1956 he met Margot Liberty, who was teaching school in Montana. Under a grant from the Association on American Indian Affairs, she helped him record his experiences in *Cheyenne Memories.* In a review of that book the *Indian Historian* said of him, "John was a gentle and kindly man, who could not find it in his heart to feel bitterness for anyone."

## Sarain Stump, 1945-1974

Stump, a Shoshone-Cree-Salish, was a poet and artist from Canada. He illustrated two books, *Assiniboine Legends* and *Cree Legends,* and published a collection of poetry, *There Is My People Sleeping,* at the age of twenty-five—four years before his death by drowning.

## Sun Bear, 1929-

Sun Bear, a Chippewa from Minnesota, is a writer and editor of *Many Smokes,* an Indian magazine. He spent his earlier years living in the wilderness much as his ancestors did. His editorial headquarters serve as a center for encouraging Native American arts and helping Indians develop work projects. He is author of *Buffalo Hearts: A Native American's View of Indian Culture, Religion and History.*

## John Tebbel, 1902-

Of Ojibwa-Irish-English background, John Tebbel was born in Boyne City, Michigan. He has a B.A. degree from Central Michigan

University and a master's degree from Columbia University. In 1948 he was awarded the honorary degree of Litt.D. by Central Michigan. Following a career in journalism on the *Detroit Free Press, Providence Journal, New York Times, Newsweek,* and *American Mercury,* he became associate editor at E. P. Dutton & Company. He joined the faculty of New York University in 1949 and was chair of the journalism department from 1954 to 1965, excepting 1958–1962 when he was on leave as director of the university's Graduate Institute of Book Publishing. He resigned in 1965 to devote more time to teaching and writing. He has written three historical novels, seven biographies, five American histories, and two popular medicine books. Among his books are *George Horace Lorimer and the Saturday Evening Post; From Rags to Riches: Horatio Alger and the American Dream; The Life and Good Times of William Randolph Hearst;* and *The Marshall Fields.* In the area of American Indian history he has written *The American Indian Wars, The Compact History of the Indian Wars,* and a novel, *The Conqueror.*

### William Vaudrin, 1943–

Vaudrin, of Chippewa and Cree descent, was born in Akron, Ohio. He received his B.A. degree from Alaska Methodist University in 1966 and his M.F.A. from the University of Oregon in 1968. As a student in Alaska, he wintered several years with the Tanaina Indians of Pedro Bay and Nondalton villages, hunting, fishing, and trapping with them. He is currently a commercial fisherman and sled-dog racer in Bristol Bay, Alaska. He was a part-time instructor in English in 1967–68 at the University of Oregon, Eugene, and an instructor in English at Anchorage Community College, Alaska, in 1968–70. He is the author of *Tanaina Tales from Alaska* (1969) and writes poetry, short stories, folklore, and reviews for Alaskan publications.

### Gerald Robert Vizenor, 1934–

A Chippewa poet, editor, and guidance director, Vizenor was born in Minneapolis, Minnesota. He attended New York University and received a B.A. degree from the University of Minnesota, where he also has been an M.A. candidate in Asian area studies. He was a group worker for the Ramsey County Corrections Authority in

St. Paul in 1957-58 and corrections agent for the Minnesota State Reformatory in 1960-61. He also has been director of Inter-Cultural Programs at Park Rapids, Minnesota, and of American Indian Studies at Bemidji State College, Bemidji, Minnesota. Vizenor is the author of two collections of haiku in English— *Raising the Moon Vines* and *Seventeen Chiros*—and three works about modern Indian life—*The Everlasting Sky, Scenes and Ceremonies,* and *Wordarrows.* He has edited collections of Anishinabe (Chippewa) song poems and legends, entitled *Anishinabe Nagamon* and *Anishinabe Adisokan,* respectively.

### Frank Waters, 1902–

Waters is part Cheyenne and was born in Colorado Springs, Colorado, and attended Colorado College of Engineering, graduating in 1925. He has worked as a telephone company engineer, apple picker, oil field roustabout, Hollywood screenplay writer, informant-consultant for the Los Alamos Scientific Laboratory, and editor of *El Crepuscolo*, a Spanish-English newspaper in Taos, New Mexico. He is the author of *The Man Who Killed the Deer; Masked Gods: Navajo and Pueblo Ceremonialism; Book of the Hopi;* and *Pumpkin Seed Point*, among other books.

### James Welch, 1940–

Welch is a Blackfoot on his father's side and a Gros Ventre on his mother's. He attended schools on the Blackfoot and Fort Belknap Reservations in Montana before graduating from high school in Minneapolis, Minnesota. He attended the University of Minnesota, Northern Montana College, and the University of Montana, where he received his B.A. and worked in the Creative Writing Workshop. In addition to his collection of poetry, *Riding the Earthboy 40*, and his novel, *Winter in the Blood*, he has published poetry in magazines such as *Choice, Concerning Poetry, New American Review, Poetry, South Dakota Review,* and *The New Yorker*.

# II Bibliography

# Introduction to
the Bibliography

By the time any bibliography is printed it is already likely to be more or less out of date. Today the available literature by and about the American Indian is growing constantly—older works are being reissued, Native American writers are speaking out, and non-Indian writers are becoming increasingly aware of the Indian as a subject of interest to an expanding public.

To enhance the scope and timeliness of this volume, an attempt has been made to include a representative number of the newer works. Annotations of older books have been updated with current critical comments where possible. Some out-of-print books of enduring merit have been listed because they may be available in libraries or because a publisher may soon recognize their value and reprint them.

## Criteria for Selection

One of the main problems in selecting books by or about the American Indian is how to judge them. All of the criteria that apply to any good literature, of course, apply here: If it is fiction, is it a good story? Does it avoid excessive coincidence? Are the characters reasonably complex individuals rather than oversimplified stereotypes? Is the style generally sensitive rather than pedestrian? Above all, in evaluating Indian literature the important question is whether the story is true to the Indian way.

The user of this bibliography is not to assume that every book in it is necessarily recommended as a fine example of Indian life and culture. Some of the books give the white point of view, which often does not convey an accurate picture of the Indian. Yet, to provide an understanding of what happened to the Indian, it seems that the reader should learn what whites thought, erroneous though it might be. Some books seem to present a one-sided or degrading picture of the Indian, and we felt a bit uncomfortable about including them. But teachers have asked, "What about this book?" Omitting the book might only indicate ignorance of its existence; including it might serve the useful purpose of revealing the problems that at least some readers saw in the book.

In an effort to determine which books offer accurate portrayals of Indian life, we have depended on reviews by Indian scholars—such as Vine Deloria, Jr., and N. Scott Momaday—where possible, and on evaluations found in various publications developed by Indian organizations.

One such source was *Akwesasne Notes*, published in Rooseveltown, New York, by the Mohawk Nation, which carries book reviews and lists of books and recordings recommended for purchase. Some of these are critical and evaluative. The Midwinter 1976–77 issue listed fifty books, available in soft cover, which the editors regarded as a basic library of Indian literature.

The *American Indian Quarterly*, published in Hurst, Texas, by the Southwestern American Indian Society, is a scholarly journal of anthropology, history, and literature, which contains extensive critical reviews, articles, and research news. Another periodical, the *Newsletter of the Association for Study of American Indian Literature*, is quite new. Its scholarly book reviews are especially useful to teachers of Native American literature.

Three publications issued in San Francisco by the American Indian Historical Society were valuable resources: *The Indian Historian*, a fine magazine produced by Indians, carries a column of book reviews and its articles often have bibliographies of recommended reading. *Wassaja*, the "national newspaper of Indian America," includes some book reviews. *Textbooks and the American Indian*, edited by Rupert Costo, is a critique of books with emphasis on those used in history and geography classes in elementary and secondary schools.

Two publications of the Association on American Indian Affairs were utilized. *A Preliminary Bibliography of Selected Children's Books about American Indians* lists sixty-three books for children six to twelve years and older, each one read, reviewed, and recommended by a Native American. *American Indian Authors: A Representative Bibliography*, edited by Arlene Hirschfelder, is the most nearly complete bibliography of books by Indians.

Sun Bear, a Chippewa Indian, is the author of *Buffalo Hearts: A Native American's View of Indian Culture, Religion and History* (Naturegraph Publishers, Healdsburg, California, 1970), which has a list of recommended Indian books. The second and third editions of *About Indians: A Listing of Books* were another good source. These bibliographies, compiled "to provide information to the many teachers, librarians, and other people interested in books written by or about Indians," are printed in both English and French, with annotations by Canadian university students, including Indians.

By relying as much as possible on references such as these, it is hoped that this volume will serve as a reliable guide to the literature of the American Indian. When one of the books annotated below has been specifically recommended by one of the above sources, it carries a notation to that effect.

Other points entering into the selection of books in the various categories are discussed below.

## *Myth, Legend, Oratory, and Poetry*

When looking for a collection of Indian myths and legends for use in the classroom, teachers must make a number of choices. First they need to decide whether they want a general collection or a collection of myths of a particular tribe. Teachers may want to choose the latter if they are in an area where there are many students from a particular tribe or where the tribe has played an important role in the regional culture. Or, if they are teaching younger children, they may wish to choose a retelling of a single folktale from one tribe; many colorful, appealing versions are available.

In using myths, legends, and poetry we are dealing with literature in translation, with all of its attendant problems. The earliest collections and translations of legends were done by people whose orientation was primarily anthropological. Their aim was to make the stories as accurately Indian as possible. More recently, collectors who are oriented more toward literature or folklore have been publishing editions. Sometimes the teacher must choose between the most literary and the most Indian collection. Certain characteristics of legend and poetry—excessive repetition, for example—were very Indian, but sound unnatural when translated into English. As Anna Moore Shaw points out in *Pima Indian Legends*, the stories were changed as cultural traditions changed and as the tales were told in English. The teacher also may want to consider whether the translations were recorded while the people were still living in a tribal society or after the acculturation process had begun. Most early collections were made by white people, but many more recent collections have been done by Indians—for instance, Kilpatrick, Momaday, Nequatewa, Shaw, Vaudrin, and Vizenor.

Obviously it is impossible to establish hard and fast guidelines.

Individual teachers must consider their aims and the available
alternatives, and make their choices accordingly.

## Fiction

Many theories have been proposed regarding the uniqueness of the
American experience. There is no doubt that contact with the
Indian is one aspect of that uniqueness. While European writers
read reports of this experience and wrote of a noble Red Man
living an idyllic existence, American writers, influenced by American settlers hungry for land, created pictures of bloodthirsty
savages, beautiful Indian maidens, and poor, starving, vanishing
tribes.

Early American fiction writers found it impossible to see and
picture Indians as they really were. Although early white settlers
learned to grow corn, pumpkins, tomatoes, beans, squash, peanuts,
and sweet potatoes from Indian farmers and probably would have
starved without this knowledge, none of the Indian characters in
early American fiction are pictured as farmers. They are instead
shown as roving hunters and savage warriors. No early American
fiction pictures the Indian statesman and orator, even though
the Iroquois formed a powerful confederacy in the seventeenth
century. Instead of the Iroquois orator and statesman Hiawatha,
Henry Wadsworth Longfellow gave us a Chippewa Hiawatha,
romantically noble but unreal.

Recently, however, writers of adult fiction have given us more
realistic Indian characters. Led by Indian novelists N. Scott
Momaday *(House Made of Dawn)*, James Welch *(Winter in the
Blood)*, Leslie Marmon Silko *(Ceremony)*, and D'Arcy McNickle
*(Runner in the Sun* and *The Surrounded)*, non-Indian authors also
have captured more nearly the true spirit of Indian values and
thought. White authors, such as Dan Cushman *(Stay Away, Joe)*
and Thomas Berger *(Little Big Man)*, have been recognized by
Indians themselves for their ability to portray the humor of Indian
life. Serious white writers like Hal Borland *(When the Legends
Die)* and Rudy Wiebe *(The Temptations of Big Bear)*, junior
novelists such as Janet Campbell Hale and Joyce Rockwood, and
writers of elementary books such as Virginia Driving Hawk Sneve
and Byrd Baylor also have created more realistic Indians.

## Biography and Autobiography

An Indian might tell his or her story for a number of different
reasons. Some, like Geronimo and Black Hawk, told their stories
because they were leaders of their people during difficult times

and wanted later generations to understand the events as they saw them. Others, like Left Handed, Two-Leggings, and Jim Whitewolf, told theirs because they were typical members of their tribes, who wanted to record and explain a way of life that was disappearing.

Because many of the Indians who told their life stories knew little or no English, we are dependent upon their editors and translators for the chance to read their stories. Thus, in selecting Indian autobiographies, the teacher should recognize the problem of finding accurate interpretations by non-Indian editors, ghost writers, and translators of the Indians' statements and the happenings they described.

Black Elk told his story to John Neihardt with Black Elk's son Ben as interpreter. The extent to which the writer in such instances gets into the story depends somewhat upon his or her experience and training. Some who are anthropologists write extensive sections explaining ceremonies and customs; others let the subjects speak for themselves. One of the interesting methods was that of Mountain Wolf Woman, who told her story in Winnebago into a tape recorder and then translated her own words into English for editing by Nancy Lurie. Plenty-Coups, the Crow chief, told his story to Frank Linderman, who was a friend of the tribe, and as other members of the tribe or family gathered around, Plenty-Coups described what was happening and what they said.

One might ask "Who are the real authors of these autobiographies?" Publishers have been inconsistent, sometimes listing the subject as author, sometimes the editor. The Association on American Indian Affairs, in *American Indian Authors: A Representative Bibliography*, takes the stand that the Indian is the author. This bibliography follows the practice of *Books in Print*.

Another kind of autobiography is that in which the subjects tell about their experiences as they made the transition from the Indian society to the white. These are the stories of Indians who went to white schools, either because they wanted to or because they were forced. Among the earliest of these are the autobiographies of Charles Eastman, Luther Standing Bear, and Francis LaFlesche. Because the subjects were fluent in English the reader is not dependent upon possible interpretations by others.

This is not to say that autobiographies written through an editor and translator are invalid. Certainly *Black Elk Speaks* is among the finest of Indian works. But the critical reader must ask, "Who is speaking now?"

*History*

A teacher who wants to plan work in Indian culture must, of course, provide students with background in history. There is no end to the works that might be included in such a background collection. Some choices have to be made. The titles in this section are by no means an exhaustive list, only a beginning.

Junior and senior high school classrooms should have available at least one of the collections of historical documents that compare the Indians' thoughts and statements with those of the whites. Such collections were compiled by Vine Deloria, Jr., an Indian scholar, and by the Council on Interracial Books for Children. If the teacher prefers a work that combines a written summary of history with the pertinent documents, the Spicer collection will serve the purpose. At least one general history should be part of such a collection, but many histories of Indian-white relations have been grossly prejudiced and inaccurate. This bibliography includes some histories in general use (by Collier, Brandon, Hagan, Underhill) which have been recommended by some Indian group, although sometimes with qualifications. Two histories (by Andrist and by Brown) seem to be generally accepted as sympathetic toward the Indian.

Indian authors have written some histories, although most of these deal with a particular tribe. Kay Bennett's story of her family *(A Navajo Saga)* becomes a history of the Navajos during their incarceration at Bosque Redondo. John Stands In Timber, in *Cheyenne Memories*, writes of his tribe's relationships with whites in a history of the tribe.

For the teacher in an area of the country associated with the lore of a particular tribe, there are historical works about specific tribes on every reading level. A few such histories are included here: Foreman, Meltzer, and Bealer, Indians of the Southeast; Hyde, Sandoz, and Hirsch, Indians of the Midwest; Bennett and Terrell, Indians of the Southwest.

It should be noted that few books of straight history have been written for the primary grades. However, some works of historical fiction can be used to introduce young readers to a specific historical period or incident and kindle an interest in further reading. Also, the large, colorful illustrations in many history books for older readers can be used to capture the interest of younger children, even though they may need help in reading the text.

*Traditional Life and Culture*

The study of literature by and about the American Indian must be supported by some background books in traditional life and culture. Included here are a variety of anthropological studies of Indian tribes, ranging from Northey's very easy one *(The American Indian)* to Farb's controversial study *(Man's Rise to Civilization)*. In between are the scholarly studies of Josephy, Marriott and Rachlin, and Embree. There are many books that focus on the culture of a single tribe or several tribes from a particular section of the country, so only representative ones are included (for example, those by Bean, Drucker, Lowie, and Powers for older readers; by Bleeker, Clark, and Sheppard for younger).

Nothing is more vital to an understanding of the myths, legends, and poetry of the Indian than books that explain Indian religions and ceremonials. Two have been done by Indians: *The Sacred Pipe*, by Black Elk, and *The Soul of an Indian*, by Charles Eastman. Recently Indian religions have gained attention, partly because of public fascination with the use of peyote, which has figured in the ritual of the Native American Church. The popularity of the studies of Carlos Castaneda is evidence of this fascination. Somewhat less spectacular studies of peyote and its use are those by LaBarre *(The Peyote Cult)* and Marriott and Rachlin *(American Epic)*.

The study of archaeology and the pre-Columbian Indians carries with it enough mystery to challenge students. A few books of fiction—such as Steele's *The Eye in the Forest*, McNickle's *Runner in the Sun*, and Bandelier's *The Delight Makers*—require some knowledge of theories about prehistoric Indians. Many books listed in this section provide valuable information on recent archaeological discoveries. Especially useful are the easier books by Lauber *(Who Discovered America?)* and Tamarin and Glubok *(Ancient Indians of the Southwest)*, and the more advanced studies by Silverberg *(Home of the Red Man)* and Terrell *(American Indian Almanac)*.

*Modern Life and Problems*

It is possible for English teachers and their students to read Indian legends, poetry, and oratory or the life of Black Elk without any understanding of the problems of modern Indians. They can even read N. Scott Momaday's story of Abel *(House Made of Dawn)* as that of a single disturbed Indian, without really appreciating the magnitude of an Indian's problems in a white society. But if we truly believe that one aim of teaching the humanities is the development of a more sensitive human being, then we must develop the fullest possible understanding of the modern Indian's problems in many areas—education, health (physical and mental), land rights, and civil rights.

The younger reader can gain understanding of modern Indian life through the many books that picture the everyday life of a modern Indian child or tribe, usually in the form of a photographic essay. These books do not treat Indian problems in detail, yet they often give glimpses of the conflict between white and Indian values and the attempts to keep the old culture and language alive. An unusual book for elementary students that is somewhat different in approach is Marcia Keegan's *The Taos Indians and Their Sacred Blue Lake*, which takes an in-depth look at a current land struggle in New Mexico.

For the older reader, the works of Indian scholars who have studied tribal problems are especially useful. The history of the acculturation of the Indian and the resulting problems are clearly described by an Indian anthropologist, D'Arcy McNickle, in *Indians and Other Americans*, in collaboration with Harold E. Fey, a white writer. Vine Deloria, Jr., a Sioux, presents the Indian's views of many aspects of the white world in his best seller, *Custer Died for Your Sins*. In *We Talk, You Listen* he suggests principles from Indian values and philosophy that might well be adopted by the United States to solve problems of ecology, inflation, and imperialism. In *Native Americans: The New Indian Resistance*, William Meyer, a Cherokee, presents a history of the Indian resistance movement, in which he has actively participated. In *The Everlasting Sky*, Gerald Vizenor, a Chippewa, describes interviews with successful young Chippewas in which they discuss their lives and their feelings about the white world in which they have made their mark.

## Music, Arts, and Crafts

The wholeness and oneness of the Indians' life is never more apparent than in their art and music. They did not ask themselves, as modern people do, whether they had talent in these areas. Every Indian was a musician and artist. They sang at their work—whether fishing, hunting, or preparing food—and song and dance were a vital part of their religious ceremonies. They sang about love, and they sang and danced for health, for a vision of life, and before going to war.

Unlike moderns, Indians did not separate the arts from the crafts. Some of their finest design is found in utilitarian objects such as pottery and rugs. Indians of the Northwest decorated their fighting knives with iron and ivory and their fish clubs with carvings. Some of the most elaborate color and design is found in objects associated with religious ceremonials: the kachinas and sand painting of the Southwest, the masks of the Iroquois, and the totem poles of the Northwest. Some art was meant to help preserve historical records—for example, the Sioux Winter Counts and perhaps the ancient rock art found in many regions.

To the Indians, art and music were not luxuries intended mainly for the well-to-do. They made their art and their musical instruments from the materials at hand. Although some might be better sand painters or night chanters than others, all Indians made music and art.

Many of the books in this section are liberally illustrated with drawings, photographs, and paintings, making them suitable for a wide range of interests and abilities, and fascinating to all ages.

How to Use This Bibliography

The books in this bibliography are listed in alphabetical order by author's name and are arranged into seven groups according to subject-matter. Each group is subdivided on the basis of the books' suitability (in reading level or content or both) for readers of elementary school age, junior high school, or senior high school and adult. Books for elementary school readers are further categorized into those for primary (grades 1–3) or intermediate (grades 4–6). Admittedly, reading levels are difficult to assess, and those indicated here are intended only as guides.

Publishers' names have been abbreviated according to the key included in the Directory of Publishers. The publication date is the date of the particular edition being reviewed. Other editions of the book may be available, and comments made here should be applicable to those unless, of course, the book has undergone revision. Some of the books are out of print but have been included because of their merit, and because they may be available in libraries or may be reprinted.

Each annotation gives a brief summary of the book, mentioning in general its good points and its drawbacks, if any. Usually there is information about the author's experiences, knowledge of the subject, or general background if this seems relevant. Sometimes there is a cross-reference to another book located elsewhere in the bibliography, with the section title given in parentheses. Books that have been cited in bibliographies compiled by various Indian authorities carry notations to that effect. Names of these sources are abbreviated in the annotation but are fully listed in the Criteria for Selection section.

Some annotations conclude with critical comment from other reviewers. The date given for the source of the review may be at variance with the publication date of the book because the critic had access to a different edition, but this should not affect the substance of the comment.

Users of the bibliography may be a bit disconcerted by the variation in spelling of the names of some Indian tribes. The practice in each annotation has been to follow the spelling used by the author of that particular book.

# Myth, Legend, Oratory, and Poetry

## Elementary

Baylor, Byrd. **And It Is Still That Way: Legends Told by Arizona Indian Children.** Scribner 1976. Primary.

Arizona Indian schoolchildren retell in their own words forty-one legends about the beginning of the world—a time when animals talked like people, ferocious monsters were slain, and gods counseled the human race. The tales are divided into categories: Why Animals Are the Way They Are, Why Our World Is Like It Is, Great Troubles and Great Heroes, People Can Turn into Anything, Brother Coyote, and There Is Magic All Around Us. The storytellers affirm their continuity with the past and convey the timelessness of the legends by ending them with "It can happen like that now," or "And it is still that way."

"The book is an excellent opportunity to see just how important the environment was to Native Americans" (*Interracial Books for Children Bulletin* 8, no. 8:13, 1977).

Belting, Natalia. **Our Fathers Had Powerful Songs.** Illus. Laszlo Kubinyi. Dutton 1974. Intermediate.

A compilation of the poetry of many Indian groups, including Apache, Kwakiutl, Mandan, and Navajo. The rhythmic power of these people has been captured in the unusually sensitive images of songs. They deal with aspects of the Indian way of life such as birth, death, months, seasons, and ceremonies, including rainmaking, harvest, healing, and blessing. One example is the song of the Sick Moon ceremony which tells of bathing, water sports, foot races, and jokes, and of efforts to cure the pallor of the daytime moon. Delicate drawings in shades of gray further enhance the poetry.

Belting, Natalia. **Whirlwind Is a Ghost Dancing.** Illus. Leo Dillon and Diane Dillon. Dutton 1974. Intermediate.

This book contains many examples of the rich, vivid imagery of North American Indian literature: The Thompson River Indians

believe that the moon smokes a pipe and the clouds are the
smoke; the Iroquois say that Dew Eagle carries a bowl of water
on his back and spreads cooling dew over the hot earth; the
Bella Coola describe Earth-Maker's eyelashes as sun rays shining
through dusty air; to the Indians of Taos Pueblo, the stars are
nightbirds with bright breasts like the hummingbird's. The ancient lore of many other tribes is included in this collection,
which can be enjoyed by all ages. The illustrations, in pastels
and acrylics combined with glaze, are authentic Indian motifs.

Bernstein, Margery, and Janet Kobrin, retold by. Coyote Goes
Hunting for Fire: A California Indian Myth. Illus. Ed. Heffernan. Scribner 1974. Primary.

The Yana Indians of northeastern California first told this story,
which begins with a world devoid of fire, making the animals
extremely cold in the winter. Wolf, who is a very wise chief,
suggests that someone go in quest of fire. When Coyote's plans
fail, five other animals are chosen to make the search: Wolf, the
leader; Fox, who is fast and clever; Sandpiper, who can fly;
Mole, because he can see in the dark; and Weasel, because he
can move without a sound. Their attempt to steal fire from the
Wind People and their failure, in spite of the good work of
Spider, make this an interesting legend.

Bernstein, Margery, and Janet Kobrin, retold by. Earth Namer:
A California Indian Myth. Illus. Ed Heffernan. Scribner 1974.
Primary.

This myth of the Maidu Indians of California describes the creation of the earth. At a time when water is everywhere, Earth
Namer descends from the sky on a rope of feathers, landing on
the raft where Turtle is floating. Because Earth Namer has come
from the sky, Turtle knows he is magic and asks him to make
dry land. Turtle is instructed to dive to the bottom of the water
and bring back some earth, which Earth Namer rolls into a ball
that grows larger and larger and finally becomes the world. Eventually Earth Namer shows the sun its place in the sky, puts up
the stars, and finally creates people and animals. Childlike
sketches illustrate the story.

Bernstein, Margery, and Janet Kobrin, retold by. How the Sun
Made a Promise and Kept It: A Canadian Indian Myth. Illus. Ed
Heffernan. Scribner 1974. Primary.

The Bungee Indians in Canada like to tell this story to explain
the beaver's appearance. Long ago, the sun went wherever he

chose and seldom visited the earth, leaving it dark and cold. The god Weese-ke-jak thought of a plan to capture the sun in a net so that the earth would be warm—much to the sorrow of everyone, for it then became much too hot. The myth tells how Weese-ke-jak made a pact to free the sun, if it would come just close enough to earth to warm it daily. Beaver, the only animal who would brave the heat to gnaw through the net and free the sun, still has a scorched, furless tail as an emblem of his ordeal.

Bernstein, Margery, and Janet Kobrin, retold by. **The Summer Maker: An Ojibway Indian Myth.** Illus. Anne Burgess. Scribner 1977. Primary.

This Ojibway myth is about the creation of summer. All the animals are accustomed to winter and have never experienced the other seasons, but they remember ancient stories when the winds were warm and the earth was green. A fisher named Ojeeg lives on the shores of an icy lake and, because of his fur coat, is oblivious to the cold and snow. His son, however, wants to become a great hunter and dislikes cold weather because he is unsuccessful in hunting and always comes home shivering and covered with snow. Ojeeg asks his friends Otter, Beaver, Lynx, and Wolverine to go in search of summer and finally, thanks to a powerful spirit called a manitou, they are successful. The black and white pen sketches add to the myth's clarity.

"The story as retold remains authentic and holds the reader's attention. The black-and-white illustrations are also quite good" (*Interracial Books for Children Bulletin* 8, no. 8:14-15, 1977).

Bierhorst, John, editor. **The Ring in the Prairie.** Illus. Leo Dillon and Diane Dillon. Dial 1976. Primary.

A retelling of a Shawnee legend of the creation of birds. When Waupee, or White Hawk, discovers a strange circle in the remote part of the forest, he hides himself nearby in the tall grass. A basket descends from the sky and twelve sisters emerge and begin to dance. White Hawk becomes intrigued with the youngest sister, changes himself into a mouse and captures her, and she becomes his wife. A son is born but White Hawk's wife longs to return to her father. Eventually all three return to the sky, taking with them the tails, feet, and wings of every beautiful and unusual bird or animal. All the people choose some part, and become animals and birds. Waupee and his family become white hawks and descend to earth where they are found today.

"This lovely legend is exquisitely illustrated by the Dillons with cut-paper collage" (*Elementary English* 47:1036, November 1970). "Stylized, dramatic, colorful big drawings. . . . A subtle irony tints the surprisingly happy ending" (*Christian Science Monitor* 62:19, 21 November 1970).

Campbell, Maria. **Little Badger and the Fire Spirit.** Illus. David Maclagan. McClelland 1977. Primary.

Ashsinee, a young Indian girl, is visiting her grandparents in present-day Alberta. As the grandfather tells an ancient story, the book returns to the days when the earth was young and the people and animals all spoke one language. Little Badger, the blind boy, is befriended by the wise and gentle Grey Coyote and asks him to find a way to keep warm when the weather is freezing. Grey Coyote admits that there is a way but it is dangerous, for the Fire Spirit is guarded by four strange creatures—Mountain Goat, Mountain Lion, Grizzly Bear, and Rattlesnake. Little Badger's words and actions win the confidence of the animals, illustrating the power of the spirit of peace and brotherhood. The illustrations portray both the present life of Ashsinee and the bygone days of the legend.

Caswell, Helen, retold by. **Shadows from the Singing House: Eskimo Folk Tales.** Illus. Robert Mayokok. C E Tuttle 1968. Intermediate.

In the ancient days, Eskimo folk tales filled with enchanting magic and strange spells were sung in the Singing House. This collection of authentic legends contains stories of why the raven's feathers are black, the origins of fog, and the guillemots, and how a wicked mother was turned into a narwhal. One tale features Qalutaligssuaq "who likes to eat children who make too much noise." The fanciful black and white sketches are by an Eskimo artist.

Chaffee, Allen, adapter. **The Story of Hiawatha.** Illus. Armstrong Sperry. Random 1951. Primary.

An adaptation of "Hiawatha," including prose and excerpts from Longfellow's poem. In the beginning, Gitche Manito, mighty god to the Indians, calls many tribes and pleads with them to live in peace. Hiawatha spends his childhood with his grandmother, Nokomis, and learns the language and secrets of the birds and animals. As he grows into manhood he sets out to punish Mudjekeewis for wronging his mother, and eventually wins the hand of Minnehaha, the lovely daughter of the Arrow-Maker in the land of the Dakotahs. The story ends with the coming of the whites and Hiawatha's departure ". . . into the fiery sunset, . . . into the purple vapors, . . . into the dusk of evening."

Clymer, Theodore. **Four Corners of the Sky.** Illus. Marc Brown. Little 1975. Primary.

An anthology of Native American poems, chants, and oratory collected and translated by Henry Schoolcraft in the nineteenth century and later by Densmore and others. History is portrayed through the text, tribal art, and symbolism. The themes vary from despair to hope and provide understanding of many Indian nations. Several poems describe the Ghost Dance religion and the hopelessness of Indians who were forced onto reservations.

Compton, Margaret. **American Indian Fairy Tales.** Illus. Lorence F. Bjorklund. Dodd 1971. Intermediate.

A new format for a collection of well-known Indian legends originally published in 1895. The tales were taken from material collected by government researchers during the 1870s and 1880s before many of the tribes were confined to reservations, and the settings range from the Pacific Coast to the Midwest prairies and the New England hills. The highly imaginative and often exciting stories describe clever giants and ghost spirits who perform feats of magic, and there are many details of Indian beliefs and ways of life. The artist has provided a significant introduction and striking illustrations.

Crompton, Anne Eliot, retold by. **The Winter Wife: An Abenaki Folktale.** Illus. Robert Andrew Parker. Little 1975. Intermediate.

In this retelling of an Abenaki folktale, an Indian hunter, alone in the cold, traps animals for their pelts and meat. One day he follows a young cow moose, who turns into a young squaw and becomes his "winter wife." Although she warns him not to marry when he returns to his people in the spring, the hunter takes a summer wife and the ensuing, suspense-filled events hold the reader's interest to the last page. The soft-hued ink and wash illustrations add to the sense of mystery.

DeArmond, Dale Burlison. **Raven: A Collection of Woodcuts.** Alaska Northwest 1975. Intermediate.

This most unusual collection of Tlingit legends is one of rare beauty. The stories are brief and to the point, in the style that an old Tlingit would use, and their hero is Raven, who often appears as a trickster. Illustrated by woodblock prints that were inspired by the Indians of the Northwest Coast but do not attempt to duplicate their art.

Erdoes, Richard, transcriber and editor. **The Sound of Flutes and Other Indian Legends.** Illus. Paul Goble. Pantheon 1976. Intermediate.

The author draws upon his many years of listening to Indian storytellers for the legends in this volume, which are mostly Sioux although a few are Cheyenne, Gros Ventre, or Crow. The introduction discusses the variety of legends and the ways in which they were told. The title piece tells how the first *Siyotanka* or flute came into existence and how it was used in courting. Other stories, some of which are humorous, describe "How the Crow Came to Be Black," "The End of the World," and "How the Sioux Nation Came into Beauty."

"Illustrator Goble has succeeded in capturing the legends' beauty and dignity in his artwork, which is surpassed in quality only by the editor's thoughtful way of compiling the stories" (*Interracial Books for Children Bulletin* 8, nos. 6,7:33, 1977).

Field, Edward, translator and editor. **Eskimo Songs and Stories.** Illus. Kiakshuk and Pudlo. Sey Lawr. Delacorte 1973. Intermediate.

Translations of Netsilik Eskimo songs and stories originally recorded by the Danish explorer Knud Rasmussen on his fifth Thule expedition. Selected poems reflect the Eskimos' daily life in a harsh land "cut off from the surrounding world by ice-filled seas and enormous trackless wastes." Others deal with family life, animals, food, hunger, and death. A valuable addition to Eskimo literature, enhanced by stone cuts in black and shades of blue.

Fox, Mary Lou (translator Melvina Corbiere). **Why the Beaver Has a Broad Tail.** Illus. Martin Panamick. Highway Bk 1974. Primary.

In this legend the beaver tricks the muskrat into lending him his flat tail, because he likes the beautiful splashing sound it makes, and then refuses to return the tail in spite of the muskrat's pleas. Based on a story told by Susan Enosse of Mantoulin Island, with an Ojibwe translation. The black and white illustrations are typical of Ojibwe art.

Harris, Christie. **Mouse Woman and the Mischief-Makers.** Illus. Douglas Tait. Atheneum 1977. Intermediate.

These Northwest Indian legends come from the land of totem poles, where people fish and hunt in summer and feast and tell stories in their great houses in the winter. These tales are about Mouse Woman, a narnauk or supernatural being, who is always trying to keep order between other narnauks and the people. Resorting to tact more than trickery, she intervenes in the affairs of a greedy porcupine hunter, a rejected suitor, and a wife held captive by the head of the Killer Whales. There are several black and white illustrations.

Harris, Christie. **Once More upon a Totem.** Illus. Douglas Tait. Atheneum 1973. Intermediate.

The Indians of the Northwest Coast—the Tlingit, Haida, Tsimshian, and Kwakiutl—share these great stories. During the long winter nights, great feasts called potlatches were held, fine gifts were given, special occasions were celebrated, and the best stories were told. The three stories in this book are: "The Prince Who Was Taken Away by the Salmon," which explores the mystery of the Pacific salmon—their disappearance and return to the rivers of the West; "Raven Traveling," featuring an Indian trickster who, in this Tsimshian version, is an incurable glutton; and "Ghost Story," which deals with the natural pattern of life and death and the Indian view of the spirit world and life after death. The reader is helped to understand the reasons for the stories and the nature of the storytellers and their listeners. Authentic black and white symbolic illustrations.

"Mrs. Harris has done justice to these imaginative tales, beautifully transcribing them" (*About Indians*, p. 65).

Heady, Eleanor B. **Sage Smoke: Tales of the Shoshoni-Bannock Indians.** Illus. Arvis Stewart. Follett 1973. Intermediate.

A noted folklorist has compiled tales which she heard from Shoshoni-Bannock storytellers at Fort Hall Reservation in Idaho. These stories describe an ancient world very different from today's. Because there is water everywhere, Bambooka the muskrat brings mud from the bottom of the sea so that Apa, the great Father of all, can roll it and dry it to make it into the earth. Other legends explain how the beaver and the coyote got their characteristic features and how Koat the crow brought nut trees into the Shoshoni country by dropping seeds stolen from the geese. Illustrated with black and white pictures.

Hodges, Margaret. The Fire Bringer: A Paiute Indian Legend. Illus.
Peter Parnall. Little 1972. Primary.

One of the best of many stories about the origin of fire. Coyote,
friend and counselor of the human race, and his young Paiute
companion help the people steal fire from the spirits at Fire
Mountain. After many difficulties they succeed in bringing
warmth to the world. The colorful vocabulary and vivid illustrations make this a dramatic book.

"Simply written and faithful to the spirit of the tale" (*About
Indians*, p. 68).

Houston, James. Kiviok's Magic Journey: An Eskimo Legend.
Illus. by author. Atheneum 1973. Primary.

One of the best-known stories about the folk hero Kiviok,
whose exciting adventures are recounted by Eskimos from
Greenland to Alaska. In this tale Kiviok takes beautiful Kungo
for his wife. Her white feather coat is snatched by a wicked
raven while she bathes in the lake with her sisters, who turn into
snow geese and soar into the sky, leaving Kungo behind. For
seven years she lives happily with Kiviok and their two children
but one day the wicked raven comes and takes Kungo and the
children away. The rest of this fast-moving story tells how
Kiviok sets out on a journey to rescue them.

Houston, James, editor. Songs of the Dream People: Chants and
Images from the Indians and Eskimos of North America. Illus.
by editor. Atheneum 1972. Intermediate.

The author-artist says, "I had the luck to live a good part of my
life near the Ojibwa people. I sometimes fished and gathered
wild rice with them. They were a strong link with the past: they
helped me to shape my future." Later he spent twelve years
with Eskimos. This is a comprehensive collection of chants and
images of tribes from the Eastern Woodland, Central Plains,
Northwest Coast, and Eskimo country, including information
about the songs, the significance of dreams, and the use of
secret terms, masks, and other artifacts. Illustrations are on
every page.

"Selective uses of these poems is recommended for social
studies enrichment and literature classes at the grade school and
secondary level" (*About Indians*, pp. 76–77).

Jagendorf, M. A. **Kwi-na the Eagle and Other Indian Tales.** Illus. Jack Endewelt. Silver 1967. Intermediate.

A colorful, well-researched book containing tales of heroism, song, dance, festival, and faith, from the Ojibwa, Algonquin, Menominee, Tuscarora, Cherokee, Seneca, Biloxi, Quapaw, Penobscot, Zuni, Comanche, Navaho, Sia, Ute, and Indians of Labrador and Texas. The tales deal with animals, tricksters, monsters, the origin of corn, the creation of the world, and folk heroes such as Gluskábe, a Penobscot, and Mánabus, a Menominee.

Jones, Hettie, adapter. **Coyote Tales.** Illus. Louis Mofsie. HR&W 1974. Intermediate.

These four Indian legends, displaying the many facets of the Coyote character, are adaptations from the Assiniboin, Dakota, and Skidi Pawnee, and resemble legends of the Blackfeet, Crow, Cree, Arapaho, and others. Coyote, a nomad, trickster, and four-legged buccaneer, has the charm of a likable animal and the complexity of a human being. He usually appears in the lore of the Great Plains tribes as an old man or a coyote, but also has the power to change himself into other forms. He often amuses himself by getting into trouble, usually for the purpose of tricking another out of food. In these four stories, Coyote outwits the thief who has stolen summer, matches wits with Fox, tricks a young girl, and conquers a man-eating monster. The illustrations reflect the artist's Hopi and Winnebago ancestry.

Jones, Hettie, adapter. **Longhouse Winter: Iroquois Transformation Tales.** Illus. Nicholas Gaetano. HR&W 1972. Intermediate.

A collection of Iroquois transformation tales, which were told only in wintertime. They were not told in other seasons because it was feared that passing animals, intrigued by the legends, might linger and then fail to find their winter homes when the snow fell—nor were they told even in secret, for a bird or bug might possibly be listening. These four stories are about a young chieftain who becomes a robin; a beautiful princess who becomes a fish; evil dancers who become rattlesnakes; and woodland animals who restore a hunter to life. The watercolor drawings have been well researched and add to the mood of the book.

Jones, Hettie, compiler. **The Trees Stand Shining: Poetry of the North American Indians.** Illus. Robert Andrew Parker. Dial 1971. Intermediate.

These songs from many Indian tribes include lullabies, prayers, short stories, and war chants. Part of an ancient oral tradition, they were not translated or recorded until the nineteenth century. In only a few lines they reveal a profound love of nature and a depth of wisdom. Illustrations are full-color paintings by a 1970 Caldecott Medal runner-up. Cited among American Library Association Notable Children's Books, 1971; *School Library Journal* Best Books of the Year, 1971; and Child Study Association Books of the Year, 1971.

"A celebration of the world and all its elements through Indian eyes" (*Library Journal* 96:1781, 15 May 1971). "*The Trees Stand Shining* is an impressionistic collage of North American Indian songs, chants and lullabies that mirror climates of the heart as well as of the natural world. . . . Robert Andrew Parker's illustrations are mythical and mellifluous . . . A handsomely designed and spacious book" (*New York Times Book Review*, 27 June 1971, p. 8). "The poems selected here are beautiful translations, concise and clear, and evocative of an Indian world view" (*About Indians*, p. 79).

McDermott, Beverly Brodsky. **Sedna: An Eskimo Myth.** Illus. by author. Viking Pr 1975. Primary.

The Inuit people, living in the Arctic wastes, are hungry one cold, dark winter. Sedna, the mother of all sea animals, has withheld the people's food because they have not honored her as they should have. Angakok, the man of magic, is summoned and persuaded to ask for Sedna's mercy. After Angakok goes into a trance, Sedna speaks through him, telling the people of how she has been deceived by a cunning bird and abandoned by her father, and promising them food if they will help her. Illustrated with pen and brush in tones of indigo and violet.

McDermott, Gerald, adapter. **Arrow to the Sun: A Pueblo Indian Tale.** Illus. by adapter. Viking Pr 1974. Primary.

Inspired by traditional Pueblo designs, McDermott uses geometric, highly stylized forms and warm, earthy colors to illustrate a Pueblo Indian legend. A boy, searching for his father, is transformed into an arrow and sent to the Lord of the Sun. To prove that he is the sun's child, the boy undergoes four trials, and then returns to earth to bring the spirit of the sun to the people. Bold illustrations appear on every page. Awarded the Caldecott Medal in 1975.

Maher, Ramona. **Alice Yazzie's Year.** Illus. Stephen Gammell. Coward 1977. Intermediate.

The changing world and feelings of Alice Yazzie, an eleven-year-old Navajo girl, are portrayed through twelve free-verse poems that describe the everyday joys and sorrows in her life. She shelters a lamb from the January cold, misses her home during a school trip to Disneyland, pays to see a mangy buffalo in a small cage, and cares for the coyote pup of a friend who has died. Underlying the poems is a deep regard for the Navajo way of life and there is a sadness because some traditional values are changing—as when Alice and her grandfather see Black Mountain, a Navajo holy place, being strip-mined for coal.

Marriott, Alice, compiler. **Winter-Telling Stories.** Illus. Richard Cuffari. T Y Crowell 1969. Intermediate.

Here are some of the wise and humorous Saynday legends from the Kiowa tribe. In the "Saynday-Does-Good Stories," Saynday brings the sun to his people and regulates its heat and light; he turns himself into a puppy to bring the buffalo to the Indians; punishes the deer, who killed people with their sharp teeth, by filing their teeth so they can eat only grass and leaves. In the "Saynday-Makes-Trouble Stories," Saynday gets stuck in a buffalo skull and learns to stay home and mind his own business; Coyote tricks Saynday out of a pot of prairie dog soup; and the reader learns how the bobcat got his spots. See also *Saynday's People: The Kiowa Indians and the Stories They Told* by the same author (Junior Myth).

Martinson, David. **Manabozho and the Bullrushes.** Illus. John Peyton. Duluth Indian Education Advisory Committee, 1976. Primary.

Part of an Indian-sponsored educational series that introduces younger readers to Chippewa legends and culture. The tales of Manabozho were told by Chippewas in interviews with the author, which he tape-recorded. Illustrations are by an Indian painter.

Newcomb, Franc Johnson (editor Lillian Harvey). **Navajo Bird Tales Told by Hosteen Clah Chee.** Illus. Na-Ton-Sa-Ka. Theos Pub Hse 1970. Intermediate.

These authentic folk tales preserve the flavor of Navajo lore and customs. Some of the stories tell why the hummingbird has many colors, why the mourning dove's song is sad, and why the mockingbird sings the songs of other birds. The illustrations are by Na-Ton-Sa-Ka (Harry Walters), a Navajo artist.

Parnall, Peter. **The Great Fish.** Illus. by author. Doubleday 1973. Primary.

Charlie sits at his grandfather's feet, enjoying the friendship and love of the man who tells him so many stories. The warmth of the old cabin, in contrast to the cold weather outside, provides the ideal setting for another story. This time Three Feathers tells of the silver salmon, the King of the Fish, who save the Northwest Indians from starvation. The black and white drawings add to the story.

Rockwell, Anne, retold by. **The Dancing Stars: An Iroquois Legend.** Illus. by author. T Y Crowell 1972. Primary.

This moving Iroquois legend explains the origin of the familiar constellation, the Pleiades. Seven little Indian brothers who love to play and dance in the deep forest are lured by the moon to dance up into the sky. Only the smallest boy is able to escape by running as fast as he can, with the bright star he is wearing making a shining trail behind him. He hears his mother's calls and falls to earth, making the kind of hole a star makes when it falls. When the mother weeps for her fallen star, her warm tears cause a little green shoot to spring up and it grows into a tall pine tree, who can now join his brothers in the sky.

"With her entrancing illustrations, combined with the legend itself, Anne Rockwell has given children a book they will remember for a long time" (*About Indians*, p. 27).

Shor, Pekay, retold by. **When the Corn Is Red.** Illus. Gary Von Ilg. Abingdon 1973. Primary.

A little-known legend that was found in dusty archives is retold in "poetic imagery suggesting the plight of the Indian today and a promise for tomorrow." Long ago when the Tuscarora Indians freely roamed the land and there was an abundance of fish and meat for them to eat, the Great Spirit lovingly gave them a special gift of red corn, asking only in return that they live together peacefully. But the Tuscarora failed to comply with the request and fought among their neighbors, thus causing the corn to turn white.

Sleator, William, retold by. **The Angry Moon.** Illus. Blair Lent. Little 1970. Primary.

A beautiful retelling of a Tlingit legend. Because a little girl, Lapowinsa, laughs at the moon's face she is spirited away to the sky as a prisoner. When Lupan, her playmate, realizes what has happened he shoots arrows at a star and they form a ladder, enabling him to rescue the girl. The large, full-color illustrations are based on Tlingit motifs. A 1971 Caldecott Medal Honor Book.

"While this is a children's book, it is rendered worthwhile reading for adults as well by its relatively mature prose and its colorful and beautifully stylized illustrations" (*About Indians*, p. 29).

Squire, Roger, retold by. **Wizards and Wampum: Legends of the Iroquois.** Illus. Charles Keeping. Abelard 1972. Intermediate.

An unusual collection of Iroquois legends, adapted especially for children. The first tale introduces Feather Toes as the wise and clever storyteller who trades his stories for corn. He tricks Panther into believing that he and his father are wizards and enjoy being eaten by other animals because they keep warm and cozy in the stomachs of the animals while causing them distress. Other tales deal with stone giants and other strange and wonderful creatures. The illustrations add excitement and humor.

"The tales are full of action and are highly imaginative" (*About Indians*, p. 98).

Toye, William, retold by. **The Loon's Necklace.** Illus. Elizabeth Cleaver. Oxford U Pr 1977. Primary.

A Tsimshian legend about a young Indian boy who helps his blind father kill a bear by guiding his bow and arrow. Tricked out of the meat by an old hag, the blind man visits the Loon, who is wise and magical, and pleads for the restoration of his sight so that he can feed his starving family. He is told to hold onto the bird, and together they dive into the lake twice, whereupon the blind man regains his sight. In gratitude he tosses his shell necklace to the bird and it falls on the Loon's neck, leaving beautiful white markings wherever the shells touch the black feathers. Illustrated with paper collages, paper cutouts, and linocuts.

Wood, Nancy. **Many Winters: Prose and Poetry of the Pueblos.** Illus. Frank Howell. Doubleday 1974. Intermediate.

The wisdom of venerable old people of the Pueblo Indians is recorded in poems and prose, giving many interpretations of the Indian way of life. Topics include the beauty of nature, the acceptance of the circle of life, buffalo-hunting customs, the values of a good simple life, and religious beliefs. The writing demonstrates the importance of roots to these Indians and their desperate struggle to keep them alive. The subject of aging is treated sympathetically. Illustrated with portraits by a noted painter who is deeply interested in the contemporary Indian.

### Junior High

Allen, Terry, editor. **Arrows Four: Prose and Poetry by Young American Indians.** WSP 1974.

A collection of prize-winning prose and poetry by participants in a four-year creative writing project begun in 1968 by the Bureau of Indian Affairs. Originally intended to give American Indian high school students extra opportunities to write and their teachers some training in the craft of writing, the project spread from nine secondary schools to twenty-seven secondary and fourteen elementary schools. The pieces were originally published in an annual called *Arrow*.

Allen, Terry, editor. **The Whispering Wind: Poetry by Young American Indians.** Doubleday 1972.

The young poets represented in this volume all spent a year or more in the writing program directed by Allen at the Institute of American Indian Arts at Santa Fe, New Mexico. Many of the poets' names have since appeared in other publications, among them Grey Cohoe, Alonzo Lopez, Janet Campbell, Ronald Rogers, and Emerson Blackhorse Mitchell. The poems express emotions that stem from the writers' varied Indian backgrounds, and from experiences shared by other twentieth century youth, including attitudes toward the Vietnam War and urban blight. Short biographical sketches of the writers are given.

"Most students will want this on their private shelves" (Dee Brown, *New York Times Book Review*, pt. 2, 5 November 1972,

p. 80w). "This book is an excellent collection of poems which will be thoroughly enjoyed by young people. Recommended" (*About Indians*, p. 115).

Bierhorst, John, editor. **In the Trail of the Wind: American Indian Poems and Ritual Orations.** Dell 1975.

Translated from more than forty Indian languages of North and South America, this collection contains creation songs, battle songs, love lyrics, orations, prayers, dreams, and incantations. Many selections come from rituals of birth, love, war, and death; others express themes of the Indian's love of nature, the foreshadowing of conquest, the resultant despair, and visions of a new life. The translators were recognized authorities such as Frank Russell, Paul Radin, Daniel G. Brinton, Alice Fletcher, and Frances Densmore. Includes explanatory notes, a list of sources, a glossary of tribes, cultures, and languages, and an introduction containing a brief history of Indian life from prehistoric times to the present. Illustrated with period engravings.

"An excellent book which opens up study in an area of literature previously not thoroughly explored" (*About Indians*, p. 126).

De Angulo, Jaime. **Indian Tales.** Illus. by author. Hill & Wang 1962.

The author is a professional linguist, amateur anthropologist, and philosopher who lived among the Pit River Indians for forty years. He says: "I wrote these stories several years ago, for my children, when they were little. Some of them I invented out of my own head. Some of them I remembered—at least, parts, which I wove in and out. Some parts I actually translated almost word for word from my texts." The stories are incidents that occurred during a single family's travels, at a time when animals and humans were less distinguishable than they are now. Also enjoyable by adults. On *Akwesasne Notes* basic library list.

"A rare and delightful book for both the young and old, *Indian Tales* captures the wonder, wisdom and rollicking humor of the Indian" (*About Indians*, p. 158).

Feldmann, Susan, editor. **The Storytelling Stone: Myths and Tales of the American Indians.** Dell 1965.

The editor aims to introduce the general reader and students of myth, psychology, and comparative literature to some of the most characteristic tales of the North American Indian oral tradition. The fifty-two, fairly short myths and folk tales are grouped by type, not by tribe or region, into three sections: In the Days of Creation; Trickster; and Tales of Heroes, Supernatural Journeys and Other Folktales. Also useful for high schools.

Hausman, Gerald. **Sitting on the Blue-Eyed Bear: Navajo Myths and Legends.** Illus. Sidney Hausman. Lawrence Hill 1975.

Hausman says that he "heard, found, borrowed, remade or created" the stories and poems in this collection. Introductions give general information about Navajo history, arts, myths, legends, and healing ceremonies. Provides an introduction to Navajo culture, but schools would do better to use more authentic stories that are not "remade or created" by the author. See also *Navajo Histories* by Ethelou Yazzie (this section), which is more appropriate for study.

"*Sitting on the Blue-Eyed Bear* would be a good introduction to Navajo culture for young readers" (*American Indian Quarterly* 3, no. 4:365, Winter 1977–78). "Here is an excellent text (combined with good drawings) that provides an example of exactly how Native American myths and legends should be told" (*Interracial Books for Children Bulletin* 7, no. 6:17, 1976).

Hungry Wolf, Adolf. **Legends Told by the Old People.** Good Medicine Bks 1972.

The author, a blood Indian from the Canadian Rockies, who is living as much as possible in the old way, has collected some of the legends told by old people. The legends come from a number of tribes, including the Sioux, Mandan, Hidatsa, Assiniboine, Nez Perce, Kiowa, Gros Ventre, Flathead, and various Eskimo tribes. These are stories that a grandparent or an old aunt might tell to children.

Kroeber, Theodora. **The Inland Whale: Nine Stories Retold from California Indian Legends.** Illus. Joseph Crivy. U of Cal Pr 1959.

The author has chosen nine tales from California Indians to put "into a familiar idiom, with restraint and good taste," as Oliver La Farge says in the introduction. Many of the themes appear in literature the world over: "Tesilya, Sun's Daughter" is the Hamlet story; "Butterfly Man" has elements of the Fall of Man; "The Man's Wife" is the legend of Orpheus and Eurydice; and

"Loon Woman" is the story of Achilles' heel. There is a discussion of the background, tribal origin, and use of each story, and each has a woman character, although she is not always important.

Marriott, Alice. **Saynday's People: The Kiowa Indians and the Stories They Told.** U of Nebr Pr 1965.

From 1934 to 1936 the author lived among the Kiowas, collecting historical information from the old people—their tribal organization, ceremonials, food, medicines, handicrafts—and their stories of old Uncle Saynday, their trickster hero. Also useful for a high school class wanting to make an in-depth study of the legends of one tribe and a general study of Plains Indians and their way of life. See also *Winter-Telling Stories* by the same author (Elementary Myth).

Metayer, Father Maurice, translator and editor. **Tales from the Igloo.** Illus. Agnes Nanogak. Hurtig 1972.

A collection of traditional legends from a group of Inuit known as the Copper Eskimos, a people who have for centuries occupied a harsh and forbidding land along the Canadian Arctic coast. The mysteries of the Eskimos' cold world are explained and animals and birds play an important role in these stories, which often are humorous or suspenseful. Vividly colored illustrations by an Eskimo artist provide an added dimension to each tale. On *Akwesasne Notes* basic library list.

"This collection is both a documentary and entertainment" (*About Indians*, p. 89).

Momaday, N. Scott. **The Way to Rainy Mountain.** Illus. Al Momaday. Ballantine 1972.

On a pilgrimage to his grandmother's grave, the author traveled the same route that his people, the Kiowa Indians, traveled three hundred years previously from the headwaters of the Yellowstone River to Oklahoma. Sketches recall old Kiowa legends, stories of his family and of people they knew, and historical events of the tribe. Illustrations are by the author's father. Cited in *American Indian Authors.*

"This Indian author and professor of comparative English literature at the University of California has the true gift of the epic in literature" (*Textbooks and the American Indian*, p. 261).

"It is a very human story, well written" (*About Indians*, p. 226).

Schultz, James Willard [Apikuni] (editor Eugene Lee Silliman). **Why Gone Those Times? Blackfoot Tales.** Illus. Charles M. Russell. U of Okla Pr 1974.

James Schultz lived among the Blackfeet from 1876-1903, the year his Indian wife died. From 1915 on, he returned almost every year to the reservation to renew friendships. This is a collection of his stories never anthologized before: some from journals such as *Youth's Companion* and *Forest and Stream*, some from newspapers such as the *Great Falls Tribune*, and others from manuscripts housed at Montana State University. They tell of his experiences with the Blackfoot tribe.

Schwarz, Herbert T., editor. **Windigo and Other Tales of the Ojibways.** Illus. Norval Morrisseau. McClelland 1969.

Canadian Ojibway artist Norval Morrisseau told the native legends that inspired his paintings to Herbert Schwarz, a British Canadian medical doctor, who retells them here. Morrisseau's art work, reproduced in two colors, combines the characteristics of Indian rock painting and Eskimo art.

Shaw, Anna Moore. **Pima Indian Legends.** Illus. Matt Tashquinth. U of Ariz Pr 1968.

The author, a full-blooded Pima, heard these tales in the early 1900s in her village, Gila Crossing, in southern Arizona. Over the years they were modified as cultural traditions changed and, with frequent repetition in English, entire sections were reworded or dropped. Believing the legends might disappear, she began recording them in the 1930s. The book is illustrated by a Pima artist.

"Mrs. Shaw relates stories heard from her parents and grandparents, and combines ancient Pima history with more current happenings" (*American Indian Authors*, p. 36).

Stump, Sarain. **There Is My People Sleeping.** Gray 1970.

Combining poetry and drawings, Sarain Stump, a Shoshone-Cree-Salish, has produced what he calls "ethnic poem-drawings" about his feelings and experiences. He expresses important tribal values and frustrations about the loss of a former way of life. The book has been adapted for use in many Canadian schools. Equally suitable for adults. On *Akwesasne Notes* basic library list.

"Sarain Stump, in his ethnic poem-drawings, reveals the heart and mind of his people" (*About Indians*, p. 273). "There is a very special flavor to Sarain's work, a gentleness and care with words and lines, even though he is a self-taught artist" (*Indian Historian* 4:52, Spring 1971).

Vaudrin, Bill, translator and editor. **Tanaina Tales from Alaska.** Illus. Buck Hayden. U of Okla Pr 1969.

The Tanaina are Indians of Athapascan stock who live in Pedro Bay and Nondalton villages, not far from Anchorage, Alaska. These tales are *suk-tus* or "legend-stories," told for entertainment, and are peopled with foxes, beavers, wolverines, and porcupines. All animals in the stories have human desires and weaknesses and some become humans for sinister purposes. The raven is the trickster who breaks society's taboos. Vaudrin is a Minnesota Chippewa who wintered several years with the Tanainas while studying at Alaska Methodist University, and he occasionally employs English idiomatic expressions used by the Tanaina people. Cited in *American Indian Authors*.

Vizenor, Gerald. **Anishinabe Adisokan: Tales of the People.** Nodin Pr 1970.

These Chippewa tales explain creation, the naming of children, the coming of age, marriage, and religion. First published on the White Earth Reservation in Minnesota before the turn of the century and retold here by a member of the tribe. Part II contains tales of Manabozho, the trickster folk hero. The illustrations are Ojibwa pictomyths or storytelling pictures.

Vizenor, Gerald. **Anishinabe Nagamon: Songs of the People.** Nodin Pr 1965.

The author, a Chippewa, has included songs of love, springtime, dreams, midewiwin, and war, along with extensive notes, interpretations, and explanations. Illustrations are Ojibwa pictomyths.

Yazzie, Ethelou, editor. Navajo Histories. Illus. Andy Tsihnahjinnie. Navajo Curr 1971.

This story of the unrecorded history of the Navajos is the work of many people, supervised by the Board of the Rough Rock Demonstration School in Chinle, Arizona. Here are the stories of the Four Worlds, Changing Woman, Spider Woman, the Twins, Coyote, and many other personages from prehistory. Illustrated with full-page color paintings and with photographs of the Navajo Reservation area. Text and illustrations are by contemporary Navajos.

**Senior High and Adult**

Armstrong, Virginia Irving, editor. **I Have Spoken: American History through the Voices of the Indians.** Swallow 1971.

The Indians' tradition was oral until whites began to record their words, usually in meetings or councils. This collection of the words of Indians, many of them chiefs and leaders, is presented chronologically from the seventeenth to the twentieth centuries. The emphasis is on Indian-white relations, on who owns the land, and on the history and future of the race. Ideal for a study of Indian rhetoric in a speech or English class. On *Akwesasne Notes* basic library list.

"It is a sorrowful history, full of broken promises and deceit but very real and one that should be studied by all North Americans" (*About Indians*, p. 117).

Astrov, Margot, editor. **American Indian Prose and Poetry: An Anthology.** Capricorn Pr 1962.

Songs, chants, and legends of tribes from the Eskimos of the Arctic to the Incas of Peru are included in this collection. The introduction discusses the problems of collecting and translating Indian materials, the power of the word in Indian life, and the influence of Christianity on the cultures. Said by some critics to be mainly the work of anthropologists and not truly Indian, this anthology is nevertheless listed in the supplement of *American Indian Authors*, and is recommended by Dave Warren of the Institute of American Indian Arts as a collection "useful in developing some ideas of American Indian thought."

Bierhorst, John, editor. **The Red Swan: Myths and Tales of the American Indians.** FS&G 1976.

Here are tales from more than forty Indian cultures, including some from the Eskimos. The stories come from early collectors, including Franz Boas, George Bird Grinnell, Henry Rowe Schoolcraft, and A. L. Kroeber, and they are organized by themes such as Dream Father, From the Body of Our Mother, and War. Most of the tales appear as they were originally collected, although a few have been rewritten.

Borich, Michael. **The Black Hawk Songs.** U of Ill Pr 1975.

Michael Borich, an Iowa high school teacher of Sac and Fox background, writes a series of songs in monologue form, based on events in Black Hawk's life. He uses images from nature to tell of past glories, lost lands, and broken treaties. Borich's first submitted poem was published in *The New Yorker*. Although in this volume he imitates the rhythms of traditional songs and chants, Borich has not yet achieved the restraint of language that is characteristic of those forms and which gives them their distinctive quality.

Brandon, William, editor. **The Magic World: American Indian Songs and Poems.** Morrow 1971.

The editor's objective was to collect only the songs and poems that he regarded as being good literature, acknowledging that "My only criterion has been, do the lines feel good, moving." He has given no attention to the works as ethnological information. His translations come from nineteenth- and twentieth-century collectors, including A. L. Kroeber, Frank Russell, Frances Densmore, Natalie Curtis, H. R. Roth, Ruth Benedict, Washington Matthews, Alice C. Fletcher, Francis LaFlesche, Henry Schoolcraft, and Arthur C. Parker. On *Akwesasne Notes* basic library list.

"Most of the translation into the conventions of modern poetry is quite competent" (*About Indians*, p. 131).

Clark, Ella Elizabeth. **Indian Legends of Canada.** McClelland 1960.

These tales of Canadian Indians, including tales from tribes ranging into the United States along the border, are organized under headings such as: Tales of Long Ago, Culture Myths, Nature Myths, Beast Fables, Myths and Legends of Landscape Features, Personal Narratives, and Historical Traditions. In some instances the editor gives the source of the story, especially if it comes from a particular storyteller. A useful introduction describes storytelling in the tribe. Because the collection is intended for use in schools, an effort has been made to select legends that are most interesting and suitable for this purpose. Tales that have brutal or erotic themes have been excluded.

Clark, Ella Elizabeth. **Indian Legends from the Northern Rockies.** U of Okla Pr 1967.

A collection of the legends, myths, personal narratives, and historical traditions from the twelve Indian tribes who have lived in the present states of Idaho, Montana, and Wyoming. The arrangement is according to six linguistic groups: Nez Perce,

Salishan, Kutenai, Shoshone, Algonquin, and Sioux. From 1950 to 1955 the collector, now professor emerita of English at Washington State University, listened to old Indians of the Northwest recount tales handed down to them, and then wrote them down to preserve them for generations to come. Recommended also for junior high school use.

Coffin, Tristram P., editor. **Indian Tales of North America: An Anthology for the Adult Reader.** Am Folklore Soc 1961.

Calling himself "a folklorist trained in the history of literature," Coffin has assembled these stories which he says are neither for scholars nor for children, but for adult readers who want good reading. The collection is organized into three parts: The Way the World Is, What Man Must Know and Learn, and The Excitement of Living. There is a useful introduction in which the editor compares Indian tales to tales from the European tradition—such as Beowulf, Chaucer's *Troylus and Cryseyde*, and the twentieth century stories of Chekhov, Mansfield, and Woolf.

Cronyn, George W., editor. **American Indian Poetry: An Anthology of Songs and Chants.** Liveright 1970.

The editor attempts to choose songs with as little European influence as possible. There are songs and chants from the Eastern Woodlands, from the Southeast, Great Plains, Southwest, Northwest, and Far North, including love songs, work songs, funeral dirges, religious songs, and chants used at traditional feasts. Originally published in 1918, "The book is actually *about* Indian poetry and chants, and translations into English (an entirely different medium) from some native languages. It leaves much to be desired, but its value exists in the historical development of Indian poetry as seen by the non-Indian and as represented in this book, in comparison with the poetry and songs of the Native, as these are now emerging in current publishing by Indian editors and Indian publishers" (*Indian Historian* 4:51, Spring 1971).

Day, A. Grove, editor. **The Sky Clears: Poetry of the American Indians.** U of Nebr Pr 1964.

More than 200 poems have been gathered from about forty North American Indian tribes, with translations from students of Indian lore and life such as Franz Boas, Daniel G. Brinton, Natalie Curtis, Frances Densmore, Alice Cunningham Fletcher, Washington Matthews, Frank Russell, Herbert H. Spinden, and William Thalbitzer. The editor chose the selections because the translations were literary rather than literal. There is an introductory essay about Indian poetry and the editor comments about the poetry of the tribes from various regions: Eskimos, Totem-Pole Makers of the Northwest, Horse Nations of the Plains, Hunters of the Eastern Woodlands, Mayas, and Aztecs. Cited in the supplement of *American Indian Authors*.

Desbarats, Peter, editor. **What They Used to Tell About: Indian Legends from Labrador.** McClelland 1969.

The Montagnais-Naskapi, who inhabit the Labrador peninsula and northern Quebec, were among the first to greet explorer Jacques Cartier, but their land was harsh and the whites passed it over as a place to settle—until recently, when Churchill Falls began to be harnessed for power. Students under the direction of Rémi Savard, anthropologist at the University of Montreal, were sent to Labrador to record the legends of these people, which had remained fairly free of white influence. Desbarats, a Quebec journalist and broadcaster, selected these tales from those recorded by the students.

Dodge, Robert K., and Joseph B. McCullough, editors. **Voices from Wah' Kon-Tah: Contemporary Poetry of Native Americans.** Intl Pub Co 1976.

Here are works by the best Native American poets—Ted Berrigan, Alonzo Lopez, Emerson Blackhorse Mitchell, N. Scott Momaday, Duane Niatum, Simon Ortiz, and James Welch—along with some young poets' works that have appeared in publications edited by their teacher, T. D. Allen, at the Institute of American Indian Arts. As Vine Deloria writes in the foreword, "Once savored this poetry may brush away the years and tell you more about the Indian's travels in historical experience than all the books written and lectures given." Recommended by Charles G. Ballard, "A Selected Bibliography on Native American Literature," 1975 NCTE Spring Institutes on "Teaching Minority Literatures at All Levels."

"Contains the work of some new poets: Ray Young Bear, Donna White Wing, Marnie Walsh, Bruce Severy and others." (*Akwesasne Notes* 8:40, Late Autumn 1976).

Eastman, Mary. Dahcotah: Or Life and Legends of the Sioux around Fort Snelling. Illus. Captain Eastman. Ross 1962.

As the wife of army officer Seth Eastman, who was stationed at Fort Snelling for seven years during Minnesota's territorial period, Mary Eastman observed and studied Sioux customs and manners. This is a group of legends, stories of actual people such as Wabashaw and Shah-Co-Pee, and descriptions of ceremonies. The writing conveys her feeling that Indians are uncivilized and that the tribe is vanishing, and shows her particular concern about the treatment of women. First published in 1849.

Emerson, Ellen Russell. Indian Myths, or Legends, Traditions, and Symbols of the Aborigines of America, Compared with Those of Other Countries, Including Hindostan, Egypt, Persia, Assyria, and China. Ross 1965.

A scholarly and valuable study of Indian myths compared with those of other peoples. It has some limitations because the author lacked access to the work of more recent folklorists and ethnographers, but she made good use of the work of early scholars such as George Catlin, David Cusick, Mary Eastman, Albert Gallatin, George Copway, and Henry Schoolcraft. Myths of different nations are compared on such themes as the god of air, the four spirits of the winds, birds, star worship, the sun, the origin of man, legends of the dead, language, and animals. First published in 1884.

Gaddis, Vincent H. American Indian Myths and Mysteries. Chilton 1977.

Gaddis begins his book by questioning the usually accepted view that Native Americans originally were Mongolian peoples who crossed the Bering land bridge during glaciation periods. Part One of the book cites examples of other possible origins found in the legends and mythology of various tribes, and offers archaeological evidence that some of these may be true. He discusses common ways of living and common themes from the stories of widely dispersed peoples. A story of a lost continent, perhaps Atlantis, exists in many tribes from the Pueblos to the Blackfeet. Stories of a great cataclysm recur in the legends of peoples from Central and South America and in the Flood narrative in the Bible. The Apache's name for the Great Spirit is Ammon-Ra, the same as that of an ancient Egyptian god. In Part Two Gaddis examines supernatural happenings among Indian tribes: the mystery of the shaking tent, the curse of Tippecanoe which predicts death in office of every American president elected at twenty-year intervals, and medicine-man magic. Students interested in the occult will find here a wealth of carefully documented information.

Grinnell, George Bird, editor. **Blackfoot Lodge Tales: The Story of a Prairie People.** U of Nebr Pr 1962.

The editor began collecting the tales of the Blackfoot Indians after reading columns in *Field and Stream* by J. W. Schultz, who lived among these Indians and married one. Grinnell heard the tales from venerable members of the tribe. Some of the stories resembled those current among the Ojibwas and other eastern Algonquian tribes. One story, "Worm Pipe," parallels "Orpheus and Eurydice" and another is parallel to part of the *Odyssey*. The last part of the book is a history of the Blackfoot people. First published in 1892.

Grinnell, George Bird, editor. **By Cheyenne Campfires.** U of Nebr Pr 1971.

After receiving his degree from Yale, the editor, a trained naturalist, made many trips to the so-called unmapped West. After 1890 the Cheyenne Indians became his favorite tribe and for the next forty years he visited them every summer. As he shared their hardships, he listened to their tales. This collection is divided into war stories, stories of mystery, hero myths, the earliest stories, culture hero stories, and stories of Wihio, the trickster. The introduction to each section gives background material about Cheyenne life, customs, and values.

"A realistic presentation of the pre-white culture of the Cheyennes" (*About Indians*, p. 178).

Grinnell, George Bird, editor. **Pawnee Hero Stories and Folk Tales, with Notes on the Origin, Customs and Character of the Pawnee People.** U of Nebr Pr 1961.

Grinnell first became acquainted with the Pawnees in 1870. About one-half of the book contains their stories and folk tales, and the other half is composed of notes on the tribe—their relationships, origin and migrations, customs, warfare, religion, and late nineteenth century history. First published in 1889.

Hamilton, Charles Everett, editor. **Cry of the Thunderbird: The American Indian's Own Story.** U of Okla Pr 1972.

This is an unusual collection, containing selections either written by Indians or told by Indians to whites. Arrangement is according to themes such as Around the Campfire, Game Trails, Wilderness Sports, the Great Spirit, On the Warpath, and the White Man's Road. Included among the authors are Black Elk, Charles Eastman, Chief Luther Standing Bear, Don C. Talayesva, George Copway, Wooden Leg, and William W. Warren. The collection is illustrated by native artists and includes information about Indian authors and a bibliography of works written or dictated by Indians. Since the collection originally was done in 1950, it contains nothing by or about modern Indians.

"Illustrated entirely by Indian artists, this collection includes about 100 stories and speeches written or dictated by North American Indians" (Supplement, *American Indian Authors*, p. 42). "This is a very informative book with excerpts from over fifty Native American authors, many of whom were great orators and leaders in war and peace" (*About Indians*, p. 180).

Johnson, E. Pauline [Tekahionwake]. **Legends of Vancouver.** Illus. Ben Lim. McClelland 1961.

The author was the daughter of the great Mohawk chief, George Henry Martin Johnson. As a girl, when she was known as the "Mohawk Singer" for her writing and reading of poetry, she met Chief Joe Capilano of the Siwash tribe. After moving to Vancouver she collected the stories and legends of the Siwash people there, and this volume contains their tribal stories which are mainly about unusual natural occurrences.

Johnston, Basil, editor. **Ojibway Heritage.** McClelland 1976.

A Canadian Ojibway scholar has collected the mythology and songs of his people and information on their customs, values, and ceremonies. His materials come from fellow Ojibways living in Ontario. Chapter headings include The Vision of Kitche Manitou, The Nature of Plants, The Nature of Animals, The Midewewin, Man's World, The Vision, and Father Sun and Mother Earth.

Katz, Jane B., editor. **I Am the Fire of Time: The Voices of Native American Women.** Dutton 1977.

This is the first collection of the writings of Native American women, containing examples of songs, poetry, prose, prayer, narrative, and oral history. Part I contains works from the tribal world—songs, myths, and true stories of women's life in the tribe. Part II consists of works of modern Indian women. Illustrated with twenty-four photographs.

Kilpatrick, Jack Frederick, and Anna Gritts Kilpatrick. **Run toward the Nightland: Magic of the Oklahoma Cherokees. S Meth U Pr 1967.**

A Cherokee husband and wife discuss the place of magic in Cherokee life: incantations and rituals that bring success in hunting and fishing, control the wind and rain, help to grow corn, and bring success in marriage and war and good luck in lawsuits. There are also examples of dark magic, incantations that bring revenge by misfortune, insanity, and death. Music is included for all of the incantations.

Kroeber, A. L. **Yurok Myths. U of Cal Pr 1976.**

During 1901-08 when he was just beginning his career as an anthropologist, the author traveled to the country of the Yurok Indians in northern California along the Klamath River. From thirty Yurok informants, he collected over 150 myths and variations. This unique collection is arranged by informant rather than by theme or type of tale, and each informant is described. The collector felt that the informant's family, personality, and relationship to other members of the tribe affected the tales told and the emphases placed on characters and events.

"The major strength of *Yurok Myths* is that it makes available for the first time an important body of material which can no longer be regathered" (*American Indian Quarterly* 3:256, Autumn 1977).

Levitas, Gloria, Frank Robert Vivelo, and Jacqueline J. Vivelo, editors. **American Indian Prose and Poetry: We Wait in the Darkness. Putnam 1974.**

An anthology of Indian poetry and prose divided into three sections: Before the Coming of the Whites, After the Whites Came, and The Present. Within each section there are geographical divisions. A valuable introduction and bibliographies add to the book.

"The editors exhibit a sound academic approach in their selection and arrangement of material" (*American Indian Quarterly* 2:33, Spring 1975).

Lourie, Dick, editor. **Come to Power: Eleven Contemporary American Indian Poets. Crossing Pr 1974.**

This is the poetry of eleven modern young Indians. Some of

them are quite unknown but others are among today's leading
Indian poets: Ray Young Bear, Leslie Silko, and Duane Niatum.
A brief biographical sketch and statement about writing accompanies each poet's section. On *Akwesasne Notes* basic library
list.

"This slender anthology of recent poetry and prose by young
contemporary American Indians is a welcome addition to the
materials available on American Indian literature" (*American
Indian Quarterly* 2:254, Autumn 1975).

McLuhan, T. C., editor. Touch the Earth: A Self-Portrait of Indian
Existence. PB 1972.

A selection of oral and written statements by Indians from the
sixteenth to the twentieth century, revealing their feelings and
relationships with the earth, nature's creatures, and their homeland, as the "hairy man from the East" encroached upon their
land. This vivid history ranges from the Indians' early desire to
share to their later desperation and anger at broken promises.
Illustrated by more than fifty photographs by Edward S. Curtis,
taken early in the twentieth century. The quotations and pictures are presented without editorial comment from the collector.

"The psychology of the Indian's mind is clearly shown, most
notably in the emotional descriptions of deep attachment to
Mother Earth" (*About Indians*, p. 219).

McTaggart, Fred. Wolf That I Am: In Search of the Red Earth
People. HM 1976.

In 1970–71 McTaggart began collecting stories from the Mesquakie people of Iowa, who once were the large and powerful
tribe known as the Fox. The project was to be his Ph.D. dis-
sertation at the University of Iowa, but McTaggart soon
discovered that he was learning about a way of life, or a way of
looking at life. The book includes some of the stories he was
told (excepting information and stories withheld because they
were sacred), but more important are his experiences with
various members of the community as they talked about themselves and their tribe.

Maestas, John R., editor. Contemporary Native American Address.
Brigham 1976.

A number of fine collections of old Indian oratory exist, but
the oratory of contemporary Indian leaders is less accessible,
making this a valuable volume. Part I deals with issues of con-

cern to the Native American—for example, sovereignty, tribal government, land claims, the Bureau of Indian Affairs, the American Indian Movement. Part II is organized around styles and kinds of speeches—inaugural and commencement addresses, testimonies, oral tradition, and history and inspirational speeches. Some of the better-known Indian leaders who have speeches in this volume are Robert Bennett, Peter MacDonald, Vernon Bellecourt, LaDonna Harris, N. Scott Momaday, Rupert Costo, and Chief Dan George.

Marriott, Alice, and Carol K. Rachlin. **American Indian Mythology.** NAL 1972.

The myths of twenty North American tribes, selected from their field data by two well-known anthropologists. The myths are grouped by themes such as the world beyond ours (creation stories), the world around us, the world we live in now, and the world we go to. Pictures of artifacts, designs, powwows, and religious ceremonials add to the book. With each tale is a brief introduction to the tribe. Cited in the supplement to *American Indian Authors.*

"While this book will be enjoyed at its fullest by the student of anthropology, nevertheless it is of value to the young adult in terms of enriching his own knowledge of Indian Culture" (*About Indians,* p. 223).

Marriott, Alice, and Carol K. Rachlin. **Plains Indian Mythology.** T Y Crowell 1975.

Thirty-one stories by eleven Great Plains Indian tribes, each with a valuable introduction telling of other versions and where they occur, and giving details about the tribe, story situation, and often the storyteller's name and background. There are four groupings: The Beginnings: The Great Myths; The Little Stories: How and Why; Horseback Days; and Freedom's Ending. The book is illustrated by photographs of people, scenes, and items worn or used by these tribes.

"It is to their [the editors'] credit that they have tried to make available the simple essence of the Indian folk literature" (*Wassaja* 4:15, March 1976).

Masson, Marcelle. **A Bag of Bones: The Wintu Myths of the Trinity River Indian.** Naturegraph 1966.

These stories are primarily in the English of a man who spoke Wintu in his family. Grant Towendolly had been chosen by his

father to become the next chieftain of the northern Wintu of
the Trinity River area in northern California. Although he attended an elementary school in the San Francisco Bay area,
most of his education came through periods of fasting and
solitude in the mountains, by learning to recognize and use
medicinal plants, and by listening to the myths and legends of
his people. Fearing that the legends would die, he wrote them
down. Marcelle Masson learned of them through her husband,
who grew up with Towendolly, and the stories are presented
here with only a few changes in spelling and punctuation. Cited
in *American Indian Authors*.

Mélançon, Claude (translator David Ellis). **Indian Legends of
Canada.** Gage Pub 1974.

These tales of Canadian Indians were collected in French from
all parts of Canada and then translated into English. When the
first Europeans came to Canadian shores they discovered,
through legends such as these, that the Indian already had stories similar to their own stories of Jonah, Jupiter, Siegfried,
Cinderella, and a great flood. The book is divided by geographical area: the Atlantic Coast and Eastern Woodlands, the Prairies,
and the Pacific Coast. The collector is a member of the Royal
Canadian Society.

Milton, John R., editor. **The American Indian Speaks: Poetry,
Fiction and Art by the American Indian.** Dakota Pr 1969.

Writings and paintings from tribes located mainly in the western half of the United States. The works were solicited by the
editor, and those artists who responded were published. Among
the well-known Indian artists represented are poets James
Welch, Simon Ortiz, Emerson Blackhorse Mitchell, and Patty
Harjo; prose writers Louis Ballard, Kay Bennett, and Bea
Medicine; and painters Oscar Howe and Jose Rey Toledo. This
publication provides access to a number of modern Indian poets
and prose writers whose works are otherwise difficult to find.
The reproductions of Indian art are also a bonus.

Momaday, Natachee Scott, editor. **American Indian Authors.** HM
1972.

This is the first collection of works by Indian authors compiled
especially for the classroom. It contains a good balance of
legends, poetry, biography, history, and short stories. Each
selection has a number of discussion questions by the editor,

who, besides being a well-known Indian teacher and author, is the mother of Pulitzer Prize-winning novelist N. Scott Momaday and wife of Kiowa artist Al Momaday. The collection provides a ready-made unit of short selections for the classroom. Ancient times are represented by four legends, the words of Chief Joseph, and chapters from Two Leggings, Black Elk, and Charles A. Eastman; the modern period is represented by Emerson Blackhorse Mitchell, Durango Mendoza, N. Scott Momaday, Vine Deloria, Jr., and James Welch.

"*American Indian Authors* is recommended for English courses in high school. It raises questions concerning past Indian life, relationships, and values and presents as well the contemporary issues faced by Indians" (*About Indians* p. 226).

Momaday, N. Scott. **The Gourd Dancer.** Illus. by author. Har-Row 1976.

This collection includes an earlier publication, *Angle of Geese*, composed of spare, dignified poems drawn from the writer's Indian background, among them "Headwaters," "Rainy Mountain Cemetery," and "Earth and I Gave You Turquoise." Additional sections are "The Gourd Dancer," with more poems with Indian themes, and "Anywhere Is a Street into the Night," a collection of more general poems. Some of these lyrics are personal, offering glimpses of relatives and friends, while others have images of animals, natural forces, and the Great Spirit.

Neihardt, John G. **The Twilight of the Sioux: The Song of the Indian Wars; The Song of the Messiah.** U of Nebr Pr 1971.

Originally entitled *A Cycle of the West*, this book begins with fourteen episodes telling of the struggle for the bison pastures west of the Missouri, including the epic Battle of the Little Bighorn in 1876. The point of view shifts from the Indian camp to the white man's camp, showing heroism on both sides. *The Song of the Messiah*, which closes with the Battle of Wounded Knee, tells of the Ghost Dance, the end of the last great dream. The author spent six years as a youth among the Omahas and he is most effective when he describes the moods of the times in an Indian village, in the soldiers' camp, or in a pioneer's cabin. Printed sources and information from a number of Indians who had experienced the wars were used to document the poems.

"In the second poem, the work is at its best in the description of messianic visions, a subject not inappropriate to poetry" (*About Indians*, p. 235).

Nequatewa, Edmund (editor Mary-Russell F. Colton). **Truth of a Hopi: Stories Relating to the Origin, Myths, and Clan Histories of the Hopi**. Northland 1973.

A Hopi Indian discusses the origin, myths, and history of a group of Hopi clans, beginning with their emergence from the underworld and ending with the story of how Hotevilla and Bakabi were founded and how the clans were divided between the Friendlies and the Hostiles. The reader gains insight into the Hopi mind, where legend and history run together. Useful to the student doing special work on the Hopi and their legends.

Niatum, Duane. **Ascending Red Cedar Moon**. Har-Row 1973.

Duane Niatum, better known to modern poetry readers as Duane McGinnis, is a member of the Klallam tribe in Washington. He says that his poetry has been influenced by his exposure to Oriental culture during the time he was in the Navy in Japan, by his interest in both painting and music, and by his Indian ancestry. One cycle of poems in this collection, "Legends of the Moon," is in memory of his great-aunt and her father, whose name, Niatum, the poet has taken. Other poems are seasonal celebrations, tributes to other tribes, love lyrics, and tributes to other poets.

"The best of his poems show a uniqueness of experience, a uniqueness and clarity of vision worth writing from and of; they are the work of a promising young poet" (*American Indian Quarterly* 1:300, Winter 1974-75).

Niatum, Duane, editor. **Carriers of the Dream Wheel: Contemporary Native American Poetry**. Illus. Wendy Rose. Har-Row 1975.

This is a collection of the works of fifteen Native American poets and one Hawaiian. Representative of the best-known poets are N. Scott Momaday, James Welch, and Simon Ortiz, but the poems from younger and lesser-known poets are equally good. There are pictures and a brief biography of each poet and drawings by Wendy Rose, one of the poets whose works appear in the volume.

"It is well produced, strikingly illustrated by one of the contributors, Wendy Rose, and spaciously conceived: three hundred pages are given to sixteen poets, each represented by at least five and sometimes as many as eighteen poems, so that the individual writer takes on real character for the reader within a fairly broad panorama of the Native American group" (*American Indian Quarterly* 3:51, Spring 1977).

O'Neill, Paul. **Legends of a Lost Tribe: Folk Tales of the Beothuck Indians of Newfoundland.** Illus. Jon Fraser. McClelland 1976.

The Beothuck Indians, called "red men" because they customarily painted their bodies with red ochre, were a fascinating tribe whose legends died with them in the nineteenth century. The author has reconstructed their folk tales, basing them on the known facts about the tribe, including information given by the last Beothuck, a woman who died in 1829. The themes are universal in mythology and fairy tales; for example, the English tale "Jack and the Beanstalk" resembles the Beothuck "Legend of the Stars and Trees." Also appreciated by intermediate readers.

Parsons, Elsie Clews, editor. **American Indian Life.** Illus. C. Grant LaFarge. U of Nebr Pr 1967.

This is a series of fictional tales of variable quality, written by well-known anthropologists, each of whom contributed a tale about the Indian tribe he knew best. Among the eminent names are Robert H. Lowie, Paul Radin, A. L. Kroeber, Edward Sapir, and Franz Boas.

Radin, Paul. **The Trickster: A Study in American Indian Mythology.** Schocken 1972.

About one-half of this book contains Indian elaborations of the myth of the trickster, with special emphasis on the Winnebago version. The remainder is a discussion of the trickster in relation to Greek mythology and to psychology. In Indian myth the trickster is a creature who is neither good nor evil but can be blamed for the evil and praised for the good that occurs. He is often identified with animals such as the raven, coyote, hare, and spider, and has similarities to Punch and Judy and to the clown. A specialized study, useful for teachers or for mature students.

Ray, Carl, and James R. Stevens, editor. **Sacred Legends of the Sandy Lake Cree.** Illus. Carl Ray. McClelland 1971.

Translator and illustrator of these tales is the well-known Indian artist Carl Ray, who comes from the Sandy Lake Cree Reserve in northwestern Ontario. Stevens, a counselor at Confederation College of Applied Arts and Technology in Thunder Bay, Ontario, wrote down the legends as they were told to him by Ray. The stories deal with the Windigo, Thunderbirds, avenging gods, and curses being placed on adversaries. In the introduction, Stevens discusses the history and economics of the villages, education, marriage customs, religion, medicine, death, and folklore.

Rothenberg, Jerome, editor. **Shaking the Pumpkin: Traditional Poetry of the Indian North Americas.** Doubleday 1972.

Poems from many tribes are included in this collection. The title poems, "Shaking the Pumpkin," are sacred curing songs translated by the editor and Richard Johnny John, a Seneca songmaker. Among the other works are a pre-conquest Mayan play, a "sacred-clown" fertility drama of the Pueblo Indians, picture poems from the Cuna and Chippewa, a Zuni spoken narrative, and poems from the Netsilik Eskimos. The editor, who has published ten volumes of his own poetry and several volumes of translations, has chosen poems that most interest and impress him for their range of types and cultures. Although recognizing the difficulties of crossing the boundary of translation, he says in his preface, "The question for the translator is not whether but how far we can translate one another." He sees the translator as one who "attempts to restore what has been torn apart."

"As documents of cultures both past and present the poems are well worth reading" (*About Indians,* p. 256).

Sanders, Thomas E., and Walter W. Peek. **Literature of the American Indian.** Glencoe 1973.

A comprehensive collection, with scholarly comments by the authors on every possible aspect of Indian life, history, and religion from pre-Columbian days to the present. Sections include pre-Columbian religions, heroes and folk tales, pre-Columbian poetry, the history of the League of the Iroquois, oratory, native religions after the Christian invasion, biography and autobiography, and current voices in poetry, prose, and protest. The editors are Indians—Sanders a Cherokee and Peek a Narragansett and Wampanoag—and also scholars. This collection provides the English teacher with a wide and varied selection of short works.

Schwarz, Herbert T., editor. **Elik and Other Stories of the Mac-Kenzie Eskimos.** Illus. Mona Ohoveluk. McClelland 1970.

Schwarz, a medical doctor who works on the DEW line from Greenland to Alaska, has used his contacts to collect authentic Eskimo tales. *Elik* is one of them. The first part of the book contains stories and the second part is composed of anecdotes about the storytellers, relating where and how Schwarz met each of them. Illustrated by an Eskimo artist.

Slickpoo, Allen P. **Nu Mee Poom Tit Wah Tit: Nez Perce Legends.** Illus. Leroy L. Seth. Nez Perce 1972.

This is a collection of Nez Perce legends, prepared by the tribe and set in a mythical time, before human beings roamed the world. The characters are animals, although they have human qualities and are sometimes called people. Collected in the Nez Perce language and translated into English, the tales are intended either to teach or to entertain. There are six groups of stories, dealing with the world's origin, disobedience, vengeance, shrewdness, greed, and bravery. Coyote, the trickster, is the principal character, and the stories are fast-moving and generally good humored. The illustrations in black and white by Leroy Seth, a Nez Perce, are done in the same spirit as the tales. Highly recommended by the National Indian Education Association Checklist of Current Books, March 1972.

Tedlock, Dennis, translator. **Finding the Center: Narrative Poetry of the Zuni Indians.** U of Nebr Pr 1972.

Tedlock, a Yale anthropologist, not only has translated nine Zuni narrative poems, as performed by Andrew Peynetsa and Walter Sanchez, but also has transcribed into English the rhythms, accents, and silences that actually occur in the Zuni performance. The poems are in two categories—short fables and tales, which are regarded as fiction and may be told only at night from October to March, and long narratives of "The Beginning," which are regarded as historical truth and may be told at any time of day during any season. Tedlock spent more than a year in field work, taping nearly one hundred formal Zuni narratives in preparation for this collection.

Thompson, Stith, editor. **Tales of the North American Indians.** Illus. Franz Altschuler. Ind U Pr 1966.

A carefully documented collection of tales from sources such as Franz Boas, Henry Schoolcraft, and Bureau of Ethnology publications. The stories are organized according to type: mythological stories, mythical incidents, trickster tales, hero tales, journeys to the other world, animal wives and husbands, tales borrowed from Europeans, and Bible stories. Some are from collections recorded by Europeans in the seventeenth century.

The editor, a well-known scholar of folklore, has included comparative notes and lists of motifs and sources, arranged by culture areas and tribes. Although this is a scholarly work, the tales are simply told.

"The arrangement is in accord with the compiler's theory that there are many recurrent patterns or types of tales which transcend geographic and linguistic boundaries" (Supplement, *American Indian Authors*, p. 43).

Underhill, Ruth Murray. **Singing for Power: The Song Magic of the Papago Indians of Southern Arizona.** U of Cal Pr 1976.

Living a difficult life in the Arizona desert, the gentle Papago use songs and ritual speeches for the entire range of life: for bringing rain, for planting, harvesting, and wild plant gathering, for their games, and for hunting. Interspersed with her translations of the songs are Ruth Underhill's descriptions of the life, ceremonies, and power of these poetic people, based on material which she gathered in the early 1930s while living among them.

Vanderwerth, W. C., editor. **Indian Oratory: Famous Speeches by Noted Indian Chieftains.** Ballantine 1971.

This collection of major orations of the greatest Indian chiefs demonstrates the importance of the spoken word around the council fires, where tribal affairs were settled and where negotiations between tribes and whites were conducted. Each oration is preceded by a discussion of the orator and the background of the speech. The earliest of the speeches was delivered in 1758 and the latest in 1910. The collection concentrates on the oratory delivered during the encroachment of the whites, and the speeches are generally longer or more complete than those in some other collections.

Welch, James. **Riding the Earthboy 40.** World. Times Mir 1971.

This is the first collection of the poetry of James Welch, a Blackfoot Indian living and writing at Upper Rattlesnake, Missoula, Montana. The title comes from the years when he lived on the Fort Belknap Reservation near Harlem, Montana, where his father leased forty acres from the Earthboy family. Some of the poems deal with the towns on or near the reservation and with poverty, drunkenness, and the disintegration of a way of life, but there are also themes of nature, Montana, and life. Welch's poems require a depth of experience and concentration, making them most useful for mature readers.

Witt, Shirley Hill, and Stan Steiner, editors. The Way: **An Indian Anthology of American Indian Literature.** Vin. Random 1972.

A collection of the ancient speeches of Indian leaders and orators as they were translated by Englishmen and Americans, and the contemporary speeches and articles of modern Indians on present problems. The greatness of speeches by Chief Joseph, Pontiac, Black Hawk, and Tecumseh has long been recognized by historians. Here we have also the moving words of modern Indians in oratory, poetry and prophecy. On *Akwesasne Notes* basic library list.

South Dakota Writers' Project, Workers of, compilers. **Legends of the Mighty Sioux.** Illus. Sioux Indian artists. AMS Pr 1975.

The stories in this collection were gathered by the Indian workers in the South Dakota Writers' Project. Often they were told by old men who related them in their native tongue. The collection includes campfire tales, legends of places and of hunting, and battle stories, and gives much information about the Sioux and their traditional lore. Sioux artist Oscar Howe contributed some of the drawings and designs.

Zuni People (translator Alvina Quam). **The Zunis: Self-Portrayals.** U of NM Pr 1972.

A collection of forty-six stories of Zuni myth, prophecy, and history, dealing with creation, religious rituals, masked dances, Zuni farming and hunting practices, and battles with the Navajo and the Apache. The stories are intended for moral instruction or for entertainment and are divided according to sections: society, history, fables of moral instruction, religion, and war and defense. In 1965 the Zuni tribe began to record their oral literature, using federal funds and help from universities and individuals, including Virginia Lewis, wife of the Pueblo governor, who reviewed and edited the legends for publication. Major storytellers of the tribe were asked to relate on tape the legends, myths, and history of the Pueblo.

# Fiction

Baker, Betty. **A Stranger and Afraid.** Macmillan 1972. Intermediate.

Sopete and Zabe, two Wichita boys, were taken prisoner by the Zuni when their village, Quivira, was raided. Zabe has come to love the security of the orderly life of the Cicuye pueblo, but Sopete remembers his former home and longs to return. It is with some hope and fear that Sopete views the coming of the Spaniards. The two boys serve as guides for a Spanish expedition to Quivira in search of gold and other riches and are forced to make some difficult decisions when the expedition nears their former home. The story is based on actual records of Coronado's expeditions of 1540–42.

Barnouw, Victor. **Dream of the Blue Heron.** Illus. Lynd Ward. Dell 1969. Intermediate.

In northern Wisconsin, a young Chippewa named Wabus, or Wallace White Sky, faces fierce conflicts between his traditional grandparents and his father, who works in a lumber mill. Wabus enters an Indian boarding school in 1905, only to discover that he has other problems to solve, among them learning to accept a new lifestyle. When Wabus returns home for the summer vacation, he dreams of an enormous bird—a blue heron—who crashes down through the branches of a tree and, taking on the form of a man, promises Wabus that he will become a speaker. Then, becoming a bird again, the heron carries Wabus into the sky. The vanishing forms symbolize help, strength, and success. The illustrations are by Lynd Ward, a distinguished American graphic artist and 1953 winner of the Caldecott Medal.

"Well-written . . . tastefully, realistically handled . . ." (*Kirkus Reviews* 34:982, 15 September 1965). "I have read *Dream of the Blue Heron* with genuine pleasure. It is true and real and it is a most human story. Mr. Barnouw has observed his Indians with warm humanity. We have had a lot of writing about the Indians of the Southwest, but we have almost nothing about the equally interesting people along the northern border" (Oliver La Farge).

Baylor, Byrd. **Hawk, I'm Your Brother.** Illus. Peter Parnall. Scribner 1976. Primary.

Rudy Soto, an Indian boy from an unspecified tribe in the Southwest, wants to fly more than anything else. Even as a small child, his first words were those for "flying" and "bird." Watching a hawk, he sees himself soaring into the sky. He finally steals a redtail hawk from its nest before it can fly and, in spite of its screams for help, Rudy takes the bird home, hoping for the day when the two of them will fly together. Eventually Rudy takes the tethered hawk out on his shoulder, to explore sandy washes, follow deer tracks into canyons, and gaze at Santos Mountain. He comes to realize that to be happy, the hawk must be free to fly, leaving Rudy to soar in his imagination.

"The theme of unity between people and nature is expressed in the illustrations. They are full of circular patterns which, on the one hand, capture the glorious sweep of a hawk in flight and, on the other, interrelate sky and human beings" (*Interracial Books for Children Bulletin* 7, no. 6:15, 1977).

Beatty, Hetty Burlingame. **Little Owl Indian.** HM 1951. Primary.

An Indian village in one of the great forests of New York state is the setting for this story. As a little brown owl flies over her village, an Indian mother decides to name her son Little Owl, in the hope that he will acquire the wisdom and swiftness of the bird. As Little Owl grows up he is a friend to all the animals, because they learn that he wants to make friends, not kill them. One day when frightening clouds of smoke and flames are rushing through the forest, Little Owl rides his horse through the trees to warn the animals and the Indians of the danger. Excitement and suspense add to the appeal of this story.

"Vivid, simple pictures help make this an appealing picture book for the four- to seven-year-olds. Recommended" (*Library Journal* 76:604, 1 April 1951).

Benchley, Nathaniel. **Small Wolf.** Illus. Joan Sandin. Har-Row 1972. Primary.

This "I Can Read" book gives a historically accurate picture of the time when the Canarsee Indians "sold" Manhattan Island

to the Dutch. Small Wolf, an Indian boy of an unnamed tribe
in the same locale, spends his days fishing and digging for clams
and oysters. Wanting to be a man like his father, he wanders
off to hunt and fish to prove himself, and is greatly surprised
when he comes upon the first white settlement he has ever
seen. The rest of the story tells of the unhappy effect this has
on his tribe, giving the reader insight into the Indians' tragic
loss of their hunting grounds to the whites.

Biesterveld, Betty. Six Days from Sunday. Illus. George Armstrong.
Rand 1973. Primary.

When Willie Little Horse thinks about going to boarding school
he feels a sickness in his stomach because he is afraid of the
White World. His mother tries to reassure him as she proceeds
with daily tasks of weaving, cooking, and caring for her family.
On each day before he leaves, Willie has adventures that point
out the differences and relative values of the old Indian ways
and the new. When the sixth day from Sunday arrives, Willie is
confused and afraid and is tempted to run away like a coyote,
but with the help of a kind teacher and others, Willie resolves
his unhappiness and makes a step toward learning to choose
what is best for him.

Blood, Charles L., and Martin A. Link. The Goat in the Rug. Illus.
Nancy Winslow Parker. Parents 1976. Primary.

Geraldine, a pet goat, is the unusual heroine of this Navajo
story. When her mistress, a young weaver, decides to shear her,
the process becomes a joint effort as the wool is washed in a
soapy, rich lather made from the yucca plant, and then dried,
combed, and spun. The story gives accurate information on the
Indians' use of plants for dyes, and the completion of the beautiful wool rug, which is one of a kind, brings the story to a
satisfactory ending. Colorful illustrations contribute to the
book's informativeness and humor.

"It is important for children to understand that there are
many different cultures within the borders of the U.S. *The Goat
in the Rug* gives them the opportunity to view a tradition of
one of the oldest" (*Interracial Books for Children Bulletin* 8,
no. 8:16, 1977).

Buff, Mary, and Conrad Buff. Hah-Nee of the Cliff Dwellers.
HM 1956. Primary.

This dramatic story helps younger children visualize the life of
a now-vanished people. It tells of an Indian boy and his family

who are forced by superstition to flee from their home. Hah-Nee wonders why he is ridiculed and called "funnyhead," "evil," "Ute," and "enemy," until he learns details of his infancy and why his head is round and not flat. When the Great Drought of 1276 begins and food is scarce, Hah-Nee's presence is looked upon as bad luck and Grandfather Wupa, fearing what might happen to Hah-Nee and his family members, paints a map on an animal skin to lead them to safety. Their adventures make for an exciting story. The many black and white drawings and double-page paintings give life and mystery to the southwestern landscape.

"A good story to read aloud" (*About Indians*, p. 44).

Bulla, Clyde Robert. Eagle Feather. Illus. Tom Two Arrows. T Y Crowell 1953. Primary.

Eagle Feather has no interest in going away to school because he is happy with his parents and younger brother and sister and likes the pleasant life of sheepherding and hunting. But when he visits the trading post and sees the inside of the schoolhouse, he becomes eager to find companions of his own age. Because of a careless act, it appears that Eagle Feather won't be able to attend school after all because he must go to work for his greedy cousin. To get his wish, he finally takes matters into his own hands and runs away. Navajo life is portrayed in detail as the exciting adventure tale unfolds. Tom Two Arrows, a full-blooded Iroquois, has illustrated the story with understanding and sensitivity of the Navajo culture. Three songs, which are easy to play and sing, add enjoyment to the story.

Bulla, Clyde Robert. Indian Hill. Illus. James J. Spanfeller. T Y Crowell 1963. Primary.

Kee Manygoats, a young Navajo boy, lives on a reservation with his parents. When the family leaves their hogan for an apartment in the city, Kee and his mother are unhappy because the city seems strange and ugly and they dislike the bright lights and smells. Kee's father, however, enjoys his work there and the family is forced to make some difficult decisions when the opportunity of returning to the reservation arises. The story of a strong and loving family caught between their traditional way of life and the world of white people.

"With simplicity and directness Mr. Bulla tells the story of a young Navajo boy and his difficult acceptance of city life" (*About Indians*, p. 45).

Bulla, Clyde Robert. **John Billington: Friend of Squanto.** Illus.
Peter Burchard. T Y Crowell 1956. Primary.

Growing up is a difficult time for John Billington, who is on
board the *Mayflower* sailing to America. He finds himself in
all sorts of trouble on board ship as well as in the colony after
the landing. The hardships of the first year and the constant
fear of Indians give John many problems. He tries to avoid the
distressing situations, but somehow always finds himself
involved. Squanto comes into his life and helps him and the
other settlers in many ways, but real trouble comes when John
runs into the woods in anger and is lost. The following day he
meets the Cape Cod Indians, who take him to their village.
The results of this exciting episode give a satisfying end to a
story.
   "The author is able to project the fear and curiosity that
existed between white man and Indian but it is unfortunate
that he chose to use the stereotyped broken English for
Squanto's speech" (*About Indians*, p. 46).

Capps, Mary Joyce. **Yellow Leaf.** Illus. Don Kueker. Concordia
1974. Intermediate.

Yellow Leaf, a Cherokee girl, is three years old when her family
is forced off their land. On the year-long march to reservations
beyond the Mississippi (The Trail of Tears), she is separated
from her family. Wandering alone, she finds Cagle, a white
trapper, who takes her into his cabin and raises her. Each
summer when Cagle goes off to trade his furs, Yellow Leaf
stays at an Indian village where she learns Indian ways and
wisdom. Eventually she has many adventures during her search
for her family. The story, told by her great-granddaughter, is
exciting and realistic.

Chandler, Edna Walker. **Indian Paintbrush.** Illus. Lee Fitzgerrell-
Smith. A Whitman 1975. Intermediate.

This story of Maria, half Sioux and half Mexican-American,
demonstrates the confusion and unhappiness of feeling
unwanted. Maria lives with her father's people south of Phoenix
in a Mexican-American village, but her father dies and she
moves to be with her mother's people. Maria is unhappy in
school until she begins to learn the traditional Indian ways, and
then she finds her attitudes changing. Interesting and exciting
adventures await her as she becomes involved in promoting a

romance between her teacher and Billy Lone Deer. Illustrations help to clarify the life on an Indian reservation.

Cheatham, K. Follis. **Spotted Flower and the Ponokomita.** Illus. by author. Westminster 1977. Intermediate.

Spotted Flower, a Blackfoot girl, and her two friends are searching on the prairie for a runaway dog and soon find that they are lost. Her friends are captured by the Shoshonis, but Spotted Flower manages to elude the enemy war party and survives in the woods for some time. One day she hears a new sound coming from the shadowy vines and a strange animal emerges. Its huge head, flaring nostrils, wide teeth, and long face are unfamiliar to her and she wonders if the animal is her new Spirit Power. A beautiful relationship develops between Spotted Flower and Ponokomita or the elk-dog, as she calls him. This is a fanciful story about how the Blackfeet living along the Montana and Canadian border in the early eighteenth century might have acquired their first horse.

Clifford, Eth. **The Year of the Three-Legged Deer.** Illus. Richard Cuffari. HM 1972. Intermediate.

Jesse Benton, a white frontiersman, lives contentedly with his Lenni Lenape wife and their two children on the Indian frontier in 1819. The children rescue a newborn fawn, which has one leg that was almost torn off by a panther, and nurse it back to health. The community's hostility toward Indians soon affects the family, causing them much anguish and leading to their tragic separation and exile. Descriptions of hangings may be gruesome to some readers; otherwise most readers will find this to be a sensitive, compelling story of courage.

Clymer, Eleanor. **The Spider, the Cave and the Pottery Bowl.** Illus. Ingrid Fetz. Atheneum 1971. Intermediate.

Each summer Kate, Johnny, and their mother go to the reservation to take care of their grandmother, but this summer the mother must stay in town with the children's father and work. Grandmother is unwell and sleeps much of the time, so Kate tries to do all the chores. When Johnny accidentally breaks an ancient pottery bowl, he runs away to hide his shame. A spider in a cave helps the children solve their problems and gives them a new appreciation of their Hopi heritage. The themes of old age, courage, and respect for tradition are sensitively handled.

Colver, Anne. Bread-and-Butter Indian. Illus. Garth Williams. Avon 1972. Primary.

Based on an actual incident experienced by the author's husband's great-great-grandmother, who lived in the Pennsylvania wilderness in the late 1700s. Seven-year-old Barbara, having no best friend, spends much time playing with her doll and often has doll tea parties in the woods. One day she offers some bread and butter, sprinkled with sugar, to a hungry-looking Indian and they become friends even though they cannot speak to each other. When Barbara is captured by a hostile tribe, her Indian friend helps her escape. Sensitively illustrated.

"Stories as delightful and exciting as this are hard to find" (*Saturday Review,* 23 January 1965, p. 52). "A charming story" (*New York Times Book Review,* 20 December 1964, p. 12).

Cossi, Olga. Fire Mate. Photographs by John McLaughlin. Independence Pr 1977. Primary.

This story tells of the loneliness of an Indian girl whose family calls her Yvonne, but in her heart she is Walakea. She has been told many ancient legends, and though she does not always fully understand their meanings, one story is very near and dear to her: that of the Great One, who is guardian of soul-fires. The belief is that all Indians have soul-fires which they must share with a fire mate in order to have light and warmth within the sacred circle of their being. Often, years pass before the search for a fire mate is over. One day as Walakea is walking by the roadside, a car comes along and a sack is tossed toward the very bushes where she is hiding. Opening the sack, she discovers a puppy, who becomes her fire mate. Complications arise when the lost dog, a valuable St. Bernard, is claimed by his former owners. Illustrations are black and white photographs.

Cowell, Vi. Normie's Moose Hunt. Illus. by author. Hale 1968. Primary.

This story gives the younger reader interesting insights into the traditional life of the Cree in northern Canada. A young boy tells of his family's adventures as they set out by canoe to hunt a moose, necessary to provide the family with food and clothing for the months ahead. The story effectively describes the everyday life of these people.

Dixon, Paige. **The Search for Charlie.** Atheneum 1976. Intermediate.

Jane is attending an eastern college when she receives word that her young brother, Charlie, is missing, and she immediately leaves for Montana to help in the search. Knowing her brother extremely well in spite of their age difference, she feels she will be more capable of finding him than anyone else. The search is poorly organized, so Jane decides to enlist the help of her good friend, Vic Barrett, whose Indian background and knowledge of scouting and outdoor survival techniques play an important role as they embark on the difficult and dangerous search. Their exciting adventures make for engrossing reading.

Dodge, Nanabah Chee. **Morning Arrow.** Illus. Jeffrey Lungé. Lothrop 1975. Primary.

Morning Arrow, a sensitive and loving Navaho boy, lives with his blind grandmother. There is an especially close relationship between the two, and together they find joy in simple everyday happenings. However, Morning Arrow is sad because his grandmother's shawl is "tattooed with too many holes." When he spies a beautiful turquoise shawl at the trading post, his greatest wish is to obtain it for her and the rest of the story deals with his efforts to make this wish come true. The black and white drawings and occasional insertions of Navaho phrases add authenticity to this book by a Navaho author.

Epstein, Anne Merrick. **Good Stones.** Illus. Susan Meddaugh. HM 1977. Intermediate.

During the Great Depression, twelve-year-old Sisul Osborn finds herself in a desperate situation: her dead father's white family, with whom she lives, mistreat her because she is a half-breed. Sisul's mother has taught her much over the years about the Wabanaki religion and way of life. When her mother dies, Sisul flees to the New Hampshire mountains, feeling certain she will survive because the vision of her mother seems to guide her. An unusual friendship develops between Sisul and Bruce, an aging hermit who helps her locate her mother's people in Maine. When even her Indian relatives do not accept her, an old basket-maker helps her discover a purpose in life and appreciate her Indian heritage.

Fredericksen, Hazel. **He-Who-Runs-Far.** Illus. John Houser. A-W 1970. Intermediate.

Pablo had contentedly lived all of his eleven years in the Papago village of Pavi in the Arizona mountains, never thinking that he would ever leave it. Change comes swiftly, however, when his grandparents come and take him to their village to be taught tribal ways before going to the Big School, where he will learn something of the white ways. Five years later, Pablo returns to Pavi and the rest of the story describes the heartbreaking division that comes between him and his people and how he attempts to heal it.

George, Jean Craighead. **Julie of the Wolves.** Illus. John Schoenherr. Har-Row 1972. Intermediate.

An Eskimo girl lives a life untouched by the ways of the whites until she is nine, when she goes to live with her aunt in Mekoryuk so that she can attend school. Her life as an Eskimo living in the white culture is so contrary to her basic instincts and so disheartening that, at age thirteen, she runs away and is lost on the tundra as winter sets in. The account of how she comes to live among the wolves and how she learns their ways is authentic and exciting, and the close bond between people and animals who share a hostile environment is effectively portrayed.

Goble, Paul, and Dorothy Goble. **The Friendly Wolf.** Illus. Paul Goble. Bradbury Pr 1974. Primary.

Little Cloud and his sister, Bright Eyes, go berry-picking with their mother and the other women and children. The two children slip away to go exploring in the hills, and after climbing one tall peak they lose their way. They find refuge in a cave for the night, but during the night Little Cloud awakens and realizes that a wolf is in the cave. Feeling the animal's hot, panting breath on his neck, he prays for mercy and is left unharmed. In the morning the wandering children again encounter the wolf, who assures them that he will lead them home, and the story ends with an explanation of why the wolf has remained the friend of the Plains Indians.

Goble, Paul, and Dorothy Goble. **Lone Bull's Horse Raid.** Illus. Paul Goble. Bradbury Pr 1973. Intermediate.

Lone Bull, a young Oglala Sioux, is impatient to prove himself as a warrior, despite his parents' insistence that there is plenty of time. On overhearing his father's plan to raid the Crow tribe for horses, he decides to fulfill his dream by joining the party. He and his friend Charging Bear steal away from the camp and follow the raiding party for several days, only to find that the men have been watching them all the while "as the mountain lion waits for the little wolf." Proud of his son, the father lets the boys continue traveling with the raiders. The raid itself brings exhilaration, adventure, danger, and narrow escapes, and there is a good description of the techniques Plains Indians used in their intertribal invasions. The illustrations were inspired by Plains Indian paintings of the period 1860–1900, when the story takes place.

Griese, Arnold A. **At the Mouth of the Luckiest River.** Illus. Glo Coalson. T Y Crowell 1973. Intermediate.

Tatlek, an Athabascan Indian and the son of a great hunter, has a crippled foot. Because a great hunter's son should have a strong body, others in the tribe wonder if a *yega*, or spirit, has done him harm. Or is it a sign that Tatlek will become a big medicine man? The medicine man in the tribe hates and fears the lame boy, partly because Tatlek has been friendly with the Eskimos and has learned to train dogs to carry him in a sled to the best fishing and trapping sites. The tribe fears that the Eskimos with whom Tatlek is friendly will come to kill them. The suspenseful tale develops as Tatlek arranges to change former enemies into friends. Graphic illustrations vividly portray a world of cold isolation.

Griese, Arnold A. **The Way of Our People.** Illus. Haru Wells. T Y Crowell 1975. Intermediate.

The Alaskan village of Anvik is celebrating the Feast of the First Hunt, for Kano has killed his first moose. However, the celebration brings no joy to the Indian boy, who fears that he and his family will be shamed when his secret is discovered. Venturing into the deep woods alone, he learns an important lesson from Old One: he must be unafraid of the *Nakani* or spirits, which may take human or animal form. When Kano meets Ivan, a Russian, he has the opportunity to face the challenges and dangers that lie ahead. The story takes place more than a century ago and is richly immersed in the legends and traditions of the Alaskan Indians. The illustrations capture the icy beauty of the land and the life of these people.

Hamilton, Dorothy. **Jim Musco.** Illus. James J. Ponter. Herald Pr 1972. Intermediate.

Twelve-year-old Jim Musco and his family are cast out of the Delaware tribe because Jim's father, being honest, had exposed a theft by another member of the tribe and was no longer accepted. The father, fearing harm, leaves his wife and son with some friendly whites and disappears. Jim meets a white boy and enjoys many adventures with his new friend. This is an exciting story about the Delaware Indians and the effect the Moravian Brethren had upon some of them.

Hancock, Sibyl. **The Blazing Hills.** Illus. Richard Cuffari. Putnam 1975. Primary.

This story, based on a true incident, takes place in the spring of 1846 in a German settlement in Texas. Twelve-year-old Nate and his sister Sarah see three Indians in the woods and hide in the bushes. The settlers live in fear of the Apaches and Comanches, so the men of the village go to a council meeting with them, hoping to make a peace treaty. Fearing a surprise attack from the whites that night, the Indians build signal fires on the hills and surround the settlement. Sarah comforts her terrified younger brothers and sisters while they wait for their father to return. When all remains peaceful, the fires are allowed to burn—which has led to a custom still practiced today.

Harnishfeger, Lloyd. **Hunters of the Black Swamp.** Illus. George Overlie. Lerner Pubns 1971. Intermediate.

This story of coming of age in prehistoric North America portrays Boy's eagerness to prove his courage and maturity in combat against the fierce animals of the Black Swamp. His reckless actions and refusal to follow his father's advice endanger their lives and he learns the value of caution when Man is wounded and responsibility for their safety falls to him. When mastodon hunters come to their aid, Boy is amazed at their cooperation and communication. He appreciates their ability to live together and share responsibilities. Meanwhile, left behind by the two hunters, Woman and Girl struggle alone against the wolf-gods, who threaten Woman in her dreams. Girl cleverly keeps her mother from making human sacrifices to appease them. When the strangers offer to extend protection to Boy's family and give him a new name, Takotay, he knows he has proven himself. Black and white sketches enhance the book.

"A rare find. . . . The author writes with authority about life in an Ohio valley during prehistoric times" (*English Journal* 60:531–32, April 1971).

Harnishfeger, Lloyd. **Prisoner of the Mound Builders.** Illus. George Overlie. Lerner Pubns 1973. Intermediate.

O-Tah-Wah, crippled from birth, is a young Indian hunter of prehistoric North America. Being rebellious, distrustful, and an outcast among his own people, he strays far from home, wandering into the terrible land of the Mound Builders. These sophisticated and cruel people have built a great civilization in the Ohio and Mississippi river valleys, using slave labor. O-Tah-Wah is captured and forced into slavery, where he is constantly beaten. He hopes to escape, and shares this dream with another slave, Bruin, who nurses him through a long illness. In attempting to escape, O-Tah-Wah learns of his own strength and of the meaning of real friendship. The illustrations add to the reader's interest.

Harris, Christie. **Secret in the Stlalakum Wild.** Illus. Douglas Tait. Atheneum 1972. Intermediate.

In this book a modern story and setting are combined with the ancient lore of the Old Coast Salish Indians to create a powerful fantasy. Sarah, a university student researching the religious beliefs of the Salish, comes to stay with Morann's family in British Columbia, and Morann's two sisters accompany her on her trips. Feeling left out, Morann ventures into the woods on her own, seeking answers to her own questions about the Salish beliefs. In her search for the mysterious Stlalakum Lake, Morann is brought face to face with stlalakum sprites—the spirits of the natural world—and comes to accept their powers and the lessons they can teach her. She learns that the unspoiled beauty of the Stlalakum Wild is a treasure to be preserved at all costs. The vivid characterization, lively dialogue, and beautiful drawings and descriptions of nature make this a very readable book.

Hickman, Janet. **The Valley of the Shadow.** Macmillan 1974. Intermediate.

Historical fact, based on records of Moravian missionaries in the Ohio country, is the basis for this novel of a year in the life of Tobias, a thirteen-year-old Delaware Indian boy. In 1781 the war between the English and the colonists has forced a group of Delawares, among whom Tobias and his father live, to move a number of times. Converted to Christianity by the Moravian Brethren, the group is strongly pacifist, but this in no way protects them from massacre and extreme hardship. Only two of the characters, Jonathan and Anna Rebecca, are fictitious. This is a touching story of a gentle boy who cannot accept the cruelty of war and violence.

Holling, Holling Clancy. **Paddle-to-the-Sea.** Illus. by author. HM 1969. Intermediate.

A young Indian boy living in the Nipigon country north of the Great Lakes carves the figure of an Indian in a canoe and christens him Paddle-to-the-Sea. His dream is to have Paddle Person travel down the river to the Great Lakes and on to the Atlantic Ocean. The rest of the book follows the hazardous adventures of the little canoe on its long trip to the sea.

Jones, Weyman. **Edge of Two Worlds.** Illus. J. C. Kocsis. Dial 1968. Intermediate.

Fifteen-year-old Calvin Harper, sole survivor of a Comanche massacre, stumbles across the endless prairie in an effort to return to his home. Hopelessly lost and nearly starved, he meets Sequoyah, an aged Cherokee, who gains Calvin's trust and sustains both himself and the boy by the survival techniques acquired from generations of his people. A great deal of tension, action, and Indian lore make this a book that is best summarized by Sequoyah's words, "Where two worlds meet they make a lonely place."

Kerle, Arthur G. **Whispering Trees.** North Star 1971. Intermediate.

A poignant tale of two boys who are growing up and reluctantly facing adulthood. Johnny Shawano, seeing his own culture rapidly disappearing, wants no part of the white culture but longs to grow to manhood and be like his father—an Ojibway hunter and builder of canoes. Then Johnny makes friends with a white boy, and they share many adventures and Ojibway activities. The coming of the lumber industry causes them much pain when they see the beautiful pine woods and clear streams being destroyed. The culture of the Ojibways is portrayed with great depth. Line drawings portray tools and techniques used in the deep woods of Michigan in the 1880s.

Lampman, Evelyn Sibley. Rattlesnake Cave. Illus. Pamela Johnson. Atheneum 1974. Intermediate.

Because of ill health, eleven-year-old Jamie is sent to spend four months with his Aunt Nora and her family on their Montana ranch. He goes prepared with many books about Indians, reptiles, and horses but a busy ranch schedule of daily chores leaves little time for reading. He becomes a good friend of Horse, a Cheyenne boy, and meets White Fang, Horse's grandfather, who is a source of history and Indian lore. Caught up in the old Indian's mystical beliefs, Jamie finds an ancient Indian medicine bag, dislodged by rattlesnakes from its resting place in a cave. Through the medicine bag, Jamie gains insight into the famous battle where Custer made his last stand, and with Horse's help he returns the bag to its rightful burial place.

Lampman, Evelyn Sibley. The Year of Small Shadow. HarBraceJ 1971. Intermediate.

Shadow is an eleven-year-old Cayuse boy whose father has been sent to prison for borrowing a horse. A white lawyer, Daniel Foster, is instrumental in having the father's sentence shortened to one year, and offers to care for Shad during that time. Although he receives kind treatment in the white home, young Shad feels alienated when he eats cakes at church socials or tries on clothing provided by the church ladies. Shad learns a great deal during the year, unaware that he has taught many things to the white people and earned their respect and affection as well.

Lenski, Lois. Indian Captive: The Story of Mary Jemison. Illus. by author. Lippincott 1941. Intermediate.

A fictionalized account of Mary Jemison, a white girl who is captured by the Seneca Indians in 1758, adopted by Red Bird, and renamed Corn Tassel because of her golden hair. At first she longs to escape, but by the end of the story she has grown to love her Indian tribe so much that she decides not to return to her own people. There are carefully documented descriptions of Indian everyday life and values, and drawings of objects used by the Senecas at that time.

"Useful as a book to read aloud, as a supplement to class work or to enjoy simply for its story" (*About Indians*, p. 212).

Lyons, Oren. **Dog Story.** Illus. by author. Holiday 1973. Intermediate.

This is a story of a beautiful relationship between a young Indian boy and a dog who are drawn to one another from the moment they first meet. The boy longs to have the dog for his very own. When the animal finally accepts the boy, they become partners in the serious business of hunting for the fatherless family. The misunderstanding that develops in the story, its resolution, and the climax will enthrall any young dog lover. The black and white drawings add depth to the story.

McGaw, Jessie Brewer. **Painted Pony Runs Away: As Little Elk Tells It in Indian Picture Writing.** Nelson 1958. Primary.

The pony of Little Elk, a Cheyenne boy, runs away and while searching for it Little Elk is captured by the Sioux. He slips away from the village, recovers his pony, and as he is escaping, he rescues a Sioux boy from a canyon. The outcome has a happy ending for the young reader.

"Written in pictographs on tan paper with each picture translated into English, this is an interesting book, especially for the beginning reader" (*About Indians*, p. 22).

Miles, Miska. **Annie and the Old One.** Illus. Peter Parnall. Little 1971. Primary.

Developing the concepts of love of family, reverence for age, and acceptance of death, this story focuses on Annie, a Navajo, and her aging grandmother. Annie wonders about life and death and believes that as long as the rug her mother is weaving stays on the loom, her grandmother will be with them. Each day Annie unravels some of the weaving, thus hoping to keep her grandmother that much longer, but the Old One explains that time's passage is inevitable, and death is a part of life. Annie soon understands and realizes that she too must grow up and learn to work the loom. Detailed, authentic line and wash illustrations. A 1972 Newbery Honor Book.

Momaday, Natachee Scott. **Owl in the Cedar Tree.** Illus. Don Perceval. Northland 1975. Primary.

Haske, a Navaho boy, has a special love for the trader's black horse, Night Wind. As he herds sheep he has much time to dream about the day when he will own a horse. When the boy goes to school, Old Grandfather is distressed because he feels his grandson is not learning truths the Ancients taught. However, Haske's Christmas gift to his teacher is a painting inspired by a story Grandfather told of his past, of an attack on his people by the Kiowas and Comanches. How this incident helps Haske realize his dream of owning Night Wind makes a satisfying story. The culture of the Navahos is ably portrayed by the well-known Indian author and artist.

Nelson, Gladys Tirrell. **War Drums at Eden Prairie.** Illus. by author. North Star 1976. Intermediate.

The Elliot family, living on the Minnesota frontier during the Civil War, is caught up in the conflicts between the Upper Sioux Agency Indians and the whites who treat them unjustly. Young Winston Elliot forms a friendship with Dan, son of a white missionary and his Sioux Indian wife. Dan and Winston have many unexpected adventures when they are suspected of spying and are captured by Red Middle Voice's band. The story vividly describes the Sioux uprisings, the settlers' flights to safety, and other episodes of Minnesota history.

O'Dell, Scott. **Island of the Blue Dolphins.** Dell 1960. Intermediate.

Karana, daughter of an Indian chief, lives on the Island of the Blue Dolphins off the coast of California. When a dangerous tribe of Aleuts comes to hunt sea otter and kills most of the native men, the tribe flees the island in fear. Karana, seeing her six-year-old brother Ramo still on the island as they are leaving, jumps overboard to join him, even though a storm is approaching and they cannot be rescued. Ramo is killed by wild dogs soon afterward. Alone on the island, Karana tames the leader of the wild dogs, survives storms, earthquakes, and enemy Aleuts, and finally is rescued. The story is based on a true account of the Lost Woman of San Nicolas, who was alone on that island from 1835 to 1853. Awarded the Newbery Medal in 1961. See also *Zia* by the same author (this section).

"A sensitively written novel worthy of reading aloud for its human values as well as for the adventure and excitement" (*About Indians*, p. 240).

O'Dell, Scott. **Sing Down the Moon.** HM 1970. Intermediate.

In 1864 the U.S. government forced the Navajo people of Arizona to migrate to Bosque Redondo in New Mexico, three hundred miles away. This book tells the tragic story of the Long

Walk from the viewpoint of Bright Morning, a fourteen-year-old
girl. In spite of being uprooted from their home, Bright Morning
and her husband possess inner strength and hope, and eventually manage to escape and begin a new life. A Newbery Honor
Book and winner of the Hans Christian Andersen Medal. Cited
by the *New York Times* as an Outstanding Book of the Year.
   "Beautifully written, intensely moving" (*Bookworld* 4,
pt. 2:23, 8 November 1970). "There is a poetic sonority of
style, a sense of identification and a note of indomitable
courage and stoicism that is touching and impressive" (*Saturday
Review*, 14 November 1970, p. 38). "Beautifully written, this
is an interesting and adventurous story for young readers of
life in Canyon de Chelly in the 1860s" (*About Indians*, p. 241).

O'Dell, Scott. Zia. HM 1976. Intermediate.

A young California Indian girl is caught between two worlds—
that of her mother's tribal past and the world of the Santa
Barbara mission. The strongest force in Zia's life is her determination to find her dead mother's sister, Karana. When Zia and
her brother Mondo find a boat cast upon the beach, they use it
to make the dangerous journey to San Nicolas Island where
Karana lives. Their struggles against the wind and waves and
their capture by a whaling boat force them to abandon their
plan. Karana is eventually rescued by an old sea captain hunting
for otter and is brought to the mission. Isolated by her ignorance of the language spoken and unable to adjust to mission
life, Karana leaves to live alone with her dog, Rontu-Aru. The
decisions Zia makes about her own life are greatly affected by
Karana's gift of love and freedom. The story is told with simplicity and occasional touches of humor. See also *Island of the
Blue Dolphins* by the same author (this section).

Oldenburg, E. William. **Potawatomi Indian Summer**. Illus. Betty
   Beeby. Eerdmans 1975. Intermediate.

Anticipating an adventure, six children explore a cave near
their homes on Lake Michigan and suddenly find themselves
transported backward in time three hundred years, when there
were no roads, automobiles, or power boats. They meet many
Indians—some peaceful and some not—and learn first-hand how
the Potawatomi Indians lived. The children share in the excitement of celebrations, contests, and dances, and are threatened
by the danger of Mohawk attacks. The suspenseful conclusion

will delight the reader. Watercolor illustrations add to the fantasy.

O'Meara, Walter. **The Sioux Are Coming.** Illus. Lorence Bjorklund. HM 1971. Intermediate.

Big Turtle warns his brother's family of the impending arrival of the hostile Sioux, who are making their way through country beyond Lake Superior and down the Otter River. Quickly Kawa gathers his wife and their son and daughter, and together they take flight in their canoe. Only a few days' journey ahead of the enemy there is sudden disaster. A broken canoe and a twisted knee force the young son, Wanito, to take charge of the family. Finding the right materials to make a new canoe is a challenge for the family. Wanito's dream of a small white bird leading him to a beautiful stand of white birch trees finally provides the solution. Authentic illustrations give additional information.

Peake, Katy. **The Indian Heart of Carrie Hodges.** Illus. Thomas B. Allen. Viking Pr 1972. Intermediate.

An unusual friendship develops between Carrie Hodges, child of white ranchers in California, and Foster Gant, a desert-seasoned old lion hunter. He presents her with a puppy and, as the years pass, Carrie's sense of kinship with animals and her intense interest in Indian ways grow stronger. On his visits to the ranch, Foster tells Carrie about the magical relationships between Indians and animals and the Indian belief in animal spirits. The girl begins her own search for her special animal spirit, hoping that it will reveal itself to her in due time, and carries magical fetishes to establish further contact with the spirits. The book moves quickly to an incredible climax when she discovers that a favorite coyote has been shot.

Penney, Grace Jackson. **Moki.** Avon 1960. Intermediate.

Moki, a young Cheyenne girl, sees her older brother become a brave hunter and gain recognition from the tribe. But all she can do is help her mother and grandmother look after her little brother and feed her pet, Rabbit Person. She tries to go in search of a vision, like her brother, but that only brings shame to her family because girls are not meant to wander far from the tribe. One day, however, she finds a way to make a name for herself. Indian lore and Cheyenne values are woven into the story.

Perrine, Mary. **Nannabah's Friend.** Illus. Leonard Weisgard. HM 1970. Primary.

This is the story of a young Navajo girl's struggle to grow up. It begins when Nannabah is to take the sheep toward the canyon by herself for the first time. When Nannabah reaches the canyon she is afraid and longs to be with her family. To ease her loneliness, she uses mud to make a small hogan and two dolls named Little Sister and Baby Brother, but they are small comfort because they neither speak nor hear. She returns home with the sheep when the "sun is standing over the tallest rock." The next morning when Nannabah leaves with the sheep she discovers a real friend, another girl who is also tending sheep.

"An entertaining story perceptively written which describes a step in the growing process that every child must go through but which is emphasized in this quiet desert setting" (*About Indians*, p. 24).

Schweitzer, Byrd Baylor. **One Small Blue Bead.** Illus. Symeon Shimin. Macmillan 1965. Primary.

The author's lyrical style conveys a sense of curiosity about the past as she speculates on the history of a small turquoise bead found in the desert sand of the Southwest. She carries the reader backward in time, telling the story of a prehistoric cave-dwelling tribe living in isolation from the outside world. As the others around the campfire mock and stare at him fearfully, an old man wonders if there are other people like themselves elsewhere. A boy who shares the same dream volunteers to do the old man's work when the man leaves to explore and seek contact with other peoples. The tribe's vision is soon expanded when he returns with a boy from another tribe who wears "one small blue bead." Line and wash drawings in warm, earthy colors capture the Indians' activities and the setting.

"Beautifully illustrated. A pleasure to read" (*About Indians*, p. 28).

Sneve, Virginia Driving Hawk. **The Chichi Hoohoo Bogeyman.** Illus. Nadema Agard. Holiday 1975. Intermediate.

Mary Jo and her two Native American cousins become frightened as an unkempt, strange-looking man haltingly moves toward them and tries to grab them. They jump into their canoe and battle the strong Sioux River current to reach the safety of their grandparents' house. Because they had been told stories of powerful spirits who make unusual things happen, the girls call the old man the "chichi hoohoo bogeyman" after the evil spirits of the Sioux, Hopi, and whites. The girls' unusual adventures and the mystery of the menacing figure are exciting. Illustrations are by an Eastern Cherokee.

Sneve, Virginia Driving Hawk. High Elk's Treasure. Illus. Oren Lyons. Holiday 1972. Intermediate.

Joe High Elk and his sister Marie are caught in a raging storm and seek shelter in the cave of their ancestor, Steps High Like an Elk. Hoping that their filly, Star, will be the beginning of a great herd of horses, they are dismayed when she breaks away from them and disappears into the woods. In anger, Joe smashes his fist into the wall of the cave. There he discovers High Elk's treasure—an old bundle wrapped in leather—which leads to a suspenseful conclusion.

"A well-written, fast-paced adventure story which will hold the interest of young readers" (*About Indians*, p. 98). "There is plenty of action, adequate characterization, a well-developed setting, and good family relationships" (*Bulletin of the Center for Children's Books* 26:98, February 1973).

Sneve, Virginia Driving Hawk. Jimmy Yellow Hawk. Illus. Oren Lyons. Holiday 1972. Intermediate.

Ten-year-old Jimmy is tired of being called Little Jim. According to Sioux custom, boys can earn new names—which they carry throughout life—good names through a deed of valor and bad ones through a disgraceful act. The highlight of Jimmy's life occurs when his father announces to everyone, "Hey, look here, Jimmy Yellow Hawk trapped this mink all by himself!" He wins the admiration of everyone, and is no longer Little Jim. The story conveys the contemporary Indians' pride in their heritage while accepting some of the white civilization. The author spent her childhood on the Rosebud Sioux Reservation in South Dakota. 1971 winner of the Council on Interracial Books for Children award for the best manuscript by an American Indian author.

"Since the author has a reservation background, the flavor of the narrative as well as that of the effective black-and-white illustrations is authentic" (*Horn Book* 48:383, August 1972).

Sneve, Virginia Driving Hawk. **When Thunders Spoke.** Illus. Oren
Lyons. Holiday 1974. Intermediate.

Fifteen-year-old Norman Two Bull considers himself too smart
to accept some of the old beliefs of his ancestors, but he loses
his assurance when he finds an ancient relic, a *coup* stick. When
he brings the relic home, his mother, who has recently joined
the church, refuses to have the "heathen" thing in the house. At
the father's insistence the *coup* stick is hung on the wall, and
immediately it changes and glows with color, and even
Norman's mother is convinced of its power. Haunting illustrations are by an Onondaga Indian.

Sobol, Rose. **Woman Chief.** Dial 1976. Intermediate.

Based on fact, this is the story of an Indian girl who becomes
the only female chief of the Crow Nation. Born a Gros Ventre
of the Prairie, she is captured during a Crow raid when still a
child and is raised by a Crow warrior. He respects and encour-
ages her unusual abilities and trains her as a warrior, urging her
to compete with the boys because she is uninterested in girls'
games. Eventually she earns the name Woman Chief for her
brave deeds and her achievement as a hunter and warrior. Many
are eager to serve with her and her name is honored by her
people, but her efforts to achieve peace between the Crows and
the Gros Ventres end tragically.

"The author's knowledge of the Crow and of Native Americans in general is superficial" (*Interracial Books for Children
Bulletin* 8, no. 3:16, 1977).

Steele, Mary Q., and William O. Steele. **The Eye in the Forest.**
Dutton 1975. Intermediate.

A young Adena Indian novitiate sets off on a journey with his
priest-teacher to search for the Sacred Eye of the Adena—the
ancestral home of their people. The gods had revealed to them
that they must return to this sacred place if their tribe is to
prosper once more. They are captured by the Primitives and
experience many dangers before they find the Eye—the earthworks known as the Old Stone Fort in present-day Tennessee.
The authors have reconstructed the culture and religious beliefs
of the pre-Columbian Adena culture of early Ohio on the basis
of findings from Adena burial mounds. Also suitable for more
mature readers.

Steele, William O. **The Man with the Silver Eyes.** HarBraceJ 1976. Intermediate.

The story of Talatu, which means "the cricket" in Cherokee, is set against the backdrop of the Revolution and the tensions of frontier living in 1780. Talatu has always hated the whites, who have taken the Indians' land and driven them into the deep wilderness. He is shocked when his great-uncle tells him he must spend a year with Shinn, a white man, in the settlement of Wantauga. As the year progresses, Talatu maintains his hatred for the peace-loving Quaker and dreams of joining his warrior uncles in attacks on the white settlers. Talatu comes to learn a great deal about himself as Shinn transforms him from a suspicious and sullen boy into a courageous young man.

Teal, Mildred. **Bird of Passage.** Illus. Ted Lewin. Little 1977. Intermediate.

Two short stories are linked in this volume by the use of the great blue heron as a symbol of survival. In the first story an Indian boy and his mother who are fleeing southward to escape raiding whites take refuge in a worn-out dugout as they push closer to the Georgia marshes and Sapelo Island. Getting to see the blue heron becomes Juanillo's goal and symbolizes his determination to survive. In the second story an English cobbler and his ailing wife and daughter encounter hardships as they settle near the Gloucester marshes of New England. Tragedy occurs, but the girl looks to the powerful bird for inspiration as she grows up, and finds freedom and strength from her surroundings. The author gives evidence of an extensive knowledge of the life of the marshes.

Terris, Susan. **Whirling Rainbows.** Doubleday 1974. Intermediate.

Thirteen-year-old Leah Friedman, who is adopted by a pair of college professors, thinks of herself as a "fat, blue-eyed Jewish Indian." She is sent to a camp one summer where she hopes to "discover her Indian roots" in the wilderness of Wisconsin, home of her Chippewa mother. She finds herself unaccepted by the other girls and tries in many ways to win their approval. Her special canoeing skills prove valuable to all the girls when they undertake an extended canoe trip from the camp, and Leah, by her knowledge of many Indian tribes, is able to correct the other girls' many misconceptions about Indians. How she proves herself makes an exciting story.

Van der Veer, Judy. Higher Than the Arrow. Illus. F. Leslie
Matthews. Avon 1975. Intermediate.

Francie, a young Indian artist with growing talent, loves the
mountain called Higher than the Arrow. On the mountain she
befriends a young coyote that has been caught in a trap, and
from this she finds inspiration for a statue of Saint Francis
with a coyote. In many ways Francie is much like any modern
teenager, yet she is proud of her California Indian heritage and
plans always to remain on the reservation. A well-told story,
illustrated with striking woodcuts.

Warren, Mary Phraner. Walk in My Moccasins. Illus. Victor Mays.
Hale 1966. Intermediate.

Hal and Myra Littlejohn adopt five Sioux children. The story
is told from the viewpoint of twelve-year-old Melody, who
worries that her new parents may not want to keep her and
her siblings. The town at times shows its prejudice and the
children's new mother is often short with them, but gradually
the Littlejohns and the children learn to accept one another.
There is a bit of the everything-turns-out-all-right approach to
life and perhaps some stereotyping of Indians as being poor and
dirty.
 "This moving book portrays the stereotype image of the
Indians' living condition in comparison to white middle-class
America" (*About Indians*, p. 285).

Witter, Evelyn. Claw Foot. Illus. Sandra Heinen. Lerner Pubns
1976. Primary.

Claw Foot, a young Sioux, feels that nature has played a cruel
joke on him by giving him a twisted, misshapen foot. His name
is a constant reminder of his weakness, and he is determined to
earn a new name by performing a great act of courage. Red
Duck, the strongest boy in the camp, constantly finds opportunities to harass Claw Foot. Big Owl, a wise warrior, kindly
advises Claw Foot that he must use wisely the abilities he has,
and not feel sorry for those he lacks. Earning the right to own
and train a long-dreamed-of stallion and using it on a dangerous
mission in enemy Crow territory provide an exciting and
satisfying conclusion.

Young, Biloine, and Mary Wilson. How Carla Saw the Shalako
God. Illus. Anne Samson. Independence Pr 1972. Primary.

Marie, a Zuni, and Carla, a Chicana, develop an interesting
friendship in spite of past problems between their people. As

summer changes into fall their friendship grows, and they watch Marie's father shearing sheep, see Johnny Edaakie setting turquoise into silver jewelry, and explore ruins of old Zuni villages where they find interesting pieces of ancient dishes. With the arrival of Shalako, the special Zuni holiday, Carla finds that she cannot attend the ceremony because it is only for the Zuni, but the story ends satisfactorily. Illustrated in color.

Young, Biloine, and Mary Wilson. **Jennie Redbird Finds Her Friends.** Illus. Anne Samson. Independence Pr 1972. Primary.

A young Chippewa girl moves from the Red Lake Reservation to a large city, where she has many adjustments to make. During a field trip with her new classmates, she is able to explain the museum scene showing the everyday activities of the Chippewa Indians. Her parents help the children at school learn to appreciate the Chippewa culture. Colorful illustrations.

Young, Biloine, and Mary Wilson. **The Medicine Man Who Went to School.** Illus. Anne Samson. Independence Pr 1972. Primary.

Jimmy Bicente, a young Navajo sheepherder living in New Mexico, is proud of his heritage. When he visits a trading post he is amazed at hearing other Navajo boys speaking English and realizes they have learned this in school. Jimmy's father wants his son to become a medicine man, which requires learning songs, prayers, and sand painting, but he eventually allows Jimmy to attend school. A warm picture of Navajo family life.

## Junior High

Annixter, Paul, and Jane Annixter. **Buffalo Chief.** Holiday 1958.

As the story opens, Hawk, a young Oglala Sioux, and his father, a Sioux holy man, view the birth of a buffalo bull. In later years the bull and his herd are faced with extinction by the coming of the whites, especially those after hides. Similarly, Hawk and his tribe foresee the disappearance of their way of life. The shift of viewpoint from animal to human characters is skillfully done. The Battle of the Little Bighorn figures in the story and there are excellent descriptions of Indian ceremonials and customs.

"Due to an overly dramatic style of writing, Hawk is something of an Indian superhero. Even so, this is an exciting tale of adventure which presents an accurate picture of life on the

Great Plains and the interdependence of Indian and buffalo"
(*About Indians*, p. 115).

Armer, Laura Adams. **Waterless Mountain.** Illus. by author and
Sidney Armer. McKay 1931.

Younger Brother, a sensitive, beauty-loving Navajo boy, is in
training under his uncle to become a medicine priest. Throughout the story there are tales of the mystery and magic that are
a part of the religion of the Navajos of northern Arizona, and
there is practical knowledge also, about the growing of plants
in the arid wastes of the Navajo country. The author spent
many years in the Southwest, painting Indian legends as well
as recording them. 1932 winner of the Newbery Medal.

"The Navajo legends are most effectively used throughout
the book. In parts, the story seems to cross the lines of believable reality and sheer fantasy; all in all, a good book to read"
(*About Indians*, p. 116).

Arnold, Elliott. **Broken Arrow.** Hawthorn 1954.

In the late 1850s, Tom Jeffords is given the responsibility of
getting the mail through Apache country to Tucson. He learns
the Apache language and goes to see the famed Indian leader,
Cochise, who has only recently learned of the treachery of the
whites. The two men become friends and blood brothers and
the mail goes through, but because Jeffords' men negotiated
Apache Pass when others failed, Jeffords is often considered a
renegade. In spite of this, General Howard takes Jeffords with
him on a campaign to arrange a peace with Cochise. An adaptation of Arnold's adult novel *Blood Brother.*

Balch, Glenn. **Indian Paint.** Schol Bk Serv 1972.

Little Falcon, son of Chief War Cloud of the Piños Indians, is
allowed to choose a black mare from his father's herd for his
own horse. His father thinks Little Falcon makes a poor choice,
but the boy knows that the black mare is with colt and the
sire is the painted wild stallion. He risks attack by mountain
lions and wolves and a bitterly cold winter in order to gain the
confidence of the colt. There is little information about tribal
customs but a great deal about the taming and care of a wild
colt and about Indian survival tactics in the wilderness.

"Although the book is not particularly well written and
many episodes seem contrived, it will be enjoyed by young
people" (*About Indians*, p. 121).

Bonham, Frank. **Chief.** Dutton 1971.

Henry Crowfoot is known as "Chief" because he is the great-great-grandson of Chief Buffaloboy and the hereditary leader of the small Santa Rosa Indian tribe. While attending high school, Chief lives with his cousin in a parolee house near his derelict uncle-guardian. Chief dreams of obtaining better conditions and facilities for his tribe through documents that have passed down to him from Chief Buffaloboy. An accidental fire in the high school chemistry lab and a down-and-out attorney, who at first is more of a problem than a help, figure in the implausible plot of this novel as Chief tries to authenticate his documents. The story fails to focus on the real problems of Indians today. Also for older readers.

"Bonham is closely in touch with contemporary youth culture, as is seen in the language used and in his insight into the way young people think. Many valuable lessons are to be learned from this highly interesting story" (*About Indians*, p. 63).

Boyce, George A. **Some People Are Indians.** Illus. Yeffe Kimball. Vanguard 1974.

A series of short stories about the Navajos by a man who spent thirty years as a teacher to the Indians. Modern young people usually are the main characters. Through them the reader discovers a great deal about tribal ceremonies, hunts, and life at the trading post. A nonfiction section, "Cultural and Historical Backgrounds," contains some misplaced humor.

"This book lacks the flavor of the Navajo, and has lost the traditional meaning and the fun of the superb tales told by the Navajos themselves" (*Wassaja* 3:17, January-February 1975).

Butler, Beverly. **A Girl Named Wendy.** Dodd 1976.

While attending the Indian mission school, Wendy, a fifteen-year-old Menominee girl, receives a note in which her mother tells of her separation from Wendy's father. This means that Wendy and her younger sister, Jill, will live in Milwaukee with Aunt Brenda and her white husband, Uncle Lew. Although she makes friends in Milwaukee and learns to love Uncle Lew, she and Jill really want to return to the Menominee Reservation, where their mother is living with Granny, a medicine woman. Wendy finds her identity after a number of experiences— running away in a storm; returning to the reservation with

Russell, a militant Native American; the illness of her sister; and becoming better acquainted with her elders.

Capps, Benjamin. **The White Man's Road.** Ace Bks 1972.

Joe Crowbone tries to discover what it is to be a man in the Indian-white society of the 1870s and 1880s. The book incorporates almost every kind of Indian character of the time: Great Eagle, the white soldier's friend; Freddy Bull, who has gone to Carlisle Indian School; Mad Wolf, who will never surrender but lives on the reservation, using the rations his granddaughter collects from the whites; and Joe's Comanche mother, who waits for her white husband to return. Joe is an interesting adolescent boy, trying to determine who he is, much as modern adolescents do—but in a very different and confusing world.

Clifford, Eth. **Search for the Crescent Moon.** Illus. Bea Holmes. HM 1973.

In a story inspired by a true incident, Joshua Bright, a Quaker, sets off on a journey to find his twin sister, Sarah, who had been captured by Indians at the age of five. Joshua, as the only remaining son, had promised his mother that he would find his sister if it took the rest of his life. Although he has made many unsuccessful trips over the years, this time he is more hopeful. He is accompanied by his fifteen-year-old grandson, Tobias, who longs to become an artist, and they have many unexpected adventures as they search for the crescent moon—the identifying birthmark on Sarah's palm.

Coatsworth, Elizabeth. **Sword of the Wilderness.** Illus. Harvé Stein. Macmillan 1966.

In 1689 King Louis XIV of France is at war with William and Mary of England, and, in America, British colonists are having boundary disputes with the French of Canada. The Abenakis, an Algonquian Indian tribe, know that British prisoners are of value to the French so they capture Seth Hubbard, with several others, from the village of Pemaquoit. The first days are harrowing for the captives, with long marches, running the gauntlet, and little food. After several months, however, Seth learns to admire and respect his captors. He falls in love with Keoka, a captive English girl, who would prefer to remain an Indian if it were not for Seth.

"While she seems to be objective in her presentation of Indian ways, her Indian characters are unconvincing, leaving the reader with a subtle uneasiness in terms of their value system and its worth" (*About Indians*, p. 147).

Cone, Molly. Number Four. HM 1972.

"I wanna be an Indian / I wanna be red / I wanna be free / Or I wanna be dead." This poem describes the feelings of Benjamin Turner, a young Indian boy living on the West Coast. The story, a fictionalized account of real events, takes place mainly at Douglas High School, where at first Benjamin does so well that most people say "he isn't like an Indian at all." He begins to change when he sees his people on the reservation, forgotten and pushed aside. To encourage them to regain their lost pride, he tries to form an Indian culture club but is told that such an organization is not permissible because it would discriminate against the whites. He rebels, and Benjamin's struggle with this problem, common to young Native Americans today, comes to a crisis when he leads a group of students on an unauthorized trip to an archaeological dig near the ocean.

Doughty, Wayne Dyre. Crimson Moccasins. Trophy. Har-Row 1972.

In a story that takes place in 1777–78, a Miami Indian boy named Quick Eagle participates in all of the symbolic and meaningful rituals of his people. During the ritual of the Circle, where the Manhood Testing is intensified, Quick Eagle learns the true story of his past and slowly begins to understand the meaning of all his dreams. The book builds to an exciting conclusion, holding the reader's attention to the last page. Also suitable for mature readers.

"This author's . . . novel is full of power and depth; and is written in a style which will transfix the reader" (*Library Journal* 91:2704, 15 May 1966). "It's an excellent portrayal of human relations, and one which will suit the idealism of teenagers" (*Kirkus Reviews* 34:311, 15 March 1966). "Characters and environment are deftly sketched. Excellent reading" (*About Indians*, p. 160).

Ellis, Mel. Sidewalk Indian. HR&W 1974.

Charley Nightwind, falsely charged with murder during an Indian protest in Milwaukee, flees by night to a far northern

Indian reservation, the home of his forefathers. He has always been a city Indian and is ignorant of the ways of the woods and his ancestors. On the reservation, he meets Betty Sands, an Indian girl who teaches him survival techniques. The police have been following him, however, so his flight continues and he hides himself on Spirit Flowage, a mysterious lake of floating islands and the source of many Indian legends. Complications set in as Charley becomes involved in a dangerous plan to dynamite a dam which has flooded the fertile valley that once fed all members of the Lost Nation Tribe. A suspenseful and exciting story based on the dilemma faced by many Indians—the conflict between modern and traditional Indian life and values.

Ellis, Mel. **The Wild Runners.** HR&W 1970.

Wild runners are creatures of both the natural and the human world, who must search for their identity because they are not accepted by the "normal and ordinary" creatures in either world. In this modern story set in northern Wisconsin the main characters are a half-blooded boy, North Main, and a coy-dog (hybrid of a hound and a coyote) which he finds in the woods. Both the boy and the animal are hunted by Joel Manning, a warden, for reasons that do not become clear until the end. The passages about nature are detailed and interesting. In recommending the book, however, the teacher should be aware of the detailed description of a coy-dog's birth and a passing reference to the element of human rape.

Forman, James. **The Life and Death of Yellow Bird.** FS&G 1973.

Yellow Bird is the son of General George Custer and a Cheyenne maiden. Because of his light hair and other white characteristics and because his father was white, Yellow Bird grows up never quite feeling a part of his tribe. Only when he is accepted into the tepee of Worm, father of Crazy Horse, does he gain recognition for his visions. Yellow Bird's story begins at the Battle of the Little Bighorn and then, after an episode with Bill Cody's Wild West Show, it concludes with the Massacre at Wounded Knee. The book sharply contrasts the avarice of the whites with the spirituality of the Indians.

Forman, James. **People of the Dream.** Dell 1974.

One of the most admirable of the great nineteenth century chiefs was Chief Joseph of the Nez Perces. This historical novel begins as young Joseph visualizes the changes in store for his people in the beautiful Wallowa Valley of Oregon, when first the gold miners and then the settlers move in. When the army orders his people to leave their home, Joseph chooses the peaceful way and leaves with his followers. But they are pursued until finally, burdened by the death of his brother and the suffering of his people, Joseph delivers his famous "I will fight no more forever" speech to General Howard. A moving story, also suitable for senior high school students.

Fuller, Iola. **The Loon Feather.** HarBraceJ 1940.

In the early 1800s, Oneta, daughter of the Shawnee leader Tecumseh and a Chippewa mother, spends her girlhood on Mackinac Island in Lake Huron with the family of her mother's second husband, a French trader. She encounters the problems of a racially mixed society of Indians, Americans, and French. The novel has a rich historical background of fur trading, commerce, and cultures.

Gugliotta, Bobette. **Katzimo, Mysterious Mesa.** Illus. Lorence F. Bjorklund. Dodd 1974.

The story of a summer in the life of Carl Bibo, half Jewish and half Indian, who in 1925 at the age of thirteen visits his mother's pueblo, Ácoma, for the first time. He meets his cousins Horace and Wilbert, participates in the gallo race, learns to ride an Indian pony, and learns about the sacred rainmakers' ceremonies, the whib contest, and the powers of the Cacique. His cousin Horace, who vents his hostility toward Anglos on Carl, threatens to spoil the summer until together they climb to the mysterious mesa of Katzimo. Although not an Indian herself, the author is related to the Bibo family and visited the pueblo a number of times, where she tape-recorded the family experiences that serve as the basis for this story. See also *Ácoma: Pueblo in the Sky* by Ward Alan Minge (Junior Traditional Life and Culture).

Haig-Brown, Roderick. **The Whale People.** Illus. Mary Weiler. Morrow 1963.

This is a story of the pre-Columbian Hotsath tribe of the Nootka Indians, whale hunters of the Pacific Northwest. One day the men of the tribe arrive home from a whaling trip and announce that the chief has died. For several years the tribe suffers while young Atlin prepares himself, physically and spiritually, to take over for his father. He learns to prove himself, not only as a brave whaler but as a diplomat in relationships with a neighboring tribe. The book contains colorful detail from Indian rituals, with source material cited in the index.

"The action of the whale hunt fails to save this volume from its underdeveloped characters who appear to lack motivation" (*About Indians*, p. 180).

Hale, Janet Campbell. **The Owl's Song**. Avon 1976.

After his best friend commits suicide, fourteen-year-old Billy White Hawk leaves his reservation in Idaho to live in California with his half-sister and attend high school. His art class goes quite well, but generally he finds hostility and persecution in the mostly black school. One day in music appreciation class Billy finds an opportunity to respond, but it turns out unhappily and he realizes that he belongs back in Idaho with his father and his people. The author is a member of the Coeur d'Alene tribe of northern Idaho.

"A sensitive portrayal of a 14-year-old's struggle to remain Indian" (*Akwesasne Notes* 7:45, Early Winter 1975).

Hamilton, Virginia. **Arilla Sun Down**. Greenwillow 1976.

Arilla Adams is the twelve-year-old daughter in a mixed black and Indian family. In many ways she is like any seventh grader in a small midwestern town—disobeying her mother by going to the forbidden roller skating rink, fighting with her brother, and objecting to housework. But she is different because her brother Jack has decided to be the Indian warrior who rides his horse and defies white policemen, because her mother is black and teaches dance, and because her father is part black and part Indian. The story with its Indian imagery is told partially through Arilla's free-association memories of her past, as she searches for her identity in the present—making it a contemporary chronicle about a family which the reader will not soon forget.

Harris, Christie. **Raven's Cry**. Illus. Bill Reid. Atheneum 1966.

The Haida Indians live on the Queen Charlotte Islands, practicing matrilineal succession, carving remarkable totem poles, and celebrating important events with lavish potlatches. Then come the whites with their liquor, guns, disease, and acquisitiveness. Epidemics strike Haida communities, disagreements and jealousies develop, and finally the whites' medicine and religion seem to tell the tribes that the totem pole and potlatch are evil. The last Haida chief is an artist who, seeing his tribe dying out, wants desperately to save its culture through his carvings. The novel focuses on the last three Eagle Chiefs and their contact with the whites. Black and white line drawings are done in Haida style by the last chief's grandnephew.

"The book gives in simple language a sensitive account of the Haida Indians of British Columbia" (*About Indians*, p. 182).

Harris, Christie. **Sky Man on the Totem Pole?** Atheneum 1975.

The Northwest Indian legend of Temlaham tells of a Sky Man who comes to Earth and carries off the Indian princess, Skawah, returning her to Earth years later with six grown children. Their descendants carry the legend with them as they search for paradise, or Temlaham. Many episodes are explained in a fascinating fusion of Indian legends and science fiction.

Harris, Christie. **West with the White Chiefs.** Illus. Walter Ferro. Atheneum 1965.

Although the elder Louis Battenote is the best guide and buffalo hunter in the Saskatchewan Country in 1863, the fur traders of Hudson's Bay Company refuse to hire him because he has killed a half-breed. However, the sickly Viscount Milton and Dr. W. B. Cheadle hire Battenote and his Assiniboine family to guide an expedition from Fort Pitt in West Canada, across the Rockies to Fort Kamloops, and finally to Victoria. Through the eyes of the young Louis Battenote the reader experiences the rigors of this early crossing of the Rockies and also the return of dignity and respect for the older Battenote and his family. A factually based story filled with personality clashes, racial antagonisms, and humor. Cited in *A Preliminary Bibliography of Selected Children's Books.*

Highwater, Jamake. **Anpao: An American Indian Odyssey.** Illus. Fritz Scholder. Lippincott 1977.

Anpao, son of the Sun, is a brave young man in love with the beautiful Ko-ko-mik-e-is, who is already promised to the Sun. She tells Anpao that she will marry him if he will journey to the Sun and obtain permission, and, as proof that permission was granted, he must ask the Sun to remove the scars from his face. Before the Sun will remove the scars, however, Anpao must save his stepbrother, Morning Star. Although the character

Anpao is Highwater's creation—a kind of Indian Ulysses—the hero's adventures are based on legends of Indians of the northern plains, where the author grew up, and on a few stories from the Southwest.

"It is a fine piece of work, truly reflective of the oral tradition and the rich heritage of Native American storytelling. Its publication ought to be considered an event of importance" (N. Scott Momaday, book jacket).

Hillerman, Tony. **Dance Hall of the Dead.** Avon 1975.

Ernesto Cato, a Zuni boy who is the Little Fire God in the Shalako ceremony, is found dead a few days before the ceremony is to take place. Lieutenant Joe Leaphorn, a Navajo policeman, is given the responsibility for finding Ernesto's best friend, a Navajo boy named George Bowlegs, thought by many to be a little crazy. As two more murders occur, the finger of guilt points alternately at George, his father Shorty, a community of hippies who live nearby, and two archaeologists who are digging in the vicinity. Leaphorn's search for the key to the mystery leads him to try to understand the Zunis' Shalako ceremony, since some aspects of the murders seem to be related to it. The book contains a wealth of information about both Navajo and Zuni life and culture.

Ishmole, Jack. **Walk in the Sky.** Dodd 1972.

The Montagne family, Mohawk Indians, are ironworkers who work on high bridges and skyscrapers in New York City. But young Joey, a high school boy, cannot forget the day his father, Big Joe, fell from a tall building and died. His uncle, Mike, is sure Joey will enter the trade practiced by his forebears, but Joey fears high places and is more interested in being a student and a singer. When Joey has an opportunity to sing professionally for two weeks in the Village, he and Mike come to an understanding. The characterization of Joey's girl, Birdie, and of a black high school teacher and his wife contribute to an interesting story about urban Indians. Winner of the Edith Busby Award.

Johnson, Annabel, and Edgar Johnson. **The Burning Glass.** Har-Row 1966.

Fifteen-year-old Jeb lies ill in his father's wagon, which is heading west to Santa Fe. A doctor advises the family to delay because the boy probably will die soon. But Jeb, who would rather go north with the mountain men than go to Santa Fe, runs away in spite of his fever and weakness. He joins the French fur trader Armand Deschute, who becomes his idol and teacher, and they share the hardships and treachery of the trapper's trade in 1833. The book is written from the white boy's point of view. The best-developed Indian character is Cuts-the-Turnip, the strange Crow boy who wants Jeb for a brother but enjoys making him the brunt of some rather cruel jokes. Equally appealing to high school readers.

Keith, Harold. **Rifles for Watie.** T Y Crowell 1957.

Young Jeff Bussey longs for the life of a Union soldier during the Civil War, but he soon becomes aware of the cruelty and savagery of some army men. The war loses its glamor as he sees his young friends die. When he is made a scout, his duties take him as a spy into the ranks of Stand Watie, leader of the rebel troops of the Cherokee Indian Nation. He makes friends among the enemy and falls in love with Lucy Washbourne, beautiful part-Cherokee girl and rebel sympathizer. Good Civil War fiction, including a picture of the talented civilized tribes who had recently been forcibly transplanted from their homes in the East. 1958 Newbery Medal winner.

Kjelgaard, Jim. **Wolf Brother.** Holiday 1957.

In 1884, when the Indian reservations were new and the Hawk Apaches were independent, freedom-loving people, Jonathan, a sixteen-year-old Apache, returned home from school with the words of Father Harvey in his ears: "Continue to learn. Be a teacher." But, after running into trouble with the local soldiers, he is forced to flee the reservation and join Cross Face's band of Apache outlaws, who have refused to settle on a reservation. Jonathan becomes Wolf Brother and has time to reflect on what he has learned, what he is experiencing, and what possible solutions there may be for his people. The novel is based on the author's study of the history of Arizona, his native state. Although it tells little about the Apache way of life, it does picture the difficulties of the transition to the reservation.

"A well-written tale of the early days of reservations which realistically presents the problems facing the Indian" (*About Indians*, p. 205).

Knudson, R. R. **Fox Running.** Illus. Ilse Koehn. Avon 1977.

Kathy "Sudden" Hart is a gold-medalist Olympic runner who, at nineteen, feels she is finished as a runner. Then one day she and her coach see a young Indian girl running along a highway. They persuade the girl, Fox Running, to return with them to Uinta University where she can develop her ability, but the discipline of wearing track shoes, waiting for the gun to start the race, and running on an inside track interferes with her running. In addition, as Kathy discovers, Fox Running can read her native Mescalero Apache but not English. Kathy begins teaching her to read, and Fox Running in turn teaches Kathy the fun of running out-of-doors among trees, as her Apache ancestors did.

Lampman, Evelyn Sibley. Bargain Bride. McElderry Bk. Atheneum 1977.

When she was ten, Ginny had been married to Stephen Mayhew for a price, but she remained with her cousins until she was fifteen. Shortly after Mayhew claims her, he dies suddenly. To avoid living on the Oregon frontier alone, Ginny takes in Nona, a Molalla Indian who has been deserted by her husband, and her baby. Because Ginny's friends would disapprove of an Indian in her home, she tells everyone that her cousin is with her. Only eighteen-year-old Jeth knows that this is not true. A number of suitors come in the spring to help the young widow put in the crops and one of them, Pastor Gilbert, intends to court her—until he learns that she is harboring an Indian. This experience helps Ginny realize who it is that she really wants to marry. Although the reader learns little about Nona and her tribe, the book portrays the prejudice and bigotry that sometimes existed on the frontier.

Lampman, Evelyn Sibley. Cayuse Courage. HarBraceJ 1970.

The Cayuse Indians have emigrated to the beautiful Oregon Territory, where Dr. Marcus Whitman and his wife, Narcissa, come as missionaries. Samuel, a young Cayuse, and his grandfather attend services at the mission but they also hold to certain native beliefs, including faith in their medicine man. When Samuel's hand is caught in a white man's trap and gangrene sets in, the medicine man fails to cure him, but Dr. Whitman saves him by performing an amputation. When the white man's disease, measles, attacks the tribe and Samuel's good friend, Amos, dies, the tribe sees this as poison brought by Dr. Whitman and decides that the family must be wiped out. This is the Whitman Massacre of 1847, seen through the eyes of an Indian boy.

"A thoroughly absorbing story which realistically portrays the events leading up to the Whitman massacre from the point of view of the Cayuse . . . Highly recommended" (*About Indians*, p. 208).

Lampman, Evelyn Sibley. Navaho Sister. Illus. Paul Lantz. Double-day 1956.

Sad Girl, a twelve-year-old Navaho, is sent from her grand-mother's hogan in Arizona to the Chemawa Indian School in Oregon. There she learns the white people's ways and language and finds a family. The book presents interesting conflicts between Navaho and white values in a mid-twentieth century setting, but the ending is a bit too pat to ring true.

"Young girls will easily identify with Sad Girl's inner feelings, making this book an important addition to the few good books of fiction available on the problems of the young Navajo living today" (*About Indians*, p. 208).

Lampman, Evelyn Sibley. The Potlatch Family. McElderry Bk. Atheneum 1976.

Plum Langor, a high school freshman and a Pacific Coast Chinook Indian, feels that her friends look down on her because of her race. On the bus to and from school she sits with Mildred, a fat girl with whom no one else will sit. One day Plum's half-brother, Simon, returns home from a long hospital-ization following the war. He interests his family and a number of others in the tribe in reviving the old Indian customs and sharing them with white tourists and friends. As the summer passes, the family and the tribe find success and pride in sharing their Indian heritage with others. An easy book about an Indian family whose values and concerns are mainly white.

Lampman, Evelyn Sibley. White Captives. Atheneum 1975.

Based on a true account, this novel begins in 1851 as the Royce Oatman family, including seven children, migrate to New Mexico with a group of fifty Mormons to establish a new home. Quarrels break out, and members leave the party. Eventually the Oatman family is traveling alone, when it is attacked by Tonto Apaches. Olive and Mary are taken slaves; the rest, it is thought, are killed. The girls are kept for a year by the Apaches and then are sold to the Mohaves. Although slaves, the girls become almost like members of the family of Mohave Chief

Espaniol. Mary, who is tubercular, dies during a famine, but Olive is rescued through the efforts of her brother Lorenzo who, as it turns out, had not died with his family after all. The book shows both the good and the bad in Indians and whites.

Lauritzen, Jonreed. **The Ordeal of the Young Hunter**. Illus. Hoke Denetsosie. Little 1954.

In this modern story, a young Navajo, Jadih Yazhi or Little Antelope, has a great ambition to ride a buckskin pony belonging to Mr. Jim, the white trader, in order to kill a cougar that has killed many of his people's sheep. But his family needs food, and Mr. Jim has promised that if Jadih will dance at the powwow in Santa Fe, he may win a prize that will help replace the sheep. Asked to dance for money and entertainment rather than for strength and wisdom, the boy wrestles with the conflict between his own culture and that of the whites. Illustrated by a Navajo artist.

Levitin, Sonia. **Roanoke: A Novel of the Lost Colony**. Atheneum 1973.

The plot of this novel offers a fictitious solution of one of the mysteries of American history—the disappearance of the colony that was established in 1587 on Roanoke Island off the coast of Virginia. The leader, John White, went back to England for supplies and was detained by England's battle with the Spanish Armada. When he returned to America years later, the colony was gone. This is a story of what might have happened. William Wythers, a sixteen-year-old runaway apprentice, joins the expedition that leaves England for Roanoke. In the New World he makes friends with Manteo, an English-speaking Indian, and his sister Telana and others in the Indian village. Relationships with the Indians worsen because the British are blamed for a measles epidemic and a rat infestation. William differs with his fellow colonists over the prejudices that develop. He falls in love with Telana and, in the final destructive days of the colony, throws in his lot with her and her people—suggesting an explanation of the stories of fair-skinned Indians that were told to the settlers at Jamestown in 1607.

McCracken, Harold. **The Great White Buffalo**. Illus. Remington Schuyler. Lippincott 1946.

Before he can be initiated into manhood, Wakan, "the Dreamer," must go out and prove himself. But he returns with such a strange story that the tribe does not believe him—a story of his friendship with a white buffalo, which is sacred to the Dakotas. When the tribal medicine man attempts to prove the story, no trace can be found of the White One, so Wakan is banished from his tribe. He finds the white buffalo and lives near him until both are captured by the Cheyennes. Among them he wins honor, but thoughts of his own tribe plague him. When the Cheyennes go to war, however, he is able to do a heroic deed for his own people and finally win favor with them. The story takes place before the destruction of the buffalo and before the Indians had horses. Told from an Indian's point of view.

"An exciting and informative story of Indian life on the plains before the arrival of the white man" (*About Indians*, p. 215).

McGraw, Eloise Jarvis. **Moccasin Trail.** Coward 1952.

Eleven-year-old Jim Keath has run away from his Missouri farm home with his trapper uncle. Clawed by a bear, he is nursed back to health by the Crow Indians and adopted by them. One day he runs away to join trapper Tom Rivers, but the beaver are scarce. A note comes from his brother Jonnie, informing him that their parents are dead and that Jonnie and their younger brother and sister, Daniel and Sally, are moving west. Only Jim is old enough to sign the homesteading papers, so he meets his family and they homestead in the Willamette Valley. Jim has difficulty refraining from joining the Indians. A fine adventure story of adolescents trying to survive alone on the frontier in 1844. A Junior Literary Guild Selection.

"This excellent book for young people gives a clear presentation of the problems and conflicts of two merging cultures" (*About Indians*, p. 218).

McNichols, Charles. **Crazy Weather.** U of Nebr Pr 1967.

In this modern story, filled with Indian customs and legends, a fourteen-year-old white boy, named South Boy by his Mojave nurse, is bored because there is nothing to do. His father is away buying cattle and his mother is at the Pacific Coast for her health. His Mojave friend, Havek, decides to go name-traveling because there is trouble among the neighboring Paiutes, and this is his chance to do a brave deed and so obtain an adult name. South Boy accompanies him and, for a time, lives as an

Indian—an experience that helps him discover who he is. Also
suitable for more mature readers.

"The background is wholly accurate: I do not note one error
of fact or construal, nor one false note as to attitude" (A. L.
Kroeber, in *American Anthropologist* 46:394, July 1944).
"While the book can be read and enjoyed sheerly for its
adventure, the mature reader will find more in subtleties of plot
and character development" (*About Indians*, p. 220).

McNickle, D'Arcy. **Runner in the Sun: A Story of Indian Maize.**
Illus. Allan C. Houser. HR&W 1954.

Salt is a young cliff-dwelling Indian of the Southwest before
the days of the white settlers. Because he has been chosen
as a successor to the holy man of the pueblo and because his
Turquoise Clan is endangered by a conspiracy of the Spider
Clan, Salt is sent to the Land of Fable (Mexico) to obtain a
more vigorous strain of corn. After many escapades en route to
what is traditionally the land of his forebears, he returns with
the corn and with a young slave girl as his mate. This represents
a strengthening of the tribe by bringing in new blood. In addition, Salt brings information about a rich area, unlike their own
harsh land, where crops can more easily be irrigated. Thus the
novel, by an Indian author, plays upon the mystery of the
deserted pueblos of the Southwest, speculating upon what
might have caused the inhabitants to leave, and examining
the alleged link between the Aztecs and early southwestern
Indians.

Marriott, Alice. **Indian Annie: Kiowa Captive.** Hale 1965.

Young Annie Donovan's family are Confederate sympathizers,
and after the Civil War they move from Tennessee to Texas.
During a Kiowa raid Annie is taken captive and becomes the
much-loved daughter of Sahnko and Maa. Her only connection
with her past life is through her Quaker friend, William George.
She learns Kiowa ways and falls in love with Black Wolf. By the
time she finds her white parents again, she and Black Wolf have
decided to marry and to teach on the reservation. Based on
actual events and people.

Montgomery, Jean. **The Wrath of Coyote.** Illus. Anne Siberell.
Morrow 1968.

The boy Kotola, who later becomes the legendary Chief Marin
of the Miwok Indians, is fascinated by the Spanish and their

ships when they first arrive at his home shores in 1775, near present-day San Francisco. He does not realize that they have come to settle. As the Miwok world is gradually subdued by the Spanish and taken over by the Spanish mission, Kotola sees his son captured and chained, and finally his entire village is wiped out. Rich in Indian lore and illustrated with woodcuts. Also appealing to older readers.

"This is a very sympathetic account, albeit imagined, of a people who are now practically destroyed as a group" (*Indian Historian* 2:37, Fall 1969). "A well-written novel describing one of history's saddest episodes" (*About Indians*, p. 228).

Peck, Robert Newton. **Fawn.** Dell 1977.

This story takes place in 1758, at the time of the battle between the French and British for Fort Ticonderoga. Fawn Charbon is the son of a Mohawk mother and a Frenchman, Henri Charbon, who had originally come to the New World as a Jesuit priest. As the British troops move toward the Fort, Henri Charbon decides to help his fellow Frenchmen and, if possible, return to France. He feels that his son belongs more to his Mohawk grandfather than to him, but Fawn's vigilance saves his father's life during the battle and proves to Henri that there is as much of himself of the Mohawk in his son. In the course of the novel, Fawn and Ben Arnold, a British youth, discover new identities as Americans.

Richter, Conrad. **A Country of Strangers.** Knopf 1966.

Stone Girl, a white girl living in the late 1700s, is captured by the Indians and raised as one of their own in a loving family. She marries Espan, a Delaware, and bears a child, Otter Boy. Because she is white and her son is a half-breed, they may be forced to return to the white world. To avoid this she flees from her Indian village. After hearing of her husband's death she returns to her white family, but they do not believe that she is theirs and reject her and her son. After the boy dies, aid finally comes from True Son who, like her, belongs to neither the white nor the Indian world. See also *The Light in the Forest* by the same author (this section).

Richter, Conrad. **The Light in the Forest.** Bantam 1953.

For eleven years True Son, a white boy, has been a captive of the Delaware Indians, but he has been adopted by them and feels that he is Indian. A treaty, however, demands that he

return to his white family, which he does reluctantly. The conflict of values becomes so unbearable that with the help of his
Indian cousin, he escapes to return to the Indians. The memory
of the one member of his white family whom he loves, his
younger brother Gordie, stays with him. When he is asked by
his Indian tribe to lure a boat of white people into a trap, he
sees a child like Gordie in the front of the boat and is unable to
carry out his mission. True Son leaves his Indian tribe, unable to
find a place for himself in either white or Indian society. Also
suitable for older readers. See *A Country of Strangers* by the
same author (this section), which is a sequel to this story.

"On the whole, Indian life and customs are presented
accurately" (*About Indians*, p. 253).

Rockwood, Joyce. **Long Man's Song.** HR&W 1975.

Soaring Hawk, a young Cherokee, is an apprentice medicine
man, before the coming of the white man. His lineage is in
danger of dying out because his only sister, Redbird, is ill, and
only the women of a Cherokee clan can carry on the line.
Soaring Hawk confidently diagnoses Redbird's illness as an
invasion of angry fish spirits, but when the illness clearly
becomes more serious, he perceives it to be the result of someone's evil conjuring. As the young apprentice struggles to understand the mystery, the reader becomes engrossed in the myths,
legends, and mystery of the ancient world of the Cherokees.
The author is a trained anthropologist with first-hand
knowledge of the Cherokees.

Rockwood, Joyce. **To Spoil the Sun.** HR&W 1976.

In the early sixteenth century, Rain Dove, a Cherokee girl of
eleven, is living with her family and tribe among the foothills
of the southern Appalachians. This is the story, told in her own
words, of her growing-up and of her two marriages—first to
Mink, the spiritual leader of the village, and then to Trotting
Wolf, with whom she has three children, only one of whom
survives. Then stories of ships arriving with strange white men,
thought to be the Immortals, come to Rain Dove's village.
Finally the white people's fever, smallpox, almost wipes out the
village, but Rain Dove and her family are among the few who
survive. Based on actual records of the early Cherokees.

Sandoz, Mari. **The Horsecatcher.** Westminster 1957.

This novel portrays the struggle of a boy to be himself, a non-
fighter in a warrior society. Young Elk is a· Cheyenne youth

who has brave warriors on both sides of his family, but he does not want to kill; his great love is catching and taming the wild horses of the prairies. He hopes to prove his prowess in this way and win the favor of the beautiful Red Sleeve, but his first efforts at this dangerous task end in humiliation. When Young Elk finally captures a beautiful white stallion, his people are being attacked by the Kiowa. By freeing the horse he is able to bring peace between the two tribes and receives the name of Horsecatcher from his people. A number of Indian values are emphasized. Cited in *A Preliminary Bibliography of Selected Children's Books.*

"A good book which doesn't present the Indian as a superman" (*About Indians*, p. 261).

Sandoz, Mari. **The Story Catcher.** Illus. Elsie J. McCorkell. G&D 1963.

Lance, an Oglala Sioux, wants to be a storyteller and historian, but such a person in his tribe has the status of a great hunter or warrior, and he is still a young and impetuous youth. He often goes on dangerous missions to prove himself. While trying to make pictures of the Arikara Indians (the Rees), he encounters a small Ree child whom he adopts as a brother and takes home, bringing danger to the tribe. Adventures, hardships, and disappointments occur before the village finally gives him the new name of Story Catcher. Set in the late nineteenth century and dedicated to the Bad Heart Bull family—a long line of story catchers—this novel demonstrates the conflict of individualism with community responsibility. Cited in *A Preliminary Bibliography of Selected Children's Books.*

"This is a well-written novel which captures the spiritually rich and physically stark life of the Plains Sioux" (*About Indians*, p. 262).

Schellie, Don. **Me, Cholay & Co.: Apache Warriors.** Four Winds. Schol Bk Serv 1973.

The narrator, Joshua Thane, is seventeen when he leaves Chicago for Arizona Territory in 1870. A year later he is working at Camp Grant when the peaceful Apaches under Chief Eskiminzin, who have settled near by, are attacked by prominent citizens from Tucson and by Papago Indians. Joshua's good friend, the thirteen-year-old Apache Charlie, disappears. While in Tucson on an errand for his employer, Joshua finds Charlie, who has a plan to rescue his little sister, Chita, held captive in the Papago village. In recovering Chita, Charlie also frees four other Apache children and Joshua helps him deliver the children to Chief Eskiminzin—a journey that takes them across the Arizona desert with a party of murderous, Apache-hating white men in pursuit. The book is based on history but is highly romanticized. Joshua tells the story in an artificial backwoods dialect.

Sneve, Virginia Driving Hawk. Betrayed. Holiday 1974.

In 1862, Chief Little Crow leads his Santee Sioux in an uprising in southern Minnesota. In the raid on the community of Lake Shetek, Sarah Duley and her mother, sister, and neighbors are captured by White Lodge and his warriors. The Santee take their captives with them as they flee westward, living a life of hunger, cold, and destitution. In the Teton Sioux camp, Charger, descendent of Meriwether Lewis, has a vision that he should rescue the white captives. Taking with him some young Teton braves, called "Fool Soldiers" by their tribesmen, Charger and his brother-friend, Kills and Comes, barter for the captives with guns, blankets, and horses and finally obtain their release.

Stephens, Peter John. Towappu: A Puritan Renegade. Atheneum 1966.

Young Timothy Morris is alone in his home in the wilderness in 1674 when men from Plymouth Colony with whom his father has quarreled come to take him prisoner. In fear, he escapes to friendly Indians and finally to his father's friend, King Philip, the great Algonquian leader. He fears the growing tension between Plymouth Colony and the king, and tries to serve as a mediator between the two factions. Eventually he learns that his father has been attempting to help Philip unite the tribes with the French. The book has several well-developed Indian characters. Cited in *A Preliminary Bibliography of Selected Children's Books.*

"An emotion-filled story which shows well the conflicts faced by the Indians and the white man in the early days of colonization" (*About Indians*, p. 272).

Thompson, Eileen. White Falcon: An Indian Boy in Early America. Illus. Leonard Everett Fisher. Doubleday 1977.

In 1537 Spanish slave traders capture nine families from a tribe in northwestern Mexico, among them the family of thirteen-year-old White Falcon. The slaves' trip to Mexico City is so difficult that White Falcon, a brother, and a sister are the only members of his family who reach the capital city. After learning some Spanish and becoming very fond of Fray Luis, White Falcon joins Coronado's expedition to the pueblos of Cibola, (modern Zuni) in search of gold and wealth. He serves as an interpreter and remains for a time to help the Cibolans resist the Spaniards. Using historical records, the author has reconstructed the story of Bartolomé, "the lad from Petatlan" who accompanied Esteban, Coronado's Moorish slave, to Cibola.

"This piece of historical fiction is well written and well researched" (*Interracial Books for Children Bulletin* 8, nos. 4, 5:31, 1977).

Walker, Diana. **Never Step on an Indian's Shadow.** Abelard 1973.

Teresa Denys, a white fifteen-year-old from Montreal, spends her summer vacation with her married sister, who lives in Moosonee near James Bay in northern Canada. There she meets Michael Big Canoe, a Cree boy who runs a freighter canoe ferry; Richard McCorkell, a white engineer at the weather station considerably older than she; and Toby, a small Cree boy living in poverty in the Indian village with his grandmother. From Michael she learns about the discrimination and bitterness against the Indians, and from Toby she learns the tragedy of being poor and helpless. At times she clashes with her sister and Richard over the bigotry of the community. The book's message is that the races must remain separate because they are somehow very different, and that Teresa has more in common with a white man ten years older than with an Indian boy her own age.

Witheridge, Elizabeth. **Just One Indian Boy.** Atheneum 1974.

Andy is a Chippewa boy growing up on a northern Minnesota reservation, trying to find his way in a white world without losing his Indian heritage. Difficult situations in his first year of high school force him to run away. He seeks a job in a lumber camp and finds it to be not much better than school. After he returns to school and receives more education than he had thought possible, his partial adjustment to city life takes place. The novel is based on actual events in the lives of several Indian boys who lived in places mentioned in the story.

Wood, Nancy. **The Man Who Gave Thunder to the Earth: A Taos Way of Seeing and Understanding.** Doubleday 1976.

Taos mythology and legend are incorporated into a book primarily about the Old Man, but also about the Mountain, the Young Boy, the Old Woman, the Wily Coyote, the Magpie, and other characters. There is a brief introduction by D. H. Lawrence on "The Vast Old Religion of Taos." The stories are divided according to the themes of identification, purification, expansion, and full circle. By a writer who has long been fascinated with the heritage and culture of Native Americans, and of the Taos Pueblo Indians in particular.

### Senior High and Adult

Arnold, Elliott. **The Camp Grant Massacre.** S&S 1976.

When First Lieutenant Royal Emerson Whitman is assigned to Camp Grant near Tucson, Arizona Territory, in November of 1870, there are strong feelings against the Apaches because many local people have had relatives killed by the Indians. But the Aravaipa Apaches, led by Chief Eskiminzin, are ready to make peace. Whitman hopes to settle them near the Camp, but the Indians' water source there dries up and they move four miles away. The whites' anger increases because they see the United States government supplying and protecting "murderous Apaches." A vigilante group attacks the peaceful Aravaipa Apaches, killing 125, mostly women and children, and taking many more children slaves. Despite Whitman's efforts to secure the children's return, the Apaches' belief in him is destroyed. With his usual skill as a writer of historical fiction, Arnold has created a truly tragic hero.

Bandelier, Adolf Francis. **The Delight Makers.** HarBraceJ 1971.

Written in 1890 by a distinguished archaeologist, this is a revealing story of the superstition and intrigue that were part of the Queres Indian culture of the Rito de los Frijoles—and which may explain why they deserted the pueblo. A mother and son incur the displeasure of the Delight Makers or Koshare, a semi-secret society whose supposed rain-making power gives it a position of authority in the tribe. The boy Okoya, his uncle Hoyoue, the witch Shotaye, and Okoya's mother are all splendid characters. Detailed descriptions of the daily life of these

Indians before the coming of the whites—their ceremonies, mourning, warfare, clans, secret societies, and family life—make this a fascinating novel, although it is long and sometimes wordy. The geography, ethnology, and archaeology are as accurate as was possible at the time, but Bandelier was unaware that the Navajo or Dinne—enemies of the Queres in his book—did not arrive in those areas until the fifteenth century and probably were not strong enough to engage in warfare until the seventeenth century. Also, it is doubtful that any Indians knew about scalping at the time of Bandelier's novel.

Baylor, Byrd. **Yes Is Better Than No.** Scribner 1977.

Some Papago Indians who live in the slums of Tucson, Arizona, have left their reservation for the excitement of the city. But their values and way of life are at odds with the dominant Anglo society, especially its welfare system, and absurd situations arise. Mrs. Domingo wins a swimming pool at a local fair; because she needs a house, she puts a roof over the pool. Maria Vasquez and her five children are evicted from her house; her welfare payments are stopped because she has no address. Finally, some Chicago Indians come to organize the Papagos into a Red Power Movement. As a result, the Domingos' swimming pool is filled with water, and Maria flees to the reservation because the local paper pictures her as one who insists on sleeping outdoors with her children, in opposition to the welfare department. This novel is both humorous and sad.

Berger, Thomas. **Little Big Man.** Fawcett 1969.

At age 111, Jack Crabb—frontiersman, Indian scout, gunfighter, buffalo hunter, adopted member of the Cheyenne tribe, and only white survivor of Custer's Last Stand—tells his story to the author. Taken from his parents by Cheyenne Indians, he grew up knowing the Indians and their world better than the ways of his own white people. The story is in the tradition of American frontier humor and of Indian tragedy. One of the strong Indian characters is Chief Old Lodge Skins. Other well-known figures from the Old West who appear in the story are Wild Bill Hickock, Wyatt Earp, General Custer, and Calamity Jane. On *Akwesasne Notes* basic library list.

"An excellent historical novel dealing with the ways of life and death on the western frontier between 1852 and 1876" (*About Indians*, p. 126). ["One of three books that] give a good idea of the intangible sense of reality that pervades the Indian people" (Vine Deloria, Jr., *Custer Died for Your Sins*, p. 16 [see Senior Modern Life]).

Blevins, Winfred. **Charbonneau: Man of Two Dreams.** Avon 1976.

A romanticized story of Jean-Baptiste Charbonneau, the son of Sacajawea, girl guide for the Lewis and Clark expedition. Born during the trip, the boy earns the affection of Captain William Clark for his intelligence. Partly to repay Sacajawea for her valuable services, Clark offers to educate Paump, as her son is called, and Sacajawea agrees to the plan, against her husband's wishes. Paump already speaks four languages, and Clark convinces him that he can contribute to the world if he will perfect his language skills, but in spite of his natural love of learning, Paump dislikes his teachers. On a trip downriver he meets Prince Paul of Württemberg, who invites him to Europe. There Paump experiences the music, life, culture, and languages of the Continent. But he finally decides to settle down with his people, the Shoshone, and raise a family and live near his mother. The book accepts the theory that Sacajawea survived her lonely trip across the prairies, fleeing from her husband's cruelty back to her people.

Borland, Hal. **When the Legends Die.** Bantam 1972.

Because Tom Black Bull's father killed a man who stole from him, his wife and young son flee with him into isolation on Horse Mountain, where they live in the traditional Indian manner. Tom's father dies in an avalanche and later his mother dies of illness. For a time young Tom lives by himself in the old ways with a young bear as his brother, but Blue Elk, a fellow Ute, persuades him to attend reservation school. After a while he joins Red Dillon, a dishonest promoter, as a bronc buster and learns to cheat at meets as Red wants him to. But after Red's death he is on his own, riding hard and taking out his anger against the world and white society on the horses. After a serious injury, he returns to Colorado to the old life. The book, set in the early twentieth century, makes beautiful use of Indian lore and love of nature and gives a vivid impression of a young Indian boy's reaction to injustice. On *Akwesasne Notes* basic library list.

The book "gives a good picture of Indian youth" (Vine Deloria, Jr., *Custer Died for Your Sins*, p. 16 [see Senior

Modern Life] ). "A good novel, sensitive to the Indian's human search for identity" (*About Indians*, p. 129).

Butterworth, F. Edward. White Shadows Among the Mighty Sioux. Illus. Alta Adkins. Independence Pr 1977.

A biographical novel of Frank Grouard, captive of Sitting Bull's Hunkpapa Sioux and later United States Army scout with General George Crook. The son of an American missionary father and a Polynesian mother, Grouard is left in the United States to fend for himself at a very young age. He is captured while riding for the Pony Express, but eventually becomes the adopted brother of Sitting Bull and marries his sister, White Fawn. He gradually earns the respect and trust of the tribe, but when conditions within the tribe deteriorate following the Battle of the Little Bighorn, he decides to try for help from the Bureau of Indian Affairs. This decision forces him to leave the tribe and throw in his lot again with his own people. The novel gives evidence of considerable research about the Sioux and their culture.

Capps, Benjamin. A Woman of the People. Fawcett 1971.

In 1854, nine-year-old Helen Morrison lives with her family on the frontier in Texas. One day she and her younger sister Katy are captured by Comanche Indians and the rest of the family is killed. Adopted by the family of Lance Returner, Helen becomes Tehanita and decides to work hard at being a good Comanche, to learn their ways and eventually to escape to her own people with Katy. But one day young Burning Hand leaves nine horses as a marriage proposal. As she watches her young husband grow in wisdom and prestige during the hard times when whites kill their buffalo and attack their settlements, she realizes that she is a Comanche wife and that her place is with the tribe. A sympathetic picture of Comanche Indians.

Carlisle, Henry. The Land Where the Sun Dies: A Novel of the Seminole Wars. Putnam 1975.

This is a novel of white people involved in the Seminole Wars of the early nineteenth century. The main character is Eliza Hutchins, a distant kinswoman of Andrew Jackson, whose family survives only because Jackson gives her impoverished father an appointment as Indian agent to the Seminoles. Both Eliza and her father differ from Jackson in their strong human-

itarianism toward the Seminoles and the escaped Negroes who
have become part of the tribe. Eventually Eliza marries her
cousin, Laird Caffrey, who is sent to Florida with the U.S.
militia, and she finds herself pleading for compassion for the
Seminoles. Laird finally responds by protecting a last group of
Seminoles and Negroes on their move West. Although it is good
historical fiction, the book focuses on Eliza and her struggle
to reconcile her sympathy for the Indians with her feelings for
Laird who must fight them, and it tells little about the Seminoles and their feelings toward the Removal.

Carter, Forrest. **Gone to Texas**. Delacorte 1975.

After his young wife and son die in a fire in Missouri during pre-
Civil War days, Josey Wales becomes a fugitive whose only
goals are survival and revenge. He flees from Missouri to the
area of the Five Civilized Nations where he is joined by his
friend Lone Watie, Cherokee relative of the Indian leader,
Stand Watie. In order to survive, Josey steals and kills until
there is a price on his head. He becomes a kind of Robin Hood
of the Civil War period, protecting the innocent, including Little
Moonlight, a mistreated Cheyenne woman, and Laura Lee
Turner, a white woman, and her grandmother. The five of them
move southward into Texas, searching for a new life. Written by
a Cherokee, this is escapist literature which pits Indians and the
oppressed against the establishment, represented here by the
law and the military. See also *The Vengeance Trail of Josey
Wales* by the same author (this section).

Carter, Forrest. **The Vengeance Trail of Josey Wales**. Delacorte
1976.

When a gambler, Ten Spot, and his girl Rosie, sign an affidavit
saying that the outlaw Josey Wales is dead, they free Wales from
his past and allow him to marry and settle down on a ranch in
Texas. But when a power-hungry Mexican, General Escobedo,
rapes and murders Rosie and imprisons Ten Spot, Josey goes
back to his old life on a trail of vengeance. Among the people
he rescues from Escobedo's violent followers is a young Apache
girl. In appreciation, Geronimo and his Apaches assist Josey in
carrying out his revenge. In this second episode in the saga of
Josey Wales, the forces of good—personified by Josey, Ten
Spot, and the young Apache—again do battle with the forces of
evil, as represented by the military. See also *Gone to Texas* by
the same author (this section).

Cather, Willa. **Death Comes for the Archbishop**. Random 1971.

Cather's masterpiece tells of incidents in the life of Father Jean Latour as he carves a bishopric out of nineteenth century New Mexico. The bishop and his vicar, Father Joseph Vaillant, travel hundreds of miles in order to say Mass among Indian tribes and Mexicans. In the beginning, Father Latour seems to feel that Indians are extremely difficult to convert to Christianity and that they are easily corrupted by liquor and trickery. Later the priest recognizes the selfishness and dishonesty of whites in their relationships with Indians and regrets that as a priest, he cannot interfere with government affairs. Although written from the white's point of view, the novel ends on a note of sympathy for the Indian. Published in 1926.

Cooper, James Fenimore. **The Deerslayer**. Sig. NAL 1963.

A very young Natty Bumppo, illiterate but trained in Christian ethics by the Moravians, finds his values challenged at Otsego Lake by the selfish and cruel Tom Hutter, and by Hurry Harry and Hutter's beautiful daughter Judith. The Indians in this novel, set in the 1740s, are definitely superior to Tom and Hurry—who scalp for glory, but cannot be blamed for it because they know no better. The Indians Natty Bumppo, Chingachgook, and his fiancée, Hist, are noteworthy and generally admirable characters. Published in 1841.

Cooper, James Fenimore. **The Last of the Mohicans: A Narrative of 1757**. Sig. NAL 1962.

In 1757 two young women, Cora and Alice, try to join their father, Colonel Munro, the commander of Fort William Henry, which is besieged by Montcalm. The girls are captured, rescued, and recaptured. Good Indians, like Chingachgook and Uncas, protect them. Uncas falls in love with Cora, but Magua, the villain of the story, also wants her. The struggle ends in the deaths of both Cora and Uncas. Published in 1826, this novel became Cooper's most famous work. The story precedes *The Deerslayer* by about fourteen years.

Many have felt Cooper's Indians to be romanticized, but George Bird Grinnell, who lived with Indian tribes over a period of sixty years, said, "The Indian of Cooper—with his bravery, his endurance, his acuteness, his high qualities of honesty, generosity, courtesy and hospitality—has been laughed at for half a century. Yet every man who has mingled much with the In-

dians in their homes has known individuals who might have sat
for the portraits which Cooper drew of some of his aboriginal
heroes" (*Pawnee Hero Stories and Folk Tales*, p. xiii [see Senior
Myth]).

Corle, Edwin. Fig Tree John. Liveright 1971.

To escape living on a reservation, the Apache Agocho, later
known by the whites as Fig Tree John, and his wife, Kai-a,
settle near the desolate Salton Sea in 1906. There their son,
N'Chai Chidn, later known as Johnny Mack, is born. Following
his wife's murder, Agocho tries to bring up Johnny in the
Apache ways, but there are none of their people around for
ceremonials. Johnny wanders to neighboring ranches and is
fascinated by the white world. Finally he marries a white girl
and builds a home near his father, and intense conflict between
Fig Tree and his daughter-in-law results in tragedy.

"It is most dramatic, utterly true, and yet not once does the
author intrude on the reader's absorption in the tale. At the
time we were all busy applauding Hemingway and Lewis and
Dreiser and Steinbeck a man wrote a book that ranks with their
best" (Frederick Manfred in *Minneapolis Tribune*, 23 May
1971, p. 9E). "Corle brilliantly portrays the character of Fig
Tree John, displaying a deep-rooted knowledge of the Indian
psychology, value system and cultures in his ability to criticize
non-Indian characters as they appear to Fig Tree John" (*About
Indians*, p. 151).

Craven, Margaret. I Heard the Owl Call My Name. Dell 1974.

Mark Brian, a young Anglican priest who does not know he is
incurably ill, is sent by his bishop to serve at Kingcome, a
Kwakiutl community in British Columbia. In this harsh, isolated environment, Mark, the only white person in the village,
struggles to understand the Indian way of life. A deep respect
grows between him and the Indians, and he comes to understand their drinking problems and their sorrow over the decline
of their old ways. From them he learns to accept death as a part
of life, as signified by the salmon's triumphant journey up-
stream.

"About a young priest with two years to live, and the
Kwakiutl People who teach him much about life—and who are
paying the price for the death of their nation in the process"
(*Akwesasne Notes* 7:45, Early Winter 1975).

Cushman, Dan. **Stay Away, Joe.** Stay Away 1968.

Big Joe Champlain, a Purple Heart Marine in World War II and
Korea, son of an Assiniboine mother and a Cree and French
father, returns home to Montana. His stepmother, a Gros
Ventre Indian, and his sister want to join the white community
and get ahead on white terms. Joe uses his hero status to get
free drinks, borrow money, and buy an expensive car. He gradually sells parts of the Buick, which is not paid for, to finance
his wild life, and ends up living in the car's shell when his stepmother puts him out of the house because he may ruin his
sister's chances for a good marriage. The conflict between Joe
and his stepmother and sister is humorously mediated by his
charming father, who understands both his son and his wife.
The story could end tragically but does not.

"*Stay Away, Joe,* by Dan Cushman, the favorite of Indian
people, gives a humorous but accurate idea of the problems
caused by the intersection of two ways of life" (Vine Deloria,
Jr., in *Custer Died for Your Sins,* p. 16 [see Senior Modern
Life]). "No one interested in the fun and frustration of what
it is to be an American Indian today should miss it" (*ASAIL
Newsletter* 2:15, Spring 1978).

Derleth, August. **Wind over Wisconsin.** Scribner 1938.

In 1831 young Chalfonte Pierneau has the only estate owned
by a white man along the Wisconsin River on Sac Prairie. He
and his father trap and trade with the Sac (Sauk) Indians and
are especially friendly with Black Hawk. The Prophet, Black
Hawk's brother, has promised that if the Sacs must fight for
their land, the Ottawas, Chippewas, Kickapoo, Potawatomi, and
Winnebagos will join them in combat. Chalfonte counsels Black
Hawk to negotiate with the whites and not fight them, but the
chief refuses. As tension grows, Chalfonte fortifies his estate,
but his wife is fatally wounded in a surprise attack from the
Sioux. Although Chalfonte broods over Black Hawk's fall and
the resulting changes, he learns to accept a new way of life with
the coming of white settlers. Black Hawk is not a well-developed character in this historical novel; the book is mainly about
the passing of a way of life with the downfall of the Sacs.

Edmonds, Walter Dumaux. **Drums Along the Mohawk.** Bantam
1947.

Gil and Lana Martin go as newlyweds to Deerfield on the frontier in the Mohawk Valley. Their struggles to survive and pro-

tect their property during the Revolutionary years 1776–1784 make an epic novel. Iroquois Indians are allied to the British Loyalists and so are to be feared by the Colonists, from whose viewpoint the story is told. Although the best-developed Indian characters—Blue Back and Gohota—are admirable and capable, the general impression of the Indians is one of savagery. They are usually pictured as dirty and smelly, many with bloody scalps hanging from their belts. There is no evidence of the tribes' dilemma as they fight for their lands and way of life, not knowing which political group could be trusted to help them. Published in 1936.

Fall, Thomas. The Ordeal of Running Standing. Bantam 1971.

Running Standing, a Kiowa living in Oklahoma, resists the Jesus Road and the whites' way until the beautiful Cheyenne, Crosses the River, goes to Carlisle to attend school. He follows her, and there, as Joe Standing and Sara Cross, they fall in love and marry. But they separate on their wedding night because he is offered work with a petroleum company, while she insists on returning to the reservation to help their people. Joe works for the company while studying law, hoping to sell mineral rights and buy a controlling interest in the company for the Indians. At home, Sara helps her people develop their allotment land. Tragedy occurs, however, because Joe cannot learn enough to outwit dishonest and greedy whites. Set in the early twentieth century, the book effectively characterizes an Indian's struggle to remain Indian while being lured by white people's promises. Although slow-moving at times, the narrative develops sympathy for the Indians and gives details of Indian customs and beliefs.

"The novel is somewhat less strained and 'precious' than most novels written by non-Indians about Indians" (*Indian Historian* 4:54, Spring 1971).

Fast, Howard Melvin. The Last Frontier. Sig. NAL 1971.

In 1878 about three hundred Cheyennes, tired of their treatment at the reservation in Oklahoma, leave for their home in the Powder River Country after duly warning the officials. The United States Army attempts to capture them. After a number of skirmishes, about half of the Indians are killed but the remainder reach their destination. This version of the Cheyennes' flight is told mainly from the whites' point of view, but the author does demonstrate sympathy for the Indian cause. On *Akwesasne Notes* basic library list.

"Suspense and easy readability make Fast's book appealing to young readers as well as adults" (*About Indians*, p. 166).

Ferber, Edna. **Cimarron.** Fawcett 1971.

In 1889 Yancey Cravat, a poetry-quoting pioneer, takes his aristocratic southern wife, Sabra, to the pioneer community of Osage in Oklahoma Territory. As a lawyer he defends controversial characters, and he establishes a newspaper in which he fights for the rights of Indians. But he soon wearies of his responsibilities and leaves Sabra and their two children, returning sometimes for important events, such as the discovery of oil. Yancey's son, too, is drawn to the Osage Indians and finally, against his mother's wishes, marries Ruby Big Elk, whose Osage family has become wealthy because of the tribe's oil interests. The Indians, especially the Osage, are usually seen through the eyes of Sabra, who is prejudiced (they say "How" and usually speak in substandard English). Published in 1929.

Fisher, Vardis. **Mountain Man: A Novel of Male and Female in the Early American West.** PB 1965.

A romantic novel of the 1830s, with a great deal of violence and bloodshed. Sam Minard is a mountain man who from his youth has loved to play the classics on a mouth organ or jew's-harp. But he seeks revenge against the entire Crow and Blackfoot nations after finding his beloved wife, Lotus, beautiful daughter of the Flatheads, and her unborn child murdered, and after seeing four Indians killed with an axe by frenzied Kate Bowden because they murdered her children and captured her husband. Eventually, however, Sam's strong belief in love and an Almighty Plan cause him to become sickened of killing. The life, food, and daily routine of the Indians and the mountain men are realistically described.

Freedman, Benedict, and Nancy Freedman. **Mrs. Mike: The Story of Katherine Mary Flannigan.** Illus. Ruth D. McCrea. Berkley Pub 1968.

In 1907 Katherine Mary O'Fallon is sent to western Canada, near Calgary, to regain her health. She meets and marries Michael Flannigan, a Canadian Mountie, who is transferred first to northern Manitoba and then to far northern Alberta. There they live among the Indians and half-breeds (Beaver, Cree, and Blackfoot), sharing in their neighbors' celebrations and experiencing their tragedies in fires, plagues, illness, and death.

There are some sympathetic pictures of the half-breed Sarah and the Indians Oh-Be-Joyful and Jonathan, but the emphasis is on the love between Katherine and Mike. A twentieth-anniversary selection of the Literary Guild.

"The book is very enjoyable and well worth reading" (*About Indians*, p. 171).

Fuller, Iola. The Shining Trail. Popular Lib 1951.

Tomah—a close friend of Black Hawk, the great Fox and Sauk chief—marries Wenona, a Sioux Indian, who has a son by a Sioux father. The family loyally follows Black Hawk as he leads his people in the hopeless struggle against the white settlers and the troops who are forcing the Indians from their homeland on the Rock River in Illinois in 1831-32. The son, Chaske, at first hopes to return to the Sioux, but is adopted by Black Hawk to replace the chief's dead son. A historical novel sympathetic to Black Hawk, his people, and their plight.

"A well-written, gripping novel for young people" (*About Indians*, p. 173).

Garland, Hamlin. The Book of the American Indian. Illus. Frederic Remington. Garrett Pr 1971.

Fifteen sketches about Indians who are forced to walk the white road in one way or another: a mother who must send her son to school; Indians who fight the building of a fence; two boys who commit suicide rather than go to a strange school. The longest of the sketches, "The Silent Eaters," is the story of Sitting Bull's resistance as a young Sioux might have told it. In these sketches Garland attempts to see things from the Indian's point of view. Remington's drawings add to but do not interpret the text. Published in 1923.

Garland, Hamlin. The Captain of the Gray-Horse Troop. Gregg 1970.

In the late 1800s, Major George Curtis of the Gray-Horse Troop is ordered to Fort Smith as an Indian agent to handle a problem between the Indians and the cattlemen. After the major's arrival a sheepherder disappears, presumably killed by Indians who were angry because his sheep were grazing on the reservation. When Cut Finger, a renegade Indian, confesses and is arrested, he is dragged to death by a mob. After this, most of the Indians and whites realize they must cooperate, and eventually the problem is solved and the Indians learn farming under the major's guidance. From the modern perspective the solutions in Garland's novel are a bit pat and unrealistic. Published in 1902.

"A powerful novel and quite generally accepted by reviewers as a truthful presentation of life on an Indian reservation in the nineties" (Albert Keiser, *The Indian in American Literature*, p. 287 [see Teacher Aids]).

Giles, Janice Holt. **Johnny Osage.** Paperback Lib 1972.

Johnny Fowler, western trader and friend of the Osage tribe, watches his friends being squeezed from their hunting grounds by the Cherokees whom the United States government is resettling in the West. He observes the growing tension between the tribes, which the weak American post at Fort Smith cannot control. Johnny finds himself at times in conflict with Judith Lovell, the girl he loves, whose teaching career is dedicated to spreading the white culture. The book contains good descriptions of Osage ceremonies, dress, hunting, and marriage customs and is historically accurate in describing the troubles of the Osages with the Cherokees, Pawnees, and whites in the 1820s.

Gillmor, Frances. **Windsinger.** U of NM Pr 1976.

Windsinger, a Navajo, is born on the night of an eclipse of the moon and, according to tribal custom, should have been killed— but he is saved by the pleadings of a white man. As an adult, Windsinger becomes a singer of healing chants and his services are increasingly in demand, which leaves his wife and two boys to herd the sheep and earn enough to keep the family together. One day Windsinger is struck by lightning and the gods tell him there will be a great flood. Upon his advice, many of his people flee to the high mesas and wait, but when the flood does not come they gradually return, feeling that Windsinger is not the prophet they believed him to be. He spends his last years alone with his wife, disillusioned that his vision proved to be false.

In the introduction to the book, N. Scott Momaday writes, "In *Windsinger* we have a true evocation of a place that is wonderful in itself, written by one possessed of its wonder."

Guthrie, Alfred Bertram. **The Big Sky.** HM 1950.

Revolting against his cruel and insensitive father, young Boone Caudill leaves Kentucky in 1830 for the West, lured by the many romantic stories told by his uncle, Zeb Calloway. Joining the French trapper and trader Jourdonnais, Boone and his friend Jim Deakins make their way to Missouri, surviving a massacre, and go on to establish themselves as mountain men. There is action, violence, and romance in Boone's attraction for young Teal Eye, daughter of the Blackfoot chief, whom he eventually marries. The story is told from the viewpoint of a white man who begins to think like an Indian. There is also a young reader's edition that omits some of the violence, but retains the beautiful descriptions.

Hail, Raven. **The Raven and the Redbird.** Raven Hail 1965.

A historical three-act play about Sam Houston and his life among the Cherokee Indians, especially his romance with Tiana, the Redbird, his Cherokee wife. The author says in the introduction, "The story is true, as told by the Old Ones. It was not entrusted to the Talking Leaves." A number of historical characters of the early nineteenth century appear in addition to Houston and Tiana, including Sequoyah, Davy Crockett, Blue Jacket the Shawnee, and Chief Oolooteka. Many Cherokee customs and historical events are discussed.

Harris, Marilyn. **Hatter Fox.** Bantam 1974.

A psychological study revolving around the problems of Indians in white society. Hatter Fox, seventeen-year-old Navajo girl, attacks Dr. Teague Summer with a knife when he visits the Santa Fe jail to treat a boy who has slit his wrists. From then on Dr. Summer dedicates his life to trying to save the girl, who is already a prostitute, drug addict, and thief. He visits her when she is sent to the women's reformatory for attacking him, and soon he is hired to try to control her. The neglect and physical and mental tortures that Hatter has endured throughout her life have caused her to feel that everyone hates her. Summer tries to help her be the kind of obedient, ambitious person the white world will accept, and almost succeeds, but again Hatter is entrapped when society insists that she be something she is not. Although a bit melodramatic, the book has special appeal for high school students.

Herbert, Frank. **Soul Catcher.** Bantam 1973.

Because of a violent crime against his sister, Charles Hobuhet, outstanding Indian college student, becomes Katsuk, the incarnation of the spirit of his ancestors. He kidnaps David Marshall, son of the U.S. Undersecretary of State, intending to sacrifice him as the innocent who must die for Katsuk's sister's death. Under the pretext of wanting to show him an Indian ceremony, Katsuk persuades David to accompany him into the wilderness and they endure a long, tense journey with a search party in pursuit. The climax comes as David attempts to save both his own life and Katsuk's. On *Akwesasne Notes* basic library list.

"Another youth, caught between two worlds, decides upon retribution for his people in a spellbinding novel you won't put down" (*Akwesasne Notes* 7:45, Early Winter 1975).

Hill, Ruth Beebe. **Hanta Yo: An American Saga.** Doubleday 1979.

Based on historical events, this novel is the result of years of research by the author and her Santee Sioux collaborator, Chunksa Yuha. The story centers around two men of the Dakotah/Lakotah tribe: Ahbleza, warrior and peacemaker, and his brother-friend, Tonweya, the scout. The time is 1769-1834, just before the whites began to have real effect on the Indian way of life. The book covers three generations, culminating in the efforts of Ahbleza and Tonweya to preserve their tribal band, the Mahto. Translated from modern English into Dakotah and then into the English of 1806, the book reflects Dakotah idiom and concepts and portrays the profound spirituality of that culture. The extensive knowledge contributed by Chunksa Yuha and the author's skill combine to produce not only a powerful portrait of two families but also a valuable record of the life and times of the Dakotah Sioux. Chunksa Yuha in a brief introduction establishes the authenticity of the entire work: "And as I reviewed the written words, I visualized a bridge across a gulf, something to bring together two races of an entirely different nature. . . . I know that this book stands alone, a book that will survive the generations. For within its pages flows . . . spiritual vitality."

Huffaker, Clair. **Flap.** Paperback Lib 1970.

The youth of a Paiute tribe near Phoenix, tired of being ignored and treated as second-class citizens, decide they need publicity. Led by Flapping Eagle and the narrator, Eleven Snowflake, they stop a road gang who are about to run over a Paiute grave; kidnap seven-eighths of a circus train; and finally, on the basis of an old treaty, attempt to assume control of the city of Phoenix. A story of young Indians who ask only one thing, "Just a human way a livin'." Some passages reveal a sensitivity

toward suffering and death, but there is much slapstick comedy
with rowdy, drunken, cursing Indians as characters. A student's
introduction to Indians and their way of life should neither
stress this book nor be limited to it. *Flap* has been made into
a film which the *Indian Historian*, Spring 1971, describes as "a
revealing mixture of slapstick and misplaced caricature." Published in 1967 under the title *Nobody Loves a Drunken Indian*.

Jackson, Helen Hunt. **Ramona.** Avon 1970.

Ramona, a half-Indian girl, grows up on a fine Spanish estate in
southern California with her stepmother, who cannot love her
because of her Indian blood. Ramona's escape with the noble
Alessandro, an Indian, and their continual flight from the encroaching Americans who force them from their lands, is a story
that touched the hearts of millions when it was published in
1884, and has moved thousands of teenagers ever since. Highly
coincidental and sentimental, the book moved the American
public to a somewhat more just treatment of California Indians.

"Mrs. Jackson's book was a story, a novel; wonderfully well
told and full of truth and feeling; but while it may have been a
relation of facts, it did not profess to treat of actual persons.
It is looked upon by many readers as a mere romance" (George
Bird Grinnell, *Pawnee Hero Stories and Folk Tales*, pp. xii-xiii).

Jayne, Mitchell F. **Old Fish Hawk.** PB 1971.

Fish Hawk, an Osage Indian facing old age and loneliness among
the whites, plans to return to the White River country, homeland of his people. But first, as a favor for a friend, he tries to
kill an old bear that is harming livestock. Because Fish Hawk
has been drinking and loads his gun improperly, his dog, Ebo,
is killed by the bear. Because of this, Fish Hawk decides to give
up drinking. Then his friend, feeble-minded Towsack Charlie,
dies of wounds inflicted by a wild boar, and Fish Hawk is left
with a decision: should he kill the boar or let it live?

"Jayne has produced a novel about a proud Indian that is a
credit to literature" (*About Indians*, p. 200).

Johnson, Dorothy M. **Buffalo Woman.** Dodd 1977.

A carefully researched novel, telling of the daily life of an
Oglala Sioux woman and her family during a difficult period in
the tribe's history. In 1820 when Whirlwind is born, her tribe
has a good life. Food is plentiful, and when she becomes a

woman at thirteen, her father can afford to hold the Buffalo
Maiden ceremony for her. But by the time Whirlwind's own
daughter is ready for the ceremony, Whirlwind's husband cannot afford it because the tribe is at war with the whites. Times
grow worse as many tribes are moved to reservations, but
Whirlwind's people are followers of Crazy Horse, and later join
Sitting Bull's Hunkpapa Sioux on the way to Canada. Shortly
before the Battle of the Little Bighorn, Crazy Horse gives
Whirlwind a new name as a reward for a brave deed. The book
contains much information on Sioux values and the Sioux way
of life. Also appropriate for some junior high school students.

Keith, Harold. **Komantcia.** T Y Crowell 1965.

In a raid on his uncle's Mexican rancho in the 1860s, fifteen-
year-old Pedro Pavon is captured by Comanches who kill his
mother. During the years that follow, he plans to escape with
his younger brother, but to do that he must learn to be the best
possible Comanche—to hunt, track, and shoot. His ability and
stamina take him from the position of beaten slave, to adopted
son of a chief, to Comanche hero. He falls in love with and wins
a beautiful part-Cheyenne, part-Comanche girl. Based on a
historical episode, the book gives descriptions of grim Indian
life, squalor, and violence that may disturb some readers, and
the brutality of Comanche life is overemphasized.

Kesey, Ken. **One Flew over the Cuckoo's Nest.** Viking Pr 1962.

A novel that deals more with racism than with Indian culture.
The main theme is the struggle between the ward nurse in a
mental hospital, who represents the conformity and regulations
of the institutional establishment, and McMurphy, a patient,
who represents freedom and individuality. Chief Bromden,
son of a full-blooded Columbia Indian chief, is the narrator. A
schizophrenic whose life of horror and abuse has made him
silent, he serves as an observer during much of the story.
Through interaction with McMurphy he gradually regains his
speech and achieves self-recognition while giving glimpses of the
tragedy of his tribe.

Kopit, Arthur. **Indians: A Play.** Bantam 1971.

In this drama, Buffalo Bill is again producing his Wild West
Show and gathers together all of the characters of his past
successes—Wild Bill Hickok, Jesse James, Billy the Kid, Ned

Buntline—as well as the victims—Geronimo, Chief Joseph, and
Sitting Bull. Gradually Buffalo Bill realizes he is powerless to
stop the murder of Sitting Bull and the resulting massacre at
Wounded Knee, leaving him to question: Where did I go wrong?

"We have in Kopit's conception of Buffalo Bill a sensitivity
of tragic proportions; the old scout is alive to himself at last,
and the hard irony of his situation is not lost upon him" (N.
Scott Momaday in *New York Review of Books* 8 April 1971,
p. 39). "There is never a dull moment in this well-written,
action-packed play of a Wild West Show. The content is such
that one reading will not be enough, and the reader will feel im-
pelled to search for deeper meanings" (*About Indians*, p. 205).

La Farge, Oliver. The Enemy Gods. Popular Lib 1937.

Beginning in 1919, the story covers the life of a Navajo boy—
War-Encircling, rechristened Myron Bigay—from childhood to
early manhood. He attends school, remaining over vacation
because his mother has remarried and life in the hogan is un-
pleasant. When the authorities and others decide he should go
home, he joins Navajo ceremonies and soon determines not to
return to school. Then his Christian girl friend, Ethel, marries
someone else and returns to the old ways, and the government
wants to use him to convince his people to break up their
tribes, which are being called communistic. Myron has a spiritual struggle to determine who he is and what is right. The
novel is critical of the whites' attempts to remake the Navajo
culture. It provides a well-developed picture of adolescent
tensions which senior high students may understand.

"A devastating attack on the ignorance, stupidity, and brazen
racism of government officials, politicans, and missionaries"
(D'Arcy McNickle, *Indian Man: A Life of Oliver La Farge*,
p. 102).

La Farge, Oliver. Laughing Boy. HM 1959.

Laughing Boy, a young Navajo, falls in love with an orphan,
Slim Girl, who has been sent to government schools. She does
not know the true Navajo ways or their "trail of beauty." After
their marriage, their life in her house is happy until Laughing
Boy begins to suspect her of infidelity. She is eventually shot by
one of her lovers. Published in 1929. Awarded the Pulitzer Prize
for fiction, 1930. On *Akwesasne Notes* basic library list.

"Throughout his life La Farge looked contemptuously upon
the Indian people as an inferior brand of human being who, if

not properly controlled, would be certain to hurt himself"
(Vine Deloria, Jr., *Custer Died for Your Sins*, p. 208). "[The
author's attitude in *Laughing Boy* is] clearly that of an outsider
looking in from a defined social position upon an alien world
and seeing many admirable characteristics" (D'Arcy McNickle,
*Indian Man: A Life of Oliver La Farge*, p. 57). "An excellent
novel that displays an adequate knowledge of the Navajo lifestyle and tradition" (*About Indians*, p. 206).

Lee, Larry. **American Eagle: The Story of a Navajo Vietnam Veteran.** Packrat Pr 1977.

Two-Luke Dancer, a Navajo Vietnam veteran returning to his
home in Canyon de Chelly, finds that his only relative, his
grandfather, is dying, and had to sell his valuable squash-blossom
necklace to a disreputable trader. Two-Luke's anger is so great
that he single-handedly destroys the trader's store. Following
his grandfather's death, he gets into further trouble with the law
by stealing a helicopter and causing another one to crash, and
by scalping but not killing an arrogant hunter. Two-Luke is not
fully believable as a Navajo; he is rather an angry, fast-living war
veteran who responds to his hatreds with acts of violence. The
book moves too swiftly, lacking sensitivity and subtlety, and
has an unsatisfactory ending.

Lott, Milton. **Dance Back the Buffalo.** PB 1968.

The setting is the Rosebud Indian Agency in South Dakota and
the time is 1889–1890, the period of the tragic Ghost Dance
and the massacre at Wounded Knee. The characters are Turning
Hawk, a Sioux chief; his daughter, Blue Fawn; her husband,
Crazy Walking; and their children, especially Little Wound, who
is both deaf and blind. White characters include the scholar
Westland Roberts, who wants to know about the old ways, and
the missionary, Martin, and his wife and daughter. The themes
are the terrible tragedy of misunderstanding, deprivation, and
fear which results in the massacre of so many innocent people,
and the growing understanding and love among individuals of
the two races.

"The novel is one of the warmest and most understanding of
all those dealing with the Indian. The sacred articles and lore,
the deep conviction of the Indian's closeness to the country,
the rigid effort of the military to carry out rigid and hampering
orders, all of these seem freshly realized" (Paul Engle in *Chicago
Sunday Tribune*, 8 November 1959, p. 3).

McNickle, D'Arcy. **The Surrounded.** U of NM Pr 1978.

Archilde Leon, half Salish (Flathead) Indian and half Spanish, returns to his father's ranch after marginally supporting himself for a year by playing the violin. The big house in which his Spanish father lives contrasts sharply with the dirt-roofed log cabin occupied by his mother. Archilde plans to visit only a short time and leave, but he is attracted by an opportunity to study the violin with the local priests, and by his love for a local girl. He becomes increasingly entangled in his family's problems: his father dies, his brother is shot by a game warden, and his mother kills the warden. Archilde wants to escape from the oppression, but each new incident further enmeshes him in the desperate life of his people. The author is a well-known Flathead Indian historian and anthropologist.

Manfred, Frederick. **Conquering Horse.** Sig. NAL 1959.

No Name is a young Sioux who has tried unsuccessfully to have a vision, and until he does, he cannot ask for his sweetheart's hand. Finally, with his competitor, Circling Hawk, he sets out in search of his vision, which, when it comes, reveals to him many hardships and tragedies. The tasks given him in the vision lead to adventures filled with Indian lore, humor, customs, and religion. This novel is rich in symbolism and offers deep insights into the Indian mind. The legend of the Pacing White Stallion, which runs throughout western lore from earliest times, is a major theme. An adult book of interest to mature students.

Means, Florence Crannell. **Our Cup Is Broken.** HM 1969.

At her Hopi home on the third mesa, Sarah feels the tension between the white's world and the Hopi's. Uncle Abraham on her father's side has been baptized a Christian; on her mother's side, Aunt Kawasie follows the most superstitious of Hopi beliefs, offering sacrifices to Masa-w, god of the underworld. By the time she is twelve Sarah is an orphan and is taken in by missionaries. At school in Kansas, she learns to like the cleanliness and comfort of the white world and falls in love with Kirk, but his family's opposition breaks up the affair. In disappointment, she returns penniless to her mother's mesa home, but finds it difficult to accept the villagers' ancient religion. She is raped by a Hopi boy and, trying to be an Indian, she bears the baby alone, and finally marries Bennie, a Christian. The author has spent much time among the Hopis and Navajos and has a Hopi

name and a Hopi "granddaughter." The book will appeal especially to older, thoughtful readers. See also *No Turning Back*
by Polingaysi Qoyawayma (Senior Biography).

"This is a well-written book for the more mature reader
which dramatizes the resultant problems of cultural separation"
(*About Indians*, p. 224).

Momaday, N. Scott. **House Made of Dawn.** Sig. NAL 1969.

This novel covers the seven years 1945–1952 in the life of Abel,
a World War II veteran who returns to the reservation where his
grandfather lives and where the ancient beliefs and traditions
are still strong. But the unreality, for him, of the old life eventually leads him to commit a murder. After prison he is relocated
in Los Angeles, where in spite of a kindly social worker and a
good friend, he finds he cannot succeed on the job. He also
becomes involved with the Los Angeles Holiness Pan-Indian
Rescue Mission, where peyote rituals are held. After a severe
beating he returns once more to the reservation in time to see
his grandfather die. Cited in *American Indian Authors*. Awarded
the Pulitzer Prize for fiction, 1969. On *Akwesasne Notes* basic
library list.

"It is a beautiful book. Because of its indefinite plot line it is
a book for discriminating readers. Its great strengths are in the
development of the main character and the imagery and detail,
especially from the natural world" (*Textbooks and the American Indian*, p. 261). "The peculiar and special beauty of this
small book is not particularly in its story line. It is rather in the
mood, the haunting language, the acutely intimate knowledge
of personal reaction, with which its pages are filled" (*Indian
Historian* 2:38, Summer 1969).

Mowat, Farley. **The Snow Walker.** Bantam 1977.

A series of short stories, varying in theme and characters, about
life in the Arctic among the Polar Eskimos. In one story, a
white man who comes as a stranger to the North finds love and
satisfaction, until his religious beliefs conflict with those of the
natives; in another, an Eskimo in his boat is blown off course
and lands in the Hebrides, where he finds love and companion-
ship. One of the most moving stories, "Dark Odyssey of Soosie,"
demonstrates the corruption of a bureaucracy that moves Eskimo families for its own profit. The viewpoint generally is one of
admiration for the Innuit and contempt for whites.

Nasnaga. Indians' Summer. Har-Row 1975.

The author, a "member of the Shawnee Nation," has used the bicentennial celebration as the time-frame of this novel about a coalition of Indian tribes into an American Indian nation, called Anishinabe-waki. The coalition declares war on the United States and wins its bluff because it controls key energy resources and the Minuteman missiles that are trained on Washington, D. C. The revolution is supported in the United Nations by Third World nations. Throughout the story, the author has various characters deliver lectures on the American Indian world view.

"Nasnaga does focus on one of the central issues in contemporary Indian affairs, the status of Indian communities as sovereign nations, but for a discussion of that issue the reader is better referred to Vine Deloria's more cogent and exciting treatment in *Behind the Trail of Broken Treaties: An Indian Declaration of Independence*" (*American Indian Quarterly* 1:295, Winter 1974–75).

Neihardt, John G. When the Tree Flowered: A Fictional Autobiography of Eagle Voice, a Sioux Indian. U of Nebr Pr 1970.

Eagle Voice was a young man of the Sioux at the time of the Battle of the Little Bighorn. This is his story, filled with Sioux customs, religion, and history, as told in his own words to the poet John Neihardt. Running throughout the narrative is Eagle Voice's boyhood attraction to Tashina, a little girl in the tribe. Finally, after Wounded Knee, she becomes his wife. The story has many passages of fine writing and shows Eagle Voice as a warm, sincere human being with a great sense of humor.

Patton, Oliver B. The Hollow Mountains. Popular Lib 1976.

On her way to marry Lieutenant Tom Royal at Camp Grant, Samantha Allyn is captured by Apache Indians. Taken by the tribe into the Huachuca Mountains, she becomes the security for the tribe; the army will not bother the Apaches for fear they will kill her. When Samantha is finally released, Tom Royal and frontier society cannot accept what she has had to do in order to save her life. Tom requests a transfer to the north, and Samantha tries to remain independent in an inflexible society that leaves few opportunities for any woman, especially for one of doubtful character.

Pratt, Theodore. Seminole. Duell 1954.

Gideon Sauny is among the first Americans to migrate to Florida after the withdrawal of the Spanish in 1821. On the way his father dies and the young white man is aided in burying him by two young Seminoles, Osceola and Wildcat. From then on, Gideon, as a hunter and scout for the United States Army, finds himself often in contact with the great chief Osceola. After he rescues Osceola from a beartrap, the two young men become blood brothers. As the brave Seminole resistance increases, Gideon is torn between loyalty to his government and loyalty to Osceola. He finds himself the victim of Andrew Jackson's Indian policies when, under a flag of truce, he brings Osceola in for talks, only to have both Osceola and Wildcat taken prisoner. Based on the outdoor drama *Seminole* by the same author (this section), the book has vivid descriptions of Seminole ways, including the Green Corn Dance.

Pratt, Theodore. Seminole: A Drama of the Florida Indian. U Presses Fla 1953.

A play written for outdoor amphitheater presentation, but adaptable for school or community theaters, this is the story of the Seminole leader, Osceola, and his treacherous capture by the United States Army after being brought in under a flag of truce. Two white characters, Gideon Sauny, Osceola's friend and the man who brings him in, and Blaze Paget, are fictional. The others—the seminoles (Osceola, Morning Dew, and Wildcat) and the whites (General Wiley Thompson, General Joseph M. Hernandez, and Lieutenant R. H. Peyton)—are historical. The plot closely follows historical documents of 1821–1837 despite conflicting accounts.

Rosen, Kenneth, editor. The Man to Send Rain Clouds: Contemporary Stories by American Indians. Illus. R. C. Gorman and Aaron Yava. Vin. Random 1975.

A number of years ago the editor initiated a search for Indian writers of short stories. He began in the Southwest, and after finding about forty contemporary stories he chose nineteen for inclusion in this book. Among the contributors are Leslie Silko, Simon Ortiz, Anna Lee Wolters, and Opal Lee Popkes. The authors' tribal affiliations include Pueblo, Apache, Navajo, and Pawnee/Otoe.

"These short stories evoke the grim reality of contemporary Indian life and vivify the magic perspective of non-white culture, the modern survival of a vital and ancient heritage" (*American Indian Quarterly* 1:210, Autumn 1974). "Highly recommended" (*Indian Historian* 7:50, Winter 1974).

Ruesch, Hans. **Back to the Top of the World.** PB 1977.

This novel continues the story of the Polar Eskimos Papik, his wife Vivi, their daughter Ootuniah, and their son Ernenek. The Eskimos feel the growing influence of whites. Papik in anger kills a white man for slaughtering great numbers of baby seals, and is jailed for a short time and then released because of a legal technicality. Later, a bulldozer hits their igloo and injures Papik, forcing the family to spend months at the Snow White infirmary. This is the family's first contact with the whites' way of life; they learn about the Place Where One Gets Stoned, and such things as saunas, nylon jackets, and airplanes. See also *Top of the World* by the same author (this section).

Ruesch, Hans. **Top of the World.** PB 1973.

This is a lusty story of the Polar Eskimos Ernenek and Asiak, and their children, Ivaloo and Papik. Because of the Eskimo code of honor, Ernenek accidentally kills a white man who refuses Asiak when Ernenek wants to lend her to him. The code also forces the aging Ernenek to wrestle a bear to prove to southern Eskimos that he is still a man. After his death, Asiak, as an aging widow, follows the dictates of custom and walks into the frozen wilderness to die on an ice floe. The coming of the whites upsets the Polar Eskimo code. During the years when the community's men are leading an expedition of white men to explore the North, the women are influenced by white missionaries to become Christians. When the men return, the half-learned Christian doctrines cause disruption of families and eventual violence. Hardship and tragedy are mingled with humor and dignity in this gripping novel. See also *Back to the Top of the World* by the same author (this section).

Seidman, Robert J. **One Smart Indian.** Putnam 1977.

At thirteen, Tumbling Hawk, a Cheyenne who wants to be a warrior, is captured and adopted by Colonel Benjamin Hyde. The boy takes the name of Tom Hyde and agrees to go East to school, hoping to learn about whites and in this way help his people. In spite of much frustration he makes friends, goes on to Yale, and finally obtains a job in Washington, D.C., during the Civil War. He is sent throughout the South to persuade the Indian tribes to remain loyal to the Union. His experiences among the tribes cause him to decide to return to his own people and to help them take advantage of the divisions among the whites. The plot is weakened by some implausible details, but the character of Tom, caught in the conflict between the two groups that he loves, remains one of the book's strong points.

Sergel, Christopher [Ta-Tunka He Luta]. **Black Elk Speaks.** Dramatic Pub 1976.

Although it is based on John Neihardt's book by the same title, this play is not a dramatization of the Neihardt book because many incidents and emphases are missing—for instance, the descriptions and significance of Black Elk's vision and his power to heal, the Sioux legends that Black Elk tells during the book, and Black Elk's travels with Buffalo Bill's Wild West Show. In place of these important elements, the dramatist has added the arrival of Columbus, a rather long section on the Santee Uprising in Minnesota, and a section on the massacre of the Cheyenne at Sand Creek. The only portions which the play has in common with Neihardt's book are the brief treatments of the Battle of the Little Bighorn and the massacre at Wounded Knee, and a few of Black Elk's speeches.

Silko, Leslie Marmon. **Ceremony.** Viking Pr 1977.

Tayo, young half-breed from the Laguna Reservation, has been a prisoner of the Japanese during World War II but is now in a veterans' hospital in Los Angeles. In his delirium he relives his experiences in the jungles of the South Pacific, and those of his earlier life on the reservation when his mother brought shame to his family. When he is discharged and returns home, his family, which has lost another son in the war, finds it difficult to accept his illness. His friends, who are also veterans, turn to drinking and violence to solve their problems, but Tayo resorts to the ceremonies, stories, and beliefs of his past. The author, who is of mixed Laguna Pueblo, Mexican, and white ancestry, grew up on the Laguna Reservation where the novel takes place.

"Leslie Silko's *Ceremony* is an extraordinary novel. . . . Her talent is real and remarkable" (N. Scott Momaday, book jacket).

Simms, William Gilmore (Joseph V. Ridgely, editor). **Yemassee: A Romance of Carolina.** Coll & U Pr 1964.

This novel takes place in the South, particularly in Carolina, beginning in 1715. It has parallel plots—that of the colonists, which ends in their triumph, and that of the Yemassees, which pictures the doom of their race. The Indians' story centers on the noble chief, Sanutee, and his family. The chief has been the colonists' friend but he now sees that their way of life is degrading and he must fight them to the finish. His son, Occonestoga, has fallen victim to the whites' liquor and can do no more than serve the whites as a slave. The totem which Occonestoga wears on his skin must be cut out because he no longer has a tribal identity, but his mother saves him from this disgrace by killing him. The literary style is that of the 1830s, when the book was published, and may seem unduly wordy to some modern readers.

Steuber, William. **Go Away Thunder.** Wisconsin Hse 1972.

A novel of the Menomini Indians in the days before the whites came, when they lived without the wheel, iron, money, or a system of writing. Two Bears is newly married to Kimewan and is joyously awaiting the birth of Little Son when his tribe asks him to go on a long journey with Low Red Moon to a gathering of many tribes. The two men survive unusual experiences and dangers, only to find that they must deal with serious trouble within their tribe when they return. Because of corruption and fear among the people, the cowardly Strikes Oak has become both chief and medicine man. The novel pictures the Menomini as an extremely superstitious tribe, especially frightened of thunder.

Storm, Hyemeyohsts. **Seven Arrows.** Har-Row 1972.

The author, who claims to be a Cheyenne Shield Maker, trained by the elders of the tribe in the Sun Dance and the Medicine Wheel, tells a number of stories about tribal members living in the last century. The main characters are Hawk, Night Bear, and Green Fire Mouse—Peace Chiefs who are opposed to the growing belligerence of some members of their tribe. The stories of the people are interwoven with the teaching stories, legends, and allegories of the tribes. The novel is difficult because it is episodic, with frequent interruptions for lesson stories, and contains numerous characters. It has also been cited for its inaccuracies, especially by Indian readers. Profusely illustrated with pictures from the E. S. Curtis collection and the National Audubon Society and with paintings of Cheyenne shields and designs.

"There are so many irreligious and irreverent inaccuracies in this book that a committee of the Northern Cheyenne is now examining it in detail, detecting every error and misrepresentation that exists. . . . The color plates [of the symbolic shields] are a solid disaster, in extremely poor taste, and in fact the end result desecrates the Cheyenne religion" (*Indian Historian* 5:41, Summer 1972).

Straight, Michael Whitney. **A Very Small Remnant.** Knopf 1963.

In 1864 in a negotiated peace, Major Ned Wynkoop brings Black Kettle and his Cheyennes into Old Fort Lyon in Colorado. The Indians are settled in their village on Sand Creek, as instructed, when the fanatical Colonel Chivington, who at first agreed to peace, attacks and massacres large numbers of Black Kettle's people. Chivington is at first a hero, but in a court of inquiry a small group, including Wynkoop, reveal the truth about the massacre, in spite of the personal danger and the assassination of one of their colleagues. The story, which is based on fact, is told from the viewpoint of Ned Wynkoop, who becomes an Indian agent to make amends for his unintentional betrayal of Black Kettle and his people.

Stuart, Colin. **Shoot an Arrow to Stop the Wind.** Popular Lib 1971.

Colin, a teenager, lives most of the year with his family in Oregon, where he is considered to be white, but during the summer he goes to the Kinnikinnick Valley in Montana, where everyone knows he and his family are "breeds." His great-grandmother, Aunt Nora-Lassie, a full-blooded Blackfoot, lives in the tribal lodge. Colin has mixed feelings of pride and doubt about his ancestors and he is not sure how his white girl friend feels about people of mixed breeding. But then he meets the beautiful Cree girl Julie Dupree. The novel frankly examines a modern teenager's pride, doubts, and fears, and should appeal to mature high school readers.

Stuart, Colin. **Walks Far Woman.** Dial 1976.

Walks Far Woman, a Blackfoot Sioux, tells her colorful life story to her grandson's fiancée. The narrative begins in 1874 with Walks Far Woman killing the warrior who has killed her husband and sister and fleeing to her Sioux relatives. She marries Horse Ghost, survives the Battle of the Little Big Horn, and kills her husband when he threatens to abandon her. She then marries a rancher of mixed blood who provides her with her first house. After he is killed by thieves, she marries Elk-Hollering, part Cree and part Blackfoot. They finally settle on Montana land to avoid living on a reservation. Throughout the book, Walks Far Woman receives guidance at propitious moments from two supernatural protectors, and she is often portrayed as a superwoman.

"One redeeming feature of this novel is the care the author has taken to incorporate both Sioux and Blackfoot customs as well as accounts of the rigorous routine of the Plains Indian woman. . . . Unfortunately, if he had hoped to produce a believable novel about a Plains Indian heroine during the late nineteenth century, he has failed" (*American Indian Quarterly* 3:265, Autumn 1977).

Vaughan, Carter A. The Seneca Hostage. Popular Lib 1969.

Jonathan Lewis, English gambler and man-about-town, comes to the United States in 1753 to claim the proceeds from an inheritance, only to find himself taken prisoner by the warlike Seneca Indians. With the aid of his good friend Li-solu, he discovers the secret plans of the French in Quebec and warns Benjamin Franklin of their tactics in cultivating the Iroquois. Consequently he and William Johnson, friend of the Mohawk Joseph Brant, are able to help the colonists negotiate a treaty of friendship with the Iroquois Nation. The book overplays the atrocities, especially the Senecas' belittling of and cruelty toward women. Some Indians—especially Li-solu—emerge as friendly, intelligent, and clever, but the overwhelming impression is of terror, torture, and bizarre rites, giving a one-sided picture of the Senecas.

Walsh, M. M. B. The Four-colored Hoop. Putnam 1976.

Mildred Shoots-Eagle, an Arikara Indian, learns very early in life about the cruelty of whites when her village is destroyed and the survivors are sent to a reservation. After she witnesses the violent deaths of her parents, she visits an elderly relative who possesses the powers of "the medicine" which, when used for good, is a beneficent gift, but when used for evil, brings harm to its possessor. Since Mildred finds that she must sometimes use the powers for evil and punishment, she must lose what she loves most, her small son. An interesting subplot to the main theme of a strong Indian woman's struggles against the white people's world concerns Mildred's relationships with three generations of Muellers—white farmers whose land overlaps hers. It suggests that, with some flexibility and affection, the people of two very different races and cultures can enrich and support each other.

Waters, Frank. **The Man Who Killed the Deer.** PB 1971.

Martiniano, part Pueblo and part Apache Indian, is an outcast because he has been forced to attend government schools and no longer follows the old ceremonialism. In addition, he has killed a deer out of season and injured a Mexican who tried to take over his mountain adobe. This is the story of his sin and gradual redemption, and of the conflict between worldly experience and tribal training. Published in 1942. A mature book, well worth study by senior high school classes. On *Akwesasne Notes* basic library list.

"Indian and non-Indian relationships and problems are presented here, setting the background for the Indian viewpoint" (*About Indians*, p. 287).

Welch, James. **Winter in the Blood.** Har-Row 1974.

The unnamed narrator of this adult novel is a Montana Blackfoot and an embodiment of the dispossesed, lonely, aimless, and frustrated people of the world. His father and brother, whom he loved, died too young, and the cattle ranch which should have been his has gone to his stepfather. His world is that of the reservation, the ranch, and the Montana towns where he gets drunk and sleeps with women he later cannot remember. Although the hopelessness of his life is somewhat relieved by the dignity of his elderly grandmother and his discovery of his grandfather, his old way of life is gone. The author, a Blackfoot and Gros Ventre poet, has produced a sensitively written first novel that should be recommended mainly to mature, well-read students.

"There is much that is particularly genuinely Indian in this novel, ranging from history to current Reservation folkways" (Sidner J. Larson, *Indian Historian* 10:24, Winter 1977). "More directly than either of the other novels [*House Made of Dawn* and *Stay Away, Joe*], *Winter in the Blood* conveys to its readers a sense of loneliness, the desolation, the aimlessness, and the frustration which characterize the lame narrator who has no name" (*American Indian Quarterly* 1:202, Summer 1974).

West, Jessamyn. **The Massacre at Fall Creek.** HarBraceJ 1975.

In Indiana in 1824, four white men and a boy massacre two Indian braves, three squaws, and four children who were peacefully collecting maple sugar. The Northwest Territory Indian agent, John Johnson, and John Calhoun, Secretary of the Interior, feel that the Indians can be controlled only by demonstrating that white men can be tried and convicted for such murders. Through the eyes of Hannah, daughter of lay preacher Caleb Cape, the reader observes the trial and its effect on the community. Two bright young lawyers sent into the community both fall in love with Hannah. The novel is based on a "little known and long-forgotten record." Although it deals mostly with the attitudes of the white population toward the Indians, it is a revealing picture of the tensions on both sides at that time.

Wiebe, Rudy. **The Temptations of Big Bear.** McClelland 1973.

Big Bear, a Plains Cree Indian living in southern Saskatchewan in the late nineteenth century, is portrayed as a noble and greatly wronged leader who is struggling to keep his people off reservations, while recognizing that fighting the white government is futile. The author, a Canadian, has used historical characters and has relied heavily upon documents that describe the signing of treaties, the arrival of the whites, the disappearance of the buffalo, the Frog Lake massacre, the military campaign against the Crees, and the chief's trial and imprisonment. There are fictionalized accounts of Big Bear's meeting with Crowfoot and Sitting Bull, and of his attempts to unify the various tribes. The contradictory figure of Big Bear is presented from the viewpoint of both friend and foe, leaving readers to reach their own conclusions about his character. Various narrative techniques are used including interior monologues, stream of consciousness, and sarcasm. 1973 winner of the Canadian General's Award.

# Biography and Autobiography

Antell, Will. **William Warren: The Story of an American Indian.** Dillon 1973. Intermediate.

William Warren's father was an American fur trader and his mother was of French and Ojibway descent. He served as an interpreter and go-between for government agents and the Ojibways, and although Indians were not allowed to vote, he was elected to the Minnesota Territorial Legislature in 1850. He wrote *The History of the Ojibways*, which describes tribal customs and records the legends of his people, and it was published posthumously in 1855. Warren died of lung disease at the age of twenty-eight and was laid to rest in a city cemetery in St. Paul—and not in the wilderness country he had loved. This biography is by a Chippewa of the Mississippi band, who writes with sensitivity and understanding of Indian life. Illustrated by photographs.

Baker, Donna. **Frederic Remington.** Childrens 1977. Intermediate.

A complete and interesting biography. Born in 1861, Frederic Remington spent his early years in New York and developed a strong interest in horses. He was educated at a boarding school and a military academy, where his comical drawings of officers and teachers were the beginning of his interest in art. Travels in the West gave him opportunities to observe the frontier and the Indians, and provided the inspiration for his paintings and sculptures. A chapter devoted to Indian life features color reproductions of many of his works. Black and white photographs of Remington and his family are included.

Bulla, Clyde Robert. **Pocahontas and the Strangers.** Illus. Peter Burchard. T Y Crowell 1971. Intermediate.

This biography of Pocahontas erases the stereotype learned by so many young Americans. Her life as an Indian, her gradual rejection of the harsh ways of her tribe, and her life among white people have been carefully researched, and new perspectives of her personality and life emerge. This is a moving account of the stress and sorrow she experienced as she tried to live in two worlds—first in her own Indian world and then in the alien world of the English.

Cutler, Ebbitt. **I Once Knew an Indian Woman.** Illus. Bruce Johnson. HM 1973. Intermediate.

A book about an unforgettable Indian woman. Madame Dey, an Iroquois, lived in a small French-Canadian resort village in the Laurentians, where the author was her childhood friend. We learn how Madame Dey left the reservation to marry, how she managed to raise her family in spite of her itinerant husband, and how she took in an unwanted child out of kindness. But one final, noble—and perhaps slightly bizarre—act sets her apart as a great lady.

Davis, Russell, and Brent Ashabranner. **Chief Joseph: War Chief of the Nez Perce.** McGraw 1962. Intermediate.

This is the true and stirring story of an Indian chief who wanted peace but, because of circumstances, became instead one of the great fighting chiefs of the Western Indian wars. The biography begins as Chief Joseph prepares to assemble the last council for peace, and he remembers an old saying: "Never sell the bones of your father." When the Indians are ordered onto the reservation, he sees only misery and trouble ahead. However, Too-hul-hul-sote, the Dreamer priest, sees war as the way to regain their lands, and Chief Joseph is forced into retaliating when Indians suffer atrocities at the hands of the white settlers. The authors describe the victory at White Bird Canyon, the sufferings of the Nez Perce as they flee along the Lolo Trail through the Bitterroot Valley and the Yellowstone in their race toward Canada, where Sitting Bull and freedom await. After the pathetic race ends in surrender, Chief Joseph speaks his now-famous words: "Hear me, my chiefs. My heart is sick and sad. From where the sun now stands, I will fight no more—forever."

"This well-written biography of a great Indian leader is well worth reading by young adults and adults alike" (*About Indians*, p. 157).

de Leeuw, Adèle. Maria Tallchief: American Ballerina. Illus. Russell Hoover. Dell 1975. Intermediate.

This is the life story of Betty Marie Tallchief from Oklahoma, who through extremely hard work and determination became a famous ballerina. Her father was an Osage Indian; her mother was of Scottish-Irish-Dutch ancestry. Proud of her American heritage and her American training, she chose the professional name Maria Tallchief instead of a Russian-sounding name, as many ballet artists have done. As a dancer, her most awesome performance was "Firebird," and she is known as America's own prima ballerina. Drawings and several photographs are included.

Deur, Lynne. **Indian Chiefs.** Lerner Pubns 1972. Intermediate.

This group of biographical sketches includes Indian leaders who were involved in the long struggle to defend themselves against invasion by whites. Most of these chiefs were military leaders and fighting men but some were statesmen, inventors, religious leaders, or educators. Some, like King Philip, Black Hawk, Osceola, Crazy Horse, and Cochise, were Indian patriots. Sequoya was a great leader of his people and invented the Cherokee alphabet. Other Indians discussed are Pontiac, Joseph Brant, Tecumseh, Gall, Sitting Bull, Geronimo, and Joseph. Excellent pictures, charts, maps, and photographs are included.

Fall, Thomas. **Jim Thorpe.** Illus. John Gretzer. T Y Crowell 1970. Primary.

This biography of the Indian decathlon champion begins when Thorpe, great-grandson of Chief Black Hawk, is a boy on a ranch in Oklahoma Territory. With his twin brother Charlie he competes in various sports, always winning the contests at the Indian boarding school. The first of many sad happenings comes to Jim when his brother contracts an illness that turns into pneumonia. Charlie's death sends Jim into deep despair and he leaves the school, only to be sent back again. After several repititions of this, the father allows him to remain at home with the promise that he will attend Haskell Institute the following fall. His many adventures at school, his victories in the Olympic Games, and the loss of his Olympic medals, make his story hard to forget. All sports enthusiasts will enjoy reading about this great athlete.

"The author portrays convincingly how, out of his early experience came the skills which later made him famous" (*New York Times Book Review*, 24 May 1970, pt. 2, p. 39).

Felton, Harold W. **Nancy Ward, Cherokee.** Illus. Carolyn Bertrand. Dodd 1975. Intermediate.

The story of an unusual Cherokee Indian in the early nineteenth century. Nancy's father, Sir Francis Ward, married Tame Doe of the Wolf Clan of the Cherokees, a sister of Chief Attakullaculla. Nancy became the wife of Kingfisher and fought bravely at his side during a battle, earning her the title "Beloved Woman" of the nation. The account of Nancy's life is set against a background of the Cherokees' struggle to retain their land and dignity. This strong, noble woman's contributions to the tribe included the introduction of cattle and dairy products. She opposed war, and believed that the white colonists should have the right to live their lives as they saw fit, hoping that the Cherokees would have the same right. These hopes ended tragically when the Cherokees were forced westward on the "Trail of Tears." Informative black and white drawings.

Garst, Shannon. **Crazy Horse: Great Warrior of the Sioux.** Illus. William Moyers. HM 1950. Intermediate.

This is the story of Crazy Horse, one of the most heroic Indian warriors and chiefs, who fought to the death to save his Sioux people and their land and freedom. His early name, Has-ka or "light-skinned one," implied weakness of character which he later overcame with a premonition of future leadership. Crazy Horse possessed the amazing ability to organize a group of Indian warriors into a great army. Descriptions of the brutality of Custer's last fight and the massacres of thousands of Indians paint a picture of a dark period in U.S. history.

"The author draws a noble portrait of Crazy Horse, a leader who is against scalping, and not boastful" (*About Indians*, p. 174).

Johnston, Johanna. **The Indians and the Strangers.** Illus. Rocco Negri. Dodd 1972. Primary.

Short stories of Squanto, Powhatan, Massasoit, Philip, Tammany, Pontiac, Joseph Brant, Sacajawea, Tecumseh, Black Hawk, Sequoya, and Crazy Horse relate some of the happenings of the time when there was a steady push westward by white people.

The biographies portray proud, courageous Indians eager to preserve their way of life. Black and white woodcuts add to these historical accounts. Excellent, concise material for the young reader.

Katz, Jane B., editor. **We Rode the Wind: Recollections of Nineteenth-Century Tribal Life.** Lerner Pubns 1975. Intermediate.

An outstanding collection of authentic American Indian literature recalling life in many tribes in the nineteenth century. Legends, folk traditions, autobiographical accounts, and historical narratives are included. In selections from *Indian Boyhood*, Charles A. Eastman tells of his transition from life as a Santee Sioux to white society and gives excellent accounts of the training of a Sioux boy. John Stands In Timber tells about the law-giving process of the Cheyenne Chiefs' Council. Two-Leggings describes the making of a Crow warrior. Luther Standing Bear of the Oglala Sioux tells of home, family, and social customs, the Sioux religion, and their reverence for nature. Excerpts from Black Elk's narratives deal with his visions, the importance of the Sun Dance to the Sioux, and his despair at the loss of traditional culture on the reservation. Waheenee reveals the mind of a Hidatsa woman through her recollections of youth, marriage, and childbearing experiences. Views of life among the Chippewas, Anishinabe, and Kiowa Apaches round out this highly recommended, well-illustrated book.

McGaa, Ed. **Red Cloud.** Dillon 1971. Intermediate.

An impressive biography of Red Cloud, written by a fifth-generation descendant. During the years when the Indian people were losing their land to the white people in the westward movement, Red Cloud was the great leader of the Lakota. His story is that of a man who earned the respect of his enemies by his courage, honesty, and dignity. He continually strove to save the lands of his people through his visits to the Great White Father. The author predicts the fulfillment of Black Elk's vision of the fifth generation of Lakota returning to life, like a holy tree, to shade people of other races. Illustrated with photographs of Red Cloud and his contemporaries.

"Simply but forcefully written, this book should be included in every school library" (*About Indians*, p. 84).

Marriott, Alice. Sequoyah: Leader of the Cherokees. Illus. Bob Riger. Random 1956. Intermediate.

This biography includes a discussion of the early history of the Forerunners (the Old, True Cherokees) and how their ancestors arrived in the Smoky Mountain region. It tells how Nathaniel Gist, a respected white trader from a leading Baltimore family, entered into "marriage by tribal law" to Wut-teh, an important Cherokee chief's daughter. From this union, Sequoyah, the Lame One, was born. The boy grew up under the influence of his grandfather and developed an interest in crafts, which became his profession as an adult. By watching white soldiers reading their mail, Sequoyah grasped the importance of writing. The story of how he undertook the difficult task of developing a system of writing in the Cherokee language gives the reader a feeling of having met a great man.

"This interesting, well-written account of the life and work of Sequoyah gives an insight into his character and personality as well as into the life and customs of the Cherokee people" (*About Indians*, p. 86).

Milton, John R. Oscar Howe. Dillon 1972. Intermediate.

Oscar Howe, the Yanktonai Sioux painter, was born in 1915 and spent his early years on the Crow Creek Reservation in South Dakota. At the age of seven he was sent to the Purri Indian School where he suffered social isolation because of a disfiguring skin disease. By the time he was ten he was nearly blinded by trachoma. In spite of his handicaps, Howe was graduated from Santa Fe Indian School, and continued to develop his artistic skills. After various minor jobs, he was given a project with the regional Works Progress Administration, which provided opportunities for painting murals, and led to his increasing success as an artist. His experiences took him from teaching high school to being a university professor. Howe's story shows how he has adjusted to the white world while retaining the enduring spirit of the Dakota Indians which he captures so vividly in his paintings.

Moody, Ralph. Geronimo: Wolf of the Warpath. Illus. Nicholas Eggenhofer. Random 1958. Intermediate.

This story begins with the raids of the desert Apaches, whom the Mexicans regarded as their most dreaded enemy. It is the life story of a boy who was first called Goklya and then Geronimo—a name that later became synonymous with terror.

His early training—walking long distances barefoot, hunting desert rats, and playing games of hiding and crouching stone-still—toughened him for the raids that were to make him famous. Accounts of his battles after he achieved warrior status show his fearless character. The book ends with this comment: "While Geronimo cannot be honored as a hero, he will always stand as a landmark in American history. He was the last Indian leader who tried, through warfare, to turn back the tide of white civilization."

"This book presents a distorted view of the courageous but desperate resistance of Geronimo and his followers against white invasion. Definitely not recommended" (*About Indians*, p. 229).

Moyer, John W. **Famous Indian Chiefs.** Illus. James L. Vlasaty. Rand 1972. Intermediate.

A collection of biographical sketches, compiled by a staff member at the Field Museum of Natural History. It gives interesting information about the chiefs' backgrounds, their tribes, and their importance to their people. Dates are given, to help the reader relate the biographies to events in American history. Included are Red Jacket, Black Hawk, Tecumseh, Yoholo-Micco, Osceola, Red Cloud, Dull Knife, Sitting Bull, Geronimo, Chief Joseph, and Quanah Parker. There are full-page color portraits of each of the subjects.

Nelson, Mary Carroll. **Annie Wauneka.** Dillon 1972. Intermediate.

Annie Dodge Wauneka, daughter of a great Navajo leader, is a respected modern-day crusader for her people. As a young girl she helped nurse her classmates through a disastrous flu epidemic. Her fight against tuberculosis in her tribe helped to eliminate what was once the leading cause of death, and her emphasis on disease prevention as well as cure has resulted in better living conditions for the Navajos. She was awarded the Medal of Freedom, highest civilian honor, in 1963, and was the first woman ever elected to the Navajo Tribal Council. Her achievements have earned her the love of her people and the respect of all who know her.

Nelson, Mary Carroll. **Maria Martinez.** Dillon 1972. Intermediate.

This is the life story of Maria Martinez, a famous Pueblo Indian potter, interwoven with expressions of her people's great respect for their religion. Maria's interest in pottery began at an early age when an aunt showed her the technique. As a young married woman, she was encouraged by two scientists to develop her skill, and subsequently her husband, Julian, perfected a firing technique that produced the world-famous blackware pottery. Maria used her art to honor her ancestors. Her story is aptly summarized in the citation that was read when she was awarded a medal at the Minnesota Museum of Art in 1969: "Maria is a native American who, working in the age-old way of her people, has achieved recognition for herself and for those in the industrial society of the twentieth century."

Nelson, Mary Carroll. **Michael Naranjo.** Dillon 1975. Intermediate.

Michael Naranjo, a Pueblo Indian and son of a Baptist minister, grew up observing nature and exploring the country around Santa Clara, his birthplace. Part of his boyhood was spent in Taos, where he learned about tribal ceremonies and holidays such as the feast of San Geronimo and the pranks of the Chifonetti. During summers on the Verner farm in Texas he made lasting friendships. After restless years of looking for a vocation, Michael was drafted into the army in 1967 and served in Vietnam, where a grenade explosion blinded him. Determined to create an independent life, he found an outlet for his emotions by creating wax figures and casting them in bronze. His famous sculpture "Eagle Dancer" was presented to President Nixon and Naranjo's art has continued to win awards. He says, "I wouldn't want to trade shoes with anyone. Does it matter if you're brown or white or black? First you have to accept what you are. I'm happy to be an Indian. Do I have to wear feathers to show I'm an Indian? My work deals with soul. I know where I'm going now. It kind of took the blindness to find it."

O'Connor, Richard. **Sitting Bull: War Chief of the Sioux.** Illus. Eric von Schmidt. McGraw 1968. Intermediate.

Sitting Bull, the great Sioux chief who defeated Custer at the Battle of the Little Bighorn, is portrayed in this book as a poet and diplomat as well as a man of war. In his early years he was named Slow because he was deliberate and thoughtful, but his dream was to be a warrior and he earned the new name of Sitting Bull at the age of fourteen through his deeds of bravery. He showed himself to be a man of mercy when he saved the life of an Assiniboine boy in battle and adopted him as a brother. In his later years Sitting Bull realized that the victory over

Custer's forces marked the end of the free-roaming Sioux way of life, and strove to give his people a sense of pride in their heritage.

"The author gives a fascinating account of Sitting Bull and his world" (*Times* [London] *Literary Supplement,* 5 December 1968, p. 1380).

Patterson, Lillie. **Sequoyah: The Cherokee Who Captured Words.** Illus. Herman B. Vestal. Garrard 1975. Primary.

"Words are like wild animals. I must learn to capture them. I will catch them and tame and put them in writing." These are the words of a lame Indian scholar who invented the Cherokee alphabet. Sequoyah worked in his Tennessee village as a trader, blacksmith, farmer, and craftsman, and earned the distinction of being the best silversmith in the Cherokee Nation. But he dreamed of doing greater things. Watching a group of white soldiers reading their mail, and seeing some of them laughing and some crying, he realized they were using "talking leaves" to send their thoughts. How he developed written symbols for the Cherokee language, and how he and his daughter Ah-yoka demonstrated them to the chiefs is an engrossing story which establishes Sequoyah as a great man who gave his people a syllabary and their first newspaper, *Cherokee Phoenix.*

Paul, Frances Lackey. **Kahtahah.** Illus. Rie Muñoz. Alaska Northwest 1976. Intermediate.

The author, who taught Tlingit children in a government school in Juneau, Alaska, early in this century, wrote this biography to satisfy her students' need to read about their own way of life. Kahtahah was a real person who in her ninetieth year still brimmed over with life, love, and interest in others. Episodes from her life story are intertwined with Tlingit legends. Descriptions of various customs such as naming ceremonies, burial practices, and festivities offer the reader accurate information not found in many other sources. Well worth reading for its accounts of exciting adventures and for the details on tribal customs, myths, and social structure.

Stember, Sol. **Heroes of the American Indian.** Fleet 1971. Intermediate.

This concise biographical collection gives a bird's-eye view of Indian history from the days of Columbus to the incident at Wounded Knee as revealed in the lives of prominent Indian

leaders. There are short, readable accounts of important conflicts between the Indians and whites, and highlights from the
lives of Indian military, religious, and educational leaders, including King Philip, Popé, Pontiac, Tecumseh, Sequoyah, John
Ross, Osceola, Black Hawk, Geronimo, Cochise, Red Cloud,
Crazy Horse, Sitting Bull, Chief Joseph, and Wovoka. Illustrated
with many photographs and old prints.

Supree, Burton, and Ann Ross. **Bear's Heart: Scenes from the Life
of a Cheyenne Artist of One Hundred Years Ago with Pictures
by Himself.** Lippincott 1977. Intermediate.

This biography is unusual because of Bear's Heart's own illustrations, drawn during his imprisonment at Fort Marion, St.
Augustine, Florida. His story began during the harsh winter
of 1874-75, when many Plains Indians left their reservations in
an attempt to reclaim their traditional way of life. Many of the
Indians, including Kiowas, Comanches, Arapahos, Cheyennes,
and one Caddo, were captured by the United States Army and
imprisoned for approximately three years. Bear's Heart recorded the prisoners' journey from Fort Sill to Florida in detailed sketches. Prison activities—catching sharks, attending
church, and camping on Anastasia Island—are depicted. Commentary by Jamake Highwater points out that the drawings
helped bring about a renaissance of American Indian painting in
the twentieth century. The authors show that Bear's Heart was
too trusting to realize that his culture was undergoing a process
of "assimilation and annihilation."

Tobias, Tobi. **Maria Tallchief.** Illus. Michael Hampshire. T Y
Crowell 1970. Primary.

"She flew, she whirled, she slashed through space like a flaming
arrow." This statement describes the beauty and grace of the
dancing of Maria Tallchief, a famous ballerina from the Osage
tribe. This book tells of her childhood in Oklahoma, of her
family's move to California, and her difficult choice between
two loves—music and ballet. Her decision was a happy one, for
she developed into an exciting performer with many successes
to her credit. In "The Firebird," she proved her greatness. She
danced the Queen of the Swans in "Swan Lake," and the Sugar
Plum Fairy in "The Nutcracker." She was described as a musical
dancer and was awarded many honors. A hometown celebration
at the height of her career brought out leaders of the Osage
tribe and the governor of Oklahoma. At an Indian ceremony

held in her honor, she was given the special title Wa-Xthe-Thonba and was made a princess of the Osage Indians.

"This informative and well-illustrated book presents a good biographical sketch of a famous contemporary Indian woman" (*About Indians*, p. 104).

Voight, Virginia F. **Red Cloud: Sioux War Chief.** Illus. Victor Mays. Garrard 1975. Intermediate.

This is a biography of the famous Oglala Sioux, whose brave deeds were represented by the many feathers on his war bonnet. The story begins with a sky blazing with fire, and the prediction that a great chief is about to be born. The baby is Two Arrows, who becomes the great war chief, Red Cloud. Included are accounts of buffalo hunts, horse-stealing raids, battles, and negotiations with the whites in the effort to save the Sioux's beloved homeland. The author portrays Red Cloud as a brave warrior in battle and a respected chief in peace, whose desperate attempt to stop the whites' invasion ended in futility. The great chief's deep concern for his people is epitomized thus: "I think of them sleeping and waking, for they are always on my heart." Historically accurate illustrations.

Williams, Neva. **Patrick des Jarlait: The Story of an American Indian Artist.** Lerner Pubns 1975. Intermediate.

Des Jarlait was born in 1921 and spent his early years on the Red Lake Indian Reservation in Minnesota, a place with beautiful, tall trees and clear lakes. His story is a record of the life of the Chippewa Indians around the seasons—winter hunting expeditions, springtime gathering of maple syrup in the "sugar bush," summertime games, and fall harvesting of wild rice. There is an account of his school days and how his experiences in high school strongly influenced his choice of a career. In his lifetime of fifty years, this American Indian artist received national acclaim for his striking paintings of Chippewa Indian life, several of which are reproduced here.

Wolfe, Ellen. **William Beltz.** Dillon 1975. Intermediate.

Introductory chapters dealing with the everyday life of the Eskimo provide insight into the effects of the coming of the whites, particularly during the gold rush. As William Beltz grew up in the mining towns of northern Alaska, he observed unequal treatment of native Indians and Eskimos. Part Eskimo himself, he worked to improve conditions and to obtain equal rights for his people. His accomplishments included the presidency of the Alaska Carpenters Union and membership in the territorial senate. In 1958, when statehood was declared, he was unanimously elected president of the first senate of the state of Alaska. An impressive biography of a great leader.

## Junior High

Allen, Terry D., and Don B. Allen. Navahos Have Five Fingers. U of Okla Pr 1970.

For many years the author and her husband were fascinated by the lifestyle and country of the Navahos. During brief excursions into the Navaho country they came to know school teachers, missionaries, traders, Indian Bureau personnel, and a few English-speaking Navahos. In 1955 they were invited to serve briefly as caretakers for the Tselani Health Center, a small outpost of the Ganado Presbyterian Mission. There they became involved in ambulance service, recreation, and Bible teaching for the Navahos. Illustrated with photographs supplied by the principal of Ganado High School.

Bennett, Kay. Kaibah: Recollections of a Navajo Girlhood. Illus. by author. Westernlore 1964.

Told from the point of view of Kaibah, this is the story of a young Navajo girl growing to adulthood from 1928 to 1935. After Kaibah's father died, Mother Chischillie managed to keep her family together by raising sheep, with occasional help from the older married children in the family. Until she left home to go to school, Kaibah tended the sheep during the winter in the Cross Hills area and in the mountains during the summer. The book pictures the life of a Navajo family—their festivals and dances; their sorrows and tensions when children are taken away to attend school and learn white ways. Cited in *American Indian Authors.*

Carter, Forrest. The Education of Little Tree. Delacorte 1976.

Five years old and orphaned, Little Tree went to live with his Cherokee grandparents in their Tennessee log cabin. From them he learned the Cherokee way—to take from the land only what is needed. He learned to hunt and to help Granpa at his still. He learned of the bond between his grandparents and other Cherokees, like Pine Billy and Willow John—people who had shared the tragedy of the Trail of Tears and then had either gone West and returned, or had retreated into the mountains. Later on, Little Tree suffered a brief and cruel stay in an orphanage but was rescued by Granpa. This is a moving story of the Cherokee education of Forrest Carter, the author of *The Vengeance Trail of Josey Wales* and *Gone to Texas* (see Senior Fiction).

Clark, Ann Nolan. **Journey to the People.** Viking Pr 1969.

In ten essays a well-known writer of juvenile books recalls her experiences as a teacher among the Zuni, Navajo, Pueblo, Sioux, and Guatemala Indians. The introductory piece discusses four basic Indian concepts—their feelings about the land and about work, time, and spiritual life. The author's essays are the result of fifty years of memories of working among people whose traditions and customs differ from her own.

Cooke, David Coxe. **Tecumseh: Destiny's Warrior.** Messner 1959.

The Shawnee chief Tecumseh dreamed of creating a confederation of all tribes of the North American continent into an Indian nation. Tecumseh had a carefree boyhood until he and his mother found his father murdered in the snow. He swore vengeance and began to perfect his riding and shooting skills; later realizing the importance of judgment, he became a great orator and tried diplomacy rather than bloodshed. During the War of 1812 he allied himself with the British, and when he died, his vision of an empire died with him. The author became interested in Indians at New York University when he discovered that many writers were unfair or inaccurate in telling the Indian story. An honorary member of the Chickasaw and Cherokee tribes, he has done research in a number of states and has written other books about Indians.

Crary, Margaret. **Susette La Flesche: Voice of the Omaha Indians.** Hawthorn 1973.

Susette La Flesche's father, Iron Eye, was the progress-minded chief of the Omaha Indians who built a wooden house for his family and determined that all of his children should obtain a good education in schools run by whites. After attending the mission school, Susette received further education in Elizabeth, New Jersey, and returned to her reservation to teach. When the Omahas' neighbors and relatives, the Poncas, were forcibly moved to Oklahoma by the government, Susette took up their cause and went on a lecture tour with her brother, Francis,

Standing Bear of the Ponca, and Thomas Tibbles, a journalist from the *Omaha World Herald*. As a result, the Poncas were returned to their land.

"A stirring portrait of interracial conflict that unfolds to reveal unbelievable inhumanity" (*Best Sellers*, 15 May 1973, p. 97).

Eastman, Charles Alexander. Indian Boyhood. Dover 1971.

The author, whose Indian name is Ohiyesa, tells about growing up as an Indian in the late 1800s when, he feels, Indians were really free to live as they wanted. He tells of their customs, religion, legends, and sacrifices, and especially their early training and values. His father, who had become a Christian, urged him to go to school so that he could survive in white society. His autobiography, published in 1902, is a fine picture of Sioux Indian life, which he describes as "recollections of my wild life." Cited in *American Indian Authors*.

"Although this autobiography is fairly interesting, the author seems in places to use strange words in describing his people" (*About Indians*, p. 163).

Eber, Dorothy, editor. Pitseolak: Pictures out of My Life. U of Wash Pr 1972.

Pitseolak is one of the most famous of the Cape Dorset, Baffin Island, Eskimo graphic artists. Dorothy Eber, a Montreal journalist, interviewed Pitseolak with the help of Eskimo interpreters and tape-recorded her story, including her birth, childhood, marriage, and the births of her children. She describes her delight in the old life—the games the Eskimos played, dances, life in camp, building an igloo, and fishing and hunting. She concludes with comments on her current way of life—her warm house, her pleasure in drawing and in her children—and also the problems in the community, especially with young people. The book has the Eskimo language beside the English translation and contains many examples of Pitseolak's work. Also appropriate for high school students and adults.

"The words tell honestly the story of the Eskimo and his acculturation as one woman saw it" (*About Indians*, p. 246).

Eckert, Allan W. Blue Jacket: War Chief of the Shawnees. Little 1969.

In 1771 a seventeen-year-old white boy was captured by Shawnees in what is now West Virginia. Adopted into the tribe, he was named Blue Jacket from the blue shirt he was wearing when captured, and he became such a good fighter and leader that he was made war chief of the Shawnee Nation. As such, he was dedicated to preventing the whites from taking over Indian land and life. He led the Shawnees against the armies of George Rogers Clark and Mad Anthony Wayne and at one point was forced to kill his own brother Charley. The book contains all that is known about his life. Much dialogue is taken from historical records, with additions by the author where there is no record.

"A well-written, fast-moving account of the Shawnee Indian war during the American Revolution which will appeal to youngsters for its excitement" (*About Indians*, p. 163).

Farnsworth, Frances Joyce. **Winged Moccasins: The Story of Sacajawea.** Illus. Lorence F. Bjorklund. Messner 1954.

This book grew out of years of research on the Indian girl guide, Sacajawea, who accompanied Lewis and Clark on their expedition to the Northwest. The story of her life with them is well known, but there is uncertainty about what happened to her afterwards. From the slight historical evidence about Sacajawea's later life, the author has put together what is probably her entire story—her life among the Shoshones; her life in slavery among the Minatarees and Mandans; her marriage to the French trader, Charbonneau; her trip with the explorers; and her later life in St. Louis, among the Comanches, and finally again with her sons among her own people. As important as her aid to Lewis and Clark was, her chief work was among her own people, helping them adjust to the new life which the white man brought. Cited in *A Preliminary Bibliography of Selected Children's Books.*

"A highly fictionalized account of Sacajawea that reinforces the stereotype of the Indian. . . . Not recommended" (*About Indians*, p. 166).

Garst, Shannon. **Buffalo Bill.** Illus. Elton C. Fox. Messner 1948.

This is the story of the great buffalo hunter, scout, and friend of the Indians. Of special interest for a unit on Indian culture is the account of the production of the Wild West Show, its travels to Europe, and Cody's version of the arrest and shooting of Sitting Bull during the time of the Ghost Dance. Fast-paced and readable. For another treatment of Buffalo Bill, see *Indians: A Play* by Arthur Kopit (Senior Fiction).

Garst, Shannon. Sitting Bull: Champion of His People. Illus. Elton C. Fox. Messner 1946.

A fictionalized biography which covers Sitting Bull's adventurous boyhood, his growing uneasiness about the increasing number of white settlers, and his futile fight to preserve the Indian way of life. Custer at Little Bighorn is pictured as a man who disobeyed orders because of his desire for glory and for the presidency. The book is well documented, telling the story with frankness and without anger.

"Written from the Indian point of view, this book gives the reader an insight into the hardships and joys of a people who lived by the law of the land" (*About Indians*, p. 175).

Haverstock, Mary Sayre. Indian Gallery: The Story of George Catlin. Four Winds. Schol Bk Serv 1973.

In 1830 George Catlin, a Philadelphia painter of miniature portraits, left his wife and comfortable home to travel to the West with Captain William Clark. He visited the Sioux, Iowas, Sacs, Kansas, Blackfeet, and Mandans, making friends and painting pictures of scenes, chiefs, and tribal members. Subsequently he made other trips West, during which his admiration and concern for Indians grew, and whenever he returned East, crowds flocked to see "Catlin's Indian Gallery." The people admired his paintings, but few heeded his warnings about the fate of the Indian, even though he told them of his Mandan friends who died of smallpox, and of the treacherous capture of Osceola of the Seminoles. On tours in England and France, Catlin met the same indifference. This version of his life is also suitable for older readers. Illustrated with many of Catlin's pictures in black and white.

Hoffman, Virginia, and Broderick H. Johnson. Navajo Biographies. Illus. Hoke Denetsosie, Andy Tsinajinnie, and Clifford Beck, Jr. Navajo Curr 1970.

A collection of biographies of Navajo leaders beginning with Narbona, born in 1766, and his son-in-law, Manuelito, who led his people in their desperate struggle to retain their lands and independence during the nineteenth century. The concluding story is the biography of Ramond Nakai, Navajo tribal chairman elected in 1962. The book was written to help Navajo children understand their history and their leaders, but other children will be equally fascinated by the wealth of information about

Navajo life and history. Illustrated by Navajo artists and by photographs.

Hollmann, Clide. **Pontiac, King of the Great Lakes.** Hastings 1968.

Following the surrender of the French to the British in the New World in 1763, the Indians were denied gifts, rum, and firearms. Pontiac, the Ottawa chief, recognized the danger in the unrest, and organized the tribes to protect the Indian lands and way of life. A persuasive orator and brilliant strategist, he plotted to attack Fort Detroit, but was the victim of treachery by his Indian allies.

"A fine book which combines history, Indian culture and biographical information in an interesting manner, providing an accurate picture of the man and his times" (*About Indians*, p. 190).

Howard, Helen Addison, and Dan L. McGrath. **War Chief Joseph.** Illus. George D. McGrath. U of Nebr Pr 1964.

No Indian chief was less deserving of the persecution he and his people received than the brilliant, soft-hearted, and peace-loving Chief Joseph of the Nez Perce. The Nez Perce War of 1877 was the last important contest between the Indians and the United States Army. As a brilliant military strategist, Joseph knew better than anyone that the odds were against him. A scholarly, interesting biography requiring average or better reading ability. See also *I Will Fight No More Forever* by Merrill Beal (Senior Biography).

"For the mature reader, this biography gives an account of Chief Joseph's intelligence, military genius and powers which make him one of America's great Indian heroes" (*About Indians*, p. 193).

Jakes, John. **Mohawk: The Life of Joseph Brant.** Illus. Roger Hane. Macmillan 1969.

The great Mohawk chief Joseph Brant was born in 1742 along the upper Ohio River. His father may have been Sir William Johnson, an unofficial representative of the British king among the Indians; but it is equally possible that his father was Nickus Brant, a Mohawk chief. Young Joseph was educated by Johnson and lived in his household. He visited England in an attempt to gain assurance from the Crown that no more Indian lands would be taken by settlers, and he believed that the whites' way offered the only hope for his people. This biography of the chief emphasizes his youth.

"In this accurate and interesting biography the author concentrates on the issues of war and the conflicting values which Joseph Brant was forced to cope with because of his background" (*About Indians*, p. 199).

Josephy, Alvin M., Jr. The Patriot Chiefs: A Chronicle of American Indian Resistance. Viking Pr 1969.

Nine of the famous Indian chiefs who challenged the coming and progress of Europeans and Americans are represented in this collection: Hiawatha, King Philip, Popé, Pontiac, Tecumseh, Osceola, Black Hawk, Crazy Horse, and Chief Joseph. A chapter on each patriot describes his reactions to threats to Indian "freedom, rights of conscience, personal security, means of existence and life itself." The Indians thought of these leaders as good and brave men, but the whites saw them as enemies. On *Akwesasne Notes* basic library list.

Kroeber, Theodora. Ishi, Last of His Tribe. Illus. Ruth Robbins. Parnassus 1964.

Ishi is a member of the Yahi tribe living in the foothills of northern California near the turn of the century. White invaders had diminished their number until only the boy Ishi, his mother, grandparents, Elder Uncle, cousin Tushi, and their friend, Timawi, remained of the People. Eventually the other members of the tribe either died or were lost in fleeing for their lives, but Ishi stumbled into the corral of a slaughterhouse outside of Oroville and was rescued by a man from the university museum who became his friend. On *Akwesasne Notes* basic library list. See also *Ishi in Two Worlds* by the same author (Senior Biography).

"A beautiful and haunting story . . . This is a moving and memorable book" (*A Preliminary Bibliography of Selected Children's Books*, p. 13).

Lawson, Marion. Proud Warrior: The Story of Black Hawk. Illus. W. T. Mars. Hawthorn 1968.

Black Hawk's story begins while his people are living in Saukenuk, their summer village on the Mississippi. During Black Hawk's childhood years, a blue-eyed child named Keokuk was born into the tribe, which was seen as a bad omen. When Black

Hawk grew older and assumed leadership of his tribe, he gave his support to the British in the War of 1812, while Keokuk, a talented orator, argued that the tribe should support the Americans and move west into Iowa. On the advice of the Prophet, a Winnebago adviser, Black Hawk tried to unite the Fox, Potawatomi, Winnebago, and Chippewa tribes, but they would not join him and he finally was forced to surrender for the good of his people.

"The author has done justice to a great Indian leader, presenting a book which will be enjoyed by anyone reading it, young adult and adult alike" (*About Indians*, p. 211).

Lee, Betty. **Lutiapik.** McClelland 1975.

In 1957 a public health nurse from Toronto, Dorothy Knight, spent one year at Lake Harbour on Baffin Island in the Arctic. Since there was no resident doctor, she found that she had to diagnose and cure all kinds of ailments, from impetigo to meningitis. She learned to order enough drugs and other supplies to last over a very long period, because boats sometimes could not reach the community for months at a time. She also became accustomed to finding people ill or dead from malnutrition in isolated Eskimo villages. The story is told from the viewpoint of a white nurse and the descriptions of Eskimo villages and life are detailed and vivid.

Myers, Elizabeth P. **Maria Tallchief, America's Prima Ballerina.** G&D 1966.

Betty Marie Tall Chief is the daughter of an Osage Indian father from Fairfax, Oklahoma, and a white mother of Scotch-Irish descent. In 1925, when Betty Marie was born, each Osage Indian was receiving $15,000 a year from the large oil field discovered on the Osage reservation in 1897. Her father owned many buildings in Fairfax including the Tall Chief Theater. When Ruth Tall Chief discovered that her two daughters had unusual musical talent, she persuaded her husband to move to Los Angeles where their talents could be properly developed and recognized. From that move came other steps along the road that led Betty Marie to become Maria Tallchief—lessons with Madame Bonislava Nijinska, sister of the great Nijinsky; work with the Ballet Russe; marriage for a time to choreographer George Balanchine; and a position as prima ballerina with the New York City Ballet Company.

Red Fox, Chief. **The Memoirs of Chief Red Fox.** Fawcett 1971.

This biography purports to be the life of a nephew of Crazy Horse, who at one hundred years of age told his story, but it has been exposed as a fraud. The book had gone through seven hardcover printings and a paperback edition when *The New York Times* accused its author and publisher McGraw-Hill of plagiarism. The book was based on twenty-five pages from *The Wounded Knee Massacre* by James McGregor, written some thirty years earlier, which Chief Red Fox admittedly purchased from a printer in St. Paul, Minnesota, for $100. In view of the author's acknowledged plagiarism, it is doubtful that any of the book can be trusted.

Roland, Albert. **Great Indian Chiefs.** Macmillan 1966.

Here are short biographies of nine great Indian chiefs with descriptions of their accomplishments: Hiawatha, Powhatan, Philip, Popé, Pontiac, Maquinna, Tecumseh, Sequoyah, and Sitting Bull. These men might have founded great civilizations had the whites not come to engulf them with their society. The book is sympathetic and well written and concludes with a chapter on Indian leaders of today. Cited in *A Preliminary Bibliography of Selected Children's Books.*

"An interesting book of biographical sketches for young people" (*About Indians*, p. 256).

Schoor, Gene. **The Jim Thorpe Story: America's Greatest Athlete.** Archway 1967.

Jim Thorpe, born in 1888, a great-grandson of Black Hawk, became one of the greatest athletes America has every known. Schoor reviews his career from his days as a football player for Carlisle Indian School to his rise to glory as an Olympic decathlon champion. It came to an end when it was discovered that he had once played summer league baseball for a small sum of money, making him ineligible for the Olympic trophies he had won in 1912. Some fictionalized conversations have been added where information did not exist.

"The book is exciting, colorful, humorous and sad, telling about justice and injustice" (*About Indians*, p. 263).

Sun Bear. **Buffalo Hearts: A Native American's View of Indian Culture, Religion and History.** Naturegraph 1970.

A small introductory book about Indians by a Chippewa editor and owner of *Many Smokes*, an Indian magazine. Over half of the pages are devoted to short biographies of Indian leaders: Chief Joseph, Red Cloud, Pontiac, Logan, Mangus Colorado, Quanah Parker, Cochise, Osceola, Powhatan, and Crazy Horse. The rest of the book discusses Indian legends, medicine, beliefs, and war. Illustrated with photographs from the Smithsonian Institution.

Waltrip, Lela, and Rufus Waltrip. **Indian Women: Thirteen Who Played a Part in the History of America from the Earliest Days to Now.** McKay 1964.

Little has been written on Indian women, but here are thirteen women who have played important roles, in their tribes, in art, literature, peace, and human rights: Big Eyes, who made a map for Coronado's travels in the Southwest; Pocahontas, who saved the Jamestown colonists; Sacajawea, who guided the Lewis and Clark expedition; Wenema, who negotiated for peace with the whites; Cynthia Ann Parker, who bridged two cultures; Sarah Winnemucca, interpreter, teacher, and peacemaker; Indian Emily, who saved a garrison; Tomassa, interpreter and peacemaker; Neosho, who fought a hand-to-hand battle; Dot-so-la-lee, Maria Martinez, and Pablita Velarde, who made contributions in art, crafts, and literature; Annie Dodge Wauneka, who worked for better health conditions; and Virginia Klinekole, who led her people to higher standards of living and better understanding of peace and good will. Some fictionalized detail and conversation.

"Each sketch is well written and easy to read. ... The book also helps bridge the gap between Indians and non-Indians" (*About Indians*, p. 285).

Wyatt, Edgar. **Cochise: Apache Warrior and Statesman.** Illus. Allan Houser. McGraw 1953.

Cochise, the famous nineteenth century Apache leader, wanted peace and protected the whites, but his aims were thwarted by bigoted American army officers who declared that "Indians are Indians." Finally, after being falsely accused of a kidnapping, almost losing his own life, and seeing his people killed, Cochise called his fellow Apache chiefs to war against the whites. In mutual admiration, he and Tom Jeffords became blood brothers. Eventually General Oliver Otis Howard, with Jeffords, persuaded Cochise to make peace, with the provision that Jeffords would be made an Indian agent. Drawings are by a distinguished Apache artist.

"A dramatized presentation of Cochise which is exciting, informative and well written" (*About Indians*, p. 295).

Wyatt, Edgar. Geronimo, the Last Apache War Chief. Illus. Allan Houser. McGraw 1952.

The boy Gokliya was given the name Geronimo, the Mexican's cry of warning, by Mangus Colorado, who taught and encouraged him. Only after Mangus was shot did Geronimo go on the warpath, becoming known as the terror of the West. Although eventually he was captured, he rode in triumph in Theodore Roosevelt's inaugural parade. Partly fictionalized, especially in its conversations. Illustrated with drawings by a direct descendant of Geronimo.

"This is a dramatic presentation of Geronimo's life" (*About Indians*, p. 295).


## Senior High and Adult

Ball, Eve, editor (narrator James Kaywaykla). In the Days of Victorio: Recollections of a Warm Springs Apache. U of Ariz Pr 1970.

James Kaywaykla was a small boy during the turbulent 1870s and 1880s when the Apaches were fighting and fleeing rather than allow themselves to be sent to reservations. He was the only survivor of the Massacre of Tres Castillos in Mexico, in which Chief Victorio, the leader of the Warm Springs Apache, fired his last bullet and then took his own life. The remnant of the tribe eventually joined Geronimo and surrendered with him, and Kaywaykla was sent to the Carlisle Indian School—the youngest member of his tribe to go. The editor lived near the Mescalero Reservation, where she developed a great admiration for her Apache neighbors. She met Kaywaykla when he returned to the reservation one year for the Ceremonials for the Maidens and over a period of years he dictated his memories to her. Many Apache legends are woven throughout the story.

"A living biography of a people, well-remembered and well-spoken" (*Akwesasne Notes* 8:42, Early Summer 1976).

Barrett, S. M., editor. Geronimo: His Own Story. Ballantine 1971.

In 1905, four years before his death, Geronimo and his people were prisoners of war at Fort Sill. An Oklahoma school teacher persuaded the Apache leader to tell his story. Asa Daklugie, Geronimo's second cousin, served as interpreter. Geronimo told of his aggression against the Mexicans and the United States, when his name was synonymous with Indian resistance. In addition he included the creation story of the Apaches, his early life with his family, Apache religion, life as a prisoner, and his vision of the future of his people. In 1905 Geronimo was hoping for repatriation and he was careful not to anger his American captors; nevertheless, the book lists grievances against the whites. Published in 1906 as *Geronimo's Story of His Life.* Cited in *American Indian Authors.*

Beal, Merrill. I Will Fight No More Forever. Ballantine 1971.

A scholarly study of Chief Joseph and his campaign to keep his beloved Wallowa Valley as the home for the Nez Perce Indians. It covers the entire struggle—from Joseph's promise to his father, Old Joseph, that he will never give up their valley, to his eventual surrender—and continues the story with Joseph's imprisonment and his efforts to negotiate the case, ending finally in 1904 when his physician reported that he died of a broken heart. Joseph is depicted as a wise and noble leader of a tribe whose very democratic procedures often kept him from controlling the young hotheads. Cited by Sun Bear in *Buffalo Hearts.* On *Akwesasne Notes* basic library list.

Bedford, Denton R. Tsali. Illus. Dan B. Timmons. Indian Hist Pr 1972.

Tsali, a Cherokee, was among the last of his tribe remaining in North Carolina after the enactment of President Andrew Jackson's Removal Bill. While Tsali and others of his family were being interned before their trip west in 1838, his wife, who was ill, was mistreated by United States soldiers. In anger and frustration, Tsali managed to get a gun from his captors and killed one of them. The family took flight and remained in hiding for several months following the incident, until a fellow Cherokee convinced Tsali that if he and the other male members of his family would surrender, they would spare the members of the tribe who were being punished for Tsali's shooting of the soldier. Tsali did surrender and was killed, thus becoming a Cherokee hero. The author, a Minsee Indian, evokes the misery and suffering of the Removal, as well as the beauty of Cherokee customs and values. Illustrations are by a Cherokee artist.

Black Hawk (editor Donald Jackson). **Black Hawk: An Autobiography.** U of Ill Pr 1964.

In 1832 the great Sauk warrior Black Hawk led his people in a fifteen weeks' war and migration, the result of deception by chiefs and medicine men who convinced the chief that he was leading his people to an alliance with the Winnebagos, Potawatomie, and British in Canada. Black Hawk's dignity and pride are evident as he tells of great injustices done his people. When the autobiography first appeared in 1833, some critics claimed that Black Hawk was not the writer. Antoine LeClaire, the interpreter, was called an unreliable half-breed by some and a government interpreter by others. Presumably dictated by Black Hawk, translated into English by the interpreter, and put into manuscript form by John B. Patterson, a young newspaper editor, much of the rather artificial language was probably Patterson's. The introduction to this edition discusses its authenticity.

Boesen, Victor, and Florence Curtis Graybill. **Edward S. Curtis: Photographer of the North American Indian.** Dodd 1977.

This is the life of photographer Edward S. Curtis who, during the early 1900s, captured on film the Indians west of the Mississippi, while they still lived the tribal life. Encouraged first by George Bird Grinnell and then by President Theodore Roosevelt to undertake the project, Curtis received financial help from J. P. Morgan. The twenty-volume set, which he began as a young man, was completed fifty years later when he photographed Eskimos near the Arctic Circle. This biography is coauthored by his daughter, who spent two summers in the field with her father—one as a child and another when she was older. Illustrated with Curtis photographs. A companion piece to *The Vanishing Race: Selections from Edward S. Curtis' The North American Indian*, edited by Mick Gidley (see Senior Traditional Life and Culture).

Boyd, Doug. **Rolling Thunder.** Delta. Dell 1974.

In 1971 Doug Boyd, a member of the Menninger Foundation's research team, had recently been studying the Hindu, Swami Rama. Then he heard Rolling Thunder speak and saw him heal in Council Grove, Kansas, and was so impressed by the Cherokee medicine man that he asked to be allowed to study him in order to learn more about the "voluntary control of internal states." Boyd went to Carlin, Nevada, to spend several months learning about the mysteries of Indian medicine. Rolling Thunder, who had been adopted by the Shoshone tribe, made a living for his family as a railroad brakeman—and, as Boyd learned, he also healed sick people, saw into the future, read other people's thoughts, created a rainstorm, and moved objects without touching them.

"*Rolling Thunder* is a thought-provoking book, for if Rolling Thunder is right, as Doug Boyd believes he is, then most of us are missing a lot" (*American Indian Quarterly* 2:146, Summer 1975).

Brant, Charles S., editor. **Jim Whitewolf: Life of a Kiowa Apache.** Dover 1969.

The Kiowa Apaches, a small tribe of never more than 350, were related to the Apaches but followed the Kiowas closely, although they spoke very different languages. Whitewolf was born in the second half of the nineteenth century, when whites were making inroads into the tribal life. He learned English in a white school, experienced Indian medicine and healing practices, attended Methodist and Baptist services, and took part in the Native American Church and the peyote cult. Told in English and Apache to ethnographer Brant, Whitewolf's story covers his life from earliest childhood to the spring of 1949. A sociological study, for those interested in Kiowa Apache ways or in changes from tribal society to modern life. The editor also surveys the known history of the Kiowa Apaches. Cited in *American Indian Authors.*

"This book is recommended for all who wish to learn of the traditional Apache culture, including the peyote religion" (*About Indians*, p. 131).

Brown, Vinson. **Great upon the Mountain: Crazy Horse of America.** Illus. Adelbert Zephier. Naturegraph 1971.

A short biography of the great Oglala Sioux, emphasizing the spiritual crises in his life. In 1968 the author, a writer, naturalist, and student of American Indians, discovered a beautiful beaded Sioux pipe and tobacco bag, given to his doctor father in 1895 at Pine Ridge, South Dakota, for saving an Indian boy's life. A Sioux medicine man believed the objects once belonged to Crazy Horse. This, with the author's strange dreams about the chief, led him to write this biography. The illustrator is a Yankton Sioux.

Burnford, Sheila. Without Reserve. Illus. Susan Ross. Little 1969.

The author is a British housewife who moved with her pediatrician husband to Port Arthur, Canada, and found a kindred spirit in Susan Ross, a lawyer's wife. Together they spent time on an Ojibway Indian Reserve on Lake Nipigon, where Mrs. Ross sketched the Indians in their various activities and Mrs. Burnford fished and took notes. Later trips took them to more isolated reservations near Hudson Bay where they encountered Ojibway and Cree Indians. The book contains sympathetic and penetrating observations about the problems of modern Indians who live in isolated communities, often hardly noticed by whites.

"She has shown the advantages of being a common housewife without the pressures of having to draw anthropological conclusions from the content life she observed" (*About Indians*, p. 136).

Campbell, Maria. Halfbreed. Sat Rev Pr 1973.

The author was born while her parents were working a trap-line in northern Saskatchewan. Her ancestry included a Scottish immigrant great-grandfather, Cree Indians, and half-breeds. Among the latter was Gabriel Dumont, president of the provisional government established by the half-breeds of Canada in northern Canada before the Riel Rebellion of 1884. The book tells of the love, struggles, and gaiety of Maria's family of eight children and their grandparents and great-grandparents who moved in and out of the family circle. Then Maria struggled to establish herself in a job to help care for her brothers and sisters, and resorted to alcoholism, drug use, and prostitution as she faced discrimination and lack of training for a job. She salvaged her life through Alcoholics Anonymous and the Alberta Native Movement.

Carson, Kit (editor Milo Milton Quaife). Kit Carson's Autobiography. U of Nebr Pr 1966.

Carson's autobiography, in which he recounts his life as a trapper, Indian fighter, guide, and hunter, was discovered during the early 1900s. Carson, who lived from 1809 to 1868, tells of his expeditions with Fremont, his exploits in the Mexican War, and his service as an Indian agent. The book contains the usual prejudices of his day. As a guide and Indian fighter, Carson was often in conflict with Indians and made statements such as "the Indians were very troublesome." Probably one of the Indian's most disliked white men, Carson did understand some of their problems—recognizing, for instance, that "they did not want to steal from the Whites."

Cochise, Ciye "Niño," and A. Kinney Griffith. The First Hundred Years of Niño Cochise: The Untold Story of an Apache Indian Chief. Pyramid Pubns 1971.

The story of Niño Cochise is told by his ninety-seven-year-old grandson. As Niño's father, Tahza, was leading the tribe to the San Carlos Reservation in 1876, he managed to help his clan escape to the mountains of Sonora, Mexico. For several years the clan lived in relative peace under the leadership of Niño's mother, Geronimo's sister. At nineteen Niño became their chief. The tribe became involved with Mexican and American politics and their way of life gradually disappeared in war. The book contains many descriptions of Apache customs—courtship, marriage, war, religion, and death. Many historical figures appear, including Geronimo and Naiche (Niño's uncles), Tom Jeffords, Theodore Roosevelt, Pancho Villa, and Porfirio Diaz.

Crowder, David L. Tendoy: Chief of the Lemhis. Caxton 1969.

A brief biography of the chief of the mixed band of Shoshone, Bannock, and Tukuarika Indians, who lived from 1875 to 1907 on the Lemhi Reservation in Idaho. He became chief upon the death of Snag, nephew of Sacajawea and Cameahwait, who extracted a death-bed promise from Tendoy to always be a friend to the whites. Tendoy complied throughout his life, except when the whites tried to eliminate the Indian way of life. This carefully documented biography is scholarly and specialized, and also readable.

Eastman, Charles Alexander. From the Deep Woods to Civilization: Chapters in the Autobiography of an Indian. Little 1916.

Charles Eastman was a doctor at Pine Ridge during the Wounded Knee massacre. This is his story from the time when he was a refugee in Canada following the 1862 Sioux uprising in Minnesota, through his schooling at the agency school in Nebraska, to medical school at Boston University. His later life was spent in trying to bring about understanding between the Indians and whites, an effort which brought shock to him following revelations of the whites' trickery. The author measures whites by Indian standards and finds them wanting. Cited in *American Indian Authors.* See also *Indian Boyhood* by the same author (Junior Biography).

Eastman, Elaine Goodale (editor Kay Graber). Sister to the Sioux: The Memoirs of Elaine Goodale Eastman, 1885–91. U of Nebr Pr 1978.

Elaine Goodale, "a properly-brought-up New England girl," opened a day school in a Brulé Sioux village in 1885 at the request of Chief Medicine Bull. From a modern perspective, readers may disagree with some of her basic assumptions—that white civilization is superior and therefore must be forced upon the Indians, that only the English language must be spoken by children in school, and that the Indians must learn farming. But the reader must admire the woman who learned Sioux, hunted for several months in the old way with a Sioux hunting party, and was the only non-Sioux at a Ghost Dance while camping with Chief Big Foot and his tribe a short time before they were massacred at Wounded Knee. During and following the massacre, Elaine Goodale worked beside Dr. Charles Eastman who later became her husband. The discovery of this manuscript in the Smith College Library was a valuable contribution to Indian history.

Ford, Clellan S., editor. Smoke from Their Fires: The Life of a Kwakiutl Chief. Archon. Shoe String 1968.

Charles James Nowell, a Kwakiutl chief born in 1870, describes a way of life which has almost disappeared. The opening chapter portrays the Indians and their adjustment to the climate and environment. Succeeding chapters tell of birth, upbringing, school, marriage, children, and extramarital relations. Of particular interest is the discussion of the potlatch celebration. Based on material from a field trip to Vancouver Island during summer 1940, sponsored by the Department of Anthropology and Institute of Human Relations at Yale University. Cited by *American Indian Authors.*

Foreman, Grant. Sequoyah. U of Okla Pr 1959.

A short biography of the Cherokee genius who, although unlearned, unable to speak English, and crippled, developed an alphabet for writing the Cherokee language. Following the terms of the Cherokee Treaty of 1817 some of the Cherokee

Nation, including Sequoyah, moved from Tennessee to Arkansas. After developing his alphabet Sequoyah showed his people that messages could be carried back and forth, and eventually he established the first Indian newspaper, *Cherokee Phoenix.* Sequoyah reportedly died on a trip to Mexico in search of the lost Cherokee colony. Includes new source material researched by the author, a well-known historian of the Southwest.

"The 'authoritative' work on this distinguished man, by Grant Foreman, is a classic example of racial chauvinism gone wild" (John White in *American Indian Reader: Education,* p. 179).

Graves, John. Goodbye to a River. Ballantine 1971.

The author grew up near Fort Worth, Texas, and the Brazos River. In 1957 he learned that dams would be built that would alter the landscape along the part of the river he knew best. In November he took a canoe trip along the river on which he had camped, fished, and swum as a child. Landmarks reminded him of the history and lore of the area, including that of the Comanche and Kiowa Indians and their struggles with white settlers.

Grinnell, George Bird. **Two Great Scouts and Their Pawnee Battalion: The Experiences of Frank J. North and Luther H. North, Pioneers in the Great West, 1856–1882, and Their Defence of the Building of the Union Pacific Railroad.** U of Nebr Pr 1973.

Toward the end of the nineteenth century, George Bird Grinnell saw the Indians of the Plains shunted off to reservations where they lived in poverty. To demonstrate the constructive contributions which many of them had made to the development of the West, Grinnell wrote several books, including this one on the lives of his two friends, Frank J. and Luther H. North. The Norths grew up near the Pawnees and later led a Pawnee battalion in the defense of the Plains. Fighting against hostile Indian tribes, these Pawnee troops demonstrated their value to the United States Army by their loyalty and their knowledge of the terrain. Grinnell's book is based on his personal contacts with the Norths and on a manuscript of Frank North's experiences, published in the *Omaha Bee.*

"That this account is biased in favor of the Norths, who were the author's friends, and the Pawnees, whom Grinnell held in high regard, does not detract from the value of the information packed in it" (*American Indian Quarterly* 1:294, Winter 1974–75).

Hannum, Alberta. Paint the Wind. Illus. Beatien Yazz. Viking Pr 1958.

Bill and Sally Lippincott were managing the Wild Ruins Trading Post when they began providing art materials for the young Navajo artist, Beatien Yazz, better known as Jimmy Toddy. At sixteen Jimmy enlisted in the Marine Corps. This book tells of his return to the reservation, his development as an artist living in a white world with Navajo ideals, and his love affair with a simple Navajo girl who did not share his broadened horizons. As his art matured, he constantly had to deal with the conflict between his Navajo customs and values and those of the white world. A sequel to *Spin a Silver Dollar* by the same author (this section).

Hannum, Alberta. **Spin a Silver Dollar: The Story of a Desert Trading-Post.** Illus. Little No-Shirt [Beatien Yazz]. Viking Pr 1945.

While travelling through the West following graduation from the University of Chicago, Sally and Bill Lippincott decided to take over the trading post at Wild Ruins, Arizona, and make it livable. This is the personal story, often told with humor, of their many experiences with the people who came there, both Indian and white. Among them was Jimmy Toddy, a Navajo boy who drew pictures of animals, and the book closes as Jimmy goes into service in World War II. Color illustrations are by the Navajo boy artist Jimmy, otherwise known as Little No-Shirt (Beatien Yazz). For a continuation of Jimmy's story, see *Paint the Wind* by the same author (this section).

Howard, James H., editor. **The Warrior Who Killed Custer: The Personal Narrative of Chief Joseph White Bull.** U of Nebr Pr 1969.

Fifty-five years after the Battle of the Little Bighorn, White Bull, member of the Miniconjou Sioux, drew and annotated a pictograph account of his exploits in which he claims to have killed Custer. Stanley Vestal supports his claim, although other historians question it. White Bull, born in 1850 and a nephew of Sitting Bull, did take part in the battle. His story contains three views of his hand-to-hand combat with Custer, along with pictures of hunts, horse-stealing expeditions, intertribal battles, and other tribal activities. There are thirty-nine pictographs, sixteen in color, with the original Dakota text in an alphabet developed by missionary Stephen R. Riggs, and the translation by Howard, who formerly was director of the W. H. Over Dakota Museum, University of South Dakota. Of interest to those who enjoy looking at pictographs and seeing the language; the narrative is not easy to read.

Hughes, Charles C. **Eskimo Boyhood: An Autobiography in Psychosocial Perspective.** U Pr of Ky 1974.

While doing anthropological research on St. Lawrence Island in the Bering Sea, Hughes met a young Eskimo boy, Nathan Kakianak. Later, when Nathan was in his twenties and recovering from tuberculosis, he wrote down what he remembered of his boyhood for Hughes and this became the manuscript for this book, with an introduction and conclusion written by Hughes. The purpose was to describe in detail the culture and values that influenced the boy's life. Nathan's family was poor, partly because in this patrilineal society there were comparatively few men in his family to do the necessary hunting. The closeness of the uncles and cousins from his father's family often influenced the boy's actions. Since Nathan was born in 1933, World War II had quite an effect upon him and upon his society. This is a somewhat detailed study of Eskimo culture, besides being an interesting biography.

"The conflict between the demands of schoolboy role and apprentice hunter role that Nathan experienced is still relevant" (*American Indian Quarterly* 2:163, Summer 1975).

John Fire/Lame Deer, and Richard Erdoes. **Lame Deer: Seeker of Visions.** S&S 1972.

Lame Deer, a full-blooded Sioux from the Rosebud Reservation, was seventy-two when he told about his life, his visions, and his feelings to Richard Erdoes, a Viennese-born writer and illustrator. In trying to find fulfillment in a world dominated more and more by whites, Lame Deer was a rodeo clown, soldier, sign painter, potato picker, policeman, shepherd, singer, and medicine man. From him, we learn much about the Sioux way of looking at life and nature.

"Biography of recently deceased storyteller, rebel, medicine man. Lame Deer's tremendous gift of humor comes through strong" (*Akwesasne Notes* 9:32, Summer 1977).

Kelly, Fanny. **My Captivity among the Sioux Indians.** Citadel Pr 1973.

While traveling west in an emigrant train from her home in Kansas to Idaho with her husband and adopted daughter, Fanny Kelly, nineteen years old, was captured near Fort Laramie by a band of Ogalalla Sioux on July 12, 1864. While her husband worked to gain her freedom, she remained a prisoner for five months before being released at Fort Sully in Dakota Territory. Mrs. Kelly shows the typical prejudices of her time and the understandable fears of a woman in such a situation, but she also expresses some fondness for her captors. It is obvious that in her mind the whites were the superior race, and she accepts the concept of the Indian as a savage, but she is also aware of the Indian as a victim. She tells, for example, of white settlers who left crackers soaked in strychnine at a campsite for hungry Indians to find. This book must be read as a document written by a woman who was influenced by the religious, racial, and social assumptions and prejudices of her time. Published in 1872.

Kennedy, Dan [Ochankugahe] (editor James R. Stevens). **Recollections of an Assiniboine Chief.** McClelland 1972.

At the time he collected his reminiscences, Dan Kennedy was one hundred years old. He had heard tales that went back to the time when his tribe separated from the Sioux. He tells of many things learned in his early life: legends, the Sun Dance, marriage and family customs, how food was gathered, and how chiefs were chosen. He lived through the disappearance of the buffalo herds, the coming of the first white settlers to Saskatchewan and Montana, the building of the railroad, the Ghost Dance, and Wounded Knee. As a child he was captured and taken to school, where he was given a "civilized" name and had his hair cut. He later witnessed the demoralizing effects of the whites' whiskey and diseases on his tribe.

Kroeber, Theodora. **Ishi in Two Worlds: A Biography of the Last Wild Indian in America.** U of Cal Pr 1961.

Ishi, a Stone Age man, was the last of his tribe of Yahi Indians from north central California. As their rugged homeland was encroached upon by gold seekers and settlers, the Yahi desperately fought back until they gained the reputation of being "wild" Indians. The whites set out to eliminate them, but the last, Ishi, alone and starving, escaped by stumbling into the corral of a slaughterhouse. Rescued by anthropologist A. L. Kroeber, he worked at the University of California Museum, which led to the telling of this poignant story of a likable, noble human being. See also *Ishi: Last of His Tribe* by the same author (Junior Biography). Cited by Sun Bear in *Buffalo Hearts*.

"It delineates with dignity an aboriginal way of life and describes with love the character of the last representative of this life. Worthwhile reading" (*About Indians*, p. 206).

LaFlesche, Francis. **The Middle Five: Indian Schoolboys of the Omaha Tribe.** U of Wis Pr 1963.

Dedicated to "the Universal Boy," this book portrays life in a Presbyterian Indian Mission School near Omaha in the last half of the nineteenth century. The Universal Boy is present in boarding school pranks, mischief, and daydreams. The boys' interpretation of Christianity, often in light of Indian legends and values, is revealing. The superintendent and "Gray-Beard," a teacher, are no worse and no better than those in most mission schools; they have their moments of love and compassion but also their punishments, such as tying boys to posts for repentance. The author, an Omaha, was an Indian scholar and anthropologist in the Bureau of Ethnology. Of interest mainly as a picture of life in Indian schools. Published in 1900. Cited in *American Indian Authors*.

Laird, Carobeth. **Encounter with an Angry God: Recollections of My Life with John Peabody Harrington.** Ballantine 1975.

John Peabody Harrington was one of the first generation of university-trained anthropologists who worked at recording what remained of Native American languages, mythology, and culture. He met Carobeth in a class he taught, and married her because she had "one of the best linguistic ears" he had ever encountered. This is the story of their seven years together, from 1915 to their divorce in 1922. The genius that caused Harrington to send to the Bureau of Ethnology over a lifetime enough detailed notes to fill two warehouses eventually drove his wife into a love affair and marriage with George Laird, one of the most intelligent of their Indian informants. For Carobeth, the years with Harrington meant separation from her children, eighteen-hour working days, weeks of loneliness on a reservation when Harrington left to deliver a paper without telling her when he would return, unnecessary poverty which he forced her to endure so that his financial records would look good for the Bureau, and his paranoid fear that someone would steal his material. The book is lacking in details about the Indians with whom the Harringtons worked, but it gives insight into the life of one of the early ethnologists and linguists and the problems of living with such a scholar.

Lawton, Harry. Tell Them Willie Boy Is Here. Award Bks 1969.

The Willie Boy manhunt began on September 26, 1909, and lasted twenty days. A neglected young Paiute did what was customary in some tribes—he kidnapped a lovely Indian girl for his wife. In doing so he killed her father, who was opposed to the marriage because they were distantly related. During his desperate flight, Willie Boy was forced to kill his sweetheart when she became too weak to follow. In public opinion, the girl became associated with the lovely Ramona. The book describes President Taft's visit to Riverside, which by then was known as Willie Boy Country, and his insensitivity to regional interests and history. When rumors grew that Willie Boy was leading an uprising a manhunt was organized, and Willie Boy was found dead from his own bullet.

"Harry Lawton has assembled an impressive amount of documentation covering newspaper articles, authentic photographs, interviews with surviving posse members and their descendants, files of law enforcement agencies, etc. Sifting out the more implausible details and carefully weighing the different kinds of evidence, he published the result of his studies in a synthesis which makes for fascinating reading" (*Indian Historian* 1:26, Winter 1968).

Lee, Nelson. Three Years among the Comanches: The Narrative of Nelson Lee, the Texas Ranger. U of Okla Pr 1967.

From 1840 to 1855 Lee rode with the Texas Rangers, fighting outlaws and Indians. While driving a herd of horses to California he was captured by Comanches and spent three years as a slave to chieftains. Before he escaped by murdering the chief who owned him, he had ample opportunity to observe his captors' customs, family life, ceremonials, and treatment of their prisoners. These observations are the basis for this exciting and often violent story of life among the Comanche warrior chiefs. Published in 1859.

Leforge, Thomas H. (as told to Thomas B. Marquis). **Memoirs of a White Crow Indian.** U of Nebr Pr 1974.

Thomas Leforge began life as an "Ohio American," but chose to "die a Crow Indian American." Attracted by stories of gold, Leforge's father took his family to the West, where the young boy made contact with the Crow Indians. He married first a young Crow woman named Cherry, and after her death he married Magpie Outside. Leforge worked as a laborer and as a night watchman at the agency before enlisting as a private in the company of Crow scouts in the United States Seventh Infantry. After twenty years with the Crows, he returned to the white world in 1887 and moved to the Pacific Northwest and Alaska, where he made two unsuccessful marriages with white women. In 1912 he returned to the Crows and lived with his children by his two Crow wives. Dr. Thomas B. Marquis, the Crow Agency physician to whom Leforge told his story, has been described as one of the few whites to whom the Crows would speak freely.

Left Handed (editor Walter Dyk). **Son of Old Man Hat: A Navaho Autobiography.** U of Nebr Pr 1967.

Left Handed tells a very frank and sometimes earthy day-to-day story of his life. Born in 1868, he knew little about his mother, and his real father is never mentioned. But any older member of the tribe might be father, mother, uncle, or grandfather to him. Left Handed's sexual awakening, learned from animals as well as humans, and his growing knowledge of tribal customs and values make this a valuable anthropological study. Dyk, a student of ethnology, describes the factual, sometimes humdrum, existence of a Navaho through words translated by an interpreter. Of interest for its portrayal of how a Navaho of the last century lived and thought. Cited in *American Indian Authors.*

Leslie, Robert Franklin. **In the Shadow of a Rainbow: The True Story of a Friendship between Man and Wolf.** Sig. NAL 1975.

In spite of having a college degree, Greg Tah-Kloma, a young Chimmesyan of the Tsimshian band, preferred the wilderness of British Columbia to white civilization. Náhani was a silver queen wolf, leader of a pack which many hunters of the area regarded as outlaws and killers. Hunters wanted to kill Náhani for her magnificent silver fur. One day while panning gold, Greg was visited by Náhani and her pack, and thus began a friendship that lasted for three years as the Indian spent his time searching for the she-wolf in the wilderness to protect her from hunters and continue the relationship. The author, of Scottish and Cherokee ancestry, says that he met Greg and wrote the book from a diary that the young man kept of his experiences with Náhani. The reader can only accept the author's word that Greg Tah-Kloma and his diary actually exist. There is no picture of him in the book. The book is not strong on Indian culture but it is an unusual story.

Linderman, Frank B. Plenty-Coups: Chief of the Crows. Illus. H. M. Stoops. U of Nebr Pr 1962.

Born in 1848, Plenty-Coups was eighty when he told his story to Linderman. At twenty-nine he fought with General Crook on the Rosebud against the Sioux, Cheyenne, and Arapaho—traditional enemies of the Crow. Because Plenty-Coups wanted to tell only of the old days, the story ends with the passing of the buffalo. The narrative is told in the chief's own words, with Linderman interspersing descriptions of everyday happenings and other information. As a trapper, hunter, and cowboy, Linderman had studied Indians and their habits for more than forty years and was known to the Crows as Sign-Talker. In a postscript he tells of Plenty-Coups' part in helping his people adjust to white ways. Cited in *American Indian Authors* and by Sun Bear in *Buffalo Hearts.*

Lister, Florence C., and Robert H. Lister. Earl Morris and Southwestern Archaeology. U of NM Pr 1977.

Earl Morris (1889–1956), one of the pioneer archaeologists who excavated in the Southwest, is best known for his work in reconstructing the Great Kiva at Aztec, New Mexico. He also worked at Mesa Verde and was among the first to use tree-ring dating on timbers that were part of the construction. Although this is a specialized account of his career with only incidental information about his personal life, the general reader who is curious about the Anasazi will find much information about these prehistoric people.

Lurie, Nancy Oestreich, editor. Mountain Wolf Woman, Sister of Crashing Thunder: The Autobiography of a Winnebago Indian. U of Mich Pr 1961.

This book tells how an Indian woman's life slowly changed from the "life of an illiterate Indian food gatherer to a responsible church member who lives in a modern house, travels on Pullman trains and believes in a Christian heaven." Mountain Wolf Woman was born in 1884, lived to be seventy-five, and related her story during the last year of her life, telling it first on tape in the Winnebago language and then translating it herself. Among the most moving incidents are her arranged marriage, which she feared and hated, and her conversion to the peyote cult. The personality of a very strong woman becomes evident. Extensive notes by the editor are based on her experience as an anthropologist. The subject looked upon the editor as a niece, as she had been adopted by her cousin, Mitchell Redcloud Senior, when he was a patient at University Hospital in Madison, while Ms. Lurie was a student.

"This book is informative about Winnebago culture in Wisconsin and Nebraska" (*American Indian Authors*, p. 30). "It is a pleasant change to read the thoughts of an Indian woman and to have knowledge of the quality of life experienced by her" (*About Indians*, p. 231).

McCracken, Harold. **Frederic Remington: Artist of the Old West.** Lippincott 1947.

First biography of Remington, who went west to seek his fortune at nineteen, four years after the Battle of the Little Bighorn. After his second trip west he began illustrating books and editing articles. In 1890 his illustrations for Longfellow's *Song of Hiawatha* established his reputation; the same year he joined a scouting party into the Badlands, narrowly escaping the Massacre of Wounded Knee. Thirty-two color reproductions of Remington's paintings include studies of soldiers, cowboys, ranchers, Indians, horses, and buffaloes.

McNickle, D'Arcy. **Indian Man: A Life of Oliver La Farge.** Ind U Pr 1971.

From his youth as an undergraduate at Harvard, when he first traveled to the Southwest, to his settling there following his second marriage, La Farge devoted his life to Indian studies and to Indians. At first he accepted the government view that Indians must be assimilated, but he later believed that the Indian culture and heritage must be preserved. His biographer is a Flathead Indian scholar, professor of anthropology, and former administrator with the Bureau of Indian Affairs. Although many Indians have been critical of La Farge, McNickle is sympathetic: "What doubtless was his most significant contribution was that he brought Indians into the consciousness of Americans as something other than casual savages without tradition or style." See also *Laughing Boy* by Oliver La Farge (Senior Fiction).

Marquis, Thomas B. Wooden Leg: A Warrior Who Fought Custer. U of Nebr Pr 1962.

Marquis, agency physician for the Northern Cheyennes, tells Wooden Leg's story of the Cheyenne side of the Battle of the Little Bighorn in 1876. In old age, Wooden Leg recounts with love and nostalgia the customs of his tribe and compares them to those of the Sioux. He explains the problems of adjusting to reservation living; especially poignant is his experience when ordered to give up one of his two wives. Many of Wooden Leg's points are corroborated by other Cheyennes who survived the Battle of the Little Bighorn, but the account provoked controversy because some Indian heroes—Crazy Horse, Crow Wing, and Gall—are given little credit by the Cheyenne. Cited in *American Indian Authors* and by Sun Bear in *Buffalo Hearts*.

Marriott, Alice. Maria: The Potter of San Ildefonso. Illus. Margaret Lefranc. U of Okla Pr 1970.

Maria Martinez and her husband, Julian, are Pueblo Indians who became legends because of their pottery—which brought economic survival and fame to their pueblo, San Ildefonso. This is the story of the couple's working together to re-create the ancient pottery of their people, the pieces of which were found in an excavation. Their development of the unique black-on-black ware is a success story but there was tragedy in their personal lives, caused by dissension in the pueblo, Julian's drinking, and the loss of a child. A simply told story of a noble woman, including much about the customs and life of the pueblo. Accurate drawings of bowls, designs, pottery-making techniques, and life at the pueblo enrich the book.

Mathews, John Joseph. Wah'Kon-Tah: The Osage and the White Man's Road. U of Okla Pr 1967.

The author, an Osage, has used a journal kept by Major Laban J. Miles, Osage agent during 1878-1931, as a framework for comment on relationships between the whites and the Osage. He interprets the journal in terms of his knowledge of the tribe. In it the agent describes some of the events of his life—the dispensing of justice, helping the Indians adjust to the encroachment of white civilization, witnessing the excitement of an oil strike. Miles loved life on the reservation and wrote with sensitivity of its sights and sounds.

Mitchell, Emerson Blackhorse, and T. D. Allen. Miracle Hill: The Story of a Navaho Boy. U of Okla Pr 1967.

Broneco, a young Navaho, describes his life, from birth in a hogan to his coming of age, including his curiosity about the white world and his attempts to become a part of it. At the Institute of American Indian Arts the youth took a creative writing course from Mrs. T. D. Allen, and from it came this book about a boy's experiences, emotions, attitudes, and aspirations. Although the instructor and her student spent two years in converting Navaho thinking into English, some readers may feel the need for further editing. Cited in *American Indian Authors*.

"This book was written by a Navaho boy, with the help of his teacher, Mrs. T. D. Allen, who has most felicitously left the original manuscript untouched. It is a revealing and touching story of a young Navaho and his life in two worlds—his own and that of western European culture" (*Textbooks and the American Indian*, p. 261).

Moisés, Rosalio, Jane Holden Kelley, and William Curry Holden. A Yaqui Life: The Personal Chronicle of a Yaqui Indian. U of Nebr Pr 1977.

Rosalio Moisés, a Yaqui man, was born in southern Sonora, Mexico, in 1896, a period of relative calm for his people. By 1900, however, Mexican soldiers had killed some 400 Yaquis, and the survivors were scattered and left to starve. Rosalio went to live in the United States and learned English, but he worried about the plight of his people and in 1932, after his second wife's death, he returned to his homeland. Two years later, he served as interpreter for Professor William C. Holden's ethnographic expedition to the Rio Yaqui country. Afterward he kept in touch with the Holden family, moving to Texas in 1951 to be near them and begin writing his story. Readers will be fascinated by the dominance of witchcraft and dreams in the everyday life of the Yaqui, and their mixture of native Yaqui beliefs with Christianity. They will be shocked by the hardships and poverty of Rosalio's life during the Mexican Revolution.

For more about the Yaqui culture, see *Journey to Ixtlan* and other books by Carlos Castaneda (Senior Traditional Life and Culture).

Momaday, N. Scott. The Names: A Memoir. Har-Row 1976.

"There are moments in that time when I live so intensely in myself that I wonder how it is possible to keep from flying apart. I want you to feel that, too, the vibrant ecstasy of so much being—to know beyond any doubt that it is only the merest accident that you can hold together at all in the exhilaration of such wonder." So writes Momaday about his childhood and especially about his young manhood on the Jemez Pueblo. In addition to tales of his ancestors—his father's Kiowa people and his mother's Cherokee and Scottish family—Momaday includes the story of his early years among his Kiowa relatives, later years in Gallup and Hobbs, New Mexico, and finally the "last best home" of his childhood, the Jemez Pueblo. Some of the writing is breathtakingly beautiful and moving; all of it is interesting and informative.

"Like all of Momaday's works, this is a book to linger over, not to skim through, to think about" (*Indian Historian* 10:50, Fall 1977).

Moulton, Gary E. John Ross: Cherokee Chief. U of Ga Pr 1978.

Although only one-eighth Cherokee, John Ross was chief of the Cherokee for more than half a century during the most trying times of his people. That period included the removal of the Cherokee from the Southeast to Indian Territory, and the Civil War Years. Using newly available sources from private collections and public depositories, the author, a professor of history, stresses the political career of Chief Ross.

Nabokov, Peter, editor. Two Leggings: The Making of a Crow Warrior. Apollo Eds 1970.

Although Two Leggings was a minor leader in his tribe, he gave his life to becoming a Crow warrior, gaining what success he had through fasting, visions, and raids. In spite of his concentration, he rose only to rank of pipeholder—roughly equivalent to a platoon lieutenant. His life, from 1851 to 1923, was typical of the Crow warrior, including such events as the Sun Dance and the accompanying self-torture, raids on Indian enemies, and scouting for the whites—which the Crows undertook in the mistaken hope that it would enable them to keep their land. Two

Leggings told his story over a period of several years while being interviewed through an interpreter by William Wildschut, acting for the Heye Museum of the American Indian. Nabokov later edited and annotated the manuscript.

"This first-hand account of the everyday life of a nineteenth century Crow Indian man provides a primary source for understanding and witnessing in action the religious and social values of a Plains Indian people" (*American Indian Authors*, p. 37). "An accurate, detailed account of an Indian's traditional life which will prove itself invaluable to ethnologists and historians" (*About Indians*, p. 233).

Neihardt, John G. Black Elk Speaks: Being the Life Story of a Holy Man of the Oglala Sioux. Illus. Standing Bear. PB 1961.

Black Elk, who was related to Crazy Horse, told his biography to the poet John Neihardt; it is a story of his visions, which gave him the power to heal and to help his people. The book includes many legends and stories of the early life of the Sioux and accounts of the Battle of the Little Bighorn and the Massacre at Wounded Knee, the Indians' struggle to remain free of the reservation, and the travels of a troop of Sioux to Madison Square Garden and to Queen Victoria's Jubilee with Buffalo Bill's Wild West Show. Black Elk's story is told with honesty; the facts are corroborated with statements from other elderly Sioux. Illustrations are by a Minneconjou Sioux. Cited by Sun Bear in *Buffalo Hearts*. On *Akwesasne Notes* basic library list.

"Long ago I would have suspected an element of the histrionic in Black Elk's words; or that Neihardt was partly inventing so balanced and rich a harmony; or that Black Elk was a solitary and exceptional mystical genius. Years of being among Indians of many societies, as one vitally related to them, have shown me otherwise. Perfection of speech goes not where literacy goes, for average men; it goes where unwritten language goes. The poetic imagery among tribal Indians was and is as unfailing as Homer's imagery" (John Collier, *The Indians of the Americas: The Long Hope*, p. 180). "This book is a must" (*About Indians*, p. 235). "Gives a moving account of Black Elk's life" (*American Indian Authors*, p. 12).

Nelson, John Young (editor Harrington O'Reilly). Fifty Years on the Trail: A True Story of Western Life. U of Okla Pr 1969.

The life and experiences of John Y. Nelson will seem bizarre to many readers, and he may have exaggerated as he told his story to Harrington O'Reilly. It is an exciting tale, jumping from one adventure and lifestyle to another during a period of tremendous change on the prairie from 1840 to 1890. Nelson spent much time among the Brulé and Oglala Sioux, where he took at least nine wives, many of whom were stolen from him. He knew and hunted with Chief Spotted Tail and served as a guide for the Mormons to Salt Lake and as an army scout against the Sioux and Cheyenne. Although he never quite understood Indian life, he preferred it to that among his own people. Published in 1889.

"Unfortunately, Nelson had a reputation as a frontier prevaricator, and although part of what he relates concerning Spotted Tail is obviously true, many of his assertions are clearly manufactured, usually with the object of making himself appear more important than he really was" (George E. Hyde, *Spotted Tail's Folk: A History of the Brulé Sioux*, p. 44).

Newcomb, Franc Johnson. **Hosteen Klah: Navaho Medicine Man and Sand Painter.** U of Okla Pr 1964.

The last Navaho medicine man, Hosteen Klah, died in 1937 at the age of seventy. Mrs. Newcomb was the wife of the owner of a trading post near where Klah and his family lived. Because she had been a student of Klah's, he allowed her to make mental notes of his sand paintings, which she later reproduced. The book covers more than a hundred years of Navaho history beginning with Chief Narbona, Klah's great-grandfather. Klah's mother had made the march to Bosque Redondo.

O'Meara, Walter. **Last Portage.** HM 1962.

As a boy in 1789, John Tanner was captured by Shawnees from his home in Kentucky, and later was bought by an unusual woman, Netnokwa, an Ottawa who was a principal chief of her tribe. Because she was old, Netnokwa decided to give up her position in the tribe and took her family to see Chippewa relatives in northern Minnesota. John spent most of the rest of his life in the area from Sault Ste. Marie to the Red River of the North. The book contains detailed information about the life and hardships of John and his family. Tragically, he attempted in later years to return to the white way of life at the Sault but failed to adjust. Frankness about the Indians' sexual customs and their hard and cruel life make this a book for mature readers. For a fictionalized account of Tanner, see *White Falcon* by Elliott Arnold (Junior Fiction).

Oskison, John. Tecumseh and His Times: The Story of a Great Indian. Putnam 1938.

This is a sympathetic biography of the great Shawnee warrior Tecumseh (circa 1786–1813), whose aim in life was to save his race from eventual destruction by trying to unite the Algonquian tribes—Ottawas, Chippewas, Wyandots, Delawares, Shawnees, and Potawatomies. His brother, the Prophet, used religious fanaticism to arouse the tribes, while Tecumseh organized them by using logic and oratory. William Henry Harrison, governor of Indiana Territory, defeated the Prophet at the Battle of Tippecanoe, and at the Battle of the Thames he defeated Tecumseh's troops after their leader was killed. The author, a Cherokee, is an admirer of Tecumseh. Cited in *American Indian Authors.*

Pelletier, Wilfred, and Ted Poole. No Foreign Land: The Biography of a North American Indian. Pantheon 1973.

Wilfred Pelletier is an Ojibwa Indian who was born in Wikwemikong on Manitoulin Island in northern Lake Huron. Ted Poole, a white friend, tape-recorded Pelletier's story during a fishing trip as he talked informally about his life and his feelings. Pelletier had tried the white world, where he had been successful as a businessman and Indian guide, but he found the experience dehumanizing. He returned to his reserve and became a political activist, attending conferences, making speeches, and trying to help the poor, but found that this, too, was insincere. The final chapter summarizes Pelletier's thoughts on being an Indian today and becoming an active part of the Indian community.

"To the reader interested in diverse philosophies of life this book furnishes a unique insight" (*American Indian Quarterly* 2:262, Autumn 1975.

Qoyawayma, Polingaysi. No Turning Back: A True Account of a Hopi Indian Girl's Struggle to Bridge the Gap between the World of Her People and the World of the White Man. U of NM Pr 1964.

Polingaysi attended the first school established for her people at their village, Old Oraibi, where she was born on a mesa in 1892. At about fourteen, she insisted that she be allowed to go with others of her tribe to the Sherman Institute in Riverside, California. Contacts with Mennonite missionaries near her home gave her access to more education. Determined to find her place between the Hopi world and the white, she finally found her role as a teacher in government Indian schools, where a new struggle for acceptance of her teaching methods awaited her. The book contains many descriptions of Hopi legend and ceremony; it is especially good in discussing the conflicts and problems the Hopi faces in adjusting to the white environment. Another Hopi woman who tells her story is Helen Sekaquaptewa in *Me and Mine* (this section). For a fictionalized treatment of the same theme see *Our Cup Is Broken* by Florence Means (Senior Fiction).

"Includes information on Hopi legend, ceremony, religion, and philosophy" (*American Indian Authors*, p. 34). "This extraordinary book will be a source of encouragement and strength to anyone undergoing a cultural change" (*About Indians*, p. 248).

Radin, Paul, editor. **The Autobiography of a Winnebago Indian.** Dover 1963.

Known only as S. B., the subject of this autobiography was born in the second half of the nineteenth century when the traditional Indian life and the white world were clashing. Reaching maturity around 1913, he tells of the education of Winnebago youth, the work of the shaman, his adolescence, initiation into the medicine dance, his marriage and sexual promiscuity, his entry into the white world, his alcoholism, the murder of a Potawatomie, his trial and stay in jail, and his experiences with the peyote cult. Part I is his autobiography; Part II is Radin's explanation of the Winnebago system of instruction. S. B. originally dictated his story to Oliver Lamere of Winnebago, Nebraska. Radin, without altering the text, translated and annotated it from his knowledge of Winnebago culture. Recommended only for older students because of its frankness.

Redsky, James [Esquekesik] (editor James R. Stevens). **Great Leader of the Ojibway: Mis-quona-queb.** McClelland 1972.

When James Redsky was a boy in southern Ontario and Manitoba seventy years before he wrote this book, he heard stories of the great leader of the Lake of the Woods Ojibway tribe, Mis-quona-queb, or Red Cloud. The chief, who probably lived in the mid-1700s, is considered the last great war leader of the Ojibway. He made his name by successfully fighting off the Sioux, who raided Ojibway villages. Tales of Mis-quona-queb became legendary and were passed from generation to generation, along with stories of his joining the Mide-wi-win, learning about the shaking tent, and telling legends of the tribe to both children and adults. Mis-quona-queb moved back and forth across the U.S.-Canadian border to Ojibway villages near what are now Warroad and Red Lake, Minnesota. Illustrated with photographs of Ojibway life as it was before the coming of the whites.

Rogers, John [Chief Snow Cloud]. Red World and White: Memories of a Chippewa Boyhood. U of Okla Pr 1974.

Way Quauh Gishig (Chief Snow Cloud) begins the account of his boyhood in 1896 when he was six years old and went to Flandreau, South Dakota, with his two sisters to attend an Indian boarding school. Six years later the three returned to their mother's wigwam near Mahnomen, Minnesota, and had to relearn their Indian language and the Indian way of life—hunting, fishing, rice-harvesting, and getting the basic materials to live. Their father had abandoned his family, so life was especially difficult. Although the author lived in the Indian world of his mother's wigwam, he also went to school, where he was exposed to the white world. At the end of his boyhood years he made contact with his father, who was living with his second wife and family at Cass Lake, Minnesota.

Sandoz, Mari. Crazy Horse: The Strange Man of the Oglalas. U of Nebr Pr 1961.

Crazy Horse was a strange, light-colored Oglala boy called "Curly," but finally earned his father's name because of his visions and bravery. He lived during troubled times for his tribe when buffalo herds were being depleted and the Indians were driven toward the hills. He died in 1877, shortly after the Battle of the Little Bighorn. The language of this biography is simple and ideally suited to the story, as the author tries to write and think like a Sioux of the period, but the book is difficult because of excessive detail. Cited by Sun Bear in *Buffalo Hearts*.

"Recommended to all educators, this book can be used as a reference for a more objective look at the Sioux wars, their causes, and after-effects as told by the Indians" (*About Indians*, p. 261).

Santee, Ross. Apache Land. Illus. by author. U of Nebr Pr 1971.

This is not a biography in the usual sense, but rather a series of sketches of Apaches the author has known or heard of, including Old Jim the Cowboy, Cochise, Geronimo, Agent Clum, and Burro Frenchy. The author gave up a career in cartooning and returned to Arizona as a horse wrangler and cowboy, where he collected incidents from his contact with the people around him, read stories about the personalities of the area, and sketched pictures of the people. Santee's stories incorporate the history, customs, and beliefs of the Apaches.

"*Apache Land* tells human stories, both the noble and the less so. Excellent writing" (*About Indians*, p. 262).

Schmedding, Joseph. Cowboy and Indian Trader. U of NM Pr 1974.

While still in his late teens, Joseph Schmedding left his home in North Carolina to travel to the Southwest. After some wandering, he went to work as a ranch hand for Richard Wetherill, in Chaco Canyon on the edge of the Navajo Reservation near Pueblo Bonito, the famous Anasazi ruins. At that time (1905 to 1908), Wetherill was engaged with the Hyde Exploring Expedition in the first well-organized attempt to accumulate data about the early Indian civilizations of the area. Schmedding then spent some time in traveling, but returned to his beloved Southwest as a trader in Keams Canyon, where he remained for about ten years. Although his account concentrates on his experiences with the Navajos, he also provides insights into the life of the Hopis in the early 1900s.

Schultz, James W. My Life as an Indian. Fawcett 1971.

Son of a staid New England family, the author was allowed to indulge his love of wild life and adventure by taking a trip west to Fort Benton, Montana, in the 1870s. There he worked with a trapper and trader and married a Piegan Blackfoot woman, Nat-ah-ki. This is an honest picture of the good and bad among both Indians and whites. Clash of values is apparent, for example, when the author describes how differently he felt, after killing a man, from the way his Indian friends thought he should feel. There also is a vivid picture of Indian agents who allowed Indians to starve after the buffalo ran out. This autobiographical material appeared originally in 1907 as a series of sketches which later were published as a book.

Scott, Lalla. Karnee: A Paiute Narrative. Fawcett 1973.

Annie Lowry was the daughter of a Paiute, Sau-tau-nee, and a white rancher named Jerome Lowry, who had married Annie's mother after rescuing her from a man who was beating her. He wanted to give his children a white education, but when he decided to leave his Indian wife and take his children with him, Annie hid in order to remain with her mother. From then on she remained in the Indian community and was married twice, each time to an Indian, and raised a number of children. Her biographer lived in Lovelock, Nevada, where Annie was born and spent most of her life. She met Annie while doing research for the Pershing County Writers' Project under the Works Progress Administration in 1936, which led to the writing of this story. "Karnee" in the title refers to the traditional Paiute home. The language of the Indian characters in the book is sometimes stereotyped.

Sekaquaptewa, Helen, and Louise Udall. Me and Mine: The Life Story of Helen Sekaquaptewa. Illus. Phillip Sekaquaptewa. U of Ariz Pr 1969.

The subject of this book grew up in a traditional Hopi family, and was given the name Helen when she went to school. There she met and married Emory, and gradually lost interest in many of the old ways and ceremonials. Her story is a bit unusual be because the break with tradition apparently caused her no emotional conflict, nor was there a violent break with her family—although there was obviously some pain and disappointment. A chapter of particular interest tells how the village of Old Oraibi was divided between the Hostiles and the Friendlies in 1906, an incident that is not often discussed freely. Cited in *American Indian Authors.* For other Hopi biographies see *No Turning Back* by Polingaysi Qoyawayma and *Sun Chief* by Leo W. Simmons (this section), and the fictionalized life story *Our Cup Is Broken* by Florence Means (Senior Fiction).

Sewid, James (editor James P. Spradley). Guests Never Leave Hungry: The Autobiography of James Sewid, a Kwakiutl Indian. Yale U Pr 1969.

The author is a Kwakiutl chieftain, born in 1913 into a changing and disintegrating society. He describes his schooling, his entry into the fishing industry at ten, his marriage at thirteen, his life in a remote Indian village, and his leadership of progressive Indians at the Kwakiutl Reserve at Alert Bay. First elected chief of his tribe, he is today vice president of the Native Brotherhood of British Columbia. Coming from a poverty-stricken home and a childhood during which he saw his relatives sent to prison for practicing Kwakiutl ceremonies, he has found a way to live in two cultures. His story was tape-recorded in informal interviews over a two-year period and is presented here with little editing. Cited in *American Indian Authors.*

Simmons, Leo W., editor. **Sun Chief: The Autobiography of a Hopi Indian.** Yale U Pr 1963.

Don Talayesva was born in the Hopi village of Oraibi in 1890. He spent ten years in schools in Arizona and California, but returned to the Indian ways. The book contains much information about religious ceremonies, family and clan relationships, and the supernatural beings of the Hopi world. It is primarily a sociological study. Talayesva was unaffected by the reticence he observed in the white world, and speaks a great deal about sex. Cited in *American Indian Authors* and by Sun Bear in *Buffalo Hearts.*

Sissons, Jack. **Judge of the Far North: The Memoirs of Jack Sissons.** McClelland 1973.

In September 1955 when he was sixty-three, Jack Sissons, then Chief Judge of the District Court of Alberta at Lethbridge, was asked to become the first Judge of the Territorial Court of the Northwest Territories. During 1955-1965 he flew in all kinds of weather, criss-crossing a third of Canada's land mass, to uphold two principles: that justice must be taken to every person's door and that an individual accused of crime must be tried by a jury of his peers. At points ranging from the Mackenzie Delta to Baffin Island, he presided at murder trials at which he had to understand Eskimo values, protected historic Eskimo hunting rights, and settled the inheritances of wives and children at a time when Eskimo marriages were regarded as a form of concubinage and all children of such marriages as illegitimate. Each case which Sissons adjudicated is described in terms of the human beings involved and their cultural values.

Smith, Derek G., editor. **The Adventures and Sufferings of John R. Jewitt, Captive among the Nootka, 1803-1805.** McClelland 1974.

Jewitt, a young blacksmith, left his native England aboard the *Boston* in September 1802, sailing around Cape Horn, up the coasts of South America and North America to Nootka Sound, where the ship dropped anchor to take on wood and other supplies. The local chief, Maquina, and his tribe were friendly until a dispute arose over the white captain's gift of a fowling-piece. It led to a massacre by the Nootkas of the whole party except Jewitt, whose smithery skills were useful to the tribe, and a sailmaker named Thompson. For two years the men served the chief as slaves, until another ship arrived. Jewitt was able to get a letter to the captain, who took Maquina prisoner in exchange for Jewitt's and Thompson's release. In 1824 Jewitt published his story. He was not trained in ethnology but his early record of life among the Nootka is valuable.

Smith, James. **Scoouwa: James Smith's Indian Captivity Narrative.** Ohio Hist Soc 1978.

While helping to build a road in the province of Pennsylvania in 1755, James Smith was taken prisoner by one Canasatauga and two Delaware Indians. They took him to Fort Duquesne, which was then held by the French and Iroquois, and he was adopted by the Caughnewagos, a part of the Mohawk tribe. From then on he was accepted as a member of the tribe—hunting, traveling, gathering maple sugar, and planting corn with them. He suffered winter hardships with them near Lake Erie. In 1760 he was exchanged near Lake Champlain and returned home to take part in a number of campaigns against the Indians. This journal, kept while Smith was a captive, was published in 1799 and reissued a number of times. This edition is especially useful because of the extensive notes by John J. Barsotti of the Ohio Historical Society.

Specht, Robert. **Tisha: The Story of a Young Teacher in the Alaskan Wilderness.** Bantam 1977.

Nineteen-year-old Anne Hobbs went to Alaska in 1927 to teach at Chicken, a remote gold-mining village in the Forty Mile River country. Light-skinned and gray-eyed, Anne had lived an unhappy childhood, relieved only by her love for her full-blooded Kentuck Indian grandmother. She was quite unprepared for the prejudice she found against both Indians and Eskimos on the frontier. Welcomed and entertained at first by the community, she soon was rejected and harassed when she fell in love with Fred Purdy, who was half Eskimo, and when she took into her home two orphaned Indian children. This is an exciting story, climaxed by a chase by dogsled across the frozen Alaskan landscape to rescue Chuck and Ethel, the two Indian children, who had been kidnapped by a well-meaning white man.

Standing Bear, Luther. My People, the Sioux. HM 1928.

Chief Standing Bear, a Sioux, tells about his early life in the tribal society. He was a young boy at the time of the Battle of the Little Bighorn in 1876 and was near the action at the Massacre at Wounded Knee, but was not present at the Ghost Dance because he did not believe in it. The book tells of his life at Carlisle Indian School, his marriage, and his work for the advancement of his people. A frank autobiography of a sincere and concerned leader of his people.

"Chief Standing Bear relates memories of his boyhood, giving a great deal of information about the Sioux tribe and how their chiefs are made" (*American Indian Authors*, p. 37).

Traveller Bird. Tell Them They Lie: The Sequoyah Myth. Westernlore 1971.

Traveller Bird, who claims to be a direct descendant of the man known as Sequoyah, writes a book recording the life of his ancestor, taken, he says, from more than six hundred unpublished documents by Sequoyah, plus writings of his children, grandchildren, and great-grandchildren. Traveller Bird says that—instead of being the crippled, scholarly Sequoyah, known also as George Gist, possibly the son of George Guess, an itinerant trader, or Nathaniel Gist, friend of George Washington—Sequoyah was a full-blooded Cherokee who did not invent the syllabary but rather taught it—a system that had been used for nine summers before whites came to San Salvador Island. Some critics of the book cite a number of discrepancies with known facts about Cherokee history and the author's unwillingness to make available his sources to the tribe.

"It documents the white's barbarism and the conceit of their culture. Interesting reading" (*About Indians*, p. 278). "It is very difficult and extremely painful, for this reviewer, to state that, after careful reading and re-reading, *Tell Them They Lie: The Sequoyah Myth* is an elaborate fabrication" (John White, in *The American Indian Reader: Education*, p. 182).

Trueman, Stuart, editor. The Ordeal of John Gyles: Being an Account of His Odd Adventures, Strange Deliverances &c. as a Slave of the Maliseets. McClelland 1973.

In 1689 a nine-year-old Puritan boy was captured by Maliseet braves in Maine and made a slave of the St. John River Indians, becoming the first English-speaking resident of New Brunswick.

As a slave of the Indians and later of a French seigneur, he was used as a pawn between the French and British in their fight for the New World. After nearly nine years he returned home. Although he had missed all those years of schooling, he could speak French, Maliseet, and Micmac and the languages of related New England tribes such as the Penobscots and the Passamaquoddies, in addition to his native English. And he had learned to deal with both Indians and French without encroaching upon their sensitivities. The material for his biography was reconstructed from his journal and from research into the history of the period. Fictionalized passages fill gaps where no information exists.

Vestal, Stanley. **Sitting Bull: Champion of the Sioux.** U of Okla Pr 1969.

A scholarly and well-documented story of a great Sioux chief (1834-1890), written in an interesting narrative style, uncluttered by long quotations from documents and eyewitness accounts. The book begins when the subject was a boy-volunteer called "Slow" and ends with the great chief's death because he refused to be captured—a picture of a wise, independent, and very human man. Based on the author's research and interviews with friends and family of Sitting Bull; written with sympathetic regard for the subject. Cited by Sun Bear in *Buffalo Hearts*.

Waters, Frank. **Pumpkin Seed Point.** Swallow 1969.

For three years the author lived among the Hopi Indians and this book is about his personal experiences during that time. His relationship with the two Bears (Oswald Fredericks and his wife) is especially important. The book concentrates on problems of conflict between Indian and white ways of life. See also *The Book of the Hopi* by the same author (Senior Traditional Life and Culture).

"While recognizing and deploring Hopi alienation from whites, the author still manages to join his ideas to those of the Hopi in a personal wish-vision of mankind united" (*About Indians*, p. 287).

Webb, George. **A Pima Remembers.** U of Ariz Pr 1959.

The author was born in 1893 at Gila Crossing on the Gila River Reservation about twenty miles south of Phoenix. He was graduated from an Indian Bureau boarding school, and worked as a ranch hand and a farm overseer. In 1934 he was elected to his tribe's first council. This autobiography includes the traditions, legends, games, history, and language of his people. Webb writes for two audiences: young Pimas, to acquaint them with their background and traditions; and the general white public, to present a true picture of the position of Pimas in modern American life. Cited in *American Indian Authors*.

Willoya, William, and Vinson Brown. **Warriors of the Rainbow: Strange and Prophetic Dreams of the Indian Peoples.** Naturegraph 1962.

In this book about Indian dreams the authors—Willoya, an Eskimo, and Brown, a student of Indian life—combine their own study and experiences with works by and about well-known Indian prophets and visionaries, such as Black Elk, Wovoka, Montezuma, and Plenty-Coups. Illustrations are by major Indian artists.

"A study of Indian dreams is accompanied by full-color reproductions of paintings done by Indian artists. An appendix gives the scientific basis for the study" (*American Indian Authors*, p. 39).

Woodward, Grace Steele. **Pocahontas.** U of Okla Pr 1970.

The Powhatan Indian princess, who perhaps saved the Jamestown Colony from starvation and massacre, lived only twenty-two years. Of the first twelve years of her life little is known; during the important last decade she brought the colonists gifts of food, warned them about Indian plots, and united her people and the English by her conversion to Christianity and her marriage to John Rolfe. A scholarly work, including notes on her American descendants, the English memorials, and a bibliography.

# History

Bealer, Alex W. Only the Names Remain: The Cherokees and the Trail of Tears. Illus. William Sauts Bock. Little 1972. Intermediate.

The beautiful Appalachian mountain region of Georgia was once the home of a remarkable Indian nation, the Cherokees, who had developed their own alphabet and had achieved peaceful coexistence with the whites. But the discovery of gold and the invention of the cotton gin led to the seizure of Cherokee land, an action that was approved by President Jackson, the Cherokees' former ally. Soon they were deprived of their rights and finally were exiled to Arkansas in what is known as the Trail of Tears—one of the more tragic episodes of American history. Black and white illustrations.

Goble, Paul, and Dorothy Goble. Brave Eagle's Account of the Fetterman Fight: 21 December 1866. Illus. Paul Goble. Pantheon 1972. Intermediate.

Brave Eagle, a nineteen-year-old Sioux warrior, gives a simplified account of a famous struggle between Indians and whites for a prized area of land in Wyoming. This land was reserved by treaty to the Indians for hunting purposes, but the U.S. government wanted it because the Bozeman Trail, the shortest route to the western gold fields, ran through it. Red Cloud, chief of the Oglala Sioux, and many Cheyenne chiefs were determined to fight for the integrity of their last hunting grounds. This led to a six-month battle culminating in the skirmish described in this book, in which Captain Fetterman's entire command of eighty-two men were overwhelmed by Cheyenne and Sioux warriors. The narrative, with material derived from historical documents, reflects the Indians' strong feelings against the whites for their false treaties and seizure of Indian land. Colorful illustrations inspired by Plains Indian paintings of the period.

Goble, Paul, and Dorothy Goble. **Red Hawk's Account of Custer's Last Battle: The Battle of the Little Bighorn, 25 June 1876.** Pantheon 1969. Intermediate.

This account of the Battle of the Little Bighorn is related by Red Hawk, a fictional Oglala Sioux. The book records what a Sioux warrior might have seen before and during the famous battle. Red Hawk tells of life in the encampment where many famous men are gathered, the most famous being Crazy Horse, and of seeing in the distance the blue-coated soldiers approaching on horseback. The ensuing battles are clearly re-created and illustrated with colorful drawings. The account is written from an Indian point of view and the authors have included italicized passages to explain difficult Indian expressions and concepts. The Indians in the book willingly acknowledge the bravery of Custer's men. Chief Sitting Bull says, "I tell no lies about dead men. Those men who came with Long Hair were as good men as ever fought."

Hirsch, S. Carl. **Famous American Indians of the Plains.** Illus. Lorence Bjorklund. Rand 1973. Intermediate.

The history of the Pawnee, Cheyenne, Blackfoot, Arapaho, Assiniboin, Crow, Kiowa, Ponca, and Sioux. These strong and colorful cultures, among the last to evolve on the North American continent, are characterized by a beautiful sense and expression of freedom. The horse and buffalo are seen to be essential to the Plains Indian way of life. The author explains traditions, such as the societies and clubs of the Cheyenne and the sacred Sun Dance of the Blackfeet, and changes brought by the coming of the whites, broken treaties, and the invasion of the railroad. The Indian religion of hope, the Ghost Dance, perished at Wounded Knee and the old life on the plains was gone forever. Paintings by Charles M. Russell, Frederic Remington, and Charles Wimar are reproduced in the book.

"In the vignettes, we have an epitome of the Plains Indians and their world. It is a world full of motion and meaning, worth looking into" (N. Scott Momaday, foreword, p. 12).

Jacobson, Daniel. **The Fishermen.** Illus. Richard Cuffari. Watts 1975. Intermediate.

A comprehensive book on the Northwest Indians, focusing on their origins, culture, and history. Several tribes are mentioned but the Tlingits are given special attention. Several chapters deal with the ancient fishermen and their lifestyle, and there is interesting historical material about the coming of whites and their diseases and the effects of the United States' formal possession of Alaska in 1867. A good glossary, many illustrations, and selected bibliography.

Jacobson, Daniel. **The Hunters.** Illus. Richard Cuffari. Watts 1974. Intermediate.

This book traces the history of the Indian tribes whose way of life on the plains revolved around hunting, beginning with prehistoric times when they were mammoth and bison hunters, to modern times with all their changes, notably the introduction of the horse by the Mexicans. Later tribal history includes the arrival of the Comanches and the Utes' eventual retreat into the Front Range of the Rockies and their abandonment of hunting. A discussion of the Assiniboines includes their ceremonial bison hunts, medicine lodge dances, and customs relating to birth, marriage, and death. The encroaching white civilization broke up the hunting cultures in the 1800s, confining the Comanches and Assiniboines to reservations. The Chippewa hunters, who traditionally lived between northern forests and tundra in an endless struggle for food, ended on the fringes of white society, many of them on welfare. In the Far North, the hunters remain, and the question is: "Are their days numbered?"

Moyers, William, and David C. Cooke. **Famous Indian Tribes.** Illus. William Moyers. Random 1954. Primary.

This is a simplified account of the way famous Indian tribes lived. Discussions of their homes, means of transportation, wars, and the accomplishments of great chiefs are included. Some Forest Indian chiefs mentioned are King Philip (Wampanoag), Pontiac (Ottawa), Red Jack (Seneca), and Black Hawk (Sauk). There are sections on the Plains Indian chiefs Red Cloud and Sitting Bull (both Sioux) and Desert Indian chiefs Geronimo and Cochise (both Apaches). Perhaps the two most famous Indians covered in the book are Tecumseh, chief of the Shawnee tribe, and Sequoyah, a great Cherokee. Of particular interest is the account of the peaceful Nez Perce tribe and the courage of their Chief Joseph. Descriptions of the acorn eaters of California and the woodcarvers and fishermen of the Northwest coast are also included. Some illustrations are in black and white, others are in color.

Rachlis, Eugene, and John C. Ewers. **Indians of the Plains. Am Heritage** 1960. Intermediate.

A history of the time when 50 million buffalo roamed the Great Plains, with descriptions of prehistoric artifacts and archaeological discoveries that give insight into the life of the Plains Indians, including their tribal laws, sign language, sports, and arts. It explains the importance of the horse, the buffalo, and historical events such as the coming of the railroad and the telegraph. The struggle of various tribes to retain their lands led to the warpath and episodes such as Custer's last stand, the Ghost Dance, and the tragic happenings at Wounded Knee. There is a section describing the myths about these tribes. The aim of the book is to portray modern American Indians as human beings who have been badly misunderstood and mistreated in the past and are now struggling to keep their rightful heritage alive. Paintings, prints, drawings, and photographs of the period.

Yellow Robe, Rosebud [Lacotawin]. **An Album of the American Indian.** Watts 1970. Intermediate.

Reproductions of early American paintings and etchings and many photographs accompany the text of this book, which covers Indian cultures and life from the appearance of the whites to the present day. In relatively few pages it presents a large amount of material, and a point of view best expressed by Lyndon B. Johnson in the first presidential message on American Indians ever sent to Congress (in 1968): "We must pledge to respect fully the dignity and the uniqueness of the Indian citizen. . . . For the first among us must not be the last."

## Junior High

Bennett, Kay, and Russ Bennett. **A Navajo Saga.** Naylor 1969.

Kay Bennett, a Navajo, tells the story of her family, the Kinlichine clan, under the leadership of headman Gray Hat during 1846–1870, when the United States Army attempted either to imprison the Navajos on the Bosque Redondo Reservation, to kill them, or starve them on the mountain. The tribe had been wealthy in sheep and horses taken in raids on ranches in New Mexico until the army stopped this practice and hunted them. After tremendous suffering the Navajos gave in; instead of the promised food and hogans at Bosque Redondo there was crowding, a shortage of land, and a lethal smallpox epidemic. A tragic story, told simply and movingly.

Brown, Dee (adapter Amy Ehrlich). **Wounded Knee: An Indian History of the American West.** HR&W 1974.

From Dee Brown's history of the Indian resistance to white colonization of the West, *Bury My Heart at Wounded Knee* (see Senior History), Amy Ehrlich has focused on four of the tribes—the Navaho and Apache of the Southwest; the Cheyenne and Sioux from the Plains—in presenting this simplified version of the story. Sentence structure and vocabulary have been condensed and simplified to make the book more readable for younger students. Listed in "Resources," *Akwesasne Notes* 8:42, Early Summer 1976.

"The editing is good and this version is interesting, readable and smooth" (*School Library Journal* 21:62, April 1975).

Capps, Benjamin. **The Indians.** Time-Life 1974.

A handsome collection of old photographs and paintings, many in full color, with text by novelist Capps. The book covers the history and culture of the Indians of the western United States, with emphasis on the Indians of the Plains. There are chapters on the Indians' way of life, their religion, the coming of the whites, and the Battle of the Little Bighorn. Part of *The Old West* series; a fine supplement for an Indian unit.

Collier, Peter. **When Shall They Rest? The Cherokees' Long Struggle with America.** HR&W 1973.

This is the story of the betrayal and removal of the Cherokees from the southeastern United States to Oklahoma. In recounting the part played by people such as Major Ridge and his son John, Elias Boudinot and his brother Stand Watie, and John Ross, it is sympathetic to the Cherokee plight.

"Suitable for high school use" (*Akwesasne Notes* 8:42, Early Summer 1976). "While the issues themselves are sympathetically handled, in such a way as to show the mistreatment suffered by these people, there is no accurate handling of the issues as the Cherokees see them and confront them. The book is a great improvement over some that have been published on the Cherokees, however" (*Indian Historian* 7:51, Winter 1974).

Council on Interracial Books for Children, editors. Chronicles of
American Indian Protest. Fawcett 1971.

A collection of documents that are statements of the Indians'
resistance to the encroachment of the whites, from the sixteenth century to the present Red Power movement. Many are
preceded by historical information about the circumstances that
precipitated the statements and some are followed by post-
scripts. Resistance movements that are represented by Indian
speeches and writings include Popé's uprising, 1680; Pontiac's
Rebellion, 1763; the Cherokee Removal, 1823 and 1836; the
Ghost Dance, 1890; and the Indians' occupation of Alcatraz,
1969.

Erdoes, Richard. The Rain Dance People: The Pueblo Indians,
Their Past and Present. Knopf 1976.

Words and photographs are combined to link the earliest settlers of the Southwest—the hunters of the ancient mammoths—
with modern Pueblo Indians in tracing the development of the
Cochise culture, and the Mogollon, Hohokam, and Anasazi
civilizations. Finally in 1536, Nuñez Cabeza de Vaca, a Spaniard
traveling through present-day New Mexico and Arizona, heard
from corn-growing Indians about the Seven Cities of Cibola
with their towering houses and great wealth—and thus began the
invasion of the West, first by the Spaniards and later the Americans. The author describes modern Pueblo Indians, their religions, their cultures, and their economy, and concludes with a
plea for their right to live in their own way, without inter-
ference from white people. Illustrated with photographs, most
of them by the author.

"A book about the Pueblo People who speak for themselves
simply and eloquently, forming a powerful picture of a people
struggling to preserve identity despite oppression" (*Akwesasne
Notes* 8:41, Midwinter 1976-77).

Erdoes, Richard. The Sun Dance People: The Plains Indians, Their
Past and Present. Photographs by author. Knopf 1972.

The historical picture of the changes in the way of life of the
Plains Indians—mainly the Sioux, Northern Cheyenne, and
Crow—from the period before the coming of the whites to the
present, including the effect of the introduction of the horse.
The Plains Indians' religion and generosity unfitted them for
the businesslike white world. As their buffalo and beaver dis-

appeared, they fought for their land at the Battle of the Little Bighorn and finally turned to their religion and the Ghost Dance, before their tragic defeat at Wounded Knee. The book concludes with a look at life on the reservation today with all of its problems. On *Akwesasne Notes* basic library list.

"The Plains Indians, their past and present for old and young readers. Profusely illustrated" (*Akwesasne Notes* 9:32, Summer 1977). "Erdoes's versions [of some of the battles] are not the same as those in most textbooks. Chivington and Custer both wear the black hats of the villain, and high time" (*New York Times Book Review*, 13 August 1972, p. 8).

Folsom, Franklin. **Red Power on the Rio Grande: The Native American Revolution of 1680.** Illus J. D. Roybal. Follett 1973.

Following the invasion of the Rio Grande Valley by gold-seeking Spaniards, the Pueblo people were forced to work in the Spanish fields and sweatshops. But the worst result was having another religion forced upon them. Popé, a Tewa medicine man, emerged as a leader in 1675 and was brutally whipped and thrown into a dungeon because of his activities against the Spanish. In spite of all difficulties, he met with other leaders and devised a unique plan for gaining the Pueblos' freedom. Other books have shown the Spanish viewpoint and have not credited Popé for being the great leader he was. The introduction is by Alfonso Ortiz, who was raised in the hometown of Popé and has researched the subject in depth.

"[Folsom's sources] are propaganda, and the authors posture and blubber unreliably just as do the authors of the Jesuit Relations, so mistakenly trusted by Francis Parkman. Since there are no independent or Indian sources, Folsom relies, once again uncritically, on anthropological studies of Indian culture" (*Indian Historian* 6:57, Fall 1973).

Georgakas, Dan. **The Broken Hoop: The History of Native Americans from 1600 to 1890, from the Atlantic Coast to the Plains.** Doubleday 1973.

This volume discusses the relationship between European settlers and the Indian population, focusing on the history of the Indians of the Great Plains and eastward—tribes such as the Iroquois, Seminole, Cherokee, Sioux, and Cheyenne. The book also explores the roles of several Indian leaders, including Black Elk, Crazy Horse, and Sitting Bull, in their continuous struggle against alien invasion. Many illustrations.

Georgakas, Dan. Red Shadows: The History of Native Americans from 1600 to 1900, from the Desert to the Pacific Coast. Doubleday 1973.

A bird's-eye view of the Indians of western United States, with glimpses of their culture, the lives of their great chiefs, and their struggles against the whites. Insight into the diversity of Indian cultures is gained through descriptions of customs and traditions such as the ceremonies, clowns, and dolls of the Pueblo, the agriculture and irrigation methods of the Pima and Papago, and the potlatches and totem poles of the Northwest Indians. However, the cultures of other tribes were forced into oblivion because they could not survive the invasion of white civilization. The book covers events of Indian history—such as the 300-mile trek of the Navajos to Bosque Redondo in New Mexico and the Modoc battles against the United States Army—and individuals such as Ishi, the last of the Yahi, the courageous Chief Joseph, and Apache leader Geronimo.

Gurko, Miriam. Indian America: The Black Hawk War. Illus. Richard Cuffari. T Y Crowell 1970.

"A glorious achievement" was what Europeans called the discovery and conquest of America. But the Indians, who had discovered the continent thousands of years before, saw it differently. Gurko epitomizes the struggle between the two forces with a discussion of the brief and disastrous war of Chief Black Hawk. Conflict between the two Sac leaders—Keokuk, polite and self-possessed, and Black Hawk, proud and headstrong—and bad advice from the Prophet were internal problems of the tribes. But greed for land, betrayal, and the whites' superior fighting forces finally led to Black Hawk's tragic downfall.

"This is the kind of corrective history that should be read by all high school students" (*Best Sellers*, 1 July 1970, p. 144).

Hagan, William T. American Indians. U of Chicago Pr 1961.

Hagan's history of Indian-white relations from the colonial period through the 1850s is concerned with the tragic encounter between the unequal forces of the United States government and the Indians. The book recognizes the differences among tribes, from the warlike Comanches to the gentle Papagos, who regarded war as a form of insanity. Awareness of these differences would have demonstrated to early settlers that one policy for all tribes was doomed from the beginning. Some critics claim that the book contains distortions—the main one, according to the American Indian Historical Society, being its generalization of personal characteristics presumably held in common by whole tribes.

"*American Indians* presents some useful information. If one is aware of the misconceptions existing in the book, the distortions and omissions of historic fact, it can be utilized within these limitations" (*Textbooks and the American Indian*, p. 160). "[It is among] other outstanding books of recent years" (Vine Deloria, Jr., in introduction to *Indians of the Americas* by Edwin Embree [see Senior Traditional Life and Culture]).

Icenhower, Joseph B. **Tecumseh and the Indian Confederation, 1811-1813: The Indian Nations East of the Mississippi Are Defeated.** Watts 1975.

Tecumseh, a chief of the Shawnee tribe, struggled in the early nineteenth century to unite all Indian tribes east of the Mississippi into a strong confederation to oppose further white takeover of tribal lands. But the Indians' hope for unification ended tragically with Tecumseh's death on the battlefield. The book portrays Tecumseh as a courageous and noble individual who drew praise and admiration from friend and foe alike. Interesting details about his life are provided, such as the belief that his birth was prophetic because a fiery meteor crossed the sky at the time. The book also describes the roles of well-known white leaders of the time, such as Thomas Jefferson, William Henry Harrison, and Anthony Wayne. Many illustrations and maps.

Jones, Jayne Clark. **The American Indian in America.** 2 vols. Lerner Pubns 1973.

The history of the American Indian is traced from prehistory to modern times. The geographical areas covered are the Arctic, Subarctic Woodlands, Northwest Coast, American Desert, Eastern Woodlands, and Great Plains. Volume I covers the prehistoric beginnings through the colonial period. Volume II begins in the nineteenth century when white expansion into Indian lands was condoned and thought to be inevitable and justified. A description of the removal of the Eastern tribes from their homelands is followed by an account of the so-called winning of the West. The section on the twentieth century shows the Indians experiencing a reawakening and speaking out for their rights with a united voice. The book concludes with a discussion of Amerindian contributions to society, listing well-known Indian political leaders, leaders in government administration, modern Indian warrior artists and craftsworkers, writers, musicians, dancers, entertainers, sports figures, and community leaders. A classification of Indian languages into related families is included. Many photographs and paintings help make this a valuable source for the history of the American Indian.

Jones, Kenneth M. **War with the Seminoles: 1835-1842—The Florida Indians Fight for Their Freedom and Homeland.** Watts 1975.

A comprehensive history of the Seminoles' attempt to defend their homeland and resist banishment to the West. In the nineteenth century, seven years of bloody warfare resulted from the many broken treaties and unkept promises. When the Seminoles were destroyed as a nation in Florida, many Indians were removed to areas west of the Mississippi, with those remaining seeking refuge in the Everglades. Many photographs of leaders and events.

Katz, Jane B., compiler and editor. **Let Me Be a Free Man: A Documentary History of Indian Resistance.** Lerner Pubns 1975.

An anthology of Indian writings covering the struggle against the advancing whites from 1607 through the Wounded Knee trial of 1974. It is an important alternative to standard histories written from the white viewpoint. Beginning with King Powhatan's doomed effort at peaceful coexistence, it gives highlights of the conquest years 1607-1890, including the campaigns of King Philip of the Pequots, Tecumseh of the Shawnees, and Black Hawk of the Sauks. Other important leaders who tell their stories include Chief Joseph, Yellow Wolf, Red Cloud, Black Kettle, Chief Two Moons, and Geronimo. The Sioux prophet Black Elk tells of the bitter climax at Wounded Knee, where "a people's dream died," and the account of the Wounded Knee massacre comes from Sioux Chief Standing Bear. Vine Deloria, Jr., writes of twentieth century revolt, beginning with the Indian uprising at Alcatraz, through the trial of Russell Means and Dennis Banks after the Wounded Knee occupation.

La Farge, Oliver. **A Pictorial History of the American Indian.**
Crown 1956.

Beginning with evidence of the Folsom Man of twelve to fifteen thousand years ago, this collection of 350 illustrations,
including many full-color plates, gives a panoramic picture of
the Indians. It covers their great events, heroes, modern schools,
crafts, and way of life. Prepared by the Institute of American
Indian Arts.

"Excellent material for secondary school courses in history
or for general interest" (*About Indians*, p. 207).

Meltzer, Milton. **Hunted Like a Wolf: The Story of the Seminole
War.** Dell 1972.

From 1835 to 1842, the Seminole Indians of Florida fought to
defend their homeland against invasion by American troops.
An offshoot of the Creek, the Seminoles included some freed
and escaped blacks. The whites wanted land and slaves; the
Seminoles had the land and were sheltering refugee slaves.
Through treachery and superior forces, the United States
drove four thousand Seminoles into exile until, by 1850, the
Indian removal was virtually completed. Based on solid research.
Also for senior high school students.

Smith, Rex Alan. **Moon of Popping Trees.** Readers Digest Pr 1975.

The author was asked by *Reader's Digest* to investigate and
report on the Indian problems in relation to the occupation of
Wounded Knee—at about the time when the American public
was asking what happened at Wounded Knee "the first time."
What began as an article became a book. As he traveled, studied,
and interviewed, Smith found that the truth lay somewhere
between the picture of the "pure-hearted, stalwart settler
defending his family against a horde of shrieking savages" and
that of "an Indian, noble and speaking with a straight tongue,
defending himself against brutal oppression by greedy, racist
whites." The story begins with the council on Horse Creek in
1851 between United States representatives and the southern
Lakota and the Cheyenne, and it ends in 1890 with the battle
at Wounded Knee.

Spicer, Edward H. **A Short History of the Indians of the United
States.** Van Nos Reinhold 1969.

The first half of this book is a brief history of tribes and their
movements to about 1967. The second contains significant

documents organized around themes: Indian history as seen by Indians, white policy, white viewpoints, and Indian prophets and spokesmen. Selections are based on the following assumptions: Indian history is longer than white history in America; Indian history did not stop when the whites came but continued to develop according to the uniqueness of each tribe; Indian-Indian relations are a reality; and since the 1940s there has been a renaissance of cultural development among many tribes.

"Valuable objective treatment" (*Textbooks and the American Indian*, p. 256).

Sumners, Cecil L. **Chief Tishomingo: A History of the Chickasaw Indians and Some Historical Events of Their Era (1737-1839).** Sumners 1974.

This story of Chief Tishomingo, the last great war chief of the Chickasaw Indians, is also a collection of stories and historical facts about the tribe. Tishomingo lived for more than a hundred years, from about 1737 to 1838 or 1839. He was a counselor to the tribe and knew U.S. presidents from Washington to Jackson. The author, a senator from Mississippi, reports that Tishomingo was of special help to his tribe and his country in bringing about a peaceful migration of the Chickasaw to the West. This privately published book could have benefited from careful editing.

Weems, John Edward. **Death Song: The Last of the Indian Wars.** Doubleday 1976.

Beginning with stories told him by his grandfather, a Texas pioneer, Weems has researched the lives of seven people, white and Indian, who lived through the last of the Indian wars: John G. Bourke, a liberal cavalry officer who frequently sympathized with his enemies; Robert Goldthwaite Carter, a young officer in the Fourth Cavalry who wanted to contribute to the "opening of the West"; Libbie and George Custer; Geronimo; Quanah Parker; and Satanta, Kiowan "orator of the Plains." A very human picture of the drama, tragedy, and changes in the lives of these people during 1867-1890, although somewhat lacking in continuity. Emphasis is on the Kiowas, Comanches, and Apaches.

Senior High and Adult

Ambrose, Stephen E. **Crazy Horse and Custer: The Parallel Lives of Two American Warriors.** Illus. Kenneth Francis Dewey. Doubleday 1975.

Ambrose, a professor of history and author of several books on aspects of American history, finds many parallels in the lives of Crazy Horse and Custer, despite the vast differences that also existed. Both were aggressive men and lovers of war; they were born at about the same time and died within a year of each other; both had happy family lives as they grew up; each was humiliated at the height of his career because of a relationship with the woman he loved; both established leadership roles after their humiliation; neither man drank; and both loved the hunt and the chase on the prairies. Parallels are developed from the men's births, through the Battle of the Little Bighorn, to their deaths. A scholarly book about the interesting personal stories of two important Americans.

Andrist, Ralph K. **Long Death: The Last Days of the Plains Indian.** Macmillan 1969.

A history of the military conquest of the Plains Indians, beginning with the Santee Sioux rebellion in Minnesota in 1862 and ending with the Battle of Wounded Knee in 1890. Included are accounts of campaigns against the Nez Perces, Cheyennes and Arapahos, Kiowas, Comanches, Modocs, Bannocks, and Utes. The book vividly describes the Indians' desperation in the face of disease, starvation, and treachery of the whites and their treaties. Rather specialized; good reading for students especially interested in history. Cited by Sun Bear in *Buffalo Hearts*.

["It is among] other outstanding books of recent years" (Vine Deloria, Jr., in his introduction to *Indians of the Americas*, by Edwin Embree).

Bailey, M. Thomas. **Reconstruction in Indian Territory: A Story of Avarice, Discrimination, and Opportunism.** Kennikat 1972.

This book fills a gap in historical research. Much has been written about the Reconstruction Period east of the Mississippi River, but few studies have been done on the tragic effect of Reconstruction on the Five Civilized Nations who, before the

Civil War, had been removed from the East Coast and who had considered themselves to be independent nations during the War. After 1871 the United States dealt with the Indian republics, not as sovereign nations, but as territories subject to Congressional control. In 1898 tribal courts were abolished, and in 1901 all Indians in Indian Territory were declared citizens of the United States, an act that eliminated any independence the tribes had.

Bataille, Gretchen M., David M. Gradwohl, and Charles L. P. Silet, editors. **The Worlds between Two Rivers: Perspectives on American Indians in Iowa.** Iowa St U Pr 1978.

This collection of thirteen articles presents an accurate picture of the Native Americans in Iowa. Topics range from the archaeology and history of Iowa's earliest residents to the effect of urbanization. Also included are a bibliography and articles on errors in the literature about Iowa's Indians, the history of the Mesquakie, and the problems of modern Indians who need both white and Indian educations. A model effort which corrects erroneous information about Indians which is often perpetuated in school materials.

Blish, Helen, editor. **A Pictographic History of the Oglala Sioux.** U of Nebr Pr 1967.

Bad Heart Bull, self-appointed tribal historian, made more than four hundred drawings and notations between 1890 and his death in 1913, providing a visual record of Sioux culture. Events depicted include the Sun Dance, Sioux-Crow fights, the Battle of the Little Bighorn, the Ghost Dance, and Fourth of July Indian shows. While an undergraduate at the University of Nebraska, the editor found the ledger containing Bad Heart Bull's drawings at Pine Ridge Reservation in South Dakota and persuaded his sister, Dollie Pretty Cloud, to allow the use of the book during 1927–1940 for an annual fee. Blish interviewed He Dog and Short Bull for interpretations of the illustrations. Cited in *American Indian Authors.*

Branch, E. Douglas. **The Hunting of the Buffalo.** U of Nebr Pr 1962.

A rather detailed account of the buffalo and its place in the history of North America, beginning with early evidence of buffalo bones and the first mention of the animal in history books. The book contains accounts of the habits of the animal, how it was used by Indians and whites, and how it was hunted extensively—and the eventual realization that it was disappearing and needed to be preserved.

Brandon, William, editor. The American Heritage Book of Indians. Dell 1964.

This is the history of Indian tribes from prehistoric times until their confinement on reservations and their forced acceptance of white ways. The book covers not only Indians of the United States but also the Aztec and Mayan empires and the northern tribes such as Eskimos. It emphasizes contacts of Indian cultures with other tribes and the white world. Some critics believe the emphasis is misplaced in some instances. On *Akwesasne Notes* basic library list.

"Good overview of native Americans. Well written, can be used in high school classes" (*Textbooks and the American Indian*, p. 256).

Brandon, William. The Last Americans: The Indian in American Culture. McGraw 1974.

A revision and updating of the author's *American Heritage Book of Indians* (this section), including recent information about archaeological discoveries and the quality of modern Indian life on reservations. As in the earlier book, emphasis is on the influence of American Indian societies on the history of America. A special feature is a selection of original Indian poetry.

"Brandon has contributed an impressive chapter toward the writing of a general Indian history" (D'Arcy McNickle, *Nation*, 7 December 1974, p. 599). "I am sure . . . that many historians will want this book on their shelves as a reference. The college student and general adult reader, however, should buy the 95¢ paperback of *The American Heritage Book of Indians* and save themselves $12.00" (*American Indian Quarterly* 2:142, Summer 1975).

Brown, Dee. Bury My Heart at Wounded Knee: An Indian History of the American West. Bantam 1971.

An account of the whites' invasion of Indian lands in the late nineteenth century and their broken promises, written with sympathy toward the Indians. Incident by incident it shows the whites destroying the land, the people, and their way of life. Indian attacks on whites are viewed as a retaliation. Few books arouse such sympathy for the Indians and such guilt on the part of the whites. The reader is aided in seeing things from the Indian point of view by the use of Indian names for historical figures: Carson is Rope Thrower; William T. Sherman is Great Warrior; Custer is Long Hair. Included are quotations from testimonies of Indians who were present when the events occurred. On *Akwesasne Notes* basic library list.

"Sympathetically written, utilizing documents long known to native people and fair-minded scholars, this book is a conscience-ridden tale finally told, of extermination, broken treaties, mistreatment, and cultural genocide" (*Indian Historian* 4:26, Summer 1971). "Dee Brown lets the Indian voice be heard at last" (*About Indians*, p. 133).

Carter, Samuel, III. **Cherokee Sunset: A Nation Betrayed—A Narrative of Travail and Triumph, Persecution and Exile.** Doubleday 1976.

In a carefully documented and detailed story, Carter emphasizes the Cherokees' decision to settle on the land, to develop plantations as the whites were doing, and in general to be good American citizens. They fought alongside Andrew Jackson in 1814 and turned the tide of the Creek campaign in favor of their ally, the United States. They established schools, sent their young people North to be educated, created their own alphabet, and published their own newspaper, *Cherokee Phoenix*. But because white settlers coveted their fertile lands and the gold that was found there and because Andrew Jackson turned against them, they gave up more and more land and finally were forced to follow the "Trail of Tears" to Oklahoma. The author's purpose is to document the development of what might have become an Indian parliamentary democracy in the eastern United States, had the white Americans not intervened with their greed. He deals only briefly with the migration and the establishment of the new nation in the West.

Collier, John. **Indians of the Americas: The Long Hope.** Ment. NAL 1952.

This history begins with the Indians who crossed the Bering land bridge from Asia to North America. It develops the history and culture of the Incas and Aztecs to the time of the Spanish conquest, describes the democracy of the peace-loving Iroquois, discusses the culture of the Plains Indians, and concludes with suggestions and predictions for the future. The author served under President Franklin Roosevelt as United States commissioner of Indian affairs during 1933-1945. With sympathy toward the Indian, he hoped that non-Indians might open their minds to the quality of the Indian heritage. Recommended by the Institute of American Indian Arts for courses in American history. On *Akwesasne Notes* basic library list.

Cook, Sherburne F. **The Conflict between the California Indian and White Civilization.** U of Cal Pr 1976.

Six essays, written by a biologist in the late 1930s and published between 1940 and 1943. The subjects are: The Indian versus the Spanish Mission, The Physical and Demographic Reaction of the Nonmission Indians in Colonial and Provincial California, The American Invasion 1848-1870, Trends in Marriage and Divorce since 1850, Population Trends among California Mission Indians, and The Dietary Adptation among California and Nevada Indians. Through the use of mission archives, interviews, Federal Indian Affairs records, memoirs, travel accounts, newspapers, and local history, the author has challenged the popular and scholarly orthodoxy of his day.

Corle, Edwin. **The Gila: River of the Southwest.** Illus. Ross Santee. U of Nebr Pr 1964.

The Gila River, which flows through southern Arizona to the Colorado, was the scene of much history of the Southwest, including that of area Indians. Along its shores flourished the pre-Columbian culture of the Hohokam, knowledgeable in masonry, irrigation, agriculture, astronomy, and architecture. Some time later it was the setting for struggles between whites and Apaches, with treachery, violence, and bravery on both sides. The author combines history, geography, anecdotes, and atmosphere into a readable book.

Cortés, Carlos E., et al., editors. **Three Perspectives on Ethnicity: Blacks, Chicanos, and Native Americans.** Putnam 1976.

An anthology of documents and articles which examine the promise of America from the point of view of three minorities—blacks, Chicanos, and Native Americans. The articles are divided into six sections: the colonial and early national period, the nineteenth century wars, the impact of urbanization, the impact of institutions such as the military and education, the development of ethnic self-affirmation, and the emergence of the new militancy. The Native American viewpoint is usually represented by white writers such as Nancy Lurie, Stan Steiner, and John Collier, with the only Native American writers being Chief Joseph and Vine Deloria, Jr.

Dale, Edward Everett. The Indians of the Southwest: A Century of Development under the United States. U of Okla Pr 1949.

When the Treaty of Guadalupe Hidalgo was signed in 1848, the United States became responsible for many tribes of Indians, about which the government and the American people of the period knew little. This book traces the history of this so-called federal undertaking as it relates to the Indians of southern and central California, Nevada, Utah, Arizona, and western New Mexico. The author was a history professor at the University of Oklahoma and a member of the Meriam Commission, which studied problems of Indian education. The book is well illustrated.

Davis, Britton (editor M. M. Quaife). The Truth about Geronimo. U of Nebr Pr 1976.

Following graduation from West Point in 1881, Davis was assigned to service in Wyoming and later to San Carlos, the Apache Reservation. There he was placed in charge of training Indian scouts, whom he led in 1885–86 in the Geronimo Campaign, hunting down the Apaches who escaped from San Carlos. Davis was acquainted with the leaders of the Apache resistance—Geronimo, Loco, Chatto, Benito, Juh, Nana, and the young Mangus. While giving the army's side of the campaign, Davis's story is filled with adventure and entertainment. For a book that presents the Apaches' side of the campaign, see *In the Days of Victorio* by Eve Ball (Senior Biography).

Debo, Angie. A History of the Indians of the United States. U of Okla Pr 1970.

This history grew out of a course in Indian history which the author taught to thirty-six teachers of Indian children in Indian Bureau schools and mission schools. The history covers Eskimos and Aleuts as well as the most important tribes in the mainland United States. It begins with the first meetings of whites with various tribes, and continues through the dispossession of the

Indians, to modern times and current government Indian policy. "Miss Debo's final chapter is not yet history and the hope of which it speaks has yet to be realized" (N. Scott Momaday, *New York Times Book Review*, 7 March 1971, p. 370w).

Deloria, Vine, Jr., editor. Of Utmost Good Faith. Bantam 1972.

The author, a Sioux and a lawyer and civil rights leader, has collected documents that deal with relations between the United States government and Indian tribes, including judicial rulings, treaties, acts, and agreements, from 1830 to the present, as well as speeches by both Indians and white defenders of Indian rights. The title comes from a government ordinance of 1789. Deloria comments on the selections, which make the case that the United States has not kept "the utmost good faith" with the Indians. See also *Custer Died for Your Sins* and *We Talk, You Listen*, both by the same author (Senior Modern Life).

"Invaluable information is organized within the bounds of the book" (*About Indians*, p. 158).

Dial, Adolph L., and David K. Eliades. The Only Land I Know: A History of the Lumbee Indians. Indian Hist Pr 1974.

The Lumbee Indians live in Robeson County, North Carolina, where they have accepted the ways, language, religion, and economy of the whites while retaining their Indian heritage. This is the story of their beginnings, their struggle for recognition, and their fight against racial prejudice. They have never been placed on reservations, nor have they been wards of the state or of the federal government. Dial is a Lumbee Indian and a college administrator, and Eliades is a history professor.

"It should and probably will dissolve the Indian stereotype. Hopefully, to be buried and never-more resurrected" (*Indian Historian* 8:51, Spring 1975).

Faulk, Odie B. The Geronimo Campaign. Oxford U Pr 1969.

The Geronimo campaign ended with the surrender of the great Apache chief to Lt. Charles B. Gatewood on the banks of the Bavispe River in August 1886. The record does not end there, however, but goes on to betrayal by the United States government. Faulk writes, "Neither side wanted war, both thought they were right." The book includes much new material collected by the son of Lieutenant Gatewood, who arranged the surrender and was the only white person Geronimo trusted.

"A first-rate story . . . treated with precision and insight, confidence and sensitivity" (N. Scott Momaday, *New York Times Book Review*, 2 February 1969, p. 10).

Fehrenbach, T. R. Comanches: The Destruction of a People. Knopf 1974.

The Comanches are a tribe that has undergone less extensive research than have some other tribes. Although they destroyed the Spanish dream of empire in North America, blocked the French advance into the Southwest, and delayed the Anglo-American conquest, no study was made of the Comanches until the 1930s, and by then their folk traditions and history were lost or obscured by contacts with white civilization. Here the author discusses the probable movements of this tribe before they met the whites, then continues the history with their separation from their Shoshone cousins, when they moved onto the plains to become horse breeders, to their final destruction, when Quanah, their half-white chief, finally chose surrender and took his people to the reservation in June 1875. Fehrenbach seems to stress the cruelty of the Comanches somewhat more than necessary. The book has also been criticized for its lack of documentation and some errors of fact.

Foreman, Grant. The Five Civilized Tribes. U of Okla Pr 1971.

The Cherokees, Chickasaws, Choctaws, Creeks, and Seminoles adopted white ways and civilization much faster than other tribes. Eventually the whites coveted their property and wealth and from 1830 to 1840, by law and oppression, they forced most members of these tribes to move from the Southeast to areas of present-day Oklahoma—in what is called the Trail of Tears because of the incredible hardship and suffering of the Indians as they moved west. A carefully documented history, valuable for students researching the period or the tribes.

"[It is] among the best of the [Civilization of the American Indian Series]" (Vine Deloria, Jr., in the introduction to *Indians of the Americas*, by Edwin Embree).

Fumoleau, René, OMI. As Long as This Land Shall Last: A History of Treaty 8 and Treaty 11, 1870-1939. McClelland n.d.

For many years the Mackenzie area of the Northwest Territories was of little concern to the Canadian government; it was important mainly for the trapping which the Indians did. Then gold and oil were discovered there and the area became valuable. Two treaties have been signed between the Indians of the region and the Canadian government. In 1973 sixteen Indian chiefs claimed an interest in the area and after six months of legal procedures, Judge William G. Morrow decided that the Indians had not relinquished all claim to the land under terms of the two treaties. This study brings together all of the documents, correspondence, and memories of people involved.

Gard, Wayne. **The Great Buffalo Hunt: Its History and Drama and Its Role in the Opening of the West.** Illus. Nick Eggenhofer. U of Nebr Pr 1968.

A book full of human interest about Indians and whites, telling of buffalo hunting from 1871 to 1883 and its significance in the conquest of the West. There are facts about the animal's habits and buffalo hunting as a sport, and songs and legends of buffalo hunting. The author, a newspaper man who was interested in western history, gathered his material while following the trails of buffalo hunters across the Great Plains.

Haines, Francis. **The Plains Indians: Their Origins, Migrations, and Cultural Development.** T Y Crowell 1976.

This account begins in about the year 1200, when supposedly no tribes lived in the Great Plains although a number were moving in that direction. By 1850 twenty-seven tribes dominated the Plains. Haines traces the migration of these tribes into and through the Great Plains, noting how each tribe adjusted to the environment and how their history and culture were shaped by the droughts that came to the Southwest, and by the coming of the whites with their smallpox, guns, and horses. The author concludes his history with a study of the various tribes' participation in the Sun Dance.

"This reviewer takes objection to the constant use of the words 'nomadic' and 'roaming' in describing the movements of the tribes. . . . They traveled in search of game. . . . The author completely ignores the profound philosophy of the tribes" (*Wassaja* 4:8, May 1976).

Haley, James L. **The Buffalo War: The History of the Red River Indian Uprising of 1874.** Doubleday 1976.

In 1872-74 Josiah Wright Mooar, engaged in a successful business of hunting buffalo for hides to export, killed more than four million buffalo on the southern plains in what is now Kansas, Oklahoma, and Texas. This area had for several hundred years been the hunting grounds for the Cheyenne, Arapaho, Kiowa, and Comanche tribes, who resisted the invasion by attacking the hunters' huts. Haley examines all of the forces that led to the Buffalo War, called by General Phil Sheridan "the most successful Indian campaign ever waged." Because so many tribes and chiefs were involved, there were competing factions among the Indians as well as among the whites. Haley has used letters and reports of the period for his research.

Heidenreich, Conrad E. **Huronia: A History and Geography of the Huron Indians, 1600–1650.** McClelland 1971.

Today the area called Huronia is a tourist region of Canada encompassing most of Simcoe County, Ontario, on the shores of Georgian Bay. In the first half of the seventeenth century, its northern portion was occupied by semisedentary, agricultural Indians of the Huron Confederacy, a group belonging to the Iroquoian-speaking peoples. With an estimated population of 21,000 in about 340 square miles, Huronia was probably the most densely populated area of aboriginal Canada. This is a scholarly reconstruction of its history, grouped under six topics: Huronia as a geographical region, physical aspects of the land, population estimates, settlement patterns, the Huron subsistence economy, and the Huron-French politics and trade. Based on historical and archaeological materials and modern statistics and linguistics. 1971 winner of the Sainte-Marie Prize in history.

Heidenreich, Conrad E., and Arthur J. Ray. **The Early Fur Trades: A Study in Cultural Interaction.** McClelland 1976.

This study is a description and comparison of two early fur-trading systems in Canada: the French-Indian fur trade in the eastern Great Lakes area from the early 1600s to its destruction in 1649, and the British system as evidenced by the first hundred years of Hudson's Bay Company in western Canada. The French lived with the Indians, learned their languages, and took sides in Indian wars. The English were interested solely in furs, took no sides in Indian wars, and made no attempt to Christianize the Indian. The sources for the British trade are the diaries of Hudson's Bay Company; for the French trade, the observations of men who lived and travelled with the Indians. Funded by the Canadian Studies Foundation and the Canadian Association of Geographers. Well illustrated with maps and old engravings. Includes study questions.

Hoig, Stan. **The Battle of the Washita: The Sheridan-Custer Indian Campaign of 1867-69.** Doubleday 1976.

George Armstrong Custer won only one battle against the Indians—the Battle of Washita, against the village of Chief Black Kettle of the Cheyennes. Four years earlier, in 1864, Black Kettle's village at Sand Creek had been attacked by troops under Colonel John M. Chivington in an engagement that has generally been called a "massacre." Custer's attack in 1868 has, on the word of Custer, been considered justified. This is the first study of the events before and after the battle; its purpose is to try to determine the reasons for the attack.

Hudson, Charles M., editor. **Four Centuries of Southern Indians.** U of Ga Pr 1975.

Scholars have learned little about the earliest history of the Indians of the Southeast, although there is evidence to suggest that they had the most complex social structure of all of the tribes in the continental United States. They apparently lived in large towns, built mounds and earthworks, enjoyed rich religious and artistic achievements, and had a flourishing economy based on agriculture and hunting. The nine essays in this volume cover four hundred years, beginning with early French and Spanish relations with the Timucuan Indians in northern Florida in the sixteenth century and ending with institution-building among the Cherokees after their removal to Oklahoma. The papers are by historians and anthropologists.

"The nine papers presented in *Four Centuries of Southern Indians* suggest the rich possibilities for research in Southeastern Indian history and culture. Prefaced with a fine introduction by Professor Hudson, the papers explore the variety of past and present issues touching the lives of many tribes" (*American Indian Quarterly* 2:377, Winter 1975-76).

Hyde, George E. **Red Cloud's Folk: A History of the Oglala Sioux Indians.** U of Okla Pr 1968.

Much has been written about the resistance chiefs, such as Sitting Bull and Crazy Horse, but perhaps those who suffered most were the agency Sioux, who outnumbered the hostiles and suffered punishment and deprivation at the hands of Indian agents and the army because of their more warlike relatives. This is a history of Indians who ultimately became followers of Chief Red Cloud, beginning with earliest records of the Teton Sioux and their conflicts with the better-armed Crees, Assiniboines, and Chippewas, and ending with the establishment of Pine Ridge Reservation. During 1865–1877, the years of greatest conflict, Red Cloud was one of the greatest of Sioux leaders in battle and diplomacy. The author, a research historian, gathered his material from official reports, Indian accounts, agency employees, traders, and interpreters.

Hyde, George E. Spotted Tail's Folk: A History of the Brulé Sioux. U of Okla Pr 1961.

This biography of Brulé Sioux chief Spotted Tail is also a story of his people. Spotted Tail has been maligned by biographers of warlike chiefs such as Crazy Horse and Sitting Bull, as well as by some Indian authors, including Charles Eastman, but this book presents his side of the story. Although some will disagree with Hyde's interpretation, he maintains that Spotted Tail demonstrated characteristics of great leadership and bravery in trying to save his people without fighting the whites. He showed no fear in fighting other Indians, but Spotted Tail believed it was useless for the Indian to do battle with the whites because of their technical advantages. Based on solid research and easily read, this book presents a side of history that deserves to be told.

"[It is] among the outstanding books in [The Civilization of the American Indian Series]" (Vine Deloria, Jr., in the introduction to *Indians of the Americas*, by Edwin Embree).

Jacobs, Paul, and Saul Landau. To Serve the Devil. 2 vols. Random 1971.

The authors have studied the phenomenon of the parallel existence of democracy and racism in United States history. Volume 1, subtitled *Natives and Slaves*, discusses the subject in relation to Indians, blacks, and Chicanos. Volume 2, *Colonials and Sojourners*, discusses it in relation to Hawaiians, Chinese, Japanese, and Puerto Ricans. Each section begins with the authors' historical analysis of racism against the particular group, followed by a series of supporting documents. The authors present evidence that any minority which blocks what the whites consider their progress is punished for it. Some of the documents presented in each section are by members of the race; others are those of white people or the government. The documentary part of the Indian section contains items such as Chief Tecumseh's plea for resistance and President Jackson's warning letter to the Seminoles.

Jacobs, Wilbur R. Dispossessing the American Indian. Scribner 1972.

The author, a professor of history, discusses the clash of the Eastern Woodland Indians with Anglo-American pioneers of the eighteenth century. This is the story of the destruction of the Indians, their culture, and the ecological balance. The author's avowed purpose is "to throw more light on the ecology of the frontier and on the shadowy history of early native-white relations." Although generally sympathetic to the Indians, Jacobs calls them Stone Age people, comparing their contact with whites to that of aborigines with whites in Australia and New Guinea, and he speaks of "Indian savagery" in their counterattacks.

Jaenen, Cornelius J. Friend and Foe: Aspects of French-Amerindian Cultural Contact in the Sixteenth and Seventeenth Centuries. McClelland 1976.

Ever since Francis Parkman said that the Spanish "crushed" the Indians, the English "scorned and neglected" them, but the French "embraced and cherished" them, it has been assumed that somehow the French got along better with the Amerindians than the British and Spanish did. Jaenen, a Canadian historian, examines the meeting of the French and Indian cultures during the sixteenth and seventeenth centuries on several grounds: attitudes toward nature, evangelism and its results, social problems, barbarism and cruelty, and integration and segregation. Recognizing that perhaps the Amerindians saw the British as colonists, displacing the agricultural Iroquoian tribes, while they saw the French as traders and soldiers laden with baubles, asking only furs and hospitality, the author points out that the French still had attitudes that caused strained relations with the Indians. The French were convinced that they were at the pinnacle of a rational and Christian civilization; the Amerindians regarded the French as effeminate, weak, improvident, and domineering; the French saw themselves controlling nature while the Indians knew they were dependent on it; and the place of religion and education in Indian societies was not understood by the French. Jaenen's study differs from other such studies in its attempt to examine the Indians' view of the French as well as the French view of the Indians. 1973 winner of the Sainte-Marie Prize in history.

Jahoda, Gloria. The Trail of Tears: The Story of the American Indian Removals, 1813-1855. HR&W 1975.

The author, a student of anthropology, describes the results of President Andrew Jackson's Removal Policy, under which the Indians living east of the Mississippi were forcibly removed from their lands and resettled in the West. Cherokees, Creeks, Choctaws, Chickasaws, Seminoles, Shawnees, Delawares, Senecas and others were brutally forced to migrate, and thousands died from cold, hunger, and disease. In addition, they had to live near or among other tribes who also were suffering under the encroachment. The tragedy of this period in American history is told with sympathy for the Indians and outrage at the whites who participated in formulating and carrying out the policy. Some readers have criticized the scarcity of footnotes, insufficient use of original materials, and some errors of fact.

"The general reader, for which it was written, will learn much he should know of the darker part of our past which will balance the all too often rosy picture given of our brave pioneer forefathers and great statesmen" (*American Indian Quarterly* 3:62, Spring 1977).

Jennings, Francis. The Invasion of America: Indians, Colonialism, and the Cant of Conquest. U of NC Pr 1975.

Jennings undermines many widely held concepts about the settlement of the American continent. One is that the Europeans settled and developed a virgin wilderness. He claims that, had that been the case, European settlements would not have survived. Europeans lacked the skills to survive in a wilderness, but they possessed the skills to conquer another people, which they did. The author also refutes the claim that Native Americans were not a very large population because in their savagery they fought and killed each other. According to Jennings, it was the disease and demoralization which the Europeans brought that depleted tribal populations. Jennings first analyzes some commonly held concepts about the East Coast and its inhabitants when Europeans first began to settle, and follows with a more detailed analysis of New England as the colonists found it.

"A vigorous, extensively researched book" (*American Indian Quarterly* 2:364, Winter 1975-76). In the areas of his strengths Jennings is very good indeed. . . . The whole of his work is shaped by a heresy I applaud and wish were not so rare" (*Indian Historian* 9:26, Fall 1976).

McGee, Harold Franklin, Jr., editor. The Native Peoples of Atlantic Canada: A History of Ethnic Interaction. McClelland 1974.

A series of documents giving a history of the interaction between the native peoples of Canada, especially the Micmac, and the Europeans. The first selection presents a portion of the earliest evidence of cultural interaction, Erik the Red's Saga. Another selection tells about interaction with the Beothuk, who are now extinct. A number of letters and reports are included.

McNickle, D'Arcy. Native American Tribalism: Indian Survivals and Renewals. Oxford U Pr 1973.

The author, a member of the Flathead Tribe of Montana, traces the evolution of the whites' treatment of Indians, from the Spanish and English colonial periods to the present, in both the United States and Canada. It is his belief that Indians will adopt knowledge and technology, but that they need to fit these changes into their own ways of life. If they are not allowed tribal determination, "anger will hang in the air, like a combustible vapor, for some time to come" (p. xii). An updating and enlargement of the author's earlier work, *The Indian Tribes of the United States: Ethnic and Cultural Survival.*

"It is an excellent summary of the history of Indian-white relations in North America from the time of discovery to 1973" (*American Indian Quarterly* 1:297, Winter 1974-75).

McNickle, D'Arcy. They Came Here First: The Epic of the American Indian. Octagon 1972.

This history of American Indians by the co-founder of the National Congress of American Indians traces the tribes from their first migrations to North America across the Bering land bridge to their despair as the whites encroached upon their lands. The author speculates on the birth of the race in Asia and includes descriptions of many Indian cultures, their languages, and their ways of life. A scholarly book. Cited in *American Indian Authors.*

McReynolds, Edwin C. The Seminoles. U of Okla Pr 1967.

A small group from mixed tribes became known as Seminoles at about the time of the British occupation of Florida, 1763-83. This is a history of these people—some three thousand in all, two-thirds of whom were Indian and about one-third Negro freedmen—from the time when they struggled against dispossession to 1901 when an act made U.S. citizens of all members of the Five Civilized Tribes. A detailed military and political history. For a fictional treatment, see the novel *Seminole* or the drama by the same name both by Theodore Pratt (Senior Fiction). Cited by Sun Bear in *Buffalo Hearts.*

Meyer, Roy W. The Village Indians of the Upper Missouri: The Mandans, Hidatsas, and Arikaras. U of Nebr Pr 1977.

The history and culture of prairie Indians is often assumed to be typified by that of tribes like the Sioux and Cheyenne, who moved about, following game. But three tribes of village Indians who grew some of their food in gardens were the Mandans, Hidatsas, and Arikaras. This is their history, from prehistoric times through early contacts with whites, to the 1837 smallpox epidemic which devastated the tribes and caused them to combine forces and establish one last earth-lodge settlement, Like-a-Fishhook Village. Between 1862 and 1886 the village was broken up and the people scattered throughout the Fort Berthold Reservation. In the 1930s and 1940s the Garrison Dam forced considerable relocation. A scholarly work.

Milligan, Edward A. Dakota Twilight: The Standing Rock Sioux, 1874-1890. Lochinvar. Exposition 1976.

The thesis of this history is that, although the Sioux won the Battle of the Little Bighorn, that victory was the beginning of the disintegration of the great Sioux Nation. There is a brief discussion of the migrations of the various parts of the Sioux tribe from Minnesota into the Dakotas. The Fort Laramie Treaty of 1868 set apart a single Great Sioux Reservation. The author believes that the Sioux tried to abide by the treaty and really wanted peace, but because of a series of violations and mistakes by government officials, the Indians' lands diminished steadily until finally they were forced into battle. Custer lost, Milligan says, because his men had defective rifles. The years that followed and led up to Wounded Knee, then, were anticlimactic. The author has lived among the Standing Rock Sioux and is an adopted member of the tribe. His interpretation comes from Indian sources and materials never before considered in the history of this period.

Miner, H. Craig. **The Corporation and the Indian: Tribal Sovereignty and Industrial Civilization in Indian Territory, 1865–1907.** U of Mo Pr 1976.

Miner, a professor of history, has studied the process by which Indian tribes lost their greatest natural possession, their tribal lands, to American corporations—railway, livestock, coal, and oil companies—which sought to enter Indian Territory in order to utilize its natural resources. Because the tribes were not united in purpose and did not understand the concept of exploiting natural resources, they saw their lands disappear in the forty years from 1865 to 1907. The relationships of corporations with the Cherokees, Choctaws, and Osages are emphasized because these tribes were fairly large and had more contact with corporations than did other tribes living in Indian Territory.

Olson, James C. **Red Cloud and the Sioux Problem.** U of Nebr Pr 1975.

This account of the life of Red Cloud, the great Oglala Sioux leader, begins with the signing of the treaty at Fort Laramie in 1851 and concludes with the "dreary years" after the Ghost Dance and the Battle of Wounded Knee in 1890, as Red Cloud led his people from their traditional life of wandering to that of the reservation. He was criticized on the one hand for giving in too easily and, on the other, for obstructing his people's progress toward civilization. The author had access to new evidence from government documents. The study focuses on Red Cloud, but the viewpoint is that of the white citizens of the United States.

Oswalt, Wendell. **This Land Was Theirs: A Study of the North American Indian.** Wiley 1966.

This book sketches both the past and present-day life of ten selected tribes in the United States and Canada. The author, a professor of anthropology, begins by discussing the history and society of each tribe at the time of initial contact with the whites. His purpose is "to present descriptive accounts of various tribes free, it is hoped, of highly technical terminology, and to trace their diverse ways of life from historic contact to their extinction or to modern times." Painstaking scholarship results in a readable, nontechnical book that combines history and ethnography.

"This book will have great reference value for the serious student" (*About Indians*, p. 241).

Parman, Donald L. The Navajos and the New Deal. Yale U Pr 1976.

Under John Collier, commissioner of Indian affairs from 1933 until 1941, the Indian Reorganization Act of 1934 reversed what had been government Indian policies of detribalization and assimilation. Collier undertook to reconstitute tribal organization, restore the tribal land base, and promote the traditional language and culture of the Indians. Because the Navajos were the largest Indian population, they were the test case for new programs. The author objectively describes the contrast between the actual operation of the New Deal Indian policies on the Navajo reservation and the theories and programs as they were conceived in Washington.

Phillips, George Harwood. Chiefs and Challengers: Indian Resistance and Cooperation in Southern California. U of Cal Pr 1975.

This study concentrates on three tribes in southern California—the Cahuilla, the Cupeno, and the Luiseno—and the response of their three leaders, Juan Antonio, Antonio Garra, and Manuelito Cota, to the encroachment of the white settlers. Since most California history is written from the whites' point of view, it is always assumed that the Indians were passive observers of their destruction. But Phillips, using mainly white sources, documents three responses by Indian leaders: resistance, withdrawal, and cooperation. By the time Americans arrived in southern California, these tribes no longer were governed by headmen of traditional lineage but by powerful territorial chiefs. From the mid-1840s to the early 1860s these chiefs at various times resisted and cooperated with the Mexicans and Anglo-Americans and so determined the course of history in southern California.

Priest, Loring Benson. Uncle Sam's Stepchildren: The Reformation of United States Indian Policy, 1865–1887. U of Nebr Pr 1975.

The period from 1865 to 1887 was one of fighting and bloodshed between Indians and whites, as a number of tribes made a last desperate attempt to defend their tribal lands from white encroachment. At the same time, the United States government was making great efforts to find a way of dealing with peaceful Indians. Many decent white people recognized that injustices were occurring and pressured their legislators to do something about them. The result in 1887 was the Dawes Act, an Indian allotment bill intended to break up reservations. The author, a professor of history, has used government documents, annual reports of Indian organizations, and newspaper clippings of the time.

Prucha, Francis Paul, editor. **Americanizing the American Indians: Writings by the "Friends of the Indian" 1880-1900.** Harvard U Pr 1973.

During the last two decades of the nineteenth century, American Indian policy was dominated by a fairly small but vocal, well-intentioned group of white Christian reformers who called themselves "Friends of the Indian." Their aim was to break down the tribal structure, culture, language, and religion of the Indians, and to transform them into American citizens exactly like whites. This group urged that reservations be divided into individual homesteads for Indians, that Indians be made citizens of the United States (even if, like the Five Civilized Nations, they wanted to be a sovereign nation), and that a universal government school system be established to hasten Americanization. This is a collection of writings of people who held these views, among them Lyman Abbott, Carl Schurz, Thomas J. Morgan, James B. Thayer, Richard H. Pratt, and Henry L. Dawes. The editor has written an introduction and headnotes.

"The book is appropriate for scholarly, student or general use" (*American Indian Quarterly* 1:114, Summer 1974). "Paul Prucha's goal of recounting the history of government policies toward Native Americans should be praised rather than maligned" (*Indian Historian* 7:50, Spring 1974).

Prucha, Francis Paul, compiler and editor. **Documents of United States Indian Policy.** U of Nebr Pr 1975.

A collection of the essential laws and official statements on United States Indian policy, from George Washington's recommendations and those of James Duane in 1783 to the Menominee Restoration Act of 1973. Included among the 161 selections are treaties, fundamental laws governing Indian relations, Supreme Court decisions, presidential messages, extracts from reports of commissioners of Indian affairs and secretaries of the interior, reports of special commissions and investigating committees, and recent proposals for Indian self-determination. A brief headnote explains each document.

"Clearly Prucha's source book has the widest application because of his general approach to the subject through which he sought to make the more important documents widely available with one volume" (*American Indian Quarterly* 3:69, Spring 1977).

Prucha, Francis Paul. **Indian Peace Medals in American History.** U of Nebr Pr 1971.

For more than a century, silver medals played an important part in Indian-white relationships. The precedent of presenting peace medals to the Indians was begun by the French, British, and Spanish, and the United States government continued the practice. The Indian chiefs were honored by these because they indicated rank, and often wore their medals when posing for portraits or photographs. Prucha discusses the use of peace medals to further relationships and tells how they were designed and made. Generously illustrated.

Sandoz, Mari. **The Beaver Men: Spearheads of Empire.** Hastings 1964.

This is the story of two and a half centuries of beaver trade and the men who were important in practicing it: Chauvin, Champlain, Manuel Lisa, and La Verendrye. The Indians called them "thunder stick men" because they exploded beaver lodges and took out the dead beaver. When the whites came to the Upper Missouri in the late 1630s or early 1640s, their expanding trade brought profit for the Indians, and whiskey, conflict, encroachment on their land, and depletion of their animals. Sandoz has researched her subject carefully; interesting reading for serious students.

Sandoz, Mari. **The Buffalo Hunters: The Story of the Hide Men.** Hastings 1954.

The great buffalo hunts began about 1867, when the total number of the four great herds—the Northern, Republican, Arkansas, and Texas—was estimated at 15 million. By the late 1880s the number had diminished to fewer than a thousand. Between these dates came Indian wars, development of the buffalo-hide trade, buffalo boom towns, and building of railroads across the prairies. Many colorful characters of the West are included, such as Yellow Wolf, Spotted Tail, Sitting Bull, Wild Bill Hickok, and

Custer. With her conscientious research and flair for making history come alive, the author colorfully describes buffalo stampedes, prairie fires, and the rollicking life that were characteristic of the period.

Sandoz, Mari. **Cheyenne Autumn.** Hastings 1953.

In 1878, a band of 278 Northern Cheyennes—fewer than half of them adults—fled the Oklahoma reservation to return to their ancestral hunting grounds in Montana, 1,500 miles away. Under the leadership of Little Wolf and Dull Knife and with little ammunition and few horses, they passed undetected through settled territory with its telegraph systems, across three railroads, and through the United States Army. For a fictionalized account of the events from the whites' point of view, see *The Last Frontier* by Howard Fast (Senior Fiction). Cited by Sun Bear in *Buffalo Hearts.*

"Not only in American history but in all history it is hard to find stories as moving, noble, and dramatic as this one" (Oliver La Farge, *Saturday Review*, 12 December 1953, p. 26). "Mari Sandoz has paid noble and gracious commendation to these people in a novel that surely demonstrates her knowledge of Indian ways of thinking and living" (*About Indians*, p. 260).

Satz, Ronald N. **American Indian Policy in the Jacksonian Era.** U of Nebr Pr 1976.

Historian Satz has gathered extensive information concerning the politics and pressures that led to the Removal Act of 1830 and started the emigration of the five southeastern tribes—Choctaw, Chickasaw, Cherokee, Creek, and Seminole—to land west of the Mississippi. Government policy insisted that Indians should settle on the land, cultivate it, and become assimilated, but when they did these things and became prosperous, white farmers wanted their land. The author also analyzes the government's policies during 1830-1850 when many tried to justify "policy, not right," which had become the rule.

"The book is filled with information, data, instances of exactly what happened. One needs to remember that Mr. Satz' conclusions and determinations are those of an apologist" (*Wassaja* 4:20, October 1976).

Sheehan, Bernard W. **Seeds of Extinction: Jeffersonian Philanthropy and the American Indian.** U of NC Pr 1973.

An intellectual history that examines the period from the 1770s through the 1830s, the era of Indian reform. The author makes the assumption that white Americans' self-conceptions shaped their perceptions of Indians and directed their policies toward them. The disparity in the way the whites saw Indians and the way Indians actually were, led the American government into policies that failed—for instance, the Removal Policy, and the attempt to lead Indians from what the whites regarded as a state of savagery into civilization. Modern historians have condemned these policies because they no longer see the Indian in terms of Jeffersonian philanthropy.

"Thoroughly researched with copious citations; it is important because ideas are made central" (*American Indian Quarterly* 2:247, Autumn 1975). "The study is quite readable and well organized. However, *Seeds of Extinction* lacks a basic understanding of Indian people. Perhaps this can be explained partially by the fact that no native scholars were included in the acknowledgments" (*Indian Historian* 8:52, Spring 1975).

Smith, Derek G., editor. **Canadian Indians and the Law: Selected Documents, 1663–1972.** McClelland 1975.

Smith, an anthropologist, has collected legal documents concerning Indians in Canada and prefaced them with an introductory discussion. The documents are in four categories: the early British Colonial period, 1760–1826; preconfederation, 1663–1916; the British North American Act, the Indian Acts and allied documents; and preconfederation and postconfederation documents.

Spicer, Edward H., and Raymond H. Thompson, editors. **Plural Society in the Southwest.** U of NM Pr 1972.

A collection of papers from a five-day conference in August 1970, "Plural Societies in the Southwest," sponsored by the Weatherhead Foundation. Papers cover four aspects of Southwestern diversity: the Indian presence, Hispaño-Anglo contact, the impact of immigration, and cultural variation. The book is both historical and sociological, concluding with a number of proposals to further the good of the plural society.

Spindler, Will H. **Tragedy Strikes at Wounded Knee and Other Essays on Indian Life in South Dakota and Nebraska.** Dakota Pr 1972.

The author spent thirty years, beginning in 1929, as a teacher in the U.S. Indian Service. Twenty of those years were spent at the

Medicine Bow Indian school at the Potato Creek Indian village on the Pine Ridge Reservation, where he wrote many essays based upon his observations of the Oglala Sioux or upon information gathered from the Indians on the reservation. Part 1 of this monograph deals with historical incidents such as the Wounded Knee massacre, the last Sun Dance in 1881, and the Buffalo Dance. Part 2, the most interesting section, tells of the author's experiences as a teacher. The book ends with additional sections on historical incidents and personages whom Spindler knew.

Stands In Timber, John (editor Margot Liberty). **Cheyenne Memories.** Yale U Pr 1967.

Margot Liberty, a student of anthropology, was teaching in Montana in 1956 when she met John Stands In Timber. Already known as the Cheyennes' historian, he had kept notes about his tribe for some time and wanted to write a book. Under a grant from the Association on American Indian Affairs, the editor began recording what the Cheyenne knew and has experienced. These are his observations about tribal priests, ceremonies, battles with the Crows, troubles and treaties with the whites, the Custer fight, the Ghost Dance, and "getting civilized" in the twentieth century.

"Stands In Timber has narrated a wide range of Cheyenne experience, from legendary times to life on the Northern Cheyenne Reservation in Montana" (*American Indian Authors*, p. 37). "One can learn more about the Cheyenne and about Indians generally in this book than can be learned from most books of a more technical character. It is recommended for students of Indian history, for individuals who are merely interested, and above all for Indians who should refresh their memory as well as their racial pride in the sheer pleasure to be derived from the reading of Timber's book" (*Indian Historian* 1:21, Spring 1968).

Szasz, Margaret C. **Education and the American Indian: The Road to Self-Determination 1928-1973.** U of NM Pr 1974.

After a brief background chapter on federal Indian education during 1870-1926, the author examines the conditions that shaped Indian education in government and public schools between 1928 and 1973. In 1969 the Kennedy Report, the work of a special Senate subcommittee on Indian education, called

the education of Indian children "a national tragedy and a
national disgrace," and re-emphasized many of the problems—
high dropout rates, low achievement, and a negative self-image—
that had been revealed in 1928 by the Meriam Commission.
Using archival documents, congressional records, and interviews,
the author demonstrates that the Bureau of Indian Affairs,
Congress, and the Bureau of the Budget all share the responsibility. The 1960s and 1970s saw Indian involvement in federal
legislation on education and the first experiments in Indian-con-
trolled schools.

"The book is a valuable contribution to the study of federal
Indian policy and administration that will be useful to anyone
with a serious interest in such matters" (*American Indian Quarterly* 2:264, Autumn 1975).

Tebbel, John. **The Compact History of the Indian Wars.** Tower
1966.

A readable history of Indian wars from Powhatan to the Battle
of Wounded Knee and of the Indian's struggle to avoid walking
the whites' road. The author is an Ojibwa scholar and journalist.

"A good account for the more mature reader" (*About Indians*, p. 276).

Terrell, John Upton. **The Plains Apache.** T Y Crowell 1975.

This is the history of the Plains Apache, their life and their
raids, as described by early explorers. The author presents evidence that the Apaches crossed the Bering land bridge and then
traveled along the coast and into the central part of the United
States. Emphasis is on the period from the Apaches' encounter
with Nuñez Cabeza de Vaca in 1535 to the present, from the
perspective of the Europeans.

"Presumptions are made without substantiation; an effort is
made to follow modern political causes; and there is complete
lack of understanding in certain areas, such as religion and
religious practices" (*Wassaja* 4:10, August 1976).

Trumbull, James Hammond. **Indian Names in Connecticut.** Archon.
Shoe String 1974.

This work was published in 1881 in an edition of only 250
copies. Indian names for Connecticut locations and some
places in part of Rhode Island, formerly known as Narragansett

County, are listed alphabetically with variant spellings, the location of the place, and the derivation of the name.

Turner, C. Frank. **Across the Medicine Line: The Epic Confrontation between Sitting Bull and the North-West Mounted Police.** McClelland 1973.

In 1873 James Morrow "Bub" Walsh, a cavalry officer and an Ontario adventurer, became one of the first to volunteer for service in the newly established Northwest Mounted Police, and was made superintendent and subinspector and told to recruit men in Ontario. Nearly two years later the first Teton Sioux were chased into Canada by the United States Cavalry, and the following year saw the annihilation of Custer's forces at the Little Bighorn. Walsh, who was on leave in the United States, was ordered back to Canada to look for Sioux. He developed a friendship with Sitting Bull, but it was severely tested by pressure from Canadian Indian tribes who were resentful of the Sioux and by the political interests of the governments on both sides of the border. The author, a Canadian militiaman, has told a chapter from Sitting Bull's life about which little is known, from the viewpoint of the Northwest Mounted Police.

Underhill, Ruth Murray. **Red Man's America: A History of the Indians in the United States.** Illus. Marianne Stoller. U of Chicago Pr 1971.

This is a history of American Indians beginning with the first migrations of primitive peoples from Siberia to Alaska and continuing with the relationships between tribes and with whites. It includes highlights of the Indians' varied origins, customs, and backgrounds with materials from the fields of archaeology, ethnology, and history. Some have objected to the concepts regarding tribal origins, the extent to which warfare was part of the natives' cultural life before the whites arrived, and the use of torture by some cultures. Written for a general audience; contains many human anecdotes. Line drawings, linguistic and tribal distribution maps, and a bibliography contribute to the book's usefulness. The author, a professor emerita of anthropology, has resided on almost every U.S. Indian reservation.

"Source materials are profuse; there is a good bibliography; and the author makes every effort to authenticate her findings. However . . . there is always the crucial matter of choice" (*Textbooks and the American Indian*, p. 166).

Utley, Robert M., and Wilcomb E. Washburn (editors Anne Moffatt and Richard F. Snow). **The American Heritage History of the Indian Wars.** Am Heritage 1977.

Although Columbus, Raleigh, and the Pilgrims were all greeted cordially by the Native Americans, it was not long before savage conflicts erupted between Indians and whites. In both prose and pictures, this book answers the question of what happened, dealing with Indian-white relationships in the East and subsequent events in the West. Both authors are respected scholars of Indian history. More than 350 photographs and paintings of Indians, Indian life, soldiers, and camp life.

Van Every, Dale. **Disinherited: The Lost Birthright of the American Indian.** Morrow 1971.

In 1780 the Continental Congress regarded the Appalachians as the permanent western boundary of the republic, but fifty years later the dominion of the United States extended to the Rockies. This is a historical account of the removal to the West of the Five Civilized Tribes—the Cherokee, Creek, Chickasaw, Choctaw, and Seminole. Although they had adopted many white manners and skills, these nations met untold suffering as they were forced westward. Scholarly and well documented; most useful for special interest and research.

"A powerful story and splendid history" (*About Indians,* p. 281).

Vogel, Virgil J., editor. **This Country Was Ours: A Documentary History of the American Indian.** Har-Row 1972.

This collection of documents is designed, as the author says, to help teachers "reorient our teaching about the American Indian in history." Documents are arranged according to the historical period in which they appeared. Each section contains a brief summary of the Indian's role during the period, followed by selected documents to illustrate the most significant events or conditions. An important reference work because of the appendixes: significant dates in American Indian history, United States Indian wars, famous Americans of Indian descent, selected audiovisual aids, selected museums, government agencies concerned with Indians, Indian and Indian interest organizations, and Indian publications. Directed especially to the needs of students in junior colleges and underclassmen in senior colleges; also for advanced high school students wanting to research a special project.

Wallace, Anthony F. C. The Death and Rebirth of the Seneca. Vin. Random 1972.

The author describes his book as the story of "the late colonial and early reservation history of the Seneca Indians, and of the prophet Handsome Lake, his visions, and the moral and religious revitalization of an American Indian society." By the time the prophet reached his forties, the once powerful and respected Senecas had seen their numbers depleted by disease and war, their hunting land taken from them, and their reputation and morals ruined by the whites' liquor. Around 1800, Handsome Lake had a series of visions that resulted in the tribe's rebirth and the beginning of the religion called the Old Way of Handsome Lake. On *Akwesasne Notes* basic library list.

"A well done and important work" (*Indian Historian* 3:52, Spring 1970).

Washburn, Wilcomb E. The Indian in America. Har-Row 1975.

This history of the Indian in America from pre-Columbian times to the present is divided into three parts: the period prior to the European invasion, the time of relative equality and interaction between the red and white races, and the period of tragic consequences of the Indians' defeat. The last chapters contain an analysis of the reservation system, allotment policy, and the Indians' search for self-realization in the white people's world. The author is director of the Office of American Studies at the Smithsonian Institution.

"Because of the complexity of the subject, no single volume can ever be described as definitive in relating the entire history of the American Indian. Washburn's effort, however, deserves a place in the first rank of those who have tried" (*American Indian Quarterly* 2:24, Spring 1975).

Worcester, Donald E., editor. Forked Tongues and Broken Treaties. Caxton 1975.

A history of treaties between Indian tribes and the United States government, beginning in 1778 when a treaty was made with the Delaware, and ending in 1871 when the treaty system was abandoned in favor of so-called agreements. The articles discuss the events leading up to each treaty, and the results of the treaty in practice. Contributors besides the editor include Arthur H. DeRosier, Jr., Emmett M. Essin, Valerie L. Mathes, Ronnie M. Day, Sandra L. Myres, and Eugene McCluney.

"The most important chapters are those by Arthur DeRosier, Jr., who gives greater emphasis to the actual treaties than some of the other contributors" (*American Indian Quarterly* 3:260, Autumn 1977).

# Traditional Life and Culture

Aliki. **Corn Is Maize: The Gift of the Indians.** Illus. by author. T Y Crowell 1976. Primary.

A factual, easy-to-read book, with drawings and explanations that introduce the reader to the history of corn. The author discusses the possibility that corn evolved from teosinte. She describes the importance of corn to many Indian tribes, the ways in which it was used and stored, and the many Indian festivals and dances that centered around the corn harvest. The Pilgrims also used corn in many ways—the husks for mattresses and corn-shuck dolls and the cobs for fuel and corncob pipes. The book concludes with a list of modern products made from corn, to demonstrate the importance of this gift from the Indians.

"*Corn Is Maize* should make any Native American child very proud to be one of a people who, through great ingenuity, developed the production of such a vital crop" (*Interracial Books for Children Bulletin* 8, no. 3:14, 1977).

Baylor, Byrd. **The Desert Is Theirs.** Illus. Peter Parnall. Scribner 1975. Primary.

The eloquent writing of Byrd Baylor shows the deep appreciation the desert people have for the land and all its inhabitants. The patience of the Papagos is compared to a weed which may wait three years to bloom, "just so it blooms sometime," or to a toad who "may wait for months to leave his sand hiding place and sing toad songs after a rain." Because the animals were on the desert first, the desert people look to them for guidance, and wish to live in harmony with all the desert creatures and plants. Illustrations depict the harmony between people and animals. 1976 Caldecott Medal Honor Book.

Bleeker, Sonia. The Apache Indians: Raiders of the Southwest. Illus. Althea Karr. Morrow 1951. Intermediate.

The Apaches, fierce raiders and fighters for hundreds of years, have always been one of the most colorful of all Indian tribes. Their roaming took them over territory that is now Arizona, New Mexico, Texas, and northern Mexico. Strong government and careful observance of religious ceremony were important aspects of their well-ordered way of life. The author, a noted anthropologist, describes Apache hunting techniques, customs, and crafts in a most interesting manner. Helpful pronunciations of Apache words are included.

"A fascinating account of this important tribe written by an authority on the North American Indian" (*About Indians*, p. 39).

Bleeker, Sonia. The Cherokee: Indians of the Mountains. Illus. Althea Karr. Morrow 1952. Intermediate.

This factual book describes the famous tribe that once roamed the Great Smokies and the Cumberland Plateau. The text begins with the vivid description of a Cherokee ball game. Other customs dealing with marriage, nature rites, the function of shamans, and hunting methods are explained. Other chapters tell of Sequoya and John Ross, the first president of the Cherokee Nation, who saw the forming of the Cherokee constitution. Finally, the tragic story of the Cherokee ends with the Trail of Tears. An excellent history of a great people. Cited in *A Preliminary Bibliography of Selected Children's Books.*

"Miss Bleeker combines details of daily life with legend and history in an interesting and lively manner" (*About Indians*, p. 40).

Bleeker, Sonia. The Chippewa Indians: Rice Gatherers of the Great Lakes. Illus. Patricia Boodell. Morrow 1955. Intermediate.

A description of the traditional Chippewa way of life, in terms of one year in the life of an imaginary Chippewa family. Seasonal travel takes the Crane family to the maple sugar groves in spring, to the lake shore in summer, to the wild rice beds to work in the fall, and to the depths of the protective forests in winter. The family demonstrates its belief in the power of spirits at the birth of a baby. The text provides information on other Chippewa customs such as the building of birch-bark canoes, the training of medicine men, and recreational activities. The final chapter describes the life of the Chippewas today.

Bleeker, Sonia. **The Crow Indians: Hunters of the Northern Plains.** Illus. Althea Karr. Morrow 1953. Intermediate.

The life of the Crow Indians is vividly described, with realistic accounts of how hunts were organized and how new camps were set up. The author also describes the training and games of boys and girls, as well as Crow customs, dress, and legends. An account of tribal history to the present day rounds out this useful book.

"A vivid tribal picture which is both interesting and accurate" (*About Indians*, p. 40).

Bleeker, Sonia. **The Delaware Indians: Eastern Fishermen and Farmers.** Illus. Patricia Boodell. Morrow 1953. Intermediate.

This volume describes the history and lifestyle of the Delaware tribe, who formerly lived in what is now Pennsylvania, Maryland, Delaware, New Jersey, and southern New York. Those who lived near the Atlantic Ocean and along the Delaware River were actively involved in fishing, clamming, hunting, and canoeing. The book follows the life of one typical family as it participates in the tribe's customs and ceremonies. Today there are no full-blooded Delaware, because of many relocations, but many of the Oklahoma Indians say with pride that an ancestor of theirs was a Delaware.

"Well researched and interesting" (*About Indians*, p. 40).

Bleeker, Sonia. **Horsemen of the Western Plateaus: The Nez Perce Indians.** Illus. Patricia Boodell. Morrow 1957. Intermediate.

The introduction tells the story of Spotted Salmon, a young Nez Perce experienced in hunting and fishing for salmon. The work, games, religious ceremonies, courtship customs, and legends of the Nez Perce are described. Their history is presented from the time of their first contact with whites to the day when the United States government sent the small surviving remnant of the tribe—all that was left of many thousands—to live on reservations. The final chapters describe the life of the famous Chief Joseph. Accurate, lifelike drawings. Cited in *A Preliminary Bibliography of Selected Children's Books.*

"An accurate and appealing book which faithfully records the history and customs of a people" (*About Indians*, p. 42).

Bleeker, Sonia. **Indians of the Longhouse: The Story of the Iroquois.** Illus. Althea Karr. Morrow 1950. Intermediate.

The Iroquois Indians lived in what is now the state of New York and were comprised of five different tribes: Mohawk, Oneida,

Onondaga, Cayuga, and Seneca. These tribes later formed the important League of the Five Nations or the League of the Iroquois. The book gives good descriptions of farming, construction of longhouses, basket weaving, mask making, and ceremonials. The great Seneca leader, Handsome Lake, urged the Iroquois to return to their old way of life and to give up liquor. His teachings are still followed by many Iroquois in New York and Canada today.

"Written with objectivity, this is an interesting, authoritative account of the Iroquois people" (*About Indians*, p. 42).

Bleeker, Sonia. The Mission Indians of California. Illus. Althea Karr. Morrow 1956. Intermediate.

A fictionalized account of Little Singer, a Luiseño Indian, which effectively portrays the vanished way of life of the California Indians. Little Singer has a natural ability for learning songs and is in great demand as a ceremonial singer. He finds village life to be much the same wherever he travels: women gather acorns and edible plants, men hunt and fish, and ceremonies such as the feather dance are observed. The peaceful existence of the California Indians was abruptly changed when the Spanish arrived in 1769 and the new Spanish missions came to dominate their lives. Most of these people, including the Chumash, Gabrielino, Luiseño, and Juaneño tribes, have vanished and only remnants of the Diegueño and the Cahuilla remain. Additional details are provided by the drawings. Cited in *A Preliminary Bibliography of Selected Children's Books*.

"A fine combination of Little Singer's personal story, with the authentic description of the old way of life" (*About Indians*, p. 42).

Bleeker, Sonia. The Navajo: Herders, Weavers, and Silversmiths. Illus. Patricia Boodell. Morrow 1958. Intermediate.

This book provides much information on the Navajo way of life by telling the story of Slim Runner, a Navajo boy who becomes ill. Hoping to be cured, he is taken to a Blessingway Ceremony, where two fire swallowers plunge burning sticks into their open mouths. When Slim Runner's health does not improve he is sent to the whites' hospital, where a gift of crayons and paper helps him develop his artistic talents. Modern reservation life coexists with the ancient arts of sand-painting and the sacred myths of magic and the supernatural. Realistic illustrations.

"A good story which uses as a backdrop Navajo life and culture as it is lived on the reservation today" (*About Indians*, p. 42).

Bleeker, Sonia. The Pueblo Indians: Farmers of the Rio Grande. Illus. Patricia Boodell. Morrow 1955. Intermediate.

Through the eyes of Young Hawk, a Pueblo Indian who lived over four hundred years ago, we see the culture of his civilization in the daily life of these people before the Spanish conquest of the Southwest. Young Hawk and his tribe spend much time working in the cornfields, and look forward to a communal rabbit hunt which will provide meat for an important festival. A final chapter shows how the Pueblo Indians have adapted their old beliefs and traditions to a modern world. Included is a list of present-day Pueblo ceremonies that are open to non-Indians. Cited in *A Preliminary Bibliography of Selected Children's Books*.

"With a simplicity and ease of style Miss Bleeker has succeeded in creating an authentic picture of Pueblo life in the past and present" (*About Indians*, p. 42).

Bleeker, Sonia. The Sea Hunters: Indians of the Northwest Coast. Illus. Althea Karr. Morrow 1951. Intermediate.

The tribes covered in this informative volume are the Salish, Kwakiutl, Nootka, Haida, Tlingit, Tsimshian, and Chinook. Surrounded as they were by high mountains and the ocean, these Indians' entire existence depended on the creatures of the sea. They were fierce fighters in their wars with other tribes, but their skill as fishermen and hunters was uppermost in importance. Their closeness to nature is evident in the description of the First Salmon Ceremony and other tribal religious rituals, and in their deep respect for the animals they hunted. Cited in *A Preliminary Bibliography of Selected Children's Books*.

"Easily read, this account of the Northwest Coast tribes is both accurate and interesting" (*About Indians*, p. 43).

Bleeker, Sonia. The Seminole Indians. Illus. Althea Karr. Morrow 1954. Intermediate.

A detailed historical account of the Creek Indians of Alabama and Georgia and their migration to Florida more than two hundred years ago. They became known as the Seminole or "people who go to another country." The early chapters are told from the viewpoint of Little Owl, a fictional Seminole boy. Later chapters give an account of the life of the Seminole hero Osceola. Includes explicit information on animal life in the swamps and the building of dugout canoes and palmetto-thatched, open-walled huts called chickees. Illustrations are accurate and appropriate. Cited in *A Preliminary Bibliography of Selected Children's Books.*

"An accurate, readable account of the tragic story of the Seminole Indians" (*About Indians*, p. 43).

Bleeker, Sonia. **The Sioux Indians: Hunters and Warriors of the Plains.** Illus. Kisa Sasaki. Morrow 1962. Intermediate.

Famous for their fighting and horsemanship, the Sioux are an unusually interesting American Indian tribe. This book covers their history from their first appearance on the Great Plains in the middle 1700s through the historic battle with General Custer. The author explains in detail the importance of the buffalo and the horse to the Sioux culture and describes the Sioux methods of raiding other tribes. She also tells of their forced resistance to the whites' encroachment on their lands, and their attempts to restore their strength with the magnificent Sun Dance. Excellent descriptions and illustrations of games and dances.

"A detailed and absorbing narrative about the Sioux people" (*About Indians*, p. 43).

Brindze, Ruth. **The Story of the Totem Pole.** Illus. Yeffe Kimball. Vanguard 1951. Intermediate.

The author successfully develops the mystery and magic of totem poles, explaining their origin and uses. Because the Northwest Indians had no written language, they carved their history, legends, and exciting adventures on giant red-cedar trunks. Sometimes the totem poles were "ridicule" poles to embarrass someone who had failed to pay a debt or keep a promise or committed some other wrong. An excellent description of the potlatch or give-away party is given. The book includes legends and fictionalized accounts of historical incidents and a humorous account of how Abraham Lincoln's likeness was carved and placed on top of a totem pole. Authentic illustrations are by an internationally known Indian artist.

Clark, Ann Nolan. **Along Sandy Trails.** Photographs by Alfred A. Cohn. Viking Pr 1969. Primary.

A beautiful book that uses the device of a small Papago Indian girl's walks in the desert with her grandmother to describe the richness of bird, animal, and plant life in the desert country. "For two summer moons" the grandmother and granddaughter roam the desert while it blooms, observing the gila woodpecker, ground squirrels, quail, and other desert life. Color photographs illustrate the brief but complementary text that is almost poetry.

Clark, Ann Nolan. **Circle of Seasons.** Illus. W. T. Mars. FS&G 1970. Intermediate.

This is a sensitive account of a year in the life of the present-day Pueblo Indians. The author, who taught among them, documents the importance of the daily rituals, the times of celebration, the closeness of the people to their environment and how they use it in contrast to the white world's superficial ways. The serious approach to tribal governance, the responsibilities of their elected officials, and their reverent approach to the blend of Indian religion and Christianity are narrated with insight and understanding.

Clark, Ann Nolan. **In My Mother's House.** Illus. Velino Herrera. Viking Pr 1969. Primary.

The author has based her story of the day-to-day life of the Tewa Indians of Tesuque Pueblo on writings by school children of the tribe. The reader is given a picture of everyday happenings in a beautiful life, lived close to nature in this village near Santa Fe: the building of a home; work with animals; the gathering and use of native plants such as juniper, Indian tea, and yucca; the digging of the vital irrigation ditches, and the dancing and feasting at a corn festival. Drawings of tribal designs in black and white and in color.

"It gives to little children as no other book has a sense of knowing Indian boys and girls and the feeling of experience shared. A distinguished American book" (*New York Times*, 4 May 1941, p. 11). "Rhythm and dignity of speech mark this simple text based on the notebooks of Indian children in schools near Santa Fe. . . . The book has great beauty" (*Horn Book* 17:102, March 1941).

Dorian, Edith, and W. N. Wilson. **Hokahey! American Indians Then and Now.** McGraw 1957. Intermediate.

This book reveals a wealth of information as it tells the American Indians' story from the earliest days to the present. There are details about their possible origin, migration, languages, history, and culture, as well as their influence on geographic locations and on democracy itself, giving the reader a new appreciation of Native Americans. Extensive information is provided for the seven great regional Indian cultures: East, Woodlands, Southeast, Plains, Plateau, California, and Northwest. Many charts give detailed listings of principal tribes and their cultural traits. Information about the Indians of today concludes the collection. Black and white drawings supplement the text. Cited in *A Preliminary Bibliography of Selected Children's Books.*

"An interesting and accurate presentation which is useful for supplementary classroom reading" (*About Indians*, p. 160).

Engel, Lorenz. **Among the Plains Indians.** Lerner Pubns 1970. Intermediate.

In 1833 Alexander Phillip Maximilian, prince of the German principality of Wied, led a small party of explorers into the heart of the American wilderness. He was accompanied by a young Swiss artist, Karl Bodmer, who was to paint scenes from their journey. Shortly before their departure the group viewed a collection of oil paintings by the American artist, George Catlin, who had made an expedition along the upper Missouri only a year earlier and had painted scenes of Indian life. This volume contains paintings of these two artists, covering a variety of subjects—hunting, dances, burial customs, village scenes, sacred bundles games, and much more—with text by the author. A list of tribes and language families and a map are included.

Grimm, William C. **Indian Harvests.** Illus. Ronald Himler. McGraw 1973. Intermediate.

American Indians have been harvesting a wide variety of wild plants throughout the country. This interesting collection of plant descriptions includes many familiar foods, from prickly pears in the Southwest to cranberries in New England. The book covers the major plants used by various tribes and indicates their present availability. Ways the Indians prepared and used them are explained. Some of the familiar plants included are strawberries, cranberries, chestnuts, crabapples, juneberries, currants, gooseberries, wild rice, and maple sugar. The many beautiful, detailed, accurate line drawings which accompany the text will enable the reader to recognize the plants. Only native American plants have been included.

Harnishfeger, Lloyd C. The Collecter's Guide to American Indian Artifacts. Illus. Sandra Heinen. Lerner Pubns 1976.

This is an excellent handbook for the beginning collector of Indian artifacts. It gives the hobbyist suggestions for the first hunt and the cleansing and recording of the items, as well as practical advice on identification, classification, mounting, and display. Pointers for recognizing, naming, and classifying a number of Indian relics found in North America are included. Excellent photographs show the exact dimensions of the artifacts. Since this is a beginner's guide to the hobby of collecting Indian relics, it does not deal with specific details of classification. However, the author does list supplementary readings to aid in further study.

Hofsinde, Robert [Gray-Wolf]. The Indian and His Horse. Illus. by author. Morrow 1960. Intermediate.

This book describes the part the horse played in the life of the American Indian. The author examines the Indians' ability to train and understand horses and provides information on the kind of equipment the Indians used with them. Interesting illustrations are included. A final chapter deals with Indians and their horses today. Cited in *A Preliminary Bibliography of Selected Children's Books.*

"A highly authentic, readable book which treats briefly but well the various breeds of horses owned by the Indian, their training, care and equipment" (*About Indians*, p. 69).

Hofsinde, Robert [Gray-Wolf]. The Indian and the Buffalo. Illus. by author. Morrow 1961. Intermediate.

More than 60 million buffalo roamed the country at the time when Columbus discovered America. Having neither horses nor rifles, the Indians used great courage and cunning in hunting them. Some of their methods are described and illustrated by the author, a well-known expert on Indian life. He also provides the reader with interesting facts about buffalo medicine and buffalo dances. The final chapter tells of the efforts made by many in recent times to save the herds of buffalo.

"Another simply written description of an important facet of the Indian culture" (*About Indians*, p. 69).

Hofsinde, Robert [Gray-Wolf]. **Indian Costumes.** Illus. by author. Morrow 1968. Intermediate.

In this valuable book the author, a noted Indian expert, describes and illustrates in detail selected examples of dress from ten representative tribes. The costumes of each Indian group— whether for war, ceremonies, or everyday use—had a distinctive style. The earliest known garments of the Navahos, who were closely related to the Apaches, consisted of shoulder wraps and leggings made from grass and yucca fibers. Blackfeet made their leggings from a Hudson Bay blanket instead of buckskin; Northwest Coast Indians donned wooden armor in battle; early Seminoles ornamented their bodies liberally with tattoos. In addition to these and other interesting facts, the author provides information on how the costumes were made. He also discusses the Indian dress of today and notes how the beautiful old costumes appear in many celebrations and tourist attractions as well as in special dances.

Hofsinde, Robert [Gray-Wolf]. **Indian Fishing and Camping.** Illus. by author. Morrow 1963. Intermediate.

The author has described and illustrated Indian methods of fishing and camping. The early Indians used poles, lines and hooks, traps, spears, and nets to catch fish. The Pacific Coast tribes invented a piece of fishing equipment resembling a rake. The methods of the Ojibwa and other woodland Indian tribes are also covered. The book includes illustrated directions on making the gear, suggestions for bait, and drawings of common fish. This is a handy guide for the modern camper and a valuable addition to the knowledge of anyone interested in Indian lore.

"A fine, useful book which will interest any [child] who enjoys fishing and the outdoors (*About Indians*, p. 70).

Hofsinde, Robert [Gray-Wolf]. **Indian Hunting.** Illus. by author. Morrow 1962. Intermediate.

The wild animals of North America supplied Indians with most of their food, clothing, shelter, and fuel, so it was important for the Indians to become skillful hunters. In spite of primitive weapons, they were successful because they had intimate knowledge of the habits of the game animals. Descriptions of various methods used in hunting by the different tribes are described, such as driving animals into fenced enclosures and using artificial deer callers. The deer was hunted more widely than any other animal; other animals hunted were moose, caribou, bear, whales, and buffalo, in addition to small game such as rabbit, beaver, and muskrat. The author vividly describes the Indians' weapons, their hunting methods, and the ceremonials involved in the hunt. His beautiful and accurate drawings add to the book's interest.

"A thorough treatment of Indian hunting in an easy, readable manner" (*About Indians*, p. 70).

Hofsinde, Robert [Gray-Wolf]. The Indian Medicine Man. Illus. by author. Morrow 1966. Intermediate.

The author, who has intimate knowledge of Indian customs and rites, discusses the importance of the medicine man to the Indian culture. Most medicine men spent years studying the medicinal properties of plants, herbs, and barks. They also used prayers, tricks, and shams in their rituals. Some were prophets as well as healers, but all were respected for their wisdom and spiritual powers. Hofsinde describes the methods of medicine men from six tribal groups—Sioux, Iroquois, Apache, Navaho, Ojibwa, and Northwest Coast Indians. The author's drawings clarify his descriptions of the various tribes.

"An accurate and interesting account presented with simplicity and ease of style" (*About Indians*, p. 71).

Hofsinde, Robert [Gray-Wolf]. Indian Sign Language. Illus. by author. Morrow 1956. Intermediate.

The author of this authentic handbook on Indian sign language has written a concise text and has drawn more than two hundred illustrations. The signs for some words, such as "paddle" and "bird," are obvious, whereas others, such as "talk" and "coffee," are amusing. Indian names and totems, such as "Running Elk," "Two Moons" and "Owl Woman," are included as picture-writing signatures. An explanation of counting is also given. A large variety of familiar words are included as well as modern words such as "motion picture" and "record player." Signs for common Indian tribes and the twelve moons are also given. An index helps readers find the words.

"Easy and fun to read" (*About Indians*, p. 72).

Hofsinde, Robert [Gray-Wolf]. **Indian Warriors and Their Weapons**. Illus. by author. Morrow 1965. Intermediate.

The author, a noted authority on Indian life, discusses weapons Indian warriors used, special clothes and charms they wore for battle, and their methods of fighting. He has included information on the following tribes: Ojibwa, Iroquois, Sioux, Blackfoot, Crow, Apache, and Navaho. The information is well organized and the sketches are accurate.

Hofsinde, Robert [Gray-Wolf]. **Indians at Home**. Illus. by author. Morrow 1964. Intermediate.

A handsomely illustrated book, showing that Indian homes were not all like the tepees of the Plains Indians. Homes described in the book include the Ojibwa wigwam, the Iroquois longhouse, the Seminole chickee, the Mandan earth lodge, the Pueblo adobe, and the Northwest Indians' plank house. The book provides additional information on the customs and lifestyles of the inhabitants. The final chapter shows that some Indian homes have remained unchanged to the present day and that others have drastically changed.

"An interesting and useful book" (*About Indians*, p. 72).

Hofsinde, Robert [Gray-Wolf]. **Indians on the Move**. Illus. by author. Morrow 1970. Intermediate.

In this useful book, the author has presented concise information for the young reader on Indian methods of travel by foot and horse. He begins by discussing the possible migratory travels of the earliest men. Travel by water was quite different among the various tribes; the Northwest Indian canoes contrast sharply with the dugouts of the Plains Indians. Winter travel methods included snowshoes, several types of toboggans, and sleds. Appropriate sketches by the author accompany the text.

"As with most of the author's other volumes, a book for children, understandable, with good illustrations but only basic information" (*About Indians*, p. 72).

Hofsinde, Robert [Gray-Wolf]. **The Indian's Secret World**. Illus. by author. Morrow 1955. Intermediate.

This book offers glimpses of the traditional Indian beliefs that give special significance to dreams, tribal masks, moccasins, medicine pipes, and other cultural objects. The author explains the Indian view of dreams as actual happenings in which a person's spirit leaves the body and receives guidance for everyday work such as the decoration of moccasins, the use of masks in healing ceremonies, and the planning and painting of tepees and medicine shields. The book reveals the meaning behind many customs, such as the Cheyenne practice of cutting holes in a newborn baby's moccasins in order to frighten away Death by showing him that the baby is wearing a worn-out pair and cannot depart on a long journey. The importance of picture writing and the tools and techniques used are discussed, as well as the way in which Indians communicated messages through the positions of their robes.

"Although Mr. Hofsinde is not an Indian himself he is able to capture the spirit and feeling of the Indian and those things important to the Indian culture" (*About Indians*, p. 72). Ellsworth Jaeger, curator of education of the Buffalo Museum of Science, says, "An Indian book by Robert Hofsinde is good medicine. Although he is a white man, he thinks like an Indian. The pages of his book are alive with the tang of smoke-tanned buckskins, the sound of drums, and the swift flight of eagle feathers."

Jenness, Aylette. **Dwellers of the Tundra: Life in an Alaskan Eskimo Village.** Photographs by Jonathan Jenness. CCPr. Macmillan 1969. Intermediate.

The extensively illustrated text covers life in the Eskimo village of Makumiut, population one hundred and fifty. Almost totally isolated from the rest of the world, the people of Makumiut lead a perilous existence which is constantly at odds with the accounts of the world outside that make up their school lessons and create in them an acute sense of inferiority. This is a factual account of the author's more-than-a-year-long teaching experience; understandably, names of people and places are changed to protect their identities.

Lauber, Patricia. **Who Discovered America? Settlers and Explorers of the New World before the Time of Columbus.** Random 1970. Intermediate.

Did Columbus discover America? Did Leif Ericsson? Early traders from Asia? Fishermen from England? The ancestors of the Indians? The author raises many questions and presents numerous theories about the discovery and settlement of the Western Hemisphere. The volume is illustrated with a number of prints and maps, as well as many photographs of ancient Indian artifacts and ruins from North and South America. This fascinating book compares the implements of several early Indian tribes and examines their cultures in depth. Descriptions of archaeological finds should provide exciting reading for the young archaeologist.

Lavine, Sigmund A. The Games the Indians Played. Dodd 1974. Intermediate.

This is an excellent collection of games played by the Chippewa, Zuni, Paiute, Apache, Menominee, Cherokee, Papago, and other tribes. The Indians spent much time in games of dexterity and chance. Religious beliefs governed the rules and ceremonies of the games. Some of the Indian games were simple diversions such as jackstraws, cat's cradle, guessing games, and games of chance. The last section includes games for children. The book is illustrated with photographs and old prints.

Lavine, Sigmund A. **Indian Corn and Other Gifts.** Dodd 1974. Intermediate.

Interesting historical information and legends are contained in this volume on plants long cultivated by the Indians. According to the Omaha, corn stemmed from a woman's body. The Algonquians maintain that maize was a gift from Manabozho, creator of earth and of life. The Zuni believe maize was created when one of their ancestors gathered seeds of different colored grasses and ceremonially planted them with sticks topped with feathers. The author shows the importance of corn in the worship, music, and dance of the Indians. He describes maple sugar harvests and feasts common among the Chippewas, and traces the development of beans, squashes, various types of peppers, and peanuts in early cultures of North and Central America, showing the important contributions these people made to modern life.

Levenson, Dorothy. Women of the West. Watts 1973. Intermediate.

One of the many chapters in this volume deals with the Indian women of the Great Plains in a general way, without mentioning any specific tribe. The chapter outlines some of the traditional duties of Indian women, including the gathering and growing of food, gathering wood, caring for children and the home, and cleaning and making clothes. The task of cutting the buffalo meat, its cooking and preservation, and the treatment of the skins were also considered women's work. Photographs and contemporary prints accompanying the text make this an interesting volume.

McGovern, Ann. **If You Lived with the Sioux Indians.** Illus. Bob Levering. Four Winds. Schol Bk Serv 1974. Primary.

This factual book describing the daily life of the Sioux is written in a question-and-answer style. Some interesting facts about traditional Sioux life are presented. It is surprising to learn, for example, that each child had a second mother and father who helped take care of him; that the men sometimes had more than one wife; that a boy was expected to hunt his first buffalo before the age of ten; that the Sioux believed that there were rock spirits, tree spirits, and cloud spirits. Special ceremonies for both boys and girls are explained, as well as good manners and other customs. The Sioux sign language is described, with several signs presented in drawings. A note from the author about the Sioux Indians of today helps to clarify concepts. Excellent drawings and a glossary make this a valuable source of information about an important Indian tribe.

Molloy, Anne. **Wampum.** Hastings 1977. Intermediate.

The author's extensive research is evident in this comprehensive book on wampum. These strung beads of polished shells were used by the Indians to atone for blood spilled among brothers and to record declarations of peace; the early settlers used it as a coin of trade to rob the Indians of their lands and to pay for a bit of rum or tuition at Harvard. Interspersed in this fascinating text are little-known facts about well-known leaders of the past, including Tecumseh, Pontiac, William Penn, and George Washington. Prints and photographs illustrate the volume. An added feature is a listing of wampum belts in American and Canadian museums.

Northey, Sue. **The American Indian.** Illus. George Gray. Naylor 1962. Intermediate.

An easy general reference work for young people, giving information about what Indians were like when whites came—how they lived, played, dressed, and worshipped. It discusses Indians by sections of the country: Woodland Indians, Plains Indians, Southwest Indians, and Northwest Indians.

"A good general book for upper elementary grades" (*About Indians*, p. 239).

Payne, Elizabeth. **Meet the North American Indians.** Illus. Jack Davis. Random 1965. Primary.

This attractive, easy-to-read book introduces the reader to five different Indian tribes, describing their lifestyles, customs, and ideas. It tells of the Northwest Coast Indians' beliefs that animals are powerful spirits which give an Indian the magic power to become a chief or a medicine man. The Makah from the present state of Washington are depicted as the great whale hunters. The chapter on the quiet, peaceful Hopi tells about their use of kachinas to talk to their many gods and their use of corn, weaving, and pottery making. The Creeks' celebration of New Year includes the playing of lacrosse in July when the ripe corn is cooked for the great feast. The great buffalo hunt is portrayed vividly in descriptions of the life of the Mandan of the Great Plains. The hunting, gathering of maple syrup, and special seafood feasts of the Penobscots of New England are also described. Appropriate illustrations and a map make this a suitable book for young readers.

Pine, Tillie S., and Joseph Levine. **The Indians Knew.** Illus. Ezra Jack Keats. McGraw 1957. Primary.

The Indians of long ago knew how to do many things we do today. They could make things spring rapidly through the air, build canoes, make work easier by pulling things instead of carrying them, preserve food, start a fire without matches, fertilize plants, and use the moon as a calendar. This book demonstrates how we apply in everyday life the same principles used by the Indians.

"Easy to read and illustrated attractively. Examples which the book presents to prove points discussed are simple enough for class or home experimentation" (*About Indians*, p. 26).

Robinson, Maudie. **Children of the Sun: The Pueblos, Navajos, and Apaches of New Mexico.** Messner 1973. Intermediate.

The author explores the history, culture, and lifestyle of three tribes of New Mexico. The book shows how these "Children of the Sun" draw spiritual and physical strength from their Earth Mother. The earth is the source of clay for building Pueblo homes, turquoise stones for jewelry, and reeds for Apache baskets, among many other things. The author, who is part Cherokee Indian, grew up among the Cherokee and Choctaw of eastern Oklahoma. Her many photographs are well chosen and give a realistic portrayal of Native Americans.

Russell, Don. **Sioux Buffalo Hunters.** Illus. Bob Glaubke. Brit Bks 1962. Primary.

The life of the Sioux Indians of two hundred years ago is portrayed in this collection of stills from the educational motion picture "Indian Family of Long Ago." The film was shot on locale in South Dakota, and modern-day members of the Sioux tribe posed in the pictures wearing costumes and using artifacts from museums. The text is simply written and describes the life of the early Sioux as being full of hard, never-ending work, fear of starvation, and fear of enemies. Yet the tepee was snug and comfortable, and there was feasting, happiness, and peace.

Searcy, Margaret Zehmer. **Ikwa of the Temple Mounds.** U of Ala Pr 1974. Primary.

This book gives a fictionalized account of Ikwa, a young girl from the prehistoric Temple Mound Indian culture of Mississippi. The story centers around a frightening fire and a new home for Ikwa, and provides much information on the daily home life, customs, and beliefs of this little-known tribe, helping the younger child to envision their way of life. Ikwa's offerings to the priest of the sun god and her brother Situs's attempts to win an important game offer the older reader fascinating glimpses of the religious and cultural life of these people. The tribe's oneness with nature and their belief in omens is graphically portrayed. Easy reading and a variety of illustrations enhance this book.

Sheppard, Sally. **Indians of the Eastern Woodlands.** Watts 1975. Intermediate.

This book focuses on the most powerful and influential tribes that lived in the area from just west of the Hudson River to the Atlantic coast and from New York and eastern Pennsylvania to the Canadian border. The author gives detailed information on the customs and lifestyles of Eastern Woodland Indians, covering such areas as government, social structure, religion, arts, and mythology. The author also outlines the history of these tribes, including biographical material on great Eastern Indian heroes and leaders and examining broken treaties as well as current struggles for Indian power and trends for the future. This inclusive book will be of much value in the understanding of the culture of the Eastern Woodland tribes before and after the arrival of whites.

Showers, Paul. **Indian Festivals.** Illus. Lorence Bjorklund. T Y Crowell 1969. Primary.

This is an introduction to Indian festivals, pointing out that many of the holidays are a time for worship and for observing sacred customs. The many tribes of the United States all have their own ancient customs and celebrations, and the author has shared a few of these. The Seminoles of Florida praise the spirits when the new corn is tall; the Zuni Indians of New Mexico honor the spirits of the rain by dancing with colorful masks; the Plains Indians—Crees, Sioux, Cheyennes, Utes, and Shoshones—hold sun dances that last for many days and nights. The illustrations are helpful in further explanation of the celebrations.

Tamarin, Alfred, and Shirley Glubok. **Ancient Indians of the Southwest.** Doubleday 1975. Intermediate.

The stories of ancient tribes of the Southwest were lost for centuries, and stone and adobe ruins were all that remained of these forgotten cultures. This book tells what anthropologists have pieced together in regard to the disappearance of several of these tribes and the possible reasons for it. The authors re-create the lives of small nomadic bands of hunter-gatherers, such as the Cochise, whose few possessions always included baskets and milling stones. The Mogollon farmers succeeded the Cochise. Important features of their culture were the kiva and the chief's weapon, the atlatl, forerunner of the bow and arrow. The prehistoric Hohokam, people of the desert, built shelters inside shallow pits and had irrigation systems. In the act of survival, these ancient peoples created one of the richest of all Indian civilizations, which is still reflected in present-day Indian cultures of the Southwest. Black and white photographs and an archaeological map supplement the text.

## Junior High

Ahenakew, Edward (editor Ruth M. Buck). **Voices of the Plains Cree.** McClelland 1973.

The author tells two kinds of stories about the life of the Plains Cree: tales told to him by Chief Thunderchild of historical events, important individuals, and events of the past; and stories of Cree life as Ahenakew knew it—told by Old Keyam, a fictitious character—including tales of war, myths, and stories of hunting buffalo and grizzly bear.

Baldwin, Gordon C. **How Indians Really Lived.** Putnam 1967.

The author, an archaeologist, uses information from archaeologists and anthropologists to reconstruct details of the daily life of Indians and Eskimos before the whites arrived—covering their work, worship, hunting, fighting, and language. The book is divided by cultural areas: Northeast, Southeast, Southwest, the Plains, the Forests, California, Northwest Coast, Northern Forests, and the Arctic.

"Written in an interesting, objective manner, this basic book provides valuable information for the student of Indian culture" (*About Indians*, p. 121).

Bjorklund, Karna L. **The Indians of Northeastern America.** Illus. Lorence F. Bjorklund. Dodd 1969.

A description of the early history of the Algonkian and Iroquois people, covering their customs, dwellings, clothing, beliefs, religion, and handicrafts. Interspersed throughout are appropriate legends which explain the aspect of life being discussed. The author's father has illustrated the book with beautiful drawings depicting differences in facial features, dress, and dwellings among the various tribes.

Brown, Vinson. **Voices of Earth and Sky: Vision Search of the Native Americans.** Illus. Tony Shearer. Naturegraph 1976.

The author, trained in anthropology and zoology under famous anthropologists Robert Lowie and A. L. Kroeber, uses Native American religions to tell his own spiritual story. On a trip to Central America as a field collector of natural history, Brown met a Guaymi man, Chio Jari, who worked for him and influenced him spiritually. Later he visited other tribes and met spiritual leaders and historians such as John Stands in Timber of the Cheyenne; Eddie Box, Sun Dance chief of the Southern Utes; and Mad Bear Anderson, Tuscarora medicine man. Much emphasis is placed on the Sioux because the author's father, as a doctor at Pine Ridge Reservation, was given a sacred pipe bag that purportedly belonged to Crazy Horse, and Brown himself bought a sandstone pipe made from the sacred quarry in Minnesota. These experiences finally led Brown to pursue

his own vision on Bear Butte, South Dakota; this episode is
the climax of his story.

Brusa, Betty War. Salinan Indians of California and Their Neighbors. Naturegraph 1975.

This small monograph is part of the American Indian Map Book
series. The author emphasizes the life of the Salinans but also
includes a bit about their neighbors, the Esselen, the Chumash,
the Costanoans, and the Yokuts. She discusses the boundaries
of the Salinan territory, the economic and social life, and
aesthetic pursuits. Since little is known about this tribe, this
volume may be useful for California schools to supplement an
Indian unit.

Burt, Jesse, and Robert B. Ferguson. Indians of the Southeast:
Then and Now. Illus. David Wilson. Abingdon 1973.

A historian and an archaeologist combine their talents to write
about the southeastern Indians, beginning their history with
the arrival of the Europeans. Citing early sources, they tell
about the religion, language, lifestyle, food, crafts, games,
dances, and music of these people. The book shows their struggle over the years to maintain a semblance of dignity and
security, and portrays their needs and hopes today by quoting
many modern young people. Illustrations, a bibliography, and
an index are included.

"It is to be hoped that this book will find its way into high
school and college libraries and classes and that it will [also] be
read by adults" (H. E. Fey, *Christian Century* 90:920, 1 September 1973).

Cody, Iron Eyes. Indian Talk: Hand Signals of the North American Indian. Illus. Ken Mansker. Naturegraph 1970.

Although all people use sign language to some degree, the
Plains Indians, who did not know each other's languages, developed sign language to carry on entire conversations. This book
contains an alphabetical list of words and signs, each with a
photograph of the author or a member of his family, showing
the corresponding hand positions. The author is Cherokee, a
tribe which did not use sign language, but he became an expert
by learning it from friends, and served as a technical adviser for
movies and television. Illustrated by a Flathead Indian artist.

Eastman, Charles Alexander. **The Soul of an Indian: An Interpretation.** Fennwyn Pr 1970.

The author describes the moral principles and beliefs on which he was reared as a Sioux during the nineteenth century. He discusses the concept of the Great Mystery, relationships between man and animals, rules governing family relationships, ceremonial worship, myths and legends of the tribe, and concepts of death. Ideal for a study of Sioux Indian values. Published in 1911.

"The author presents religious life as it was before the advent of the white man, contending that the religion of the Indian is the last thing that a man of another race will ever understand" (*American Indian Authors*, p. 19).

Fergusson, Erna. **Dancing Gods: Indian Ceremonials of New Mexico and Arizona.** U of NM Pr 1970.

A popularized account of the most important dances of the Pueblo, Navajo, and Apache tribes of New Mexico and Arizona. This is hardly more than a report of what happens and deals little with the meaning of the dances. The author's personal experiences help explain some aspects of the dances and their symbolism.

Hanson, James Austin. **Metal Weapons, Tools, and Ornaments of the Teton Dakota Indians.** U of Nebr Pr 1975.

Extensive research has resulted in this comprehensive guide to the identification of typical Teton metal objects. The study adds to the understanding of the transition of the Teton Sioux from a Stone Age people to a nation dependent on white people's goods. An introductory chapter briefly outlines the history of these people, covering prereservation days, development of trade, rise and decline of trading houses, and the Tetons' relationship with the government. Other chapters deal with weapons, tools, and ornaments. Nearly two hundred drawings and photographs.

Hungry Wolf, Adolf. **Charlo's People: The Flathead Tribe of Montana.** Good Medicine Bks 1974.

Charlo became Head Chief of his tribe of Flathead Indians in 1870 and died some forty years later at the age of eighty. His people tried to keep to the old ways as much as possible, although the chief encouraged them to raise cattle and horses, grow vegetables and grain, and attend the mission church regularly. This publication contains the stories of a number of older members of the tribe whom the author knew.

Johnston, Bernice. **Speaking of Indians: With an Accent on the Southwest.** U of Ariz Pr 1970.

This is a guide for the general reader to tribes of the Southwest—their customs, art, and way of life. The author explores some of the history of the ancient tribes of the area, including a discussion of products originally grown by Indians and passed on to the whites.

Miller, Alfred J. **Braves and Buffalo: Plains Indian Life in 1837.** U of Toronto Pr 1973.

A collection of forty-one watercolor paintings, reproduced in full color, conveying the author-artist's sense of adventure, excitement, and wonder as he traveled to the Rocky Mountains in the early 1800s. The paintings and commentaries portray details of Indian life at the time, including domestic scenes, hunting techniques, stampedes, skirmishes, councils, and fur-trading episodes. An introduction by Michael Bell explains the rendezvous—a time of selling winter pelts, renewing friendships, and engaging in drunken brawls. The unfamiliar style and a number of words with variant spelling may lessen the readability but the paintings help to clarify the text.

Minge, Ward Alan. **Ácoma: Pueblo in the Sky.** U of NM Pr 1976.

This is the first book on Ácoma to be approved by the Tribal Council. It traces the social, economic, and political history of the tribe, mainly from the pueblo's first exposure to the whites over 400 years ago. The author discusses the assimilation of Spanish, Mexican, and finally United States institutions, and explains problems during this century which threaten the Ácoma pueblo and its way of life. Although some historical critics have questioned some of the facts and the sources used, the book is readable and beautifully illustrated.

O'Kane, Walter Collins. **Sun in the Sky: The Hopi Indians of the Arizona Mesa Lands.** U of Okla Pr 1957.

Although by profession he is an entomologist, the author has spent time among the Hopis, where he has developed a number of close friends. He describes the daily life of the Hopis—their agriculture in very arid lands, the construction and furnishings of their homes, their cooking, dress, and personal traits, their art, and the bringing up of their children. His discussion of the Hopi religion, myths, and ceremonies is especially vivid. Profusely illustrated with photographs.

Pope, Saxton T. **Bows and Arrows.** U of Cal Pr 1974.

The author was an instructor in surgery and research at the medical school of the University of California in 1911 when Ishi, the last of the Yahi tribe, was brought to the university. As a result of their friendship the surgeon developed a strong interest in archery, practicing with the bow and arrow under Ishi's guidance. Later he became interested in other kinds of bows and arrows, which he describes in this small book, telling how they are made and used. Some ancient non-Indian bows and arrows also are described.

Sandoz, Mari. **These Were the Sioux.** Illus. Amos Bad Heart Bull and Kills Two. Dell 1961.

A short, highly personalized book about the author's neighbors, the Sioux, in the western Nebraska Sand Hills. Beginning with her childhood experience with Bad Arm—a bloodthirsty Sioux who fought against Custer, but who picked her up, put her on his shoulders, and gave her his braids as reins—the author describes her contacts with the Sioux and her growing knowledge of them and their customs. The author played with Indian children, observed their campfires, and later heard their legends and anecdotes. From personal experience she tells how the children were taught, and describes the tribe's courtship and marriage customs and their ideas of earth and man—contrasting the fierceness of the Sioux with their gentleness in family life.

"An informative and interesting book to be enjoyed by young and old alike" (*About Indians*, p. 262).

Silverberg, Robert. **Home of the Red Man: Indian North America before Columbus.** Illus. Judith Ann Lawrence. WSP 1971.

The author discusses the life and culture of various Indian tribes before the whites' arrival, including locations of the different cultures, how they changed with time, and the artifacts typical of each. A clear introduction to the subject, although the author is not a practicing archaeologist. Useful as supplementary reading in English and history and other social sciences. A bibliography is included.

"The text perpetuates sensationalistic notions about Indian culture and the stereotype of the Indian as violent savage. Silverberg's biases betray themselves in the last chapter" (*Akwesasne Notes* 5:41, Early Winter 1973).

Tomkins, William. Indian Sign Language. Dover 1969.

Words in sign language are arranged alphabetically as in a dictionary, with drawings showing the hand positions for many of them. Hand positions for other words are explained and shown in sentences. There are brief sections on smoke signals and on the pictography and ideography of the Sioux and Ojibway. As a boy in the late 1800s, the author lived on the edge of the Sioux reservation in South Dakota where he worked the range and associated constantly with Indians. He learned some of the spoken language of the Sioux but took a special interest in the sign language by which they communicated with their neighbors—the Blackfoot, Cheyenne, and Arapaho tribes.

Wetmore, Ruth Y. First on the Land: The North Carolina Indians. Blair 1975.

A book that tries to survey—in 196 pages—twenty-eight tribes of North Carolina Indians from 10,000 B.C. to the present, including their history, wars, linguistic families, daily life, festivals, myths, and modern problems. The book was probably intended as background information for North Carolina elementary and junior high school students, and as such it may be useful, but it should be supplemented with other materials about the same tribal groups.

"Quite obviously, this book was published to satisfy the desire of the educational community and the general public for a quick, instant-information capsule about the Indians of the state. The author . . . has done her best to provide the pablum desired by unthinking schoolmasters and a gullible public" (Jeannette Henry, *Indian Historian* 8:49, Summer 1975).

## Senior High and Adult

Alexander, Hartley Burr. The World's Rim: Great Mysteries of the North American Indians. U of Nebr Pr 1967.

A scholarly and philosophical study of American Indian ritual ceremonies and dances. In his introduction the author says his purpose is "to sketch the salient features of the American Indian understanding of human life: their view of the world and the place of humanity in nature." His thesis centers on the similarity of human minds and he sees the ceremonial rites as metaphor, showing their relationship to cults around the world, such as the ancient Oriental and Grecian mystic cults, and Christianity. On *Akwesasne Notes* basic library list.

Balls, Edward K. **Early Uses of California Plants.** U of Cal Pr 1962.

One of the California Natural History Guides, which describes the ways in which Indians in California used plants before the coming of the white settlers. Plants common to California are grouped according to their use as food, drink, fiber and basketry, medicine, dye, gum, tobacco, soap, and fish poison. The final chapter discusses present-day uses of some California plants. Well illustrated with photographs in color and black and white, and drawings.

Bean, Lowell John. **Mukat's People: The Cahuilla Indians of Southern California.** U of Cal Pr 1972.

This is a small, scholarly book about the life of the Cahuilla Indians of southern California at the time the whites arrived. The author visited the area, and has used documents, interviews with members of the tribe, and geographical information to reconstruct the life of this small group before white civilization intervened.

Black Elk (editor Joseph Epes Brown). **The Sacred Pipe: Black Elk's Account of the Seven Rites of the Oglala Sioux.** Penguin 1971.

Black Elk, over ninety years old and the last of the Sioux holy men, feared the ancient religion of his tribe would disappear and asked Brown to record this account of it. He describes the rites of purification of the soul of the dead, the cry for a vision, the Sun Dance, and other rituals. Black Elk—who knew Sitting Bull, Red Cloud, and American Horse—reconstructed the religious practices for Brown while he lived with Black Elk for eight winter months in 1947–48. It is evident that the editor admires Black Elk and his people. Mainly of interest to those studying the Sioux religion in some depth. Cited in *American Indian Authors.* On *Akwesasne Notes* basic library list.

"The poetic language and religious reverence for the rites is distinctly Indian in tone and style, and in the manner of the tale-teller" (*About Indians*, p. 127).

Bryde, John F. Modern Indian Psychology. Dakota Pr 1971.

As a professor of psychology and guidance, Bryde prepared this book for use with classes of Indian students, to help them understand themselves in relation to white society. He approaches the subject by asking what values the Indian has about God, Myself, Fellow Man, and the World. He concludes that no other group has better ideas, because Indian societies are based on the following attitudes: God is merciful, I am so trustworthy that I can be given complete freedom, I am related somehow to everyone and therefore we must work together for common goals, and the earth is a holy place that should be treated reverently. The book concludes with a section on Sioux history. It is chatty in style and occasionally didactic, but will no doubt make Indian and non-Indian students proud of the First Americans.

Castaneda, Carlos. Journey to Ixtlan: The Lessons of Don Juan. S&S 1972.

The author, an anthropologist, goes on grueling desert marches, mountain hunts, and plant-gathering expeditions in order to more fully understand the world of the man of power. He is used by Don Juan as bait to attract a mountain lion in a test of courage. In the mountains and in the desert he has a series of encounters with the past and with death. The arduous tests and trials are exercises of the will, and lead to visions and experiences as the scholar forgets his rational world for a time and realizes that drugs are unnecessary in gaining understanding.

Castaneda, Carlos. A Separate Reality: Further Conversations with Don Juan. PB 1971.

Castaneda returns to Don Juan after more than two years to give him a copy of his first book. He reviews his previous experiences and their meanings and begins to realize that there is a way of seeing, in Don Juan's world, without drugs. These further glimpses of the "separate reality" of the Yaqui man of knowledge are recorded in detailed journal form.

Castaneda, Carlos. Tales of Power. PB 1976.

In the final report which Castaneda makes on his apprenticeship to Don Juan, the Mexican Indian shaman, the author describes the experiences on his excursion into the unknown (the Nagual), which represents the death of his personal self. Afterward he tries to understand his experiences rationally through conversations with his teacher. Whereas his previous books concentrated on the teacher, Don Juan, this one focuses on Castaneda's introspection. It is a book full of dreams, magic, colors, and voices, ending with Castaneda's moving farewell to Don Juan.

Castaneda, Carlos. **The Teachings of Don Juan: A Yaqui Way of Knowledge.** Ballantine 1968.

A young anthropologist's experiences as an apprentice of a Yaqui Indian sorcerer, Juan Matus or Don Juan, whom he first met in 1960 in an Arizona bus depot near the Mexican border. Castaneda visited him over a period of four years in an effort to find out from the so-called man of knowledge how to prepare and administer peyote and other drugs. In this book, which was presented as the author's master's thesis in anthropology, he explains his experiences in detail and analyzes them. Walter Goldschmidt in his foreword calls it "both ethnography and allegory."

"The information given establishes the basis for an exploration into the depths of Indian religion and for an appreciation of its value to mankind" (*About Indians*, p. 144).

Catlin, George (editor John C. Ewers). **O-kee-pa: A Religious Ceremony and Other Customs of the Mandans.** U of Nebr Pr 1976.

In 1832 George Catlin, painter of American Indian life, was among the Mandan Indians of the Upper Missouri when the four-day O-kee-pa ceremony was performed. His description of the suffering and pain which the members of the tribe inflicted upon themselves during the ceremony was so grim that some people claimed Catlin was in error. The author was forced to seek out other people who could verify the content of his pictures and his text, which led to this more fully illustrated account. It includes an introduction by John C. Ewers and testimonial statements by others who had witnessed or heard of the O-kee-pa.

Clark, Jerry E. **The Shawnee.** U Pr of Ky 1977.

The Shawnee, an Algonquian tribe, had two to four thousand members at the beginning of the historic period. This is a history of that tribe, especially that part which lived in and around Kentucky, covering their social organization, subsistence, migrations, and relations with whites. Famous Shawnees, such as

Tecumseh and his brother, the Prophet, are also discussed. The book concludes with a bibliographical essay.

Cook, Sherburne F. **The Indian Population of New England in the Seventeenth Century.** U of Cal Pr 1976.

After several years on the Pacific Coast, working on population studies of California Indians, the author returned to New England, the locale of his birth and early manhood, to study the native populations there. Using reports of missionaries and early travelers to the area, as well as government documents, he has reconstructed the Indian populations of New England in the seventeenth century. A scholarly, specialized work.

Cook, Sherburne F. **The Population of the California Indians, 1769-1970.** U of Cal Pr 1976.

This collection of essays by a social biologist climaxes forty years of interest in the demography of Indian tribes. By studying records in California missions, diets of the various tribes, and records of early diseases, Cook raised the estimate of Indian population in California to over 300,000 around 1769. He also studied the reasons for the decline after the whites began to settle the state. A scholarly, well-documented study.

Cox, Bruce, editor. **Cultural Ecology: Readings on the Canadian Indians and Eskimos.** McClelland 1973.

These essays emphasize the relationship between the cultural life of the indigenous peoples of Canada and their conservation practices, organized in terms of the five Canadian geographical regions: Great Lakes–St. Lawrence, Boreal Forest, Grasslands, Pacific, and Arctic and Barren Grounds. The largest number of articles is in the section on the Boreal Forest, which is especially rich in ecological studies. The collection has descriptions of both early and recent cultures and their effects on ecology.

Crapanzano, Vincent. **The Fifth World of Forster Bennett: Portrait of a Navaho.** Viking Pr 1973.

As a young graduate student in anthropology, Crapanzano lived for two summer months in a Navaho village with the Navaho family of Forster Bennett. This is the day-by-day journal of his observations and experiences. Forster had been married several times and still had three daughters and a son at home. This is a picture of the poverty, boredom, drugs, and alcohol that are part of the life of the reservation Indian, but Forster still hopes for a better life for his children. The reader does not really understand how the Navaho feels and thinks, however; this is rather an account of a young anthropologist's feelings about Forster and his people.

"Unfortunately the author quotes his 'subject' throughout in a sort of dim-witted pidgin English, although in his own language 'Forster Bennett' may presumably have been reasonably articulate" (*Akwesasne Notes* 4:40, Summer 1972).

Crawford, James M., editor. **Studies in Southeastern Indian Languages.** U of Ga Pr 1975.

A collection of scholarly papers on Indian languages, presented at the annual meetings of the Southern Anthropological Society in 1970 and 1971. The Southeast is here defined as anything southward from the Potomac and Ohio rivers to the Atlantic and Gulf of Mexico, and westward beyond the Mississippi river for 200 miles or more. Included among the languages of the Southeast are Algonquian, Caddoan, Iroquoian, Muskogean, Sioux, and a few language isolates.

Deloria, Vine, Jr. **God Is Red.** Delta. Dell 1975.

The author states the purpose of his book in these words: "We shall attempt to define in Western terms that nature of Indian tribal religions as they differ in their method of framing questions from a predominantly spatial conception of reality. And we shall discuss traditional Christian solutions to these questions, comparing the two types of answers to learn if any distinct differences do in fact exist." The final solution to American history, Deloria says, is a reconciliation between the spiritual owners of the land—the American Indians—and the political owners of the land—the American whites. Drawing upon an extensive literature by Christian scholars as well as the writings about Indian religions, he concludes that "for this land, God is Red."

"Those who would understand the Indian viewpoint, past and present, will find this work instructive" (*American Indian Quarterly* 1:88, Summer 1974).

Drucker, Philip. **Indians of the Northwest Coast.** Natural Hist 1955.

The Northwest Indians, ranging from British Columbia to southeast Alaska, had an especially rich culture during the nineteenth century, of which little remains except a few artifacts. The author, an ethnologist, examines the collection in the American Museum of Natural History and reconstructs the history, social structure, religious beliefs, and ceremonial patterns of tribes such as the Chinook, Haida, and Chilkat.

Drucker, Philip, and Robert F. Heizer. **To Make My Name Good: A Re-Examination of the Southern Kwakiutl Potlatch.** U of Cal Pr 1967.

Although several well-known scholars, including Ruth Benedict, Franz Boas, and Helen Codere, have made studies of the Kwakiutl, the potlatch is still not understood. Making use of two well-qualified informants from the tribe, the authors—an ethnologist and an anthropologist—studied theories of the function and nature of the potlatch.

Embree, Edwin R. **Indians of the Americas.** Macmillan 1970.

Published in 1939, this is a simply written account of the Iroquois, Pueblo, and Oglala Sioux tribes. The author considered the Native American to be nearly extinct when he wrote the book. In the introduction of this new edition Vine Deloria, Jr., writes, "It is important to understand what Embree is trying to communicate in this book since it is the feeling of life which he presents that is the most important thing we can learn in this generation."

Farb, Peter. **Man's Rise to Civilization, As Shown by the Indians of North America from Primeval Times to the Coming of the Industrial State.** Avon 1968.

An anthropological and sociological study of North American Indians, tracing representative tribes from the very primitive Shoshones to the advanced Indians of the Northwest Coast and the Aztecs. Family organization, dances, burial customs, and religion are described. The final section considers the cultural and physical destruction of the Indian by European settlers. The author's thesis is that differences and similarities in cultures can be attributed to human social behavior rather than to biology or personality. He has been criticized by some readers for molding facts into a particular evolutionary theory. Maps, drawings, and photographs from leading museums and art collections.

"The unexamined premises under which the book was written are many and the book will merely serve to reinforce existing stereotypes concerning Indians which have been so detrimental for years" (Vine Deloria, Jr., *Custer Died for Your Sins*, p. 96). "Lacks the depth of scholarship which must be expected in such a work, but it's a good introduction" (*Textbooks and the American Indian*, p. 257). "Despite certain errors, more especially ethnographically, when the author describes various phases of Indian society and family relationships, this book deserves a wide readership" (*Indian Historian* 1:30, Winter 1968). "It is extraordinary in its scope and scholarship, and for these qualities it ought to be read . . . [although it perpetuates] the conception that social complexity is the equivalent of civilization" (N. Scott Momaday, *New York Review of Books* 16:39–42, 8 April 1971).

Garbarino, Merwyn S. Native American Heritage. Little 1976.

Intended as a college text covering all Indian groups within the United States from the crossing of the Bering land bridge to the present civil rights confrontations, arranged into four sections: Prehistory, Culture Areas of North America, Native American Culture, and Conflict between Cultures. Although it may be argued that this is not a history of Indian tribes but rather an anthropological treatment, the book attempts too much in too little space, and the result is a superficial treatment of everything. For instance, the author describes what happened at Wounded Knee in 1890 in five sentences and at the Battle of the Little Bighorn in only two (and the date of the Wounded Knee massacre is wrong). The impression is that the Indian people lost their battles because they were inept and savage, but the white soldiers never were. There are bibliographies for each of the sections but most of the publications appeared before 1970, and no Indian publications are listed for the final section on contemporary Indians.

"I cannot recommend this book except as another example of the kind of compilation of misinformation and one-sided interpretation of things Indian that we have come to expect of non-Indian writers over the years. I do recommend that teachers assiduously avoid using it" (*Wassaja* 4:14, June 1976).

Gidley, Mick. The Vanishing Race: Selections from Edward S. Curtis' The North American Indian. Taplinger 1977.

Between 1907 and 1930, twenty volumes of illustrated text and twenty portfolios containing more than seven hundred large-sized photogravures by Edward Curtis were published in a limited edition entitled *The North American Indian*. From these volumes, Gidley, a lecturer in American literature, has selected choice sections and pictures, giving descriptions of varied tribal homelands and habitations, religious beliefs, tribal organization, social customs, ceremonies, arts and crafts, food, war, mythology, songs, and tales. Suggested for use with *Edward S. Curtis: Photographer of the North American Indian* by Victor Boesen and Florence Curtis Graybill (see Senior Biography).

Gilmore, Melvin R. Uses of Plants by the Indians of the Missouri River Region. U of Nebr Pr 1977.

Published in 1919 as a report of the Bureau of American Ethnology, this study is an attempt to "ascertain so far as possible the relation of the native people of the plains to one phase of their indigenous physical environment—its plant life—and their ingenuity in supplying their necessities and pleasures therefrom." A taxonomic list of plants and their uses is included.

Hurdy, John Major. American Indian Religions. Sherbourne 1971.

This book describes the religions of five representative North American Indian tribes: Hopi, Sioux, Iroquois, Kwakiutl, and Navaho. It demonstrates how the religious values in each are evident in the social life and customs of the tribes, and discusses significant aspects of Indian religions such as the Ghost Dance, peyote cults, the potlatch, and the Snake Dance.

Josephy, Alvin M., Jr. The Indian Heritage of America. Bantam 1969.

A comprehensive account of Indian origins, culture, and history from the Arctic to South America, revealing the great diversity of tribes. The author examines ancient and present-day Indians, the whites' stereotypes of Indians, and the whites' attempts to make Indians like themselves. The author does not advocate any one school of thought on cultural progression and correlation. The contributions of archaeology, ethnology, history, and other disciplines to the study are recognized, and a generous selected bibliography is included. Also useful as a source book for junior high schools.

Kluckhohn, Clyde, and Dorothea Leighton. The Navaho. Natural Hist 1946.

During the drought and depression of the 1930s there was an urgent problem of survival for the increasing population of the Navaho Reservation in Arizona and New Mexico, because of the

soil erosion that was prevalent on their lands. Aided by agrono-
mists, educators, physicians, and other specialists, the U.S.
Office of Indian Affairs developed a program to relieve the condition. This updated version of the story is a study of how
failure to allow for the cultural patterns of the Navaho led to
failure of the program. The book remains a valuable introduction to the general ethnography of the Navaho, largest tribe in
the United States.

Kroeber, A. L. Handbook of the Indians of California. Dover 1976.

An unabridged republication of Bulletin 78 of the Bureau of
American Ethnology, this monumental work is a summary of
almost everything known at that time (1925) about California
Indians: demography, language relations, social structures, religion, crafts, and ceremonies. The most important tribes, the
Yurok, Pomo, Maidu, Yokuts, and Mohave, receive the most
detailed attention. The book contains 419 illustrations, 40
maps, and an extensive bibliography.

LaBarre, Weston. The Peyote Cult. Schocken 1969.

The first extended study of peyote, its effects, and its use in
the Native American Church, based on the author's Ph.D. thesis
and supplemented with two essays bringing the study up to
1964. Photographs and drawings of leaders and rituals of the
Native American Church. Cited by Sun Bear in *Buffalo Hearts*.

Landes, Ruth. The Ojibwa Woman. Norton 1971.

An ethnological field study of social behavior on the Emo
Reserve in western Ontario, containing material gathered in
the 1930s. Topics covered include youth, marriage, occupations, and abnormalities. The book concludes with a series of
life histories of women. Much of the information was given to
the author by Maggie Wilson of Emo. An in-depth study that
also will interest the general adult reader.

Latorre, Felipe A., and Dolores L. Latorre. The Mexican Kickapoo
Indians. U of Tex Pr 1976.

The Mexican Kickapoo are an Algonquian tribe which the
French first reported finding in Wisconsin during the seventeenth century. Following the encroachment by French, English,
and Americans during the 1800s they gradually moved South.
They found some acceptance in Mexico in the state of Coahuilla
because of their service in protecting ranchers from Apache and

Comanche raids. The authors found them in their village in 1960, living in many ways as they had lived in the past. For the next twelve years the authors lived in a neighboring village, gradually gaining the confidence of the Kickapoos in order to study their life, economy, ceremonies, medicine, and traditions. An interesting study about a little-known tribe, for scholars and general readers.

Lighthall, J. I. The Indian Folk Medicine Guide. Popular Lib 1974.

The author, a botanist who was one-eighth Indian, began early in life in Illinois to learn about plants. He went with Indian doctors into the woodlands and prairies, where he assisted them in gathering roots, barks, leaves, and flowers and in manufacturing them into Indian remedies. The book describes each plant, its uses, and how to prepare it for medicinal purposes. Published in 1883.

Long, James Larpenteur (editor Michael Stephen Kennedy). The Assiniboines: From the Accounts of the Old Ones Told to First Boy (James Larpenteur Long). Illus. William Standing. U of Okla Pr 1961.

This book grew out of the pre-World War II Federal Writers' Program. Although not a full-blooded Indian, the author grew up with his full-blooded Assiniboine grandmother and half-blooded Indian mother and was steeped in Assiniboine traditions. The Old Ones told him the tales and customs of their tribe, and this book contains their legends and descriptions of war parties, courtship and marriage, hunting societies, and medicine men. The illustrator is a full-blooded Assiniboine.

   "Long interviewed and recorded twenty-five of the oldest members of the Assiniboine tribe living in the 1930s. Their facts, stories, and recollections tell of the Assiniboine way of life" (*American Indian Authors*, p. 26).

Lowie, Robert H. Indians of the Plains. AMS. Natural Hist 1954.

A distinguished anthropologist writes about the life of the Indians who inhabited the Plains from the Mississippi to the Rockies—Blackfeet, Cheyenne, Dakota, Crow, Kiowa, Mandan, Osage, Hidatsa, and Shoshone. These tribes had certain things in common because of the nature of the area in which they lived, but there were many differences. A useful handbook of information on these tribes.

McClintock, Walter. The Old North Trail: Or Life, Legends and Religion of the Blackfeet Indians. U of Nebr Pr 1968.

In 1896 the author was a member of a U.S. Forest Service expedition to northwestern Montana under Gifford Pinchot. There he became acquainted with the Blackfeet and was adopted into the tribe as a son of Chief Mad Dog, their great orator, high priest of the Sun Dance, and keeper of the Beaver Medicine Bundle. For four years he lived with the tribe, keeping accurate records of their customs, ceremonials, and life. He reminisces about his encounter with the missionary Father DeSmet and gives a wealth of information about warrior societies, songs, dances, and the effects of white civilization upon the tribe.

Marriott, Alice. The Ten Grandmothers. U of Okla Pr 1968.

The author lived among the Kiowas during the summers of 1935 and 1936, and these are stories which the elderly people of the tribe told her about their lives. Sitting Bear tells of his attempt to find out which of his sons had mystical power; Spear Woman tells of loneliness after her marriage, until her husband also married her sister who then helped with the work and kept her company. Sketches tell of later generations and their adjustments to going away to school, the coming of missionaries, and the disappearance of the buffalo. Although the same characters and families appear in all of the sketches, each one is a story complete in itself.

Marriott, Alice, and Carol K. Rachlin. American Epic: The Story of the American Indian. Ment. NAL 1970.

The purpose of this book is to show how the Indians were more greatly affected by the movements of people than they were by historical events. An extensive section discusses tribal movements in prehistoric times before contact with whites. The remainder of the book surveys the migrations, cultures, religion, wars, and adversities of the tribes up to the time of today's so-called red power. Although sympathetic to the preservation of tribal ways, the authors disapprove of the Native American Church.

"Much labor and study has gone into this work and it is recommended as a general reference for Indian history from the era of migration to the present day" (*About Indians*, p. 223).

Marriott, Alice, and Carol K. Rachlin. **Peyote.** Ment. NAL 1971.

A short study of the peyote cult from its beginning in the Mexican desert to when it was carried by the half-breed, Quanah Parker, to his people and other tribes of the Plains. Use of the drug in services of the Native American Church, the symbolic significance of objects used in the rite, and the relationship of peyote to metalwork, painting, and music are described. The authors also discuss the possible harmful effects of the drug's continued use. The authors are anthropologists who have participated in the peyote ceremony. For a shorter and easier-to-read book on the subject, see *The Peyote Cult* by Weston LaBarre (this section).

Mead, Margaret. **People and Places.** Illus. W. T. Mars and Jan Fairservis. Bantam 1970.

The author discusses five cultural groups—the Eskimo, Indians of the Plains, the Balinese, the Minoans of Crete, and the Ashanti of West Africa, emphasizing how each group developed in relation to its environment and its contact with other people. She is especially concerned with how the young learn their culture and its values. The Blackfoot and Cheyenne Indians are discussed in depth. This book has been called a "young people's encyclopedia of man."

Morey, Sylvester M., and Olivia L. Gillam, editors. **Respect for Life: Report of a Conference at Harper's Ferry, West Virginia, on the Traditional Upbringing of American Indian Children.** Illus. Warren P. Jennerjahn. Waldorf Pr 1974.

The Myrin Institute for Adult Education in 1974 invited leading Indians from widely separated tribes to spend a week in discussing traditional Indian views of bringing up children. The purpose was to "focus attention to the intuitive wisdom of the American Indian, in order to bring about greater understanding and mutual help between red man and white." Among the elders who took part were two Navajos, two Crows, a Mohawk, a Kiowa, a Laguna Pueblo, and an Arapaho, plus the various officials of the Institute. Topics such as childbirth, the discipline of the cradle board, obedience, adolescence, the role of grandparents, family and clan structure, and the home were discussed.

Morgan, Lewis Henry. **League of the Iroquois: A Classic Study of an American Indian Tribe.** Citadel Pr 1972.

Although he made money as a corporation lawyer, Lewis Morgan wanted to research the Iroquois, in order "to encourage a kinder feeling towards the Indian, founded upon a truer knowledge of his civil and domestic institutions." He researched the history of the tribe up to the time of publication—its family relationships, religion, dances, games, pottery, and language. Published in 1851. On *Akwesasne Notes* basic library list.

Niethammer, Carolyn. **Daughters of the Earth: The Lives and Legends of American Indian Women.** Collier. Macmillan 1977.

The position of the Indian woman varied greatly among the tribes. In most tribes she created the home and raised the children, but in some she led men into battle and even ruled the tribe. Through interviews with modern Indian women, the writings of anthropologists, and old songs, legends, and ceremonies, the author gathers together into one volume a great deal of information that formerly appeared in scattered sources. The book covers topics such as childbirth, courtship, widowhood, the Indian woman's economic role, and her role as witch, doctor, and warrior.

Nurge, Ethel, editor. **The Modern Sioux: Social Systems and Reservation Culture.** U of Nebr Pr 1975.

A collection of essays by anthropologists who have studied the various aspects of modern Sioux bands: their economy, diet, government, religious systems, family organization, music, and dance. The editor is an anthropology professor and each of the contributors has had extensive experience among the Sioux.

Powers, Stephen. **Tribes of California.** U of Cal Pr 1976.

On New Year's Day in 1869, Powers began a walking trip across the United States from Raleigh, North Carolina, using the so-called southern route, and arrived in San Francisco on November 3 in the same year. Having been a newspaper correspondent in Europe for several years, he wrote an account of the trip. He then turned to another project, for which he gathered material during the summers of 1871 and 1872, traveling on foot and by horseback among California Indians, collecting material on their habits, customs, legends, geographical bound-

aries, and religious ideas. Although he was not an anthropologist, his work has served as a base for all other studies of these
Indians. Published in 1877.

Powers, William K. **Oglala Religion.** U of Nebr Pr 1977.

This is a scholarly study of the Oglala Sioux—their history,
their relationship to other divisions of the Seven Council Fires
of the Sioux, and their social and cultural identity. The author,
an anthropologist, "treats continuity and change as two aspects
of the same phenomenon." Rather than assuming that Native
Americans have or will become Americanized, he concentrates
on those Oglala cultural values that have persisted. He reconstructs their religious system at the time of first contact with
whites and compares it with present-day practices at Pine Ridge
Reservation. Emphasis is on the Sun Dance, vision quest, sweat
lodge, memorial feast, and Yuwipi rituals.

Sando, Joe S. **The Pueblo Indians.** Indian Hist Pr 1975.

A Jemez man, Joe Sando, has written this history of the Pueblo
people from the Indian point of view. The inhabitants of the
nineteen pueblos of the Southwest are descendants of the aborigines of that area, estimated to have occupied their land ten
thousand years before Christ. Sando begins his history with the
oral traditions of the origins of his people, continues with the
Spanish conquest and the Pueblo Revolt, and finally discusses
the Pueblos and their relationship with the United States
government. He concludes with a chapter on elements of change
in education, the economy, and lifestyle, and biographies of
people who have shaped Pueblo history.

Tedlock, Dennis, and Barbara Tedlock, editors. **Teachings from
the American Earth: Indian Religion and Philosophy.** Liveright
1975.

This is a valuable collection of fifteen articles, some by Indians
and some by whites, on various Indian religions and philosophical beliefs. The articles are arranged under two subheadings:
Seeing and Curing, and Thinking about the World. Among the
well-known writers represented are Knut Rasmussen (on the
Eskimos), Black Elk, Ruth Underhill, James Moody, Alfonso
Ortiz, and Paul Radin.

Terrell, John Upton. American Indian Almanac. World. Times Mir 1971.

The author, an American historian who has written extensively on western history, has sifted through anthropological, ethnological, archaeological, and geological sources to create a very readable book on what is known about Indian tribes before the arrival of the whites. Dividing the United States into ten geographical regions that conform generally to prehistorical cultural areas, he discusses what is known about the earliest people and their successors in each area—their ways of life, ritual, arts, and political systems. Each section ends shortly after the historical period of that geographical area began. An absorbing discussion of the mystery-shrouded origins of the tribes.

Terrell, John Upton, and Donna M. Terrell. Indian Women of the Western Morning: Their Life in Early America. Anch. Doubleday 1976.

A study of what it was like to be a woman in the various Indian tribes of early America. The authors discuss the role of women in creation myths, the status of women, their duties, their health and physiques, the crafts at which they excelled, sexual performance, and the raising of children. The authors rely upon myths, early histories, and journals of early travelers and explorers for their information. They disprove the concept of the Indian woman as an abject drudge of her tribe's men.

Recommended by Beatrice Medicine in "The Role of Women in Native American Societies" (*Indian Historian* 8:51-53, Summer 1975). "The book will be useful to college students, interested general readers, as well as a starting place for researchers" (*American Indian Quarterly* 2:153, Summer 1975).

Thomas, Davis, and Karin Ronnefeldt, editors. People of the First Man: Life among the Plains Indians in Their Final Days of Glory—The Firsthand Account of Prince Maximilian's Expedition up the Missouri River, 1833-34. Illus. Karl Bodmer. Dutton 1976.

In 1833-34, Prince Maximilian of Wied, the German explorer and naturalist, along with Karl Bodmer, his Swiss-born artist friend traveled five thousand miles along the Missouri River to visit and record the life of the Plains Indians: Mandan, Blackfeet, Cree, Sioux, Minnetaree, Assiniboin, and Gros Ventre.

They were especially careful to record the daily life and the ceremonies—Maximilian in words, Bodmer in pictures. This collection contains newly edited and translated entries and pictures never before published—material discovered after World War II.

Waters, Frank. Book of the Hopi. Illus. Oswald White Bear Fredericks. Ballantine 1969.

Frank Waters collected the myths, legends, ceremonials, and history of the Hopi Indians during three years spent on the Hopi reservation. Some thirty older members of the tribe told their stories on tape, and White Bear translated them. The book is supplemented by answers to specific questions, personal observations of ceremonies, field trips, and historical research. It contains four sections: myths, legends (migrations of the clans), mystery plays, and history. Mainly for sophisticated readers with a special interest in the Hopi Indians. Cited by Sun Bear in *Buffalo Hearts*. On *Akwesasne Notes* basic library list. See also *Pumpkin Seed Point* by the same author (Senior Biography).

"These drawings and source materials provide an account of Hopi historical and religious views as interpreted by a Hopi artist in collaboration with a non-Indian novelist" (*American Indian Authors*, p. 20). "Waters' compilation of Hopi prophecies has been the handbook of traditionalist Indians working to reestablish ancient Indian ways in contemporary society" (Vine Deloria, Jr., in the introduction to *Indians of the Americas* by Edward Embree). "The book has been repeatedly denounced as a fabrication by many traditional chiefs, and several elders who were listed as collaborators in the preface were surprised to discover this. The taped interviews on which the book is allegedly based have never turned up despite frequent requests by the elders" (Alfonso Ortiz, *Indian Historian* 4:14, Spring 1971).

Waters, Frank. Masked Gods: Navaho and Pueblo Ceremonialism. Ballantine 1970.

This interpretation and history of Pueblo and Navaho life includes a history of the tribes, theories about their origins, their relationships with other tribes, and their historical movements. There also is an analysis of the ceremonials—Navaho songs, Pueblo dances, and the Zuni kachina ceremonials—and of the influences on the life and character of the people. Some scholars have questioned some of its facts and conclusions while acknowledging that it is a splendid and personal book. Cited by Sun Bear in *Buffalo Hearts.*

"[It is] an important, muscular, prejudiced, erroneous, angry, perceptive, misleading, stimulating book" (Oliver La Farge, *New York Herald Tribune*, 2 September 1951, p. 9).

Weslager, C. A. **Magic Medicines of the Indians.** NAL 1974.

The author, a historian, examines the cures that Indians used for all sorts of ailments. Through historical documents and actual testimonies from records left by explorers and settlers, Weslager explains the relationship between Indian medicine and religion. His main examples come from the Delaware Indians, especially Touching Leaves (Nora Thompson Dean), an herbalist and visionary living in Oklahoma. Several hundred plants and their medicinal uses are listed.

"These herbs were not used indiscriminately but were administered in a ritualistic manner . . . the author understands this relationship" (*American Indian Quarterly* 2:148–149, Summer 1975).

Will, George F., and George E. Hyde. **Corn among the Indians of the Upper Missouri.** U of Nebr Pr 1964.

This reprint of a 1917 publication is a study of the kinds of corn and its place in the lives of the Indians of the upper Missouri River area—the Arikaras, Hidatsas, Mandans, Iowas, Omahas, Otoes, Pawnees, Ponkas, Sioux, Chippewa, Winnebagoes, and Iroquois. Historical documents are cited from the earliest explorers, reporting the adoption of corn by white settlers as an essential part of their diet and economy. In addition to the use of corn as food and as an article of trade, several of the tribes held it sacred and made it the center of elaborate ceremonies.

"The editors welcome the reprinting of a most important work on *Corn among the Indians*" (*Indian Historian* 10:49, Fall 1977).

# Modern Life and Problems

## Elementary

Bales, Carol Ann. **Kevin Cloud: Chippewa Boy in the City.** Contemp Bks 1972. Primary.

Eleven-year-old Kevin is a city boy living on the North Side of Chicago, which may not seem to be unusual, but he is a Chippewa Indian. His family, forced for economic reasons to leave the reservation near Cass Lake, Minnesota, is thoroughly urbanized, yet his mother and grandmother pass on as much as possible of the Chippewa lore to Kevin and his brother and sisters. Told in Kevin's words, the book aptly conveys the Indians' innate feeling for their own kind. Both black and white and color photographs emphasize the persistence of the Indian way, even in the big city.

Blades, Ann. **A Boy of Taché.** Illus. by author. Tundra Bks 1976. Primary.

This contemporary true story of Charlie, a young Carrier Indian, takes place on Taché, an Indian reserve in northern British Columbia. Charlie feels fortunate to be living with his grandparents, Za and Virginia, as they embark on a trip to their summer dwelling to fish, trap, and pick berries. Za and Charlie decide to go inland for a few days, where Za begins to shiver and it is obvious that help is needed. Charlie goes to a camp where a phone is available and calls for a plane to land at the cabin. Later a friend assures him that his grandfather will recover, but Charlie will have to do the hunting and trapping for his grandparents. The story is based on a true incident which occurred on this reservation while the author was teaching there. Illustrations portray the present lifestyle of the people. 1972 Book of the Year, Canadian Association of Children's Libraries.

"At times the author's style lacks fluency but the material content and spirit of the text truly capture the Indian way. Ann Blades has illustrated this book with beautiful, soft-tone watercolors, which skillfully portray the essence of the people and their environment" (*About Indians*, p. 11).

Brill, Charles. **Indian and Free: A Contemporary Portrait of Life on a Chippewa Reservation.** Photographs by author. U of Minn Pr 1974. Intermediate.

This collection of 160 photographs with accompanying text presents the contemporary life of the Red Lake Band of Chippewa Indians in northern Minnesota. The freedom of the Indians' way of life is emphasized as they fish and hunt freely in the half-million acres of woodlands, lakes, and streams. Daily work, such as logging, ricing, hunting, and fishing is portrayed. In the powwow, an important part of their life, the Chippewas display their colorful costumes with beadwork of a popular floral design. Pictures of children's activities show swimming, baseball, tree-climbing, and other pastimes. Scenes of home life and wake and burial customs are included. An excellent resource on the modern life of the Chippewa Indians.

Conklin, Paul. **Choctaw Boy.** Photographs by author. Dodd 1975. Primary.

This is a biography of eleven-year-old Clifton Henry, a contemporary Choctaw boy living in Bogue Chitto in central Mississippi. He enjoys football, baseball, fishing, and watching television, and does a lively business in trading bubble gum cards. The highlight of his summer is the annual Choctaw Indian fair with its stickball tournament. The pageant, depicting the past when Choctaws were proud and prosperous, also brings sad memories of their Trail of Tears. Clifton is caught between two worlds and finds enjoyment in both.

Crowder, Jack L. **Stephannie and the Coyote.** Photographs by author. Crowder 1969. Primary.

This story tells of the daily activities of Stephannie Peaches, a seven-year-old Navajo girl. Color photographs of Stephannie and her maternal grandparents, who pose as her parents, accompany the text in English and Navajo. Related in a sympathetic manner, giving younger readers insights into the customs and lifestyle of the Navajo today.

Henderson, Nancy, and Jane Dewey. **Circle of Life: The Miccosu-kee Indian Way.** Photographs by David Pickens. Messner 1974. Intermediate.

The Miccosukee Indians of the Florida Everglades seldom left their marshy home until the 1920s. Then the opening of the Tamiami Trail, which runs through their lands, and the appro-priation of more than two million acres of Miccosukee land for the Everglades National Park brought the realization that the tribe must find new ways of living. How they finally solved their problems and how they live today are related in this book—the first ever written about the Miccosukees.

Keegan, Marcia. **The Taos Indians and Their Sacred Blue Lake.** Photographs by author. Messner 1972. Primary.

This is the story of the Taos Indians' long and determined struggle to regain their sacred Blue Lake. The land surrounding the lake had belonged to them since ancient times, but first Spain, then Mexico, and finally the United States claimed ownership. All countries had recognized that the mountain wilderness surrounding Blue Lake belonged to the Indians as their place of worship, but the United States violated this agree-ment in 1906 by making the area a national forest. This started a legal battle lasting sixty-five years. This is a thorough study of a current issue, quoting many of the Taos people involved in the controversy, and giving insight into the Taos Indians' pro-found love of nature and respect for their religion.

Kirk, Ruth. **David, Young Chief of the Quileutes: An American Indian Today.** Photographs by author. HarBraceJ 1967. Inter-mediate.

The coast of the state of Washington is the locale of this sym-pathetic picture of the Quileute Indians, who strive to keep their tribal ways while living almost entirely in the contem-porary white world. David, or Hoheeshata, at the age of eleven, is already chief of the Quileutes, having been designated chief when he was three so that he could be indoctrinated throughout his young life with the tribal ways of his people, in order to respect and further them. The Quileutes live a thoroughly modern life, while cherishing their tribal customs. Cited in *A Preliminary Bibliography of Selected Children's Books.*

Reit, Seymour. Child of the Navajos. Photographs by Paul Conklin. Dodd 1971. Primary.

The light-hearted yet disciplined life of a Navajo Indian boy in present-day America is effectively told in pictures and narrative. Young Indians, through close tribal living on one hand and carefully structured schooling on the other, learn to live in America as both members of the tribe and citizens of the white community.

Tamarin, Alfred. **We Have Not Vanished: Eastern Indians of the United States.** Follett 1974. Intermediate.

Contrary to the belief of many, the Indians of the East Coast of the United States have not disappeared; from Maine to Florida more than 115,000 of them live in some sixty tribal groups, in cities and on reservations. This is a presentation of the Indian personality as it sees itself and a description of how these Indians live today. The author describes the Indians state by state, and makes some interesting forecasts about their future.

Wolf, Bernard. **Tinker and the Medicine Men: The Story of a Navajo Boy of Monument Valley.** Photographs by author. Random 1973. Intermediate.

Six-year-old Tinker Yazzie is an Arizona boy with a special heritage, as the son and grandson of medicine men, and his ambition is to become one too. One week of his life is illustrated with photographs and a sympathetic text, beginning with Tinker returning to his home after going to school in town for a year. Daily family tasks such as watering the flocks, weaving rugs, and preparing food are pictured. Tinker's father teaches him the practices of the traditional Navajo singer and the peyote religion, and Tinker participates for the first time in a peyote ceremony. Numerous black and white photographs.

## Junior High

Akwesasne Notes. **Voices from Wounded Knee, 1973: In the Words of the Participants.** Akwesasne 1974.

This book includes transcriptions of taped conversations and pictures taken during the occupation of Wounded Knee. In the winter of 1973, several hundred Oglala Sioux moved to impeach their tribal chairman, Richard Wilson. He, in turn, called in United States Marshals and the Federal Bureau of Investigation. The Oglalas then asked the American Indian Movement for support. For seventy-one days no federal law enforcement personnel or Bureau of Indian Affairs officials had any authority in Wounded Knee. The editorial collective that produced this report with pictures included two reporters who had been working with *The Rest of the News,* an alternative radio network in Ithaca, New York, and two others who came from New York and Chicago, one to do support work and one to cover the confrontation for a newspaper. Three of these people were inside Wounded Knee during the confrontation, talking to the people there; the fourth was in Rapid City to gather tapes as they came out. On *Akwesasne Notes* basic library list.

Dorris, Michael. Native Americans: 500 Years After. Photographs by Joseph C. Farber. T Y Crowell 1975.

It took Joseph Farber five years of traveling throughout North America to collect these photographs of Indians as they live, work, and play today. From the Eskimos at Point Barrow, Alaska, Farber traveled down the West Coast and across the United States—photographing Tlingit totem poles, ceremonial dances in the Southwest, ricing in Minnesota, the funeral of a Sioux war hero, Mohawks working on high steel, and Seminole cattle-raising in Florida. Michael Dorris, a Modoc anthropologist, has provided an eighteen-page introduction.

George, Chief Dan, and Helmut Hirnschall. My Heart Soars. Hancock Hse 1974.

In a series of prose poems and prayers, Chief Dan George of the Capilano tribe of British Columbia speaks of his parents and the values they gave him, the needs of his people now, the things they value, and his own place in the tribe. He can no longer fight as a warrior chief for his tribe, but he can speak for his people. He sees them as people no longer with hands out for welfare but rather as people who can contribute to society their skills and also their values from the past—love for the earth and its creatures, respect for communal living and working with one's hands, regard for old people and old ways, and dependence on the spiritual life. Illustrated with drawings.

Halsell, Grace. Bessie Yellowhair. Warner Bks 1974.

The author's father was a Texas rancher and Indian fighter who once outwitted Geronimo. It was natural, then, that following her experience of passing as a black woman and writing *Soul Sister*, she should turn to living as a Navajo Indian. After living with several other Navajo families, she met Bessie Yellowhair and her family. She lived with them in their isolated hogan, slept on their mud floor, ate their mutton stew, and shared their silences. When Grace felt that she could pass for an Indian, she applied for a job as a housemaid in Irvine, California. She was submissive, passive, and oppressed, until finally she could no longer stand being a Navajo maid and fled from the experience.

Hirst, Stephen. **Life in a Narrow Place: The Havasupai of the Grand Canyon.** Photographs by Terry Eiler and Lyntha Eiler. McKay 1976.

For nearly a century, most of the Havasupai Indian nation have lived on 518 acres of canyon on one of the smallest and most inaccessible reservations in the world, at the bottom of the Grand Canyon. This book is the story of their life, and their struggles to regain their traditional winter homeland on the plateau above their canyon. Against overwhelming odds they won their battle for survival, and in 1975 President Ford signed a bill which returned to them the largest amount of land ever reclaimed by a single tribe. The author went to the Havasupai in 1967 to teach in their tribal school, and served as secretary and bookkeeper for the tribal council and assistant director of the Havasupai Land Use Plan. Generously illustrated with photographs.

Hungry Wolf, Adolf. **Indian Summer.** Good Medicine Bks 1975.

This book is one of a series devoted to inspiring "new people of today with the spirits and ways of the old people who lived in this land in the past." Hungry Wolf and his family create the books from their home, Good Medicine Ranch, in a valley in the Rocky Mountains of Canada. This volume contains poems and articles about old people whom Hungry Wolf has visited, and about powwows, and history.

LaPointe, Frank. **The Sioux Today.** CCPr. Macmillan 1972.

The author, a Rosebud Sioux, uses vignettes of twenty-four individuals to show what life is like for the young Sioux today— fighting poverty, unemployment, and conflict between their heritage and the dominant white culture. Shirley, who died suddenly at fourteen, left her brothers and sisters without their substitute mother; Ruth discovered her heritage through the giveaway; Ken wanted to be an Olympic runner; Louis did not want to admit that he was a Sioux. These are some of the people to be met in this book.

"Mr. LaPointe . . . does not romanticize his people. In a series of blunt profiles of representative lives, he shows how the Sioux are fighting the forces that conflict with their culture, as well as their continuing struggle against poverty and ignorance" (Dee Brown, *New York Times Book Review*, pt. 2, 15 November 1972, p. 20).

Louis, Ray Baldwin. **Child of the Hogan.** Brigham 1975.

Ray Louis, a Navajo writer and entertainer, has collected from his own works a series of poems and short poetic prose selections about the Navajo. Each selection describes a slice of the Navajo life, demonstrating the love of home, reverence for life, and respect for tribal traditions. Illustrated with photographs of Navajo territory.

Manuel, George, and Michael Posluns. **The Fourth World: An Indian Reality.** Free Pr 1974.

This book is George Manuel's vision of a world where aboriginal peoples—the Indians of the Americas, the Lapps of Scandinavia, the Polynesian and Pacific Basin peoples, the Basques of Spain, the Welsh and Celts of Great Britain, the Maori and Australian aborigines, and others who share similar status—will be on an equal footing with other peoples. This will occur when the values of these people—especially their unity with the land and their practice of making decisions for the good of the tribe rather than of the individual—are integrated into the values of all peoples. The book discusses the experiences of Manuel, a Shuswap Indian, as he worked for recognition of Canadian Indians.

"Manuel is not a historian, and is little concerned with research, footnotes, and bibliography. Instead, the authors tell what it is like to be an Indian in Canada today in language that the general public would appreciate" (*American Indian Quarterly* 2:253, Autumn 1975). "The history of any Indian Nation, or indeed that of any aboriginal people, can be read in its pages" (*Indian Historian* 7:58, Summer 1974).

Schusky, Ernest. **The Right to Be Indian.** Indian Hist Pr 1970.

This brief monograph, widely used by teachers and students in the social sciences and Native American studies since its first appearance in 1965, offers a definition of the Indian and discusses the complexities of the Indian struggle for civil rights during the early 1960s. The author, a non-Indian, states, "Civil rights problems of American Indians are particularly complex because Indians can claim special rights. Their unique rights derive from historical circumstance." In reissuing the monograph, the Indian Historical Society noted that conditions with regard to the Indian's civil rights have worsened since the 1960s.

Vizenor, Gerald. **The Everlasting Sky: New Voices from the People Named the Chippewa.** CCPr. Macmillan 1972.

A contemporary Chippewa writes about the hopes, fears, and feelings of the *oshki anishinabe*, the new people of the woodland. Using examples of people in Minnesota, he tells how they feel about their homes, families, reservations, and education. He reviews some legends of the past, and gives insight into the feelings of the old people of the tribe. He describes the young urban Indians who know little about the past, and the reservation youths who cannot face the schools they must attend. There also are interviews with college students and college graduates who seem to have succeeded but remain troubled because they exist between two cultures.

Vizenor, Gerald. **Tribal Scenes and Ceremonies.** Nodin Pr 1976.

A Chippewa writer has collected ten years of his work on problems of the modern Indian in white society. There is a discussion of the case of Thomas James White Hawk, the young Sioux accused of killing a jeweler in Vermillion, South Dakota. Other issues include the American Indian Movement, Indian education, hunting and fishing rights, paraeconomic survival, and tribal ceremonies. Vizenor, a capable spokesman for his people, also discusses the concerns of important Indian people today. Illustrated with photographs.

### Senior High and Adult

Brophy, William A., and Sophie D. Aberle. **The Indian: America's Unfinished Business.** U of Okla Pr 1969.

This is a report of the activities of the Commission on the Rights, Liberties, and Responsibilities of the American Indian, established by the Fund for the Republic to give an up-to-date appraisal of the status of the Indian. Impetus for the commission was a congressional resolution setting forth a policy of terminating the special relationship between Indians and the federal government. The report covers topics such as law, government, and economic conditions of the Indian; the Bureau of Indian Affairs; education; health; and policies that have impeded Indian development. The author is a former Commissioner of Indian Affairs. Useful in social problems classes and for students researching contemporary conditions of Indians. On Rupert Costo's list of suggested reading on the American Indian Today (*Indian Historian* 1:35, Winter 1968).

Burnette, Robert, and John Koster. **The Road to Wounded Knee.** Bantam 1974.

Burnette, tribal chairman of the Rosebud Sioux, gives his version of the reasons for the takeover of the Bureau of Indian Affairs (BIA) in Washington and the confrontations at Wounded Knee in 1972 and 1973. Koster is a white journalist who has reported on Indian activism. Burnette describes the events that precipitated the incidents and offers a nine-point program for improving circumstances among the Indians today. He is especially critical of the BIA, so-called Uncle Tomahawks (second-generation Indians who depend on white establishment approval for satisfaction), and white liberals who admire Martin Luther King but are unsympathetic toward Indians and their problems.

"He offers a nine-point program for improving the disgraceful situation of Native Americans today, a positive, though far from perfect answer, to the question asked by potential supporters— 'What can we do?'" (*American Indian Quarterly* 2:33, Spring 1975). "This is a much-needed book, considering the great amount of misinformation that has been disseminated about the event" (*Indian Historian* 7:51, Spring 1974).

Cahn, Edgar S., editor. **Our Brother's Keeper: The Indian in White America.** New Com Pr 1969.

The Citizen's Advocate Center of Washington, D. C., made a study of today's 600,000 American Indians whose lives are dominated by the Bureau of Indian Affairs. The report covers all aspects of Indian life in the United States, with emphasis on problems of education, health, and land. Its purpose is best described in the words of the postscript: "This book has attempted to provide an insight into the frustrations of that world which thwarts and penalizes individual and tribal self-realization, which rewards and perpetuates dependency, and which demands alienation from one's heritage as a price for survival."

Written partly to shock, the report is valuable for senior high research on today's problems of the Indian.

"The book is probably the best thus far in describing actual Indian opinion on certain levels and in certain sections of the country. It goes no further than that, and certainly it lacks a complete cross-section of Native American opinion" (*Indian Historian* 3:61, Winter 1970). "Everyone concerned with the political reasons for the social and economic problems confronting the contemporary American Indian student should read this book" (*About Indians*, p. 137).

Collier, John. **On the Gleaming Way: Navajos, Eastern Pueblos, Zunis, Hopis, Apaches, and Their Land—And Their Meanings to the World.** Swallow 1962.

This is an attempt to describe southwestern Indian tribes and their outlook on life; for example, the introductory chapter, Another Time Dimension, points out the tyranny of clocks in our technological society compared to the Indians' power "to endure, to create, and to outlast." The book was begun in 1946 when the author was an advisor on trusteeship to the American delegation at the General Assembly of the United Nations and trying to persuade the United States to lift the "blight of military absolutism" from the Pacific Islands. Suitable for study of the Indians of the Southwest and their ways of life. On *Akwesasne Notes* basic library list.

Deloria, Vine, Jr. **Behind the Trail of Broken Treaties: An Indian Declaration of Independence.** Delta. Dell 1974.

Deloria briefly reviews the background of treaties that have been made with Indian tribes. He then analyzes events that led to the formation of the Trail of Broken Treaties caravan, which crossed the United States in 1972, and discusses developments later that year which ended in the showdown at Wounded Knee. Deloria examines the claims that whites do or do not have, to the North American continent. He discusses the relationship of Indian tribes to the U.S. government and concludes that the tribes should be considered as independent nations under the protection of the United States.

Deloria, Vine, Jr. **Custer Died for Your Sins: An Indian Manifesto.** Avon 1970.

A Sioux Indian and former executive director of the National Congress of American Indians clearly defines Indian values and their clashes with those of the whites. He documents past mistreatment of Indians by the U.S. government, church groups, and anthropologists, and criticizes the political, social, and religious forces that perpetuate the stereotyping of his people. There is a discussion of tribal organization and the ways in which modern society might benefit from its values. Necessary reading for students or teachers interested in learning the attitudes of Indians. Cited in *American Indian Authors;* also on *Akwesasne Notes* basic library list.

"With a rare talent for writing, Mr. Deloria has expressed the views of many Indian people, and has done it well" (*Textbooks and the American Indian*, p. 260). "Highly recommended on all levels particularly for a good introduction to the ideological pressures upon the American Indian today and in the near past" (*Indian Historian* 3:62, Winter 1970).

Deloria, Vine, Jr. We Talk, You Listen: New Tribes, New Turf. Dell 1970.

In this book the author develops his thesis that the answers to a great many of America's problems—imperialism, capitalism, ecology, and inflation, for example—lie in neotribalism. The concept of individualism, he feels, is outmoded. The real need of society is an extended concept of the tribe, which can be learned from the Indian, whose way of life is the most durable and flexible of any in the country. Articulate and incisive, Deloria turns from Indian problems to the problems of the United States, and contributions the Indian way of life might make toward correcting them. On *Akwesasne Notes* basic library list.

N. Scott Momaday feels that Deloria's plea for tribalism is made in the interest of "an economic and not an ethical ideal." Momaday does not object so much to what Deloria says but rather to the fact that he does not go far enough: "In neither book [this and *Custer Died for Your Sins*] is there any real evocation of that spirit and mentality which distinguishes the Indian as a man and as a race" (*New York Review of Books* 16:39-42, 8 April 1971).

Dosman, Edgar J. Indians: The Urban Dilemma. McClelland 1976.

As a native of Saskatchewan, the author decided to study the conditions of urban Indians in Saskatoon. By the early 1960s several factors had brought about a large-scale migration of Indians and Metis (mixed bloods) into that city—an industrial and housing boom provided employment opportunities; Indians awakened to possibilities outside of the reserves; they acquired greater access to transportation; controls over the Indians by the Indian Affairs Branch broke down; and the population of Indians and Metis throughout Canada increased rapidly. Dosman concludes that, having broken the Indians, Canadian society must now accept the consequences of Indian poverty in order to develop a Canadian civilization. He suggests reasons for the failure of existing welfare programs and makes both short- and long-term proposals for improvement.

Fey, Harold E., and D'Arcy McNickle. **Indians and Other Americans: Two Ways of Life Meet.** Har-Row 1971.

A short, readable explanation of why, 450 years after the first Europeans arrived in North America, the Indians are poorer and less well educated than any other racial minority, have a shorter life expectancy, and suffer great economic and social injustice. A discussion of wars, treaties, land agreements, attempts at education, urbanization, and industrialization, and their effects on the Indian. Harold Fey, editor of the *Christian Century*, and D'Arcy McNickle, Flathead Indian, collaborate on this history of Indian-white relations. Cited by Rupert Costo in his list of suggested reading on the American Indian Today (*Indian Historian* 1:35, Winter 1968).

"Necessary for an understanding of the current situation" (*Textbooks and the American Indian*, p. 256). "At a time when authentic and accurate information was scarce, this little book filled a great need. Today it seems inadequate; accurate still, but inadequate. . . . But one must respect their approach which is useful in studying the complexities of Indian affairs today" (*Indian Historian* 4:52, Spring 1971). "This comprehensive survey reviews the contacts between Indians and European colonists, wars, treaties, land deals, educative attempts, effects of relocation, urbanization, industrialization, and contemporary self-help programs designed to help Indians retain dignity and a sense of identity" (*American Indian Authors*, p. 27).

Highwater, Jamake. **Fodor's Indian America.** Illus. Asa Battles. McKay 1975.

This is a compendium of facts and information about American Indians, and where to go to see them and their ceremonies. It includes sections on Indian history and culture, information on contemporary artists, where to shop for arts and crafts, and a

directory of Indian galleries and museums, ceremonials, costumes, and dwellings. The main section covers various Indian
nations, including that of the Eskimos and the Aleuts. One
rather obvious error, however, is the treatment of the Chippewas or Objibwas. The author says, "By treaty negotiations in
1892 they were finally located on a small reservation on the
Canadian border called Turtle Mountain." This ignores the
many Chippewa reservations in Minnesota and Wisconsin, especially the large Red Lake and Leech Lake Reservations in Minnesota, and the religious and historical center of the Chippewa,
Madeline Island in Wisconsin.

Josephy, Alvin M., Jr., editor. Red Power: The American Indians'
Fight for Freedom. McGraw 1970.

A documentary collection of twenty-four selections covering
the history of the rise of the Red Power or Indian Power movement. Beginning with a speech by Thomas L. Sloan, an Omaha
Indian, before the Society of American Indians in 1911, and
concluding with an article by Vine Deloria, Jr., from the *New
York Times Magazine* in 1970, the collection contains statements by Indians and non-Indians, excerpts of reports by congressional committees, and manifestos by Indian groups. On
*Akwesasne Notes* basic library list.

Levine, Stuart, and Nancy Oestreich Lurie, editors. The American
Indian Today. Penguin 1968.

A collection of essays on the status of the Indian today, done
primarily by anthropologists who have worked among Indians.
Two contributors are Indian—Shirley Hill Witt, a Mohawk, and
Robert K. Thomas, a Cherokee. The book contains articles on
historical background, current trends, and problems of individual tribes. The articles in this collection, from the *Midcontinent
American Studies Journal*, give a good background for understanding current Indian problems. On Rupert Costo's list of
suggested reading on the American Indian Today (*Indian Historian* 1:35, Winter 1968).

Marquis, Arnold. A Guide to America's Indians: Ceremonials,
Reservations and Museums. U of Okla Pr 1974.

A tourist guide to reservations, ceremonials, museums, and
campgrounds, with some background on Native American
history, languages, arts, and contemporary affairs. The author
is better informed about the Southwest than about other areas

and therefore devotes more space to that region. The book has a number of factual errors and oversimplifications. For example, the author includes the Mandan, Arikara, and Hidatsa among the Sioux, and, apparently using evidence of the Chippewa in Wisconsin, suggests that very little remains of Chippewa life and culture.

"Although some excellent museums and collections are listed, many miss the mark, and an inordinate number of exceptional museums are missing altogether" (*American Indian Quarterly* 1:26, Autumn 1974).

Meyer, William. Native Americans: The New Indian Resistance. Intl Pub Co 1971.

This small book, by a Cherokee long active in the struggle for Indian rights, is a history of American Indian resistance from colonial times to the present. About half of the space is devoted to modern questions, including problems with the Bureau of Indian Affairs, land and water rights, hunting and fishing rights, and self-determination. On *Akwesasne Notes* basic library list.

"The author, a native Cherokee, is active in the native rights struggle. His feelings which are shared by many other North American natives are expressed in this book" (*About Indians*, p. 225).

Morey, Sylvester M., editor. Can the Red Man Help the White Man? A Denver Conference with the Indian Elders. Myrin Institute 1970.

Papers from a June 1968 conference of Indian elders, sponsored by the Myrin Institute of Adult Education, to consider what Indians might contribute to white society. The intuitive knowledge of the Indian elders was of special interest. Topics for discussion include Indian beliefs, education, religion, myths, and legends.

Pratson, Frederick. Land of the Four Directions: A Portrait of North American Indian Life Today. Chatham Pr 1970.

In pictures and in prose, the author presents the life, problems, and hopes of modern Indians of eastern Maine and the Canadian Maritimes—Passamaquoddies, Maliseet, and Micmac. The text is divided into topics such as the land, the community, the individual, the home, children, age, and the elders.

"*Land of the Four Directions* is the first book which truly presents the way of life, the real problems, and the hopes for the future of the Indians in eastern Maine and the Canadian Maritimes. It is fully endorsed by the joint tribal councils of the Passamaquoddies" (John Stevens, in the introduction to the book, p. 10). "This is a good book, and can well be utilized as an introduction to a more comprehensive study of these peoples" (*Indian Historian* 4:54, Spring 1971). "It is seldom one finds so excellent a book that really 'says it all'" (*About Indians*, p. 248).

Steiner, Stan. The New Indians. Dell 1969.

Known as the "White Navaho," the author is a wanderer who, after World War II, set out to discover his country and himself. He traveled more than 200,000 miles in twenty years, living part of the time among Indian tribes and learning about them and the workings of their councils. This is a collection of stories about modern Indians—their hopes, disappointments, and fears about themselves, modern America, and the whites. Some stories are about Red Muslims and their hatred toward the whites; others are about Indians who are saddened by the whites' refusal to accept the good that is to be found in the Indian way of life. Appendices contain notes on the people interviewed, documents, chronology, statistics, and selected bibliography. On *Akwesasne Notes* basic library list.

"Considerable information of value for an understanding of the Indian in the world of today" (*Textbooks and the American Indian*, p. 258). "Steiner's book has had substantial influence in awakening younger Indians to the nationalistic trends of the major Indian organizations" (Vine Deloria, Jr., in the introduction to *Indians of the Americas* by Edwin Embree). "Complete with adjectival embellishments as it is, the book suffers from sensationalism. However, there is a great deal of important material concerning the attitudes and activities of Indians today" (*Indian Historian* 1:28, Summer 1968).

Steiner, Stan. The Vanishing White Man. Illus. Maria Garza. Har-Row 1976.

The main purpose of this publication is to compare and contrast Indian and white attitudes toward energy, conservation, and the relationship of people to the land they live on. The author describes a series of incidents that have grown out of the conflicting attitudes of the two races, and has collected statements or so-called testaments regarding these issues, by Indians and whites—including Alvin Dashee, vice chairman of the Hopi tribe;

Frank Tenorio, secretary of the All-Indian Pueblo Council; Grace Black Elk, Ogallala Nation; Walter Hickel, former Governor of Alaska and former Secretary of the Interior; and Senator James Abourezk from South Dakota.

"It is without a doubt Steiner's finest effort, qualitatively above his other efforts and a book that may bring a needed sobriety to the problem of Indian-white relations" (Vine Deloria, Jr., *New York Times Book Review*, 12 September 1976, p. 45).

Vizenor, Gerald. Wordarrows: Indians and Whites in the New Fur Trade. U of Minn Pr 1978.

Adopting the name Clement Beaulieu, the author combines fact and fiction in presenting a number of sketches about Indian people he has known, many of them when he was a counselor and advocate in Minneapolis. Among these Native Americans with their trials and problems in a white society are Rattling Hail, who objects to having white people provide "services" for him; Laurel Hole in the Day, who is drawn between life on the reservation and life in the city; and Roman Downwind, who was born in an abandoned station wagon while his mother was ricing and sees nothing wrong with living in his car in the city. The book closes with four chapters recounting the author's experiences as an investigator in the trial of Thomas White Hawk for murder in South Dakota. Throughout the book, words and their use in the tribal society are compared with their use in white society. From his own Native American background, the author sensitively presents the tragic dilemmas faced by individual Indian people.

Watkins, Mel, editor. Dene Nation—The Colony Within. U of Toronto Pr 1977.

In 1976 a hearing was held in Northwest Territories of Canada before Justice Thomas R. Berger of the Supreme Court of British Columbia, to consider the proposals of Canadian Arctic Gas Pipeline Ltd. and Foothills Pipe Lines Ltd. for building pipelines in the Mackenzie Valley. The Dene people of that territory are trying to live as much like their ancestors as possible; thus many of their chiefs and other leaders testified against the proposal and in favor of retaining their life as it is. This collection contains statements of the Dene people concerning their views.

Wilson, Edmund. Apologies to the Iroquois. Random 1965.

Realizing that he knew little about his neighbors, the author visited the reservations of six Iroquois Nation tribes to study their life, problems, and growing nationalism. The result was a series of articles in *The New Yorker*, which are collected in this volume along with Joseph Mitchell's "The Mohawks in High Steel." The articles are about contemporary Indians' problems, life-views, values, and needs. Written originally for an adult audience; will interest senior high students who are studying current social problems.

"[It is among] other outstanding books of recent years," says Vine Deloria, Jr., in the introduction to *Indians of the Americas* by Edwin Embree. "Part of the memorial tribute to Mr. Wilson belongs to us, for the legacy of *Apologies to the Iroquois*, which made an impact on both the Indian and the non-Indian world at a critical time in Iroquois history" (Betty Crouse Mele, *Indian Historian* 5:23, Fall 1972).

# Music, Arts, and Crafts

Elementary

Baylor, Byrd. **Before You Came This Way.** Illus. Tom Bahti. Dutton 1969. Primary.

The remarkable rock paintings of the prehistoric Indians of Arizona, New Mexico, and West Texas have inspired both the author of this book and the artist to convey the beauty and mystery of ancient times. The illustrations depict animals, the sun, moon, stars, and people engaged in activities such as hunting, dancing, or going to battle. Printed on *amatl* paper—a rough bark paper, handmade by the Otomi Indians of Puebla, Mexico—the figures resemble authentic petroglyphs. The author's spare, poetic text expresses the wonderment of later generations as they speculate upon the lives of "those who passed this way before."

"The entire book is infused with a sense of wonder and quiet reverence . . . Evocative and poetic, a distinguished book" (*Saturday Review*, 8 November 1969, p. 65). "This is not a 'fact' book . . . It is rather a work that treats the drawings for what they are—the emotional expressions of a nonliterate people . . . It is seldom that children are exposed to such a poignant commentary on any unfamiliar culture, past or present" (*Library Journal* 94:4593, 15 December 1969).

Baylor, Byrd. **They Put On Masks.** Illus. Jerry Ingram. Scribner 1974. Primary.

This book, based on authentic sources, discusses the use of masks with Indian dances and songs, and includes a description of how they were made. Many Indians still feel the power of their masks and continue to use them in the ancient, sacred ways. The cultures of many tribes are studied, including the Eskimo, Kwakiutl and other Northwest Indians, Iroquois, Navajo, Apache, Pueblo, and Zuni.

"Baylor tells of the uses and meanings of masks . . . through quiet rambling verse which calls up that sense of power and mystery given to the masks by their makers. . . . Much feeling and information of importance is communicated in the effective illustrations and poetic dramatizations" (*Booklist* 70:1102, 1 June 1974).

Baylor, Byrd. **When Clay Sings.** Illus. Tom Bahti. Scribner 1972. Primary.

Reassembled pieces of prehistoric Indian pottery, found in the deserts of Arizona, inspired this book which re-creates the past with sensitivity and eloquence. The Indians who find the pottery today believe that everything has its own spirit—even a broken pot. The many animals and birds that appear on the fragments give evidence that there were "speckled bugs, spotted bugs, bugs with shiny wings, and pinchy bugs and jumpy bugs and bugs that had a thousand legs that liked to walk through grass." The line drawings are beautifully adapted from the designs of prehistoric Indian potters of the Anasazi, Mogollon, Hohokam, and Mimbres cultures. 1973 Caldecott Medal Honor Book.

"This is a lyrical treatment of archaeology and the art of Indians of the Southwest. Great immediacy is lent by the reflections on the prehistoric people who might have used these fragments and by the parallels of thought and feeling drawn between then and now" (*Library Journal* 97:1898, 15 May 1972).

Bierhorst, John. **Songs of the Chippewa.** Illus. Joe Servello. FS&G 1974. Intermediate.

These songs were collected by ethnomusicologist Frances Densmore during the early 1900s and by ethnographer Henry Rowe Schoolcraft more than fifty years earlier. Arranged for piano and guitar, the songs include lullabies, ritual songs, dream songs, and songs about nature. A few have Chippewa words, with English translations. The melodic lines, which can be learned by young children, are exotic and unfamiliar. The source of each song and helpful notes for teachers are included. Brown-tone illustrations further enhance this collection.

Coen, Rena Neumann. **The Red Man in Art.** Lerner Pubns 1972. Intermediate.

In this collection, Indian art is surveyed from early times to the present. The examples of early symbolic art forms include a

Seneca mask, a Kwakiutl female figure, a Haida rattle, and a stone pipe from Moundville, Alabama. Paintings by whites which acquainted Europeans with Indian culture are reproduced in both black and white and color, with commentary on the artists' work. Among those represented are Gustavus Hesselius, Benjamin West, Gilbert Stuart, Peter Rindisbacher, Karl Bodmer, Seth Eastman, George Catlin, and Frederic Remington. Twentieth-century American Indian artists who have made notable contributions to the understanding of Indian culture are represented. Oscar Howe, a descendant of Plains Indians, combines a modern feeling for abstract design with the two-dimensional linear style of the early buffalo-robe painters. Fred Kabotie's vivid painting, "Hopi Corn Dance," is included. Favorite subjects for Patrick Des Jarlait, a self-taught Chippewa painter from the Red Lake reservation in northern Minnesota, are the seasonal occupations of his people. The variety of art included makes this a highly desirable aid to appreciating and understanding Indian art.

Daubney, Brian, and Ronald Reah. **Ojimite's Journey: A Story with Music.** Illus. Rita Teasdale. Oxford U Pr 1968. Intermediate.

This is a story taken from Shoshoni legends and arranged with musical accompaniment. The legend tells of the mighty chief Mirimoya who rules well and is loved and revered by his people. Evil and terror befall the people when the ruler's son, Yusinte, is carried off by Mavawok, Evil Spirit of the Black Mountains. Ojimite, a brave and noble warrior, sets out to find Yusinte. On his journey he rescues an antelope, a blue jay, and a fish from danger, and they in turn endow him with various magical powers. Eventually he reaches the kingdom of Mavawok and with his magic rescues Yusinte. The chief rewards Ojimite with the dark-eyed Dakodilla as his bride. A complete musical score is included and interwoven with the rhythmic prose of the story.

Glubok, Shirley. **The Art of the Northwest Coast Indians.** Macmillan 1975. Intermediate.

This book lavishly illustrates the art of the Kwakiutl, Tlingit, Nootka, Haida, Tsimshian, Bella Coola, Coast Salish, and other Indian tribes of the Northwest, from the Columbia River in Oregon to Yakutat Bay in southern Alaska. Radically different from the art of other North American Indians, the works depict the lifestyles of these present-day tribes, who live in distinctive houses and have adapted well to white culture. Their carvings of wood, bone, and horn are intricate and detailed, as are the paintings with which they decorate their houses, inside and out. Canoes, charms, body armor, decorated hide clothing, gods, and totem poles—all reminiscent of tribal history—illustrate in detail an informative, concisely written text.

Glubok, Shirley. **The Art of the Plains Indians.** Photographs by Alfred Tamarin. Macmillan 1975. Intermediate.

The art of the Blackfeet, Blood, Piegan, Sarcee, Crow, Sioux, Kiowa, Cheyenne, Arapaho, and Mandan is presented in illustrations ranging from simple pictographs to photographs of elaborate ceremonial dress, intricately decorated cradles and toys, beautifully carved "magic" pipes, and hide paintings of their history, including their constant fight to repel the ever-encroaching whites. The text, though brief, provides a wide-ranging account of the customs, religion, and day-to-day life of the Plains Indians.

Glubok, Shirley. **The Art of the Southwest Indians.** Photographs by Alfred Tamarin. Macmillan 1971.

The three main groups of the Southwest Indians—the Navajo, the Apache, and the desert tribes, including the Pima, Papago, and Mojave—have ancient and deeply religious cultures centered on nature. The artifacts presented in this volume, some of them centuries old, range from dance wands, wall paintings, small carved-stone fetishes, baskets, rugs, and sand paintings to rich silver work, kachina dolls and masks, ceremonial robes, and decorated pottery. The text provides information about the philosophy and daily activities of these tribes.

Hofsinde, Robert [Gray-Wolf]. **Indian Arts.** Illus. by author. Morrow 1971. Intermediate.

A concise, selective presentation of the many kinds of art developed by the Indians of America. Explanations of the origin, design, and decorations of ceremonial, personal, and household items are given along with numerous clear drawings. The pictured objects show how the Indians made use of the available natural materials—sheep horns for spoons, abalone shells for inlaid designs, stone for making pipes, grasses for weaving, and clay for making pottery. A section on the Indian arts of today is included. A handy reference for the young reader.

"While the information provided in this children's book is meager, it is good. The illustrations are especially helpful" (*About Indians*, p. 69).

Hofsinde, Robert [Gray-Wolf]. Indian Beadwork. Illus. by author. Morrow 1958. Intermediate.

For centuries the North American Indians had decorated their clothing with quill embroidery, but with the advent of European traders they learned to use colored beads and by the nineteenth century, beadwork had become one of their great arts. The author provides instructions for the construction of a bead loom and the working of attractive bead designs. There are patterns for making useful items such as coin purses, belts, and moccasins, and methods for working out original designs. Excellent sketches and directions. Cited in *A Preliminary Bibliography of Selected Children's Books*.

"The book is a good introduction to beadwork for hobby and craft enthusiasts as well as children. It is written in simple language and covers a number of basic projects" (*About Indians*, p. 69).

Hofsinde, Robert [Gray-Wolf]. Indian Games and Crafts. Illus. by author. Morrow 1957. Intermediate.

A collection of interesting games and beautiful craftwork, by a well-known expert on Indian life. Included are instructions for making simple games from readily available materials, with each step carefully described and illustrated. Some of the items are: the Zuni kick stick, the Hopi Kachina doll, the Chippewa corncob dart, the Eskimo buzz board, the Iroquois double ball and stick, the Eskimo toss and catch game, and several kinds of Indian rattles. Cited in *A Preliminary Bibliography of Selected Children's Books*.

"Detailed instructions with careful illustrations and lists of simple materials are included to aid in creating the described equipment making this book a useful addition to any craft collection" (*About Indians*, p. 70).

Hofsinde, Robert [Gray-Wolf]. Indian Music Makers. Morrow 1967. Intermediate.

The author has collected a wealth of interesting material on Indian songs and musical instruments, and he explains the importance of singing in the Indians' life. As infants, Indians were calmed by cradle songs. Later they learned songs of hunting, war, victory, prayer, harvest, and death. Various Indian instruments are described and illustrated, including the flute, which was used in courting, the drum, the tom-tom, and the rattle. The examples of authentic Indian music in the book come from the Ojibwa (or Chippewa) of northern Minnesota and were gathered by Frances Densmore and published in *Chippewa Music II*. Cited in *A Preliminary Bibliography of Selected Children's Books*.

"This unusual presentation gives the reader new insights into the daily customs of the Indian" (*About Indians*, p. 71).

Hofsinde, Robert [Gray-Wolf]. Indian Picture Writing. Illus. by author. Morrow 1959. Intermediate.

Picture writing is described as a way of expressing thoughts and recording events by marks or drawings. Many people, such as cave dwellers, Egyptians, Vikings, and American Indians, have carved or painted scenes of their exploits and hunts. Some of these drawings are crude in design; others are miniature masterpieces of primitive art. An index to the symbols offers easy access to specific words in picture writing. Sample stories are given, with the correct interpretation on later pages. A challenging and engrossing book for anyone interested in the subject.

"A simple, clear presentation" (*About Indians*, p. 72).

Hunt, W. Ben. The Complete Book of Indian Crafts and Lore. Golden Pr. Western Pub 1954. Intermediate.

This colorful book is an excellent source of information on costumes, drums and tom-toms, teepees, totem poles, and many other items from various tribes. The care of feathers and construction of war bonnets, breechclouts, aprons, and leggings are also described. Directions and patterns are given for beadwork. Finally, basic Indian dance steps are included, with appropriate costumes for each dance. There is a pronunciation guide and an interesting biographical sketch of the author. An invaluable reference book for any class interested in the crafts of the American Indians.

"An excellent book which clearly describes articles that boys and girls can make, patterned on authentic Indian costumes" (*About Indians*, p. 77).

Junior High

Appleton, LeRoy H. American Indian Design and Decoration. Dover 1971.

This book contains more than 700 examples of Indian designs found on baskets, pottery, sculpture, paintings, weaving, masks, headgear, blankets, ponchos, and other artifacts from tribes ranging from the Arctic Circle to Tierra del Fuego. The author, who spent more than twenty years in preparing the book, gathered the designs from museums. There are symbols of religion, mythology, and magic, organized geographically by clans and tribes, followed by examples of their use on artifacts and a discussion of the lore, tradition, stories, and songs that explain the motifs. Published in 1950 as *Indian Art of the Americas.*

Berlant, Anthony, and Mary Hunt Kahlenberg. **Walk in Beauty: The Navajo and Their Blankets.** NYGS 1977.

Berlant is with the Mimbres Foundation, an organization formed to excavate the villages of the prehistoric Mimbres Indians of southern New Mexico, and Kahlenberg is an art historian and museum curator of textiles. They have combined their knowledge and expertise in this readable history of the Navajo and the development of their weaving as demonstrated in the changing designs and colors. The Navajo blanket is an expression of the beliefs, culture, and experience of the people. There are sixty plates in color and many more in black and white.

Dewdney, Selwyn, and Kenneth E. Kidd. **Indian Rock Paintings of the Great Lakes.** U of Toronto Pr 1967.

Dewdney, an artist and writer, with the help of Kidd, a curator in the Department of Ethnology, Royal Ontario Museum, found and recorded Indian rock paintings from Lake Mazinaw to the Ontario-Manitoba border along the Canadian Shield. The story of Dewdney's search is exciting. More than a thousand individual drawings from about one hundred sites—most of them west of the Lakehead area of Lake Superior—are described. The authors speculate on the identity of the artists, what their materials were, and what their pictures meant.

Dockstader, Frederick J. **Indian Art of the Americas.** Photographs by Carmelo Guadagno. Mus Am Ind 1973.

This volume contains photographs of the five hundred objects in "Indian Arts of the Americas," an exhibit that toured the United States during 1973-1976. The artifacts date from 3000 B.C. to A.D. 1970. Textual matter summarizes the technology and cultures of American Indians and how they were affected by the arrival of white people. Facts are given concerning the material, date, and measurements of each article.

Garfield, Viola, and Linn A. Forrest. **The Wolf and the Raven: Totem Poles of Southeastern Alaska.** U of Wash Pr 1961.

A guide to the totem poles of southeastern Alaska. In 1938 funds became available through the U.S. Forest Service for collecting and restoring these carved memorials to the clans and the spiritual life of the people. With the cooperation of the Indians who owned them, the totems were gathered into several parks where they could be preserved and seen more easily. Each totem is described and often there is an explanation of its legend.

Hofmann, Charles. **American Indians Sing.** Illus. Nicholas Amorosi. John Day 1967.

This book begins with a discussion of the general characteristics of Indian music and ceremonies, followed by a description of the uses of song and dance among specific tribes across the United States and an examination of Indian music today. The author, a collector of folk materials for the Library of Congress, was a student of the pioneer collector of Indian music, Frances Densmore. The book contains reading lists for students and for teachers and parents, a list of recordings of Indian music, and a brief recording, which is bound into the book. Illustrated with photographs of dancers and with drawings.

Kimball, Yeffe, and Jean Anderson. **The Art of American Indian Cooking.** Illus. Yeffe Kimball. Avon 1970.

A cookbook for making authentic, easily prepared Indian foods, ranging from the turkey and corn dishes of the Southeast to the wild game recipes of the Great Plains and the seafoods of the northwestern coast. Yeffe Kimball, noted Osage artist, has been a consultant on Indian affairs and arts to the government and several magazines. Jean Anderson is with the food department of the *Ladies' Home Journal.* Cited in *American Indian Authors.*

Laubin, Reginald, and Gladys Laubin. **The Indian Tipi: Its History, Construction, and Use.** Ballantine 1971.

All there is to know about the tipi—how to make one, how to transport it, different styles used by various tribes, ceremonials and customs connected with it, how to decorate it, and its history and legends. The authors have constructed tipis and have camped in them in all sorts of weather. Their book will appeal to students who love the outdoors and camping, and to all who enjoy the history and romance of the Indian life. Photographs, sketches, and designs with color keys make this a valuable book on the subject.

"You can appreciate the elegant design of a tipi and the completeness of the culture that produced it. All the information you need, technical or traditional, is here" (*Whole Earth Catalog*).

Miller, Marjorie. **Indian Arts and Crafts: A Complete "How to" Guide to Southwestern Indian Handicrafts.** Illus. Ann Bruce Chamberlain. Nash Pub 1972.

This is a general survey of the handicrafts of the Southwest Indians—silverwork, jewelry, kachina dolls, Navajo rugs, and pottery. There is advice on identifying Indian art works and on the buying of materials, but the book is not detailed enough to be used alone, and students will find it difficult to make the articles without some background in crafts or guidance from a knowledgeable teacher. It might be used along with more complete guides to each craft, such as *Santa Clara Pottery Today* by Betty LeFree (see Senior Art).

Naylor, Maria, editor. **Authentic Indian Designs: 2500 Illustrations from Reports of the Bureau of American Ethnology.** Dover 1975.

The illustrations in this book are from nearly a century of reports of the Bureau of Ethnology. The book begins with a section on prehistoric art of the eastern United States, emphasizing the cultures in the Mississippi and Ohio river valleys. Other sections cover the Eastern Woodlands, Plains, Pacific Northwest, and Southwest. The objects illustrated are those that were actually used by the people who made them. A brief introduction gives information about éach of the cultures represented by the artifacts.

"This vast pictorial archive collection offers the beauty and vigor of 2500 Indian designs that come from all over the United States, including Alaska and the Canadian Pacific Coast" (*Indian America* 9:61, Spring 1976).

Norbeck, Oscar. Book of Indian Life Crafts. Illus. John B. Eves. Tower 1970.

This book tells how to make costumes (shirts, leggings, head-dresses), woven articles, motifs and decorations, musical instruments, pottery, games, dwellings, and items of transportation. There is a helpful bibliography of Indian craft and lore, and a list of addresses for sources of supplies.

Reynolds, Charles R., Jr., editor. American Indian Portraits from the Wanamaker Expedition of 1913. Greene 1971.

A collection of photographs from the American Museum of Natural History, where they were discovered by Reynolds, the picture editor of *Popular Photography*, in 1965. Research led to the conclusion that they were taken in 1913, on the third of the expeditions to the Indians financed by Rodman Wanamaker. All of the expeditions were led by Joseph Kossuth Dixon (who authored a book on the subject), but it is unclear whether he or a member of his staff took the pictures. A few of the portraits are of well-known Indians such as Ishi, Jack Red Cloud, and Wooden Leg of the Northern Cheyenne.

Salomon, Julian Harris. The Book of Indian Crafts and Indian Lore. Har-Row 1928.

At the suggestion of Chief Curly Bear of the Blackfeet, Salomon began gathering lore about Indian crafts which the chief felt would be lost. The author, a producer of Boy Scout Indian pageants in the United States and in Europe, intended his collection especially for scouts and scout leaders. It gives general background about the tribes and discusses the making of items such as headdresses, war shirts, moccasins, tepees, pipes, bags, and bows and arrows. Chapters on Indian games, dances, music, and Indian pageants conclude the book.

"This book on Indian culture will be helpful in stimulating an interest in Indian customs, dances and lore. Those interested in scouting and camping will find it of particular value" (*About Indians*, p. 260).

Stuart, Jozefa, and Robert H. Ashton, Jr., editors. Images of American Indian Art. Walker & Co 1977.

A former editor of *Life* magazine has chosen more than 200 photographs, in color and in black and white, as a panorama of the art of the North American Indian. The text identifies the pictured artifacts. The editor and publisher of the magazine *American Indian Art* has written a brief introduction. Prehistoric Mound Builder pottery, Northwest Indian masks coveted by the Russian czars, a nineteenth-century Eskimo whalebone carving, and twentieth-century Navajo rugs and Pueblo pottery indicate the range of subject. Ideal for classroom use.

## Senior High and Adult

Adams, Clinton. Fritz Scholder Lithographs. NYGS 1975.

Fritz Scholder, who is one-quarter Indian, was already one of America's leading painters when he began working in a new medium, lithography. This collection contains all of the ninety-two lithographs Scholder has made since he turned to the new medium in 1970. His subjects are modern Indians, mostly from the Southwest. The author of the text is the director of Tamarind Institute, the lithography workshop in Albuquerque where Scholder does most of his work.

Bedinger, Margery. Indian Silver: Navajo and Pueblo Jewelers. U of NM Pr 1973.

This is a scholarly study of the development of the silversmith's craft among the Navajo and Pueblo peoples. The author traces its history from the first appearance of silver ornaments from Mexico, to the development of iron and copper works, to the craft of the jewelry makers. Emphasis is on the Navajos, Zunis, and Hopis, who do the most work in silver, but the author also surveys contributions of the smaller pueblos. Well illustrated with both antique and modern items.

Brody, J. J. Mimbres Painted Pottery. U of NM Pr 1977.

Between A.D. 1000 and 1250 the Mimbres lived in several hundred small villages in the mountain valleys and hot deserts of New Mexico. Their villages would be commonplace excavation sites except for the remarkable pottery found in them. The author explains the techniques used by the people in making the pottery. Nearly two hundred color and black and white photographs, maps, and line drawings accompany the text of this volume, which is part of the Southwest Indian Arts series produced by the School of American Research, Santa Fe.

Bunting, Bainbridge. **Early Architecture in New Mexico.** U of NM Pr 1976.

An architectural historian at the University of New Mexico, the author traces the development of architecture in New Mexico from the original Indian multistoried pueblos, which the Spaniards found when they arrived, to the American invasion in 1848 and the arrival of the railroad in 1880, which brought new influences and materials from the East. The study ends in the early 1900s. Both paperback and hardcover editions are well illustrated with black and white photographs and diagrams.

Chapman, Kenneth M. **The Pottery of San Ildefonso Pueblo.** U of NM Pr 1970.

This is a scholarly, definitive study of the pottery of San Ildefonso, covering its origin, form, firing, and styles. Introductory material provides information about the pueblo; the author then discusses the general features of the pottery from its origins to modern times, and the work of the most famous of pueblo potters, Maria and Julian Martinez. One hundred-seventy-four color plates with descriptive material catalog all of the designs that have been used on the pottery.

Curtis, Natalie. **The Indians' Book: Songs and Legends of the American Indians.** Dover 1968.

When the author first began her pioneer work among the Indians, the singing of their songs was forbidden in government schools. Many of the Indians were afraid to sing for her, fearing government retribution. Only through her direct appeal to President Theodore Roosevelt was she able to continue her monumental work of recording the songs of Indians of the Plains, Lake Region, Northwest, Southwest, and Pueblo Indians. Both texts and music are included. Illustrated by photographs and original drawings by Indians. Revised edition published in 1907. Cited in the supplement of *American Indian Authors.*

"A source book of Indian music, songs and related history" (*Textbooks and the American Indian*, p. 261). "Those who do not have a copy of this book should have it. Every library needs it. Every scholar should require it of himself to own a copy, if

there is any interest at all in the native peoples of this land"
(*Indian Historian* 2:37, Fall 1969).

Frank, Larry, and Francis H. Harlow. **Historic Pottery of the
Pueblo Indians, 1600–1880.** Photographs by Bernard Lopez.
NYGS 1974.

Even without a potter's wheel, the Pueblo Indians of the Southwest created beautiful ceramic ware for both utilitarian and
ceremonial use. Today the vessels made during the historic
period—from about 1600, when the Spanish arrived, to about
1880, with the tourists' advent—are appreciated for the artistic
achievement they represent. The text reviews the circumstances in which pottery was made, describes how the Spanish
church officials forbade the Indians to bury the vessels with
their dead, and discusses the shift to more utilitarian vessels.
Each of the 198 pots is illustrated in color or in black and white
and is described in detail.

Grant, Campbell. **Rock Art of the American Indian.** Illus. by
author. T Y Crowell 1967.

This book deals with rock art in general, the artists, motifs,
methods of dating, and rock art in each area of the country.
Rock art abounds with fertility symbols, dream and spirit
figures, clan and power symbols, and magic motifs for hunting.
Migrations to the south and east can be traced by the presence
of the thunderbird and plumed or horned serpent. This art form
connects the Creek and Cherokee cultures with civilizations in
Mexico. The author, an archaeologist, looks at the art as both
an anthropologist and an artist.

"Owing to its wide scope, it is a cursory volume and can best
serve as an introduction to the subject for anthropology students" (*About Indians*, p. 177).

Grant, Campbell. **The Rock Paintings of the Chumash: A Study of
a California Indian Culture.** Illus. by author. U of Cal Pr 1965.

The author-illustrator of this volume is known for his studies
of early rock paintings of a number of Indian tribes. Here he
has collected many rock paintings from Chumash country in
southern California. Since many of the petroglyphs are in caves
where photography is difficult, Grant has hand-copied many of
them. A text describes the Chumash people, their culture, and
the paintings.

Heizer, Robert F., and Martin A. Baumhoff. Prehistoric Rock Art of Nevada and Eastern California. U of Cal Pr 1975.

A scholarly book, documenting the sites of early rock art in the Great Basin of Nevada and California and speculating on its meaning. The Indians living there today (Paiute and Shoshone) claim that the drawings were made by an earlier people, although they acknowledge that some may have been made more recently by tribal people in imitation of their forebears. The authors postulate that the petroglyphs may have been created as part of the hunting ceremony or as part of shamanistic ceremonies. In attempting to connect them with hunting, they have carefully documented the nature of the land around each site and the migration patterns of animals.

Highwater, Jamake. Song from the Earth: American Indian Painting. NYGS 1976.

Highwater—of Blackfoot-Cherokee parentage and a widely published writer on Indian affairs, travel, and related subjects—has turned to producing the first history of Indian painting. After describing what he calls "the otherness" of the Indian world view compared to the white view, he discusses pre-1900 art forms—rock pictographs, kiva murals, rawhide painting, and sand painting. He traces the advances in formal training for Indian artists, from the Santa Fe Indian School to Bacone Junior College and the University of Oklahoma, to the awareness of avant-garde European painting and the adoption of non-traditional styles and themes. The book concludes with interviews with nine leading contemporary Indian painters. A chronology, bibliography, directory of collections of Indian painting, and 32 color and 130 black and white illustrations help make this a valuable book.

Jernigan, E. Wesley. Jewelry of the Prehistoric Southwest. U of NM Pr 1978.

Three ancient cultures—the Hohokam, the Mogollon, and the Anasazi—inhabited the Southwest before the coming of the whites, and all three groups mysteriously disappeared. Evidence found in the areas where these people lived indicates that both men and women decorated themselves with many forms of jewelry. The author, an art historian, has surveyed the various kinds of jewelry these civilizations produced. Illustrated with color and black and white photographs and one hundred detailed drawings by the author. Part of the Southwest Indian Arts series of the School of American Research, Santa Fe.

LeFree, Betty. **Santa Clara Pottery Today.** U of NM Pr 1975.

The author, an anthropologist, conducted the field work on a technological study of Santa Clara pottery in 1968, under a grant from the Wenner Gren Foundation. The resulting monograph is a detailed study of how the pottery is made, and some of its history. The illustrations show individual potters doing various stages in the process of making this most valued of Indian pottery.

Lister, Robert H., and Florence C. Lister. **Anasazi Pottery.** U of NM Pr 1978.

This is a catalog of the pottery found or collected by archaeologist Earl Morris in the Four Corners country, where the states of Arizona, Utah, Colorado, and New Mexico meet. (Anasazi is a term used for the Pueblo Indians and their cliff-dwelling ancestors.) Each picture of a pottery vessel is accompanied by information on its size and pottery type, often with a statement from Morris about the circumstances in which he acquired it, and occasionally with comments by the authors on how and when the vessel was used or made.

Maxwell Museum of Anthropology. **Seven Families in Pueblo Pottery.** U of NM Pr 1974.

The craft of pottery making, handed down from generation to generation, is ably described in this book which traces the development of styles and techniques used by seven Pueblo families. Family histories are based on the recollections of the oldest members and they include a family tree. The text contains comments on the designs and development of pottery skills in each family, with references to the study and use of ancient Indian designs. Statements by the potters explain the development and change of the craft in their families, which include the Chino and Lewis families (Ácoma), the Nampeyos (Hopi), the Gutierrez and Tafoya families (Santa Clara), and the Gonzales and Martinez families (San Ildefonso). Illustrations in color and black and white show the progress that has been made by each family.

Navajo School of Indian Basketry. **Indian Basket Weaving.** Dover 1971.

This book describes the basic techniques of basketry: choice of materials, preparation of the reed, splicing, color, principles of design, shaping, and finishing. The text then discusses a variety of baskets and weaves from different Indian cultures. There are suggestions for weaving with shells, beads, feathers, palms, and pine needles. Black and white photographs and line drawings supplement the instructions. Published in 1903.

Newcomb, Franc J., and Gladys A. Reichard. **Sandpaintings of the Navajo Shooting Chant.** Dover 1975.

Before publishing this book in 1937, Gladys Reichard spent five summers living with the family of Miguelito, a Navajo chanter. Her purpose was "to attempt to regard matters in a Navajo spirit." During those years she witnessed the Shooting Chant three times, following it in every ceremonial detail, and met Franc Newcomb, a trader's wife, whose sandpaintings recorded from memory her first-hand impressions of the Shooting Chant. (The Navajos prohibited more permanent methods of recording the ceremony.) This book contains thirty-five plates in color and ten in black and white from Newcomb's collection, accompanied by the myths upon which the chant is based.

"Authentic forms presented in their original symbolic and mythical context" (*Akwesasne Notes* 8:42, Early Summer 1976).

Rodee, Marian E. **Southwestern Weaving.** U of NM Pr 1977.

This is primarily a catalog of the textile collection of the Maxwell Museum of Anthropology at the University of New Mexico, where the author is a curator. The largest number of samples come from the Navajo, with fewer from the Pueblo, North Mexico, and Rio Grande cultures. There are photographs of each of the 318 pieces in the collection, with information on their yarns, dyes, weaves, selvages, and sizes.

Sides, Dorothy Smith. **Decorative Art of the Southwestern Indians.** Dover 1962.

A collection of designs used on pottery, basketry, and rugs by the southwestern Indians from earliest times to the present, with emphasis on ancient designs still in use. Commentaries by Clarence Martin Smith give information about the history and occurrence of each design.

Villaseñor, David. Tapestries in Sand: The Spirit of Indian Sand-painting. Naturegraph 1966.

Villaseñor, an Otomi Indian, entered the United States at six-teen, at which time he first saw sandpainting being done for ceremonial reasons by an old medicine man on the Navajo reservation. He vowed to find a way to preserve the beauty and meaning of the ancient art, which is a vital part of the religious life and ceremonies of the cultures of the Southwest. The last stronghold of sandpainting is in the Monument Valley region.

Viola, Herman J. The Indian Legacy of Charles Bird King. Double-day 1976.

Charles Bird King was a well-known portrait artist when Thomas L. McKenney, founder of the Bureau of Indian Affairs, commis-sioned him to paint the portraits of the Indian chiefs who were being brought to Washington, D.C., as guests of the United States government. Between 1821 and 1842 he painted more than a hundred Indian leaders and the portraits were placed in the Smithsonian Institution, where the entire collection was destroyed by fire in 1858. King, however, had made replicas of the most important ones and the author has located more than sixty of these, plus sixteen charcoal sketches. In telling their story, the author (director of the National Anthropolog-ical Archives, National Museum of Natural History of the Smithsonian Institution) has also told much of the history of the era and of the nation's capital.

Walker Art Center, Indian Art Association, and the Minneapolis Institute of Art. American Indian Art: Form and Tradition. Dutton 1972.

This publication includes a catalog of some of the art exhibited at the Walker Art Center and the Investors Diversified Services Building in Minneapolis in 1972. It also contains a series of articles on the subject, by distinguished scholars such as Andrew Hunter Whiteford, Gerald Vizenor, Robert Ritzenthaler, Frederick Dockstader, and Dorothy Jean Ray.

Whiteford, Andrew Hunter. North American Indian Arts. Illus. Owen Vernon Shaffer. Western Pub 1970.

A book of color pictures of designs and objects made by North American Indians, including pottery, basketry, textiles, skin-work, woodwork, stonework, and metalwork. Brief descrip-tions accompany the pictures. The author is a professor of anthropology and director of the Logan Museum of Anthropology, where many of the examples are found, but extensive use has also been made of collections in the Field Museum of Natural History in Chicago and the Milwaukee Public Museum. On *Akwesasne Notes* basic library list.

"A little book which runs through the steps involved in pottery, basketry, textiles, skinwork, woodwork, stonework and more. Well illustrated" (*Akwesasne Notes* 9:17, Spring 1977).

Yava, Aaron. **Border Towns of the Navajo Nation.** Holmgangers 1975.

Aaron Yava is a Navajo painter and sculptor who has appeared in many exhibitions, won awards, and traveled across New Mexico and Arizona. Because he was without money and hungry at the time, he identified with others of his people who also were poor, hungry, drunk, and suffering. This book of his drawings shows a side of Indian life which the tourists who go for ceremonials and powwows either do not see or choose to ignore. The foreword, by novelist Leslie Silko, is a moving tribute to Yava's artistry.

"The introduction by Leslie Silko is particularly fine, introducing a small part of the talent of Aaron Yava, Navajo artist, astute observer of the Indian scene" (*Indian Historian* 8:51, Fall 1975).

# Directory of Publishers

A-W  Addison-Wesley Publishing Co., Inc., Jacob Way, Reading, MA 01867

A Whitman  Albert Whitman & Co., 560 W. Lake St., Chicago, IL 60606

Abelard  Abelard-Schuman Ltd., c/o Harper & Row Pubs., Scranton, PA 18512

Abingdon  Abingdon Press, 201 Eighth Ave., S., Nashville, TN 37202

Ace Bks  Ace Books, Div. of Charter Communications Inc., c/o Grosset & Dunlap, 51 Madison Ave., New York, NY 10010

AHM Pub  AHM Publishing Corp., 3110 N. Arlington Heights Rd., Arlington Heights, IL 60004

Akwesasne  Akwesasne Notes, Mohawk Nation, Rooseveltown, NY 13683

ALA  American Library Assn., 50 E. Huron St., Chicago, IL 60611

Alaska Northwest  Alaska Northwest Publishing Co., 130 Second Ave. S., Edmonds, WA 98020

Am Folklore Soc  American Folklore Society, 1703 New Hampshire Ave. N. W., Washington, DC 20009

Am Heritage  American Heritage Publishing Co., Ten Rockefeller Plaza, New York, NY 10020

AMS. Natural Hist.  American Museum Science Books. Imprint of Natural History Press. Dist. by: Doubleday & Co., Inc., 501 Franklin Ave., Garden City, NY 11530

AMS Pr  AMS Press, Inc., 56 E. 13th St., New York, NY 10003

Anch. Doubleday.  Anchor Books. Imprint of Doubleday & Co., 501 Franklin Ave., Garden City, NY 11530

Apollo Eds  Apollo Editions. Dist. by: Harper & Row Pubs., Scranton, PA 18512

Archon. Shoe String  Archon Books. Imprint of Shoe String Press, Inc., 995 Sherman Ave., Hamden, CT 06514

Archway  Archway Paperbacks, c/o Pocket Books, 1230 Avenue of the Americas, New York, NY 10020

Atheneum  Atheneum Pubs. Dist. by: Book Warehouse, Inc., Vreeland Ave., Boro of Totowa, Paterson, NJ 07512

Avon  Avon Books, 959 Eighth Ave., New York, NY 10019

Award Bks  Award Books. Imprint of Universal Publishing & Distributing Corp., 235 E. 45 St., New York, NY 10017

Ballantine  Ballantine Books, Inc., Div. of Random House, Inc., 400 Hahn Rd., Westminster, MD 21157

Bantam  Bantam Books, Inc., 414 E. Golf Rd., Des Plaines, IL 60016

**Berkley Pub**  Berkley Publishing Corp., Affiliate of G. P. Putnam's Sons, 200 Madison Ave., New York, NY 10016

**Blair**  John F. Blair Pub., 1406 Plaza Dr., Winston-Salem, NC 27103

**Bradbury Pr**  Bradbury Press. Dist. by: E. P. Dutton & Co., Inc., 2 Park Ave., New York, NY 10016

**Brigham**  Brigham Young Univ. Press, 206 University Press Bldg., Provo, UT 84602

**Brit Bks**  Britannica Books, Div. of Encyclopaedia Britannica, Inc. (Defunct)

**C E Tuttle**  Charles E. Tuttle Co., Inc., 28 S. Main St., Rutland, VT 05701

**Capricorn Pr**  Capricorn Press. Dist. by: Book People, 2940 Seventh St., Berkeley, CA 94710

**Caxton**  Caxton Printers, Ltd., P.O. Box 700, Caldwell, ID 83605

**CCPr.**  Macmillan. Crowell-Collier Press. Imprint of Macmillan Publishing Co., Inc., Riverside, NJ 08075

**Chatham Pr**  Chatham Press, Inc. Dist. by: The Dervin-Adair Co., Old Greenwich, CT 06870

**Childrens**  Childrens Press, Inc., 1224 W. Van Buren St., Chicago, IL 60607

**Chilton**  Chilton Book Co., School, Library Services, 201 King of Prussia Rd., Radnor, PA 19089

**Citadel Pr**  Citadel Press, Subs. of Lyle Stuart, Inc., 120 Enterprise Ave., Secaucus, NJ 07094

**Coll & U Pr**  College & Univ. Press, 267 Chapel St., New Haven, CT 06513

**Collier.**  Macmillan. Collier Books. Imprint of Macmillan Publishing Co., Inc., Riverside, NJ 08075

**Concordia**  Concordia Publishing House, 3558 S. Jefferson Ave., St. Louis, MO 63118

**Contemp Bks**  Contemporary Books, Inc., 180 N. Michigan Ave., Chicago, IL 60601

**Coward**  Coward, McCann & Geoghegan, Inc., 390 Murray Hill Pkwy., East Rutherford, NJ 07073

**Crossing Pr**  Crossing Press, 17 W. Main St., Trumansburg, NY 14886

**Crowder**  Jack L. Crowder, Bernalillo, NM 87004

**Crown**  Crown Pubs., Inc., 1 Park Ave., New York, NY 10016

**Dakota Pr**  Dakota Press, University of South Dakota, Vermillion, SD 57069

**Delacorte**  Delacorte Press, c/o Dell Publishing Co., 1 Dag Hammarskjold Plaza, 245 E. 47th St., New York, NY 10017

**Dell**  Dell Publishing Co., Inc., 1 Dag Hammarskjold Plaza, 245 E. 47th St., New York, NY 10017

**Delta.**  Dell. Delta Books. Imprint of Dell Publishing Co., Inc., 1 Dag Hammarskjold Plaza, 245 E. 47th St., New York, NY 10017

**Dept Ind NA Canada**  Department of Indian and Northern Affairs of Canada, Information Kiosk, Main Floor, 10 Wellington Street, Hull, Quebec K1A 0H4, Canada

**Dial**  Dial Press, 1 Dag Hammarskjold Plaza, 245 E. 47th St., New York, NY 10017

Dillon  Dillon Press, Inc., 500 S. Third St., Minneapolis, MN 55405

Dodd  Dodd, Mead & Co., 79 Madison Ave., New York, NY 10016

Doubleday  Doubleday & Co., Inc., 501 Franklin Ave., Garden City, NY 11530

Dover  Dover Pubns., Inc., 180 Varick St., New York, NY 10014

Dramatic Pub  Dramatic Publishing Co., 4150 N. Milwaukee Ave., Chicago, IL 60641

Duell  Duell, Sloan & Pearce. (Defunct)

Duluth Ind Ed  Duluth Indian Education Advisory Committee, Duluth Independent School District, Lake Avenue & Second St., Duluth, MN 55802

Dutton  E. P. Dutton, 2 Park Ave., New York, NY 10016

Eerdmans  Wm. B. Eerdmans Publishing Co., 255 Jefferson Ave. S.E., Grand Rapids, MI 49503

Fawcett  Fawcett Book Group, 1515 Broadway, New York, NY 10036

Fennwyn Pr  Fennwyn Press. Dist. by: Honor Books, P.O. Box 94, Spearfish, SD 57783

Fleet  Fleet Press Corp., 160 Fifth Ave., New York, NY 10010

Follett  Follett Publishing Co., Div. of Follett Corp., 1010 W. Washington Blvd., Chicago, IL 60607

Four Winds. Schol Bk Serv.  Four Winds Press. Imprint of Scholastic Book Services, 906 Sylvan Ave., Englewood Cliffs, NJ 07632

Free Pr  Free Press. Dist. by: Macmillan Co., Riverside, NJ 08075

FS&G  Farrar, Straus & Giroux, Inc., 19 Union Square W., New York, NY 10003

G&D  Grosset & Dunlap, Inc., 51 Madison Ave., New York, NY 10010

Gage Pub  Gage Educational Publishing, Ltd., 164 Commander Blvd., Agincourt, Ontario MIS 3C7, Canada

Garrard  Garrard Publishing Co., 1607 N. Market St., Champaign, IL 61820

Garrett Pr  Garrett Press, Inc., 250 W. 54 St., New York, NY 10019

Glencoe  Glencoe Publishing Co., Inc. Dist. by: Macmillan Co., Riverside, NJ 08075

Golden Pr. Western Pub.  Golden Press. Imprint of Western Publishing Co., Inc., Dept. M, 1220 Mound Ave., Racine, WI 53404

Good Medicine Bks  Good Medicine Books. Dist. by: Book People, 2940 Seventh St., Berkeley, CA 94710

Gray  Gray's Publishing, Ltd., Box 2160, Sidney, British Columbia V8L 3S6, Canada

Greene  Stephen Greene Press, P.O. Box 1000, Brattleboro, VT 05301

Greenwillow  Greenwillow Books, Div. of William Morrow & Co., Inc., Wilmor Warehouse, 6 Henderson Dr., West Caldwell, NJ 07006

Gregg  Gregg Press, Inc., Div. of G. K. Hall & Co., 70 Lincoln St., Boston, MA 02111

Hale  E. M. Hale & Co., 128 W. River St., Chippewa Falls, WI 54729

Hancock Hse  Hancock House Pubs., Ltd., 12008 First Ave. S., Seattle, WA 98168

Har-Row  Harper & Row Pubs., Inc., Scranton, PA 18512

HarBraceJ  Harcourt Brace Jovanovich, Inc., 757 Third Ave., New York, NY 10017

Harvard U Pr  Harvard Univ. Press, Customer Service, Harvard Univ. Press, 79 Garden St., Cambridge, MA 02138

Hastings  Hastings House Pubs., Inc., 10 E. 40th St., New York, NY 10016

Hawthorn  Hawthorn Books, Inc., 260 Madison Ave., New York, NY 10016

Herald Pr  Herald Press, 616 Walnut Ave., Scottdale, PA 15683

Highway Bk  Highway Book Shop, Cobalt, Ontario POJ ICO, Canada

Hill & Wang  Hill & Wang, Inc., Div. of Farrar, Straus & Giroux, Inc., 19 Union Square, New York, NY 10003

HM  Houghton Mifflin Co., 2 Park St., Boston, MA 02107

Holiday  Holiday House, Inc., 18 E. 53rd St., New York, NY 10022

Holmgangers  Holmgangers Press, 7200 Collier Cyn Rd., Livermore, CA 94450

HR&W  Holt, Rinehart & Winston, Inc., 383 Madison Ave., New York, NY 10017

Hurtig  Hurtig Publishers, 10560 105 St., Edmonton, Alberta T5H 2W7, Canada

Ind U Pr  Indiana Univ. Press, Tenth & Morton St., Bloomington, IN 47401

Independence Pr  Independence Press, Div. of Herald House, Drawer HH, Independence, MO 64055

Indian Hist Pr  Indian Historian Press, Inc., 1451 Masonic Ave., San Francisco, CA 94117

Intl Pub Co  International Pubs. Co., 381 Park Ave. S., Suite 1301, New York, NY 10036

Iowa St U Pr  Iowa State Univ. Press, South State Ave., 112 C Press Office, Ames, IA 50010

John Day  John Day Co., Inc. Dist. by: Harper & Row Pubs., Scranton, PA 18512

Johns Hopkins  Johns Hopkins Univ. Press, Baltimore, MD 21218

Kennikat  Kennikat Press Corp., Subs. of Taylor Publishing Co., 90 S. Bayles Ave., Port Washington, NY 11050

Knopf  Alfred A. Knopf, Inc., Subs. of Random House, Inc., 400 Hahn Rd., Westminster, MD 21157

Lawrence Hill  Lawrence Hill & Co., Inc. Dist. by: Whirlwind Book Co., 80 Fifth Ave., New York, NY 10011

LC  Library of Congress. Dist. by: Superintendent of Documents, Government Printing Office, Washington, DC 20402

Lerner Pubns  Lerner Publications Co., 241 First Ave. N., Minneapolis, MN 55401

Lippincott  J. B. Lippincott Co., East Washington Sq., Philadelphia, PA 19105

Little  Little, Brown & Co., 200 West St., Waltham, MA 02154

Liveright  Liveright Publishing Corp., Subs. of W. W. Norton Co., Inc., 500 Fifth Ave., New York, NY 10036

Lochinvar. Exposition. Lochinvar. Imprint of Exposition Press, Inc., 900 S. Oyster Bay Rd., Hicksville, NY 11801

Lothrop Lothrop, Lee & Shepard Co., Div. of William Morrow & Co., Inc., Wilmor Warehouse, 6 Henderson Dr., West Caldwell, NJ 07006

McClelland McClelland & Stewart, Ltd., 25 Hollinger Rd., Toronto, Ontario M4B 3G2, Canada

McElderry Bk. Atheneum. McElderry Book. Imprint of Atheneum Pubs. Dist. by: Book Warehouse, Inc., Vreeland Ave., Boro of Totowa, Paterson, NJ 07512

McGraw McGraw-Hill Book Co., 1221 Ave. of the Americas, New York, NY 10020

McKay David McKay Co., Inc., 750 Third Ave., New York, NY 10017

Macmillan Macmillan Publishing Co., Inc., Riverside, NJ 08075

Ment. NAL. Mentor Books. Imprint of New American Library, 1301 Ave. of the Americas, New York, NY 10019

Messner Julian Messner, A Simon & Schuster Div. of Gulf & Western Corp., 1230 Ave. of the Americas, New York, NY 10020

Morrow William Morrow & Co., Inc., Wilmor Warehouse, 6 Henderson Dr., West Caldwell, NJ 07006

Mus Am Ind Museum of the American Indian, Broadway at 155th St., New York, NY 10032

Myrin Institute Myrin Institute, Inc., 521 Park Ave., New York, NY 10021

NAL New American Library, 1301 Ave. of the Americas, New York, NY 10019

Nash Pub Nash Publishing Corp. Dist. by: E. P. Dutton & Co., Inc., 2 Park Ave., New York, NY 10003

Natural Hist Natural History Press. Dist. by: Doubleday & Co., Inc., 501 Franklin Ave., Garden City, NY 11530

Naturegraph Naturegraph Pubs., Inc., P.O. Box 1075, Happy Camp, CA 96039

Navajo Curr Navajo Curriculum Center Press, Rough Rock Demonstration School, Chinle, AZ 86503

Naylor Naylor Co. (Defunct)

NCTE National Council of Teachers of English, 1111 Kenyon Rd., Urbana, IL 61801

Nelson Thomas Nelson, Inc., 407 Seventh Ave. S., Nashville, TN 37203

New Com Pr New Community Press, 963 National Press Building, Washington, DC 20007

Nez Perce Nez Perce Tribe, Box 305, Lapwai, Idaho 83540

Nodin Pr Nodin Press, c/o The Bookmen, Inc., 519 N. Third St., Minneapolis, MN 55401

North Star North Star Press, P.O. Box 451, St. Cloud, MN 56301

Northland Northland Press, P.O. Box N, Flagstaff, AZ 86002

Norton W. W. Norton & Co., Inc., 500 Fifth Ave., New York, NY 10036

NYGS New York Graphic Society, Ltd. Dist. by: Little, Brown & Co., 200 West St., Waltham, MA 02154

**Octagon**   Octagon Books, 19 Union Square W., New York, NY 10003

**Ohio Hist Soc**   Ohio Historical Society, 1982 Velma Ave., Columbus, OH 43211

**Oxford U Pr**   Oxford Univ. Press, Inc., 16-00 Pollitt Dr., Fair Lawn, NJ 07410

**Packrat Pr**   Packrat Press, House 3, Madrid, NM 87010

**Pantheon**   Pantheon Books, Div. of Random House, Inc., 400 Hahn Rd., Westminster, MD 21157

**Paperback Lib**   Paperback Library Werner, 315 Park Ave. S., New York, NY 10010

**Parents**   Parents Magazine Press, 80 New Bridge Rd., Bergenfield, NJ 07621

**Parnassus**   Parnassus Press, 4080 Halleck St., Emeryville, CA 94608

**PB**   Pocket Books, Inc., Div. of Simon & Schuster, Inc., 1230 Ave. of the Americas, New York, NY 10020

**Penguin**   Penguin Books, Inc., 625 Madison Ave., New York, NY 10022

**Popular Lib**   Popular Library, Inc., Unit of CBS Pubns., 1515 Broadway, New York, NY 10036

**Putnam**   G. P. Putnam's Sons, 390 Murray Hill Pkwy., East Rutherford, NJ 07073

**Pyramid Pubns**   Pyramid Pubns., Inc., 9 Garden St., Moonachie, NJ 07074

**Rand**   Rand McNally & Co., P.O. Box 7600, Chicago, IL 60680

**Random**   Random House, Inc., 400 Hahn Rd., Westminster, MD 21157

**Raven Hail**   Raven Hail, P.O. Box 35733, Dallas, TX 75235

**Readers Digest Pr**   Reader's Digest Press, c/o Harper & Row Pubs., 10 E. 53rd St., New York, NY 10022

**Ross**   Ross & Haines, Inc., 639 E. Lake St., Wayzata, MN 55391

**S Meth U Pr**   Southern Methodist Univ. Press, Dallas, TX 75275

**S&S**   Simon & Schuster, Inc., 1230 Ave. of the Americas, New York, NY 10020

**Sat Rev Pr**   E. P. Dutton, 2 Park Ave., New York, NY 10016

**Schocken**   Schocken Books, Inc., 200 Madison Ave., New York, NY 10016

**Schol Bk Serv**   Scholastic Book Services, Div. of Scholastic Magazines, 906 Sylvan Ave., Englewood Cliffs, NJ 07632

**Scribner**   Charles Scribner's Sons, Shipping & Service Ctr., Vreeland Ave., Totowa, NJ 07512

**Sey Lawr. Delacorte.**   Seymour Lawrence. Imprint of Delacorte Press, 1 Dag Hammarskjold Plaza, 245 E. 47th St., New York, NY 10017

**Sherbourne**   Sherbourne Press, P.O. Box 12037, Nashville, TN 37212

**Sig. NAL.**   Signet Books. Imprint of New American Library, 1301 Ave. of the Americas, New York, NY 10019

**Silver**   Silver Burdett Co., Div. of General Learning Co., 250 James St., Morristown, NJ 07960

**Stay Away**   Stay Away Joe Pubs., P.O. Box 2054, Great Falls, MT 59401

**Stein & Day**   Stein & Day, 122 E. 42nd St., Suite 3602, New York, NY 10017

Sumners  Cecil L. Sumners, 602 North Pearl St., Iuka, MS 38852

Swallow  Swallow Press, 811 W. Junior Terrace, Chicago, IL 60613

T Y Crowell  Thomas Y. Crowell Co. Dist. by: Harper & Row Pubs., Scranton, PA 18512

Taplinger  Taplinger Publishing Co., Inc., 200 Park Ave. S., New York, NY 10003

Theos Pub Hse  Theosophical Publishing House, 306 W. Geneva Rd., Wheaton, IL 60187

Time-Life  Time-Life Books, Div. of Time, Inc. Dist. by: Little, Brown & Co., 34 Beacon St., Boston, MA 02106

Todd Pubns  Todd Publications, Box 535, Rye, NY 10580

Tower  Tower Publications, Inc., 185 Madison Ave., New York, NY 10016

Trophy. Har-Row.  Trophy. Imprint of Harper & Row Pubs., Inc., Scranton, PA 18512

Tundra Bks  Tundra Books of Northern New York. Dist. by: Charles Scribner's Sons, 597 5th Ave., New York, NY 10017

U of Ala Pr  Univ. of Alabama Press, Box 2877, University, AL 35486

U of Ariz Pr  Univ. of Arizona Press, P.O. Box 3398, Tucson, AZ 85722

U of Cal Pr  Univ. of California Press, 2223 Fulton St., Berkeley, CA 94720

U of Chicago Pr  Univ. of Chicago Press, 11030 S. Langley Ave., Chicago, IL 60628

U of Ga Pr  Univ. of Georgia Press, Athens, GA 30602

U of Ill Pr  Univ. of Illinois Press, Urbana, IL 61801

U of Mich Pr  Univ. of Michigan Press, 615 E. University, Ann Arbor, MI 48106

U of Minn Pr  Univ. of Minnesota Press, 2037 University Ave. S.E., Minneapolis, MN 55455

U of Mo Pr  Univ. of Missouri Press, 107 Swallow Hall, Columbia, MO 65211

U of NC Pr  Univ. of North Carolina Press, P.O. Box 2288, Chapel Hill, NC 27514

U of Nebr Pr  Univ. of Nebraska Press, 901 N. 17th St., Lincoln, NE 68588

U of NM Pr  Univ. of New Mexico Press, Albuquerque, NM 87131

U of Okla Pr  Univ. of Oklahoma Press, 1005 Asp Ave., Norman, OK 73019

U of Pa Pr  Univ. of Pennsylvania Press, 3933 Walnut St., Philadelphia, PA 19104

U of Tex Pr  Univ. of Texas Press, P.O. Box 7819, University Sta., Austin, TX 78712

U of Toronto Pr  Univ. of Toronto Press, 33 E. Tupper St., Buffalo, NY 14203

U of Wash Pr  Univ. of Washington Press, Seattle, WA 98105

U of Wis Pr  Univ. of Wisconsin Press, P.O. Box 1379, Madison, WI 53701

U Pr of Ky  Univ. Press of Kentucky, Lexington, KY 40506

U Presses Fla  Univ. Presses of Fla., 15 N.W. 15th St., Gainesville, FL 32603

US HEW  U.S. Department of Health, Education and Welfare, 330 Independence Ave. S.W., Washington, DC 20201

Van Nos Reinhold  Van Nostrand Reinhold Co., Div. of Litton Educational Publishing, Inc., Lepi Order Processing, 7625 Empire Dr., Florence, KY 41042

Vanguard  Vanguard Press, Inc., 424 Madison Ave., New York, NY 10017

Viking Pr  Viking Press, Inc., 625 Madison Ave., New York, NY 10022

Vin. Random.  Vintage Trade Books. Imprint of Random House, Inc., 400 Hahn Rd., Westminster, MD 21157

Waldorf Pr  Waldorf Press, Adelphi Univ., Cambridge Ave., Garden City, NY 11530

Walker & Co  Walker & Co., 720 Fifth Ave., New York, NY 10019

Warner Bks  Warner Books, Inc. Dist. by: Independent News Co., 75 Rockefeller Plaza, New York, NY 10019

Watts  Watts, Franklin, Inc., Subs. of Grolier Inc., 730 Fifth Ave., New York, NY 10019

Western Pub  Western Publishing Co., Inc., Dept. M, 1220 Mound Ave., Racine, WI 53404

Westernlore  Westernlore Books, P.O. Box 41073, Los Angeles, CA 90041

Westminster  Westminster Press, 920 Witherspoon Bldg., Philadelphia, PA 19107

Wiley  John Wiley & Sons, Inc., 605 Third Ave., New York, NY 10016

Wisconsin Hse  Wisconsin House Ltd., Box 2118, Madison, WI 53701

World. Times Mir.  World Publishing Co., Subs. of The Times Mirror Co., 280 Park Ave., New York, NY 10017

WSP  Washington Square Press, Inc., Div. of Simon & Schuster, Inc., 1230 Ave. of the Americas, New York, NY 10020

Yale U Pr  Yale Univ. Press, 92A Yale Sta., New Haven, CT 06520

# Author Index

Aberle, Sophie D., 327
Adams, Clinton, 347
Ahenakew, Edward, 45, 296
Alexander, Hartley Burr, 302
Aliki, 279
Allen, Don B., 198
Allen, Terry D., 50, 56, 90, 198, 225
Ambrose, Stephen E., 251
Anderson, Jean, 344
Andrist, Ralph K., 3, 72, 251
Annixter, Jane, 137
Annixter, Paul, 137
Antell, Will, 45, 187
Appleton, LeRoy H., 343
Armer, Laura Adams, 138
Armstrong, Virginia Irving, 18, 96
Arnold, Elliott, 11, 19, 20, 22, 24, 138, 158
Ashabranner, Brent, 188
Ashton, Robert H., Jr., 347
Astrov, Margot, 96

Bailey, M. Thomas, 251
Baker, Betty, 114
Baker, Donna, 187
Balch, Glenn, 138
Baldwin, Gordon C., 297
Bales, Carol Ann, 320
Ball, Eve, 208
Balls, Edward K., 303
Bandelier, Adolf Francis, 73, 158
Barnouw, Victor, 114
Barrett, S. M., 208
Bataille, Gretchen M., 252
Baumhoff, Martin A., 350
Baylor, Byrd, 20, 70, 77, 115, 159, 279, 337, 338
Beal, Merrill, 209
Bealer, Alex W., 72, 239
Bean, Lowell John, 73, 303
Beatty, Hetty Burlingame, 115
Bedford, Denton R., 209
Bedinger, Margery, 347
Belting, Natalia, 77

Benchley, Nathaniel, 115
Bennett, Kay, 4, 16, 46, 72, 198, 242
Bennett, Russ, 46, 242
Berger, Thomas, 70, 159
Berlant, Anthony, 343
Bernstein, Margery, 78, 79
Berry, Brewton, 26, 27
Beuf, Ann H., 27
Bierhorst, John, 79, 91, 96, 338
Biesterveld, Betty, 116
Bjorklund, Karna L., 297
Black Elk, 6, 46, 71, 73, 303
Black Hawk, 14, 70, 210
Black, Nancy B., 27
Blades, Ann, 320
Bleeker, Sonia, 73, 280-284
Blevins, Winfred, 160
Blish, Helen, 252
Blood, Charles L., 116
Boesen, Victor, 24, 210
Bonham, Frank, 139
Borich, Michael, 47, 96
Borland, Hal, 5, 8, 70, 160
Boyce, George A., 23, 139
Boyd, Doug, 210
Branch, E. Douglas, 252
Brandon, William, 5, 14, 72, 97, 253
Brant, Charles S., 211
Brill, Charles, 321
Brindze, Ruth, 284
Brody, J. J., 347
Brophy, William A., 327
Brown, Dee, 3, 72, 243, 253
Brown, Joseph Epes, 46, 303
Brown, Vinson, 6, 211, 238, 297
Brusa, Betty War, 298
Bryde, John F., 304
Buck, Ruth M., 296
Buff, Conrad, 116
Buff, Mary, 116
Bulla, Clyde Robert, 117, 118, 187
Bunting, Bainbridge, 348
Burnette, Robert, 328
Burnford, Sheila, 212

Burt, Jesse, 298
Butler, Beverly, 139
Butterworth, F. Edward, 161

Cahn, Edgar S., 328
Campbell, Maria, 47, 80, 212
Capps, Benjamin, 10, 140, 161, 243
Capps, Mary Joyce, 118
Carlisle, Henry, 161
Carson, Kit, 212
Carter, Forrest, 22, 47, 162, 198
Carter, Samuel, III, 254
Cashman, Marc, 28
Castaneda, Carlos, 73, 304, 305
Caswell, Helen, 80
Cather, Willa, 163
Catlin, George, 305
Chaffee, Allen, 80
Chandler, Edna Walker, 118
Chapman, Kenneth M., 348
Cheatham, K. Follis, 8, 47, 119
Clark, Ann Nolan, 73, 199, 285
Clark, Ella Elizabeth, 97
Clark, Jerry E., 305
Clifford, Eth, 119, 140
Clymer, Eleanor, 119
Clymer, Theodore, 81
Coatsworth, Elizabeth, 140
Cochise, Ciye "Niño," 213
Cody, Iron Eyes, 298
Coen, Rena Neumann, 338
Coffin, Tristram P., 98
Collier, John, 72, 254, 329
Collier, Peter, 243
Colton, Mary-Russell F., 108
Colver, Anne, 120
Compton, Margaret, 81
Cone, Molly, 141
Conklin, Paul, 321
Cook, Sherburne F., 255, 306
Cooke, David Coxe, 199, 241
Cooper, James Fenimore, 12, 13, 14, 16, 18, 163
Corle, Edwin, 8, 164, 255
Cortés, Carlos E., 255
Cossi, Olga, 120
Costo, Rupert, 26, 28, 68
Cowell, Vi, 120
Cox, Bruce, 306
Crapanzano, Vincent, 306
Crary, Margaret, 8, 199
Craven, Margaret, 164
Crawford, James M., 307
Crompton, Anne Eliot, 81
Cronyn, George W., 98
Crowder, David L., 213

Crowder, Jack L., 321
Curtis, Natalie, 348
Cushman, Dan, 70, 165
Cutler, Ebbitt, 188

Dale, Edward Everett, 256
Daubney, Brian, 339
Davis, Britton, 256
Davis, Russell, 188
Day, A. Grove, 98
De Angulo, Jaime, 91
DeArmond, Dale Burlison, 81
Debo, Angie, 256
de Leeuw, Adèle, 16, 189
Deloria, Vine, Jr., 15, 17, 18, 48, 68, 72, 74, 257, 307, 329, 330
Derleth, August, 165
Desbarats, Peter, 99
Deur, Lynne, 189
Dewdney, Selwyn, 343
Dewey, Jane, 322
Dial, Adolph L., 48, 257
Dixon, Paige, 121
Dobyns, Henry F., 31, 344
Dockstader, Frederick J., 26, 29, 48, 344
Dodge, Nanabah Chee, 49, 121
Dodge, Robert K., 99
Dorian, Edith, 286
Dorris, Michael, 49, 324
Dosman, Edgar J., 330
Doughty, Wayne Dyre, 141
Drucker, Philip, 73, 307, 308
Dyk, Walter, 221

Eastman, Charles Alexander, 15, 49, 71, 73, 200, 213, 299
Eastman, Elaine Goodale, 22, 214
Eastman, Mary, 100
Eber, Dorothy, 200
Eckert, Allan W., 200
Edmonds, Walter Dumaux, 14, 165
Ehrlich, Amy, 243
Eliades, David K., 257
Ellis, Mel, 141, 142
Embree, Edwin R., 73, 308
Emerson, Ellen Russell, 100
Engel, Lorenz, 286
Epstein, Anne Merrick, 121
Erdoes, Richard, 82, 217, 244
Ewers, John C., 242, 305

Fall, Thomas, 9, 166, 189
Farb, Peter, 73, 308
Farnsworth, Frances Joyce, 201
Fast, Howard Melvin, 18, 166

Faulk, Odie B., 257
Fehrenbach, T. R., 258
Feldmann, Susan, 12, 91
Felton, Harold W., 8, 190
Ferber, Edna, 167
Ferguson, Robert B., 298
Fergusson, Erna, 299
Fey, Harold E., 17, 54, 74, 331
Fiedler, Leslie A., 26, 29
Field, Edward, 82
Fire, John, 217
Fisher, Vardis, 167
Folsom, Franklin, 245
Ford, Clellan S., 214
Foreman, Grant, 72, 214, 258
Forman, James, 142
Forrest, Linn A., 344
Fox, Mary Lou, 82
Frank, Larry, 23, 349
Fredericksen, Hazel, 122
Freedman, Benedict, 167
Freedman, Nancy, 167
Fuller, Iola, 143, 168
Fumoleau, René, 258

Gaddis, Vincent H., 100
Garbarino, Merwyn S., 309
Gard, Wayne, 259
Garfield, Viola, 344
Garland, Hamlin, 168
Garst, Shannon, 4, 6, 190, 201, 202
Georgakas, Dan, 245, 246
George, Chief Dan, 50, 324
George, Jean Craighead, 122
Gidley, Mick, 24, 309
Giles, Janice Holt, 169
Gillam, Olivia L., 314
Gillmor, Frances, 169
Gilmore, Melvin R., 310
Glubok, Shirley, 73, 296, 339, 340
Goble, Dorothy, 122, 239, 240
Goble, Paul, 122, 239, 240
Graber, Kay, 214
Gradwohl, David M., 252
Grant, Bruce, 29
Grant, Campbell, 349
Graves, John, 215
Graybill, Florence Curtis, 24, 210
Grey, Zane, 17
Gridley, Marion E., 26, 30
Griese, Arnold A., 123
Griffith, A. Kinney, 213
Grimm, William C., 286
Grinnell, George Bird, 23, 101, 215
Gugliotta, Bobette, 143
Gurko, Miriam, 246
Guthrie, Alfred Bertram, 169

Hagan, William T., 72, 246
Haig-Brown, Roderick, 143
Hail, Raven, 170
Haines, Francis, 259
Hale, Janet Campbell, 10, 21, 24, 50, 70, 144
Haley, James L., 259
Halsell, Grace, 324
Hamilton, Charles Everett, 102
Hamilton, Dorothy, 124
Hamilton, Virginia, 144
Hancock, Sibyl, 124
Hannum, Alberta, 216
Hanson, James Austin, 299
Harlow, Francis H., 23, 349
Harnishfeger, Lloyd, 124, 125, 287
Harris, Christie, 83, 125, 144, 145
Harris, Marilyn, 170
Harvey, Lillian, 88
Hausman, Gerald, 92
Haverstock, Mary Sayre, 202
Heady, Eleanor B., 83
Heidenreich, Conrad E., 260
Heizer, Robert F., 31, 308, 350
Helm, June, 31
Henderson, Nancy, 322
Henry, Jeannette, 26, 30
Herbert, Frank, 170
Hickman, Janet, 125
Highwater, Jamake, 21, 23, 24, 50, 145, 331, 350
Hill, Ruth Beebe, 171
Hillerman, Tony, 146
Hirnschall, Helmut, 324
Hirsch, S. Carl, 72, 240
Hirschfelder, Arlene, 68
Hirst, Stephen, 325
Hodges, Margaret, 84
Hoffman, Virginia, 202
Hofmann, Charles, 344
Hofsinde, Robert [Gray-Wolf], 287–290, 340–342
Hoig, Stan, 261
Holden, William Curry, 225
Holling, Holling Clancy, 126
Hollmann, Clide, 203
Houston, James, 84
Howard, Helen Addison, 203
Howard, James H., 216
Hudson, Charles M., 261
Huffaker, Clair, 15, 171
Hughes, Charles C., 217
Hungry Wolf, Adolf, 51, 92, 299, 325
Hunt, W. Ben, 342
Hurdy, John Major, 310
Hyde, George E., 72, 261, 262, 319

Icenhower, Joseph B., 247
Ishmole, Jack, 146
Iverson, Peter, 31

Jackson, Donald, 210
Jackson, Helen Hunt, 12, 15, 172
Jacobs, Paul, 262
Jacobs, Wilbur R., 263
Jacobson, Daniel, 240, 241
Jaenen, Cornelius J., 263
Jagendorf, M. A., 85
Jahoda, Gloria, 264
Jakes, John, 203
Jayne, Mitchell F., 172
Jenness, Aylette, 291
Jennings, Francis, 26, 31, 264
Jernigan, E. Wesley, 350
Johnson, Annabel, 146
Johnson, Broderick H., 202
Johnson, Dorothy M., 20, 24, 172
Johnson, Emily Pauline [Tekahion-
 wake], 51, 102
Johnson, Edgar, 146
Johnston, Basil, 51, 102
Johnston, Bernice, 300
Johnston, Johanna, 190
Jones, Hettie, 85, 86
Jones, Jayne Clark, 247
Jones, Kenneth M., 248
Jones, Weyman, 126
Josephy, Alvin M., Jr., 73, 204, 310,
 332

Kahlenberg, Mary Hunt, 343
Katz, Jane B., 102, 191, 248
Kaywaykla, James, 208
Keegan, Marcia, 74, 322
Keiser, Albert, 26, 31
Keith, Harold, 10, 14, 147, 173
Kelly, Ernece B., 26, 32
Kelley, Jane Holden, 225
Kelly, Fanny, 11, 23, 218
Kennedy, Dan [Ochankugahe], 218
Kennedy, Michael Stephen, 312
Kerle, Arthur G., 10, 126
Kesey, Ken, 173
Kidd, Kenneth E., 343
Kilpatrick, Anna Gritts, 52, 103
Kilpatrick, Jack Frederick, 52, 69,
 103
Kimball, Yeffe, 344
Kirk, Ruth, 322
Kjelgaard, Jim, 147
Klein, Barry T., 32
Kluckhohn, Clyde, 310
Knudson, R. R., 147
Kobrin, Janet, 78, 79
Kopit, Arthur, 173

Koster, John, 328
Kroeber, A. L., 96, 97, 103, 311
Kroeber, Theodora, 4, 92, 204, 218

LaBarre, Weston, 73, 311
La Farge, Oliver, 5, 54, 174, 249
LaFlesche, Francis, 4, 9, 18, 52, 71,
 219
Laird, Carobeth, 219
Lame Deer, 217
Lampman, Evelyn Sibley, 21, 22,
 127, 148, 149
Landau, Saul, 262
Landes, Ruth, 311
LaPointe, Frank, 53, 325
Lass-Woodfin, Mary Jo, 32
Latorre, Dolores L., 311
Latorre, Felipe A., 311
Lauber, Patricia, 73, 291
Laubin, Gladys, 345
Laubin, Reginald, 345
Lauritzen, Jonreed, 150
Lavine, Sigmund A., 292
Lawson, Marion, 204
Lawton, Harry, 220
Lee, Betty, 205
Lee, Larry, 175
Lee, Nelson, 220
Leforge, Thomas H., 221
LeFree, Betty, 351
Left Handed, 71, 221
Leighton, Dorothea, 310
Lenski, Lois, 10, 127
Leslie, Robert Franklin, 53, 221
Levenson, Dorothy, 292
Levine, Joseph, 294
Levine, Stuart, 332
Levitas, Gloria, 103
Levitin, Sonia, 150
Liberty, Margot, 273
Lighthall, J. I., 312
Linderman, Frank B., 71, 222
Link, Martin A., 116
Lister, Florence C., 222, 351
Lister, Robert H., 222, 351
Long, James Larpenteur, 312
Lott, Milton, 175
Louis, Ray Baldwin, 326
Lourie, Dick, 103
Lowie, Robert H., 73, 312
Lurie, Nancy Oestreich, 71, 222, 332
Lyons, Oren, 8, 53, 128

McClintock, Walter, 313
McCracken, Harold, 7, 150, 223
McCullough, Joseph B., 99
McDermott, Beverly Brodsky, 86
McDermott, Gerald, 86

McGaa, Ed, 54, 191
McGaw, Jessie Brewer, 128
McGee, Harold Franklin, Jr., 265
McGovern, Ann, 293
McGrath, Dan L., 203
McGraw, Eloise Jarvis, 151
McLuhan, T. C., 104
McNichols, Charles, 19, 151
McNickle, D'Arcy, 7, 17, 54, 70, 73, 74, 152, 176, 223, 265, 331
McReynolds, Edwin C., 266
McTaggart, Fred, 104
Maestas, John R., 24, 104
Maher, Ramona, 87
Manfred, Frederick, 6, 176
Manuel, George, 54, 326
Marken, Jack W., 26, 32
Marquis, Arnold, 332
Marquis, Thomas B., 221, 224
Marriott, Alice, 10, 14, 16, 73, 87, 93, 105, 152, 192, 224, 313, 314
Martinson, David, 87
Masson, Marcelle, 105
Mathews, John Joseph, 55, 224
Mead, Margaret, 314
Means, Florence Crannell, 176
Mélançon, Claude, 106
Meltzer, Milton, 4, 72, 249
Metayer, Father Maurice, 93
Meyer, Roy W., 266
Meyer, William, 55, 74, 333
Miles, Miska, 128
Miller, Alfred J., 300
Miller, J. Hillis, 33
Miller, Marjorie, 345
Milligan, Edward A., 266
Milton, John R., 106, 192
Miner, H. Craig, 267
Minge, Ward Alan, 300
Mitchell, Emerson Blackhorse, 15, 17, 56, 225
Moffatt, Anne, 276
Moisés, Rosalio, 225
Molloy, Anne, 293
Momaday, N. Scott, 9, 17, 18, 20, 22, 56, 68, 69, 70, 74, 93, 107, 177, 226
Momaday, Natachee Scott, 17, 56, 106, 128
Montgomery, Jean, 152
Moody, Ralph, 13, 192
Morey, Sylvester M., 33, 314, 333
Morgan, Lewis Henry, 315
Moulton, Gary E., 226
Mowat, Farley, 177
Moyer, John W., 193
Moyers, William, 241
Myers, Elizabeth P., 205

Nabokov, Peter, 226
Nasnaga, 57, 178
Naylor, Maria, 345
Neihardt, John G., 5, 46, 71, 107, 178, 227
Nelson, Gladys Tirrell, 129
Nelson, John Young, 227
Nelson, Mary Carroll, 16, 193, 194
Nequatewa, Edmund, 69, 108
Newcomb, Franc Johnson, 88, 228, 352
Niatum, Duane, 57, 108
Niethammer, Carolyn, 315
Norbeck, Oscar, 346
Northey, Sue, 73, 293
Nurge, Ethel, 315

O'Connor, Richard, 194
O'Dell, Scott, 129, 130
O'Kane, Walter Collins, 300
Oldenburg, E. William, 130
Olson, James C., 267
O'Meara, Walter, 10, 131, 228
O'Neill, Paul, 109
O'Reilly, Harrington, 227
Oskison, John, 57, 229
Oswalt, Wendell, 17, 267

Parker, Arthur Caswell, 58
Parman, Donald L., 268
Parnall, Peter, 88
Parsons, Elsie Clews, 109
Patterson, Lillie, 195
Patton, Oliver B., 178
Paul, Frances Lackey, 195
Payne, Elizabeth, 294
Peake, Katy, 131
Pearce, Roy H., 12, 26, 33
Peck, Robert Newton, 153
Peek, Walter W., 110
Pelletier, Wilfred, 58, 229
Penney, Grace Jackson, 7, 131
Perrine, Mary, 132
Phillips, George Harwood, 268
Pine, Tillie S., 294
Poole, Ted, 58, 229
Pope, Saxton T., 301
Posluns, Michael, 326
Powers, Stephen, 315
Powers, William K., 73, 316
Pratson, Frederick, 333
Pratt, Theodore, 179
Priest, Loring Benson, 268
Prucha, Francis Paul, 269, 270

Qoyawayma, Polingaysi, 9, 16, 229
Quaife, Milo Milton, 212, 256

Rachlin, Carol K., 73, 105, 313, 314
Rachlis, Eugene, 242
Radin, Paul, 109, 230
Ray, Arthur J., 260
Ray, Carl, 109
Reah, Ronald, 339
Red Fox, Chief, 206
Redsky, James [Esquekesik], 58, 230
Reichard, Gladys A., 352
Reit, Seymour, 323
Reynolds, Charles R., Jr., 346
Richter, Conrad, 10, 14, 19, 153
Ridgely, Joseph V., 182
Robinson, Maudie, 294
Rockwell, Anne, 88
Rockwood, Joyce, 20, 24, 70, 154
Rodee, Marian E., 352
Rogers, John [Chief Snow Cloud], 59, 231
Roland, Albert, 206
Ronnefeldt, Karin, 317
Rose, Alan Henry, 33
Rosen, Kenneth, 59, 179
Ross, Ann, 196
Rothenberg, Jerome, 110
Ruesch, Hans, 180
Russell, Don, 295

Salomon, Julian Harris, 346
Sanders, Thomas E., 110
Sando, Joe S., 59, 316
Sandoz, Mari, 6, 7, 72, 154, 155, 231, 270, 271, 301
Santee, Ross, 231
Satz, Ronald N., 271
Schellie, Don, 22, 155
Schmedding, Joseph, 232
Schoor, Gene, 206
Schultz, James Willard [Apikuni], 94, 232
Schusky, Ernest, 326
Schwarz, Herbert T., 94, 110
Schweitzer, Byrd Baylor, 132
Scott, Lalla, 18, 232
Searcy, Margaret Zehmer, 295
Seidman, Robert J., 180
Sekaquaptewa, Helen, 16, 233
Sergel, Christopher [Ta-Tunka He Luta], 181
Sewid, James, 233
Shaw, Anna Moore, 59, 69, 94
Sheehan, Bernard W., 271
Sheppard, Sally, 73, 295
Shor, Pekay, 88
Showers, Paul, 296
Sides, Dorothy Smith, 352

Silet, Charles L. D., 252
Silko, Leslie Marmon, 20, 24, 59, 70, 104, 181, 354
Silliman, Eugene Lee, 94
Silverberg, Robert, 73, 301
Simmons, Leo W., 234
Simms, William Gilmore, 182
Sissons, Jack, 234
Sleator, William, 89
Slickpoo, Allen P., 60, 111
Smith, Derek G., 11, 23, 234, 272
Smith, James, 11, 235
Smith, Rex Alan, 249
Sneve, Virginia Driving Hawk, 53, 60, 70, 132-134, 156
Snodgrass, Jeanne O., 34
Snow, Richard F., 276
Sobol, Rose, 8, 134
Specht, Robert, 235
Spicer, Edward H., 72, 249, 272
Spindler, Will H., 272
Spradley, James P., 233
Squire, Roger, 89
Standing Bear, Luther, 60, 71, 236
Stands In Timber, John, 61, 72, 273
Steele, Mary Q., 73, 134
Steele, William O., 73, 134, 135
Steiner, Stan, 113, 334
Stember, Sol, 195
Stephens, Peter John, 156
Steuber, William, 182
Stevens, James R., 58, 109, 218, 230
Storm, Hyemeyohsts, 182
Straight, Michael Whitney, 4, 183
Stuart, Colin, 183
Stuart, Jozefa, 347
Stump, Sarain, 61, 94
Sumners, Cecil L., 250
Sun Bear, 61, 68, 206
Supree, Burton, 196
Szasz, Margaret C., 273

Tamarin, Alfred, 73, 296, 323
Tanner, Helen Hornbeck, 31
Teal, Mildred, 135
Tebbel, John, 61, 274
Tedlock, Barbara, 316
Tedlock, Dennis, 111, 316
Terrell, Donna M., 317
Terrell, John Upton, 72, 73, 274, 317
Terris, Susan, 135
Thomas, Davis, 317
Thompson, Eileen, 21, 156
Thompson, Raymond H., 272
Thompson, Stith, 12, 111
Tobias, Tobi, 196

Tomkins, William, 302
Toye, William, 89
Traveller Bird, 236
Trueman, Stuart, 236
Trumbull, James Hammond, 274
Turner, C. Frank, 275

Udall, Louise, 233
Ullom, Judith, 34
Underhill, Ruth Murray, 72, 112, 275
Utley, Robert M., 276

Van der Veer, Judy, 136
Vanderwerth, W. C., 112
Van Every, Dale, 276
Vaudrin, Bill, 62, 69, 95
Vaughan, Carter A., 14, 184
Vestal, Stanley, 4, 237
Villaseñor, David, 353
Viola, Herman J., 353
Vivelo, Frank Robert, 103
Vivelo, Jacqueline J., 103
Vizenor, Gerald, 12, 19, 62, 69, 74, 95, 327, 335
Vogel, Virgil J., 276
Voight, Virginia F., 197

Walker, Diana, 19, 22, 157
Wallace, Anthony F. C., 277
Walsh, M. M. B., 184
Waltrip, Lela, 207
Waltrip, Rufus, 207
Warren, Mary Phraner, 136
Washburn, Wilcomb E., 276, 277
Waters, Frank, 7, 9, 63, 185, 237, 318

Watkins, Mel, 335
Webb, George, 237
Weems, John Edward, 250
Weidman, Bette S., 27
Welch, James, 17, 20, 24, 63, 70, 112, 185
Weslager, C. A., 319
West, Jessamyn, 20, 186
Wetmore, Ruth Y., 302
Whiteford, Andrew Hunter, 353
Wiebe, Rudy, 20, 24, 70, 186
Will, George F., 319
Williams, Neva, 197
Willoya, William, 238
Wilson, Edmund, 336
Wilson, Mary, 136, 137
Wilson, W. N., 286
Witheridge, Elizabeth, 10, 157
Witt, Shirley Hill, 18, 113
Witter, Evelyn, 136
Wolf, Bernard, 323
Wolfe, Ellen, 197
Wood, Nancy, 90, 158
Woodward, Grace Steele, 238
Worcester, Donald E., 277
Wyatt, Edgar, 207, 208

Yava, Aaron, 354
Yazzie, Ethelou, 95
Yellow Robe, Rosebud [Lacotawin], 242
Young, Biloine, 136, 137

Zolla, Elémire, 26, 34

# Title Index

About Indians: A Listing of Books, 26, 28, 68

Ácoma: Pueblo in the Sky, 300

Across the Medicine Line: The Epic Confrontation between Sitting Bull and the North-West Mounted Police, 275

Adventures and Sufferings of John R. Jewitt, Captive among the Nootka, 1803-1805, The, 11, 234

Album of the American Indian, An, 242

Alice Yazzie's Year, 87

Along Sandy Trails, 285

American Eagle: The Story of a Navajo Vietnam Veteran, 175

American Epic: The Story of the American Indian, 73, 313

American Heritage Book of Indians, The, 14, 253

American Heritage History of the Indian Wars, The, 276

American Indian, The, 73, 293

American Indian Almanac, 73, 317

American Indian Art, 353

American Indian Authors, 17, 56, 106

American Indian Authors: A Representative Bibliography, 68, 71

American Indian Design and Decoration, 343

American Indian Fairy Tales, 81

American Indian in America, The, 247

American Indian: Language and Literature, The, 26, 32

American Indian Life, 109

American Indian Mythology, 105

American Indian Myths and Mysteries, 100

American Indian Painters: A Biographical Directory, 34

American Indian Poetry: An Anthology of Songs and Chants, 98

American Indian Policy in the Jacksonian Era, 271

American Indian Portraits from the Wanamaker Expedition of 1913, 346

American Indian Prose and Poetry: An Anthology, 96

American Indian Prose and Poetry: We Wait in the Darkness, 103

American Indian Reader: Anthropology, The, 30

American Indian Reader: Education, The, 26, 30

American Indian Religions, 310

American Indian Speaks: Poetry, Fiction and Art by the American Indian, The, 106

American Indian Today, The, 332

American Indian Tribes, 30

American Indians, 246

American Indians and Our Way of Life, 33

American Indians Sing, 344

American Indians Yesterday and Today, 29

Americanizing the American Indians: Writings by the "Friends of the Indian" 1880-1900, 269

Among the Plains Indians, 286

Anasazi Pottery, 351

Ancient Indians of the Southwest, 73, 296

And It Is Still That Way: Legends Told by Arizona Indian Children, 77

Angry Moon, The, 89

Anishinabe Adisokan: Tales of the People, 12, 63, 95

Anishinabe Nagamon: Songs of the People, 63, 95

Annie and the Old One, 128

Annie Wauneka, 16, 193

Anpao: An American Indian Odyssey, 21, 50, 145

Apache Indians, The, 280

Apache Land, 231

Apologies to the Iroquois, 336

Arilla Sun Down, 144

Arrow to the Sun: A Pueblo Indian Tale, 86
Arrows Four: Prose and Poetry by Young American Indians, 90
Art of American Indian Cooking, The, 344
Art of the Northwest Coast Indians, The, 339
Art of the Plains Indians, The, 340
Art of the Southwest Indians, The, 340
As Long as This Land Shall Last: A History of Treaty 8 and Treaty 11, 1870-1939, 258
Ascending Red Cedar Moon, 57, 108
Assiniboines: From the Accounts of the Old Ones Told to First Boy (James Larpenteur Long), The, 312
At the Mouth of the Luckiest River, 123
Authentic Indian Designs, 345
Autobiography of a Winnebago Indian, The, 230

Back to the Top of the World, 180
Bag of Bones: The Wintu Myths of the Trinity River Indian, A, 105
Bargain Bride, 22, 148
Battle of the Washita: The Sheridan-Custer Indian Campaign of 1867-69, The, 261
Bear's Heart: Scenes from the Life of a Cheyenne Artist of One Hundred Years Ago, 196
Beaver Men: Spearheads of Empire, The, 270
Before You Came This Way, 337
Behind the Trail of Broken Treaties: An Indian Declaration of Independence, 329
Bessie Yellowhair, 324
Betrayed, 60, 156
Bibliography of American Ethnology, 28
Bibliography of Nonprint Instructional Materials on the American Indian, 26, 27
Big Sky, The, 169
Bird of Passage, 135
Black Elk Speaks, 181
Black Elk Speaks: Being the Life Story of a Holy Man of the Oglala Sioux, 6, 46, 71, 227
Black Hawk: An Autobiography, 210
Black Hawk Songs, The, 47, 96
Blackfoot Lodge Tales, 101

Blazing Hills, The, 124
Blue Jacket: War Chief of the Shawnees, 200
Book of Indian Crafts and Indian Lore, The, 346
Book of Indian Life Crafts, 346
Book of the American Indian, The, 168
Book of the Hopi, 63, 318
Books on American Indians and Eskimos: A Selection Guide for Children and Young Adults, 32
Border Towns of the Navajo Nation, 354
Bows and Arrows, 301
Boy of Taché, A, 320
Brave Eagle's Account of the Fetterman Fight: 21 December 1866, 239
Braves and Buffalo: Plains Indian Life in 1837, 300
Bread-and-Butter Indian, 120
Broken Arrow, 19, 138
Broken Hoop: The History of Native Americans from 1600 to 1890, from the Atlantic Coast to the Plains, The, 245
Buffalo Bill, 201
Buffalo Chief, 137
Buffalo Hearts: A Native American's View of Indian Culture, Religion and History, 61, 68, 206
Buffalo Hunters, The, 270
Buffalo War: The History of the Red River Indian Uprising of 1874, The, 259
Buffalo Woman, 20, 172
Burning Glass, The, 146
Bury My Heart at Wounded Knee: An Indian History of the American West, 3, 253
By Cheyenne Campfires, 101

Camp Grant Massacre, The, 20, 22, 158
Can the Red Man Help the White Man? A Denver Conference with the Indian Elders, 333
Canadian Indians and the Law: Selected Documents, 1663-1972, 272
Captain of the Gray-Horse Troop, The, 168
Carriers of the Dream Wheel: Contemporary Native American Poetry, 57, 108
Cayuse Courage, 21, 148

Ceremony, 20, 60, 70, 181
Charbonneau, 160
Charlo's People: The Flathead Tribe of Montana, 51, 299
Cherokee, The, 280
Cherokee Sunset: A Nation Betrayed —A Narrative of Travail and Triumph, Persecution and Exile, 254
Cheyenne Autumn, 271
Cheyenne Memories, 61, 72, 273
Chichi Hoohoo Bogeyman, The, 60, 132
Chief, 139
Chief Joseph: War Chief of the Nez Perce, 188
Chief Tishomingo: A History of the Chickasaw Indians and Some Historical Events of Their Era (1737-1839), 250
Chiefs and Challengers: Indian Resistance and Cooperation in Southern California, 268
Child of the Hogan, 326
Child of the Navajos, 323
Children of the Sun: The Pueblos, Navajos, and Apaches of New Mexico, 294
Chippewa Indians, The, 280
Choctaw Boy, 321
Chronicles of American Indian Protest, 244
Cimarron, 167
Circle of Life: The Miccosukee Indian Way, 322
Circle of Seasons, 285
Claw Foot, 136
Cochise, 207
Collector's Guide to American Indian Artifacts, The, 287
Comanches: The Destruction of a People, 258
Come to Power: Eleven Contemporary American Indian Poets, 103
Compact History of the Indian Wars, The, 62, 274
Complete Book of Indian Crafts and Lore, The, 342
Conflict between the California Indian and White Civilization, The, 255
Conquering Horse, 6, 176
Contemporary American Indian Leaders, 26, 30
Contemporary Native American Address, 24, 104

Corn among the Indians of the Upper Missouri, 319
Corn Is Maize: The Gift of the Indians, 279
Corporation and the Indian: Tribal Sovereignty and Industrial Civilization in Indian Territory, 1865-1907, The, 267
Country of Strangers, A, 10, 153
Cowboy and Indian Trader, 232
Coyote Goes Hunting for Fire: A California Indian Myth, 78
Coyote Tales, 85
Crazy Horse and Custer, 251
Crazy Horse: Great Warrior of the Sioux, 6, 190
Crazy Horse: The Strange Man of the Oglalas, 6, 231
Crazy Weather, 19, 151
Crimson Moccasins, 141
Crow Indians, The, 281
Cry of the Thunderbird: The American Indian's Own Story, 102
Cultural Ecology: Readings on the Canadian Indians and Eskimos, 306
Custer Died for Your Sins: An Indian Manifesto, 15, 17, 18, 48, 74, 329

Dahcotah: Or Life and Legends of the Sioux around Fort Snelling, 100
Dakota Twilight: The Standing Rock Sioux, 1874-1890, 266
Dance Back the Buffalo, 175
Dance Hall of the Dead, 146
Dancing Gods: Indian Ceremonials of New Mexico and Arizona, 299
Dancing Stars: An Iroquois Legend, The, 88
Daughters of the Earth: The Lives and Legends of American Indian Women, 315
David, Young Chief of the Quileutes, 322
Death and Rebirth of the Seneca, The, 277
Death Comes for the Archbishop, 163
Death Song: The Last of the Indian Wars, 250
Decorative Art of the Southwestern Indians, 352
Deerslayer, The, 163
Delaware Indians, The, 281

Delight Makers, The, 73, 158
Demonic Vision: Racial Fantasy and Southern Fiction, 33
Dene Nation—The Colony Within, 335
Desert Is Theirs, The, 279
Disinherited: The Lost Birthright of the American Indian, 276
Dispossessing the American Indian, 263
Documents of United States Indian Policy, 269
Dog Story, 8, 53, 128
Dream of the Blue Heron, 114
Drums Along the Mohawk, 14, 165
Dwellers of the Tundra: Life in an Alaskan Eskimo Village, 291

Eagle Feather, 117
Earl Morris and Southwestern Archaeology, 222
Early Architecture in New Mexico, 348
Early Fur Trades, The, 260
Early Uses of California Plants, 303
Earth Namer: A California Indian Myth, 78
Edge of Two Worlds, 126
Education and the American Indian: The Road to Self-Determination, 1928-1973, 273
Education of Little Tree, The, 22, 47, 198
Education of the American Indians: A Survey of the Literature, The, 26, 27
Edward S. Curtis: Photographer of the North American Indian, 210
Elik and Other Stories of the MacKenzie Eskimos, 110
Encounter with an Angry God: Recollections of My Life with John Peabody Harrington, 219
Enemy Gods, The, 174
Eskimo Boyhood: An Autobiography in Psychosocial Perspective, 217
Eskimo Songs and Stories, 82
Everlasting Sky: New Voices from the People Named the Chippewa, The, 19, 63, 74, 327
Eye in the Forest, The, 73, 134

Famous American Indians of the Plains, 240
Famous Indian Chiefs, 193

Famous Indian Tribes, 241
Fawn, 153
Fifth World of Forster Bennett: Portrait of a Navaho, The, 306
Fifty Years on the Trail, 227
Fig Tree John, 8, 9, 164
Finding the Center: Narrative Poetry of the Zuni Indians, 111
Fire Bringer: A Paiute Indian Legend, The, 84
Fire Mate, 120
First Hundred Years of Niño Cochise, The, 213
First on the Land: The North Carolina Indians, 302
Fishermen, The, 240
Five Civilized Tribes, The, 258
Flap, 15, 171
Fodor's Indian America, 50, 331
Folklore of the North American Indians: An Annotated Bibliography, 34
Forked Tongues and Broken Treaties, 277
Four Centuries of Southern Indians, 261
Four-colored Hoop, The, 184
Four Corners of the Sky, 81
Fourth World, The, 54, 326
Fox Running, 147
Frederic Remington, 187
Frederic Remington: Artist of the Old West, 223
Friend and Foe: Aspects of French-Amerindian Cultural Contact in the Sixteenth and Seventeenth Centuries, 263
Friendly Wolf, The, 122
Fritz Scholder Lithographs, 23, 347
From the Deep Woods to Civilization: Chapters in the Autobiography of an Indian, 49, 213

Games the Indians Played, The, 292
Geronimo Campaign, The, 257
Geronimo: His Own Story, 208
Geronimo, the Last Apache War Chief, 208
Geronimo: Wolf of the Warpath, 13, 192
Gila: River of the Southwest, The, 255
Girl Named Wendy, A, 139
Go Away Thunder, 182
Goat in the Rug, The, 116

God Is Red, 48, 307
Gone to Texas, 162
Good Stones, 121
Goodbye to a River, 215
Gourd Dancer, The, 57, 107
Great Buffalo Hunt: Its History and Drama and Its Role in the Opening of the West, The, 259
Great Fish, The, 88
Great Indian Chiefs, 206
Great Leader of the Ojibway: Misquona-queb, 58, 230
Great North American Indians, 26, 29
Great upon the Mountain: Crazy Horse of America, 6, 211
Great White Buffalo, The, 7, 150
Guests Never Leave Hungry: The Autobiography of James Sewid, a Kwakiutl Indian, 233
Guide to America's Indians, A, 332

Hah-Nee of the Cliff Dwellers, 116
Halfbreed, 47, 212
Handbook of the Indians of California, 311
Hanta Yo, 171
Hatter Fox, 170
Hawk, I'm Your Brother, 115
He-Who-Runs-Far, 122
Heroes of the American Indian, 195
High Elk's Treasure, 53, 60, 133
Higher Than the Arrow, 136
Historic Pottery of the Pueblo Indians, 1600–1880, 23, 349
History of the Indians of the United States, A, 256
Hokahey! American Indians Then and Now, 286
Hollow Mountains, The, 178
Home of the Red Man: Indian North America before Columbus, 73, 301
Horsecatcher, The, 7, 154
Horsemen of the Western Plateaus: The Nez Perce Indians, 281
Hosteen Klah: Navaho Medicine Man and Sand Painter, 228
House Made of Dawn, 9, 18, 20, 56, 70, 74, 177
How Carla Saw the Shalako God, 136
How Indians Really Lived, 297
How the Sun Made a Promise and Kept It: A Canadian Indian Myth, 78
Hunted Like a Wolf: The Story of the Seminole War, 4, 249

Hunters, The, 241
Hunters of the Black Swamp, 124
Hunting of the Buffalo, The, 252
Huronia: A History and Geography of the Huron Indians, 1600–1650, 260

I Am the Fire of Time: The Voices of Native American Women, 102
I Have Spoken: American History through the Voices of the Indians, 18, 96
I Heard the Owl Call My Name, 164
I Once Knew an Indian Woman, 188
I Will Fight No More Forever, 209
If You Lived with the Sioux Indians, 293
Ikwa of the Temple Mounds, 295
Images of American Indian Art, 347
In My Mother's House, 285
In the Days of Victorio: Recollections of a Warm Springs Apache, 208
In the Shadow of a Rainbow: The True Story of a Friendship between Man and Wolf, 53, 221
In the Trail of the Wind: American Indian Poems and Ritual Orations, 91
Index to Literature on the American Indian: 1970, 26
Indian America: The Black Hawk War, 246
Indian: America's Unfinished Business, The, 327
Indian and Free: A Contemporary Portrait of Life on a Chippewa Reservation, 321
Indian and His Horse, The, 287
Indian and the Buffalo, The, 287
Indian Annie: Kiowa Captive, 10, 14, 152
Indian Art of the Americas, 344
Indian Arts, 340
Indian Arts and Crafts: A Complete "How to" Guide to Southwestern Indian Handicrafts, 345
Indian Basket Weaving, 352
Indian Beadwork, 341
Indian Boyhood, 15, 49, 200
Indian Captive: The Story of Mary Jemison, 10, 127
Indian Chiefs, 189
Indian Corn and Other Gifts, 292
Indian Costumes, 288

Indian Festivals, 296
Indian Fishing and Camping, 288
Indian Folk Medicine Guide, The, 312
Indian Gallery: The Story of George Catlin, 202
Indian Games and Crafts, 341
Indian Harvests, 286
Indian Heart of Carrie Hodges, The, 131
Indian Heritage of America, The, 310
Indian Hill, 117
Indian Hunting, 288
Indian in America, The, 277
Indian in American Literature, The, 26, 31
Indian Legacy of Charles Bird King, The, 353
Indian Legends from the Northern Rockies, 97
Indian Legends of Canada, 97, 106
Indian Man: A Life of Oliver La Farge, 54, 223
Indian Medicine Man, The, 289
Indian Music Makers, 341
Indian Myths, or Legends, Traditions, and Symbols of the Aborigines of America, Compared with Those of Other Countries, Including Hindostan, Egypt, Persia, Assyria, and China, 100
Indian Names in Connecticut, 274
Indian Oratory, 112
Indian Paint, 138
Indian Paintbrush, 118
Indian Peace Medals in American History, 270
Indian Picture Writing, 342
Indian Population of New England in the Seventeenth Century, The, 306
Indian Rock Paintings of the Great Lakes, 343
Indian Sign Language, 289, 302
Indian Silver: Navajo and Pueblo Jewelers, 347
Indian Summer, 51, 325
Indian Tales, 91
Indian Tales of North America, 98
Indian Talk: Hand Signals of the North American Indian, 298
Indian Tipi, The, 345
Indian Tribes of the United States: Ethnic and Cultural Survival, The, 54, 265
Indian Warriors and Their Weapons, 290

Indian Women of the Western Morning: Their Life in Early America, 317
Indian Women: Thirteen Who Played a Part in the History of America from the Earliest Days to Now, 207
Indians, The, 243
Indians: A Play, 173
Indians and Other Americans: Two Ways of Life Meet, 17, 54, 74, 331
Indians and the Strangers, The, 190
Indians at Home, 290
Indians' Book: Songs and Legends of the American Indians, The, 348
Indians Knew, The, 294
Indians of California: A Critical Bibliography, The, 31
Indians of Northeastern America, The, 297
Indians of the Americas, 308
Indians of the Americas: The Long Hope, 254
Indians of the Eastern Woodlands, 295
Indians of the Longhouse: The Story of the Iroquois, 281
Indians of the Northwest Coast, 307
Indians of the Plains, 242, 312
Indians of the Southeast, 298
Indians of the Southwest: A Century of Development under the United States, The, 256
Indians of the Subarctic: A Critical Bibliography, The, 31
Indians on the Move, 290
Indian's Secret World, The, 290
Indians' Summer, 57, 178
Indians: The Urban Dilemma, 330
Inland Whale: Nine Stories Retold from California Indian Legends, The, 92
Invasion of America: Indians, Colonialism, and the Cant of Conquest, The, 264
Ishi in Two Worlds: A Biography of the Last Wild Indian in America, 218
Ishi, Last of His Tribe, 4, 204
Island of the Blue Dolphins, 129

Jennie Redbird Finds Her Friends, 137
Jewelry of the Prehistoric Southwest, 350
Jim Musco, 124

Jim Thorpe, 189
Jim Thorpe Story, The, 206
Jim Whitewolf: Life of a Kiowa
    Apache, 211
Jimmy Yellow Hawk, 53, 60, 133
John Billington: Friend of Squanto,
    118
John Ross: Cherokee Chief, 226
Johnny Osage, 169
Journey to Ixtlan, 304
Journey to the People, 199
Judge of the Far North: The Memoirs
    of Jack Sissons, 234
Julie of the Wolves, 122
Just One Indian Boy, 10, 157

Kahtahah, 195
Kaibah: Recollections of a Navajo
    Girlhood, 16, 46, 198
Karnee: A Paiute Narrative, 18, 232
Katzimo, Mysterious Mesa, 143
Kevin Cloud: Chippewa Boy in the
    City, 320
Kit Carson's Autobiography, 212
Kiviok's Magic Journey: An Eskimo
    Legend, 84
Komantcia, 10, 14, 173
Kwi-na the Eagle and Other Indian
    Tales, 85

Lame Deer: Seeker of Visions, 217
Land of the Four Directions: A Por-
    trait of North American Indian
    Life Today, 333
Land Where the Sun Dies: A Novel
    of the Seminole Wars, The, 161
Last Americans: The Indian in Amer-
    ican Culture, The, 253
Last Frontier, The, 18, 166
Last of the Mohicans: A Narrative of
    1757, The, 163
Last Portage, 10, 228
Laughing Boy, 5, 174
League of the Iroquois, 315
Legends of a Lost Tribe: Folk Tales
    of the Beothuck Indians of New-
    foundland, 109
Legends of the Mighty Sioux, 113
Legends of Vancouver, 51, 102
Legends Told by the Old People, 51,
    92
Let Me Be a Free Man: A Documen-
    tary History of Indian Resistance,
    248

Life and Death of Yellow Bird, The,
    142
Life in a Narrow Place: The Havasu-
    pai of the Grand Canyon, 325
Light in the Forest, The, 10, 14, 19,
    153
Literature of the American Indian,
    110
Little Badger and the Fire Spirit, 80
Little Big Man, 70, 159
Little Owl Indian, 115
Lone Bull's Horse Raid, 122
Long Death: The Last Days of the
    Plains Indian, 3, 251
Long Man's Song, 20, 154
Longhouse Winter: Iroquois Trans-
    formation Tales, 85
Loon Feather, The, 143
Loon's Necklace, The, 89
Lutiapik, 205

Magic Medicines of the Indians, 319
Magic World: American Indian Songs
    and Poems, The, 5, 97
Man to Send Rain Clouds: Contem-
    porary Stories by American In-
    dians, The, 59, 179
Man Who Gave Thunder to the Earth:
    A Taos Way of Seeing and Under-
    standing, The, 158
Man Who Killed the Deer, The, 7, 9,
    63, 185
Man with the Silver Eyes, The, 135
Manabozho and the Bullrushes, 87
Man's Rise to Civilization, As Shown
    by the Indians of North America
    from Primeval Times to the Com-
    ing of the Industrial State, 73, 308
Many Winters: Prose and Poetry of
    the Pueblos, 90
Maria Martinez, 193
Maria Tallchief, 16, 196
Maria Tallchief: American Ballerina,
    189
Maria Tallchief, America's Prima Bal-
    lerina, 205
Maria: The Potter of San Ildefonso,
    16, 224
Masked Gods: Navaho and Pueblo
    Ceremonialism, 63, 318
Massacre at Fall Creek, The, 20, 186
Me and Mine: The Life Story of Hel-
    en Sekaquaptewa, 16, 233
Me, Cholay & Co.: Apache Warriors,
    22, 155

Medicine Man Who Went to School, The, 137
Meet the North American Indians, 294
Memoirs of a White Crow Indian, 221
Memoirs of Chief Red Fox, The, 206
Metal Weapons, Tools, and Ornaments of the Teton Dakota Indians, 299
Mexican Kickapoo Indians, The, 311
Michael Naranjo, 194
Middle Five: Indian Schoolboys of the Omaha Tribe, The, 4, 9, 18, 52, 219
Mimbres Painted Pottery, 347
Miracle Hill: The Story of a Navaho Boy, 56, 225
Mission Indians of California, The, 282
Moccasin Trail, 151
Modern Indian Psychology, 304
Modern Sioux, The, 315
Mohawk: The Life of Joseph Brant, 203
Moki, 7, 131
Moon of Popping Trees, 249
Morning Arrow, 49, 121
Mountain Man: A Novel of Male and Female in the Early American West, 167
Mountain Wolf Woman, Sister of Crashing Thunder: The Autobiography of a Winnebago Indian, 222
Mouse Woman and the Mischief-Makers, 83
Mrs. Mike: The Story of Katherine Mary Flannigan, 167
Mukat's People: The Cahuilla Indians of Southern California, 303
My Captivity among the Sioux Indians, 11, 23, 218
My Heart Soars, 50, 324
My Life as an Indian, 232
My People, the Sioux, 61, 236

Names: A Memoir, The, 22, 57, 226
Nancy Ward, Cherokee, 8, 190
Nannabah's Friend, 132
Native American Heritage, 309
Native American Historical Demography: A Critical Bibliography, 31
Native American Tribalism, 17, 54, 265
Native Americans: 500 Years After, 49, 324

Native Americans: The New Indian Resistance, 55, 74, 333
Native Peoples of Atlantic Canada, The, 265
Navaho, The, 310
Navaho Sister, 149
Navahos Have Five Fingers, 198
Navajo Biographies, 202
Navajo Bird Tales Told by Hosteen Clah Chee, 88
Navajo: Herders, Weavers, and Silversmiths, The, 282
Navajo Histories, 95
Navajo Saga, A, 4, 46, 72, 242
Navajos: A Critical Bibliography, The, 31
Navajos and the New Deal, The, 268
Never Step on an Indian's Shadow, 19, 22, 157
New Indians, The, 334
Newberry Library American Indian Bibliographical Series, The, 26, 31
No Foreign Land: The Biography of a North American Indian, 58, 229
No Turning Back: A True Account of a Hopi Indian Girl's Struggle to Bridge the Gap between the World of Her People and the World of the White Man, 9, 16, 229
Nobody Loves a Drunken Indian. See Flap
Normie's Moose Hunt, 120
North American Indian Arts, 353
Nu Mee Poom Tit Wah Tit: Nez Perce Legends, 60, 111
Number Four, 141

Of Utmost Good Faith, 48, 257
Oglala Religion, 316
Ojibwa Woman, The, 311
Ojibwas: A Critical Bibliography, The, 31
Ojibway Heritage, 51, 102
Ojimite's Journey, 339
O-kee-pa: A Religious Ceremony and Other Customs of the Mandans, 305
Old Fish Hawk, 172
Old North Trail: Or Life, Legends and Religion of the Blackfeet Indians, The, 313
On the Gleaming Way: Navajos, Eastern Pueblos, Zunis, Hopis, Apaches, and Their Land—And Their Meanings to the World, 329

Once More upon a Totem, 83
One Flew over the Cuckoo's Nest, 173
One Small Blue Bead, 132
One Smart Indian, 180
Only Land I Know: A History of the Lumbee Indians, The, 48, 257
Only the Names Remain: The Cherokees and the Trail of Tears, 239
Ordeal of John Gyles, The, 236
Ordeal of Running Standing, The, 9, 166
Ordeal of the Young Hunter, The, 150
Oscar Howe, 192
Our Brother's Keeper: The Indian in White America, 55, 328
Our Cup Is Broken, 176
Our Fathers Had Powerful Songs, 77
Owl in the Cedar Tree, 56, 128
Owl's Song, The, 10, 21, 50, 144

Paddle-to-the-Sea, 126
Paint the Wind, 216
Painted Pony Runs Away: As Little Elk Tells It in Indian Picture Writing, 128
Patrick des Jarlait: The Story of an American Indian Artist, 197
Patriot Chiefs: A Chronicle of American Indian Resistance, The, 204
Pawnee Hero Stories and Folk Tales, with Notes on the Origin, Customs and Character of the Pawnee People, 101
People and Places, 314
People of the Dream, 142
People of the First Man: Life among the Plains Indians in Their Final Days of Glory—The Firsthand Account of Prince Maximilian's Expedition up the Missouri River, 1833-34, 317
Peyote, 314
Peyote Cult, The, 73, 311
Pictographic History of the Oglala Sioux, A, 252
Pictorial History of the American Indian, A, 249
Pima Indian Legends, 59, 69, 94
Pima Remembers, A, 237
Pitseolak: Pictures out of My Life, 200
Plains Apache, The, 274
Plains Indian Mythology, 105
Plains Indians, The, 259

Plenty-Coups: Chief of the Crows, 222
Plural Society in the Southwest, 272
Pocahontas, 238
Pocahontas and the Strangers, 187
Pontiac, King of the Great Lakes, 203
Population of the California Indians, 1769-1970, The, 306
Potawatomi Indian Summer, 130
Potlatch Family, The, 21, 149
Pottery of San Ildefonso Pueblo, The, 348
Prehistoric Rock Art of Nevada and Eastern California, 350
Preliminary Bibliography of Selected Children's Books about American Indians, A, 68
Prisoner of the Mound Builders, 125
Proud Warrior: The Story of Black Hawk, 204
Pueblo Indians, The, 59, 316
Pueblo Indians: Farmers of the Rio Grande, The, 283
Pumpkin Seed Point, 63, 237

Rain Dance People: The Pueblo Indians, Their Past and Present, The, 244
Ramona, 15, 172
Rattlesnake Cave, 127
Raven: A Collection of Woodcuts, 81
Raven and the Redbird, The, 170
Raven's Cry, 144
Recollections of an Assiniboine Chief, 218
Reconstruction in Indian Territory: A Story of Avarice, Discrimination, and Opportunism, 251
Red Children in White America, 27
Red Cloud, 54, 191
Red Cloud and the Sioux Problem, 267
Red Cloud: Sioux War Chief, 197
Red Cloud's Folk: A History of the Oglala Sioux Indians, 261
Red Hawk's Account of Custer's Last Battle, 240
Red Man in Art, The, 338
Red Man's America: A History of the Indians in the United States, 275
Red Power on the Rio Grande: The Native American Revolution of 1680, 245
Red Power: The American Indians' Fight for Freedom, 332

Red Shadows: The History of Native Americans from 1600 to 1900, from the Desert to the Pacific Cost, 246

Red Swan: Myths and Tales of the American Indians, The, 96

Red World and White: Memories of a Chippewa Boyhood, 59, 231

Reference Encyclopedia of the American Indian, 32

Respect for Life: Report of a Conference at Harper's Ferry, West Virginia, on the Traditional Upbringing of American Indian Children, 314

Return of the Vanishing American, The, 26, 29

Riding the Earthboy 40, 63, 112

Rifles for Watie, 147

Right to Be Indian, The, 326

Ring in the Prairie, The, 79

Road to Wounded Knee, The, 328

Roanoke: A Novel of the Lost Colony, 150

Rock Art of the American Indian, 349

Rock Paintings of the Chumash: A Study of a California Indian Culture, The, 349

Rolling Thunder, 210

Run toward the Nightland: Magic of the Oklahoma Cherokees, 52, 103

Runner in the Sun: A Story of Indian Maize, 7, 54, 70, 73, 152

Sacred Legends of the Sandy Lake Cree, 109

Sacred Pipe: Black Elk's Account of the Seven Rites of the Oglala Sioux, The, 46, 73, 303

Sage Smoke: Tales of the Shoshoni-Bannock Indians, 83

Salinan Indians of California and Their Neighbors, 298

Sandpaintings of the Navajo Shooting Chant, 352

Santa Clara Pottery Today, 351

Savagism and Civilization: A Study of the Indian and the American Mind, 12, 26, 33

Saynday's People: The Kiowa Indians and the Stories They Told, 93

Scoouwa: James Smith's Indian Captivity Narrative, 11, 235

Sea Hunters: Indians of the Northwest Coast, The, 283

Search for Charlie, The, 121

Search for the Crescent Moon, 140

Searching for America, 26, 32

Secret in the Stlalakum Wild, 125

Sedna: An Eskimo Myth, 86

Seeds of Extinction: Jeffersonian Philanthropy and the American Indian, 271

Seminole, 179

Seminole: A Drama of the Florida Indian, 179

Seminole Indians, The, 283

Seminoles, The, 266

Seneca Hostage, The, 14, 184

Separate Reality, A, 304

Sequoyah, 214

Sequoyah: Leader of the Cherokees, 192

Sequoyah: The Cherokee Who Captured Words, 195

Seven Arrows, 182

Seven Families in Pueblo Pottery, 351

Shadows from the Singing House: Eskimo Folk Tales, 80

Shaking the Pumpkin: Traditional Poetry of the Indian North Americas, 110

Shawnee, The, 305

Shining Trail, The, 168

Shoot an Arrow to Stop the Wind, 183

Short History of the Indians of the United States, A, 249

Sidewalk Indian, 141

Sing Down the Moon, 129

Singing for Power: The Song Magic of the Papago Indians of Southern Arizona, 112

Sioux Are Coming, The, 131

Sioux Buffalo Hunters, 295

Sioux Indians, The, 284

Sioux Today, The, 53, 325

Sister to the Sioux: The Memoirs of Elaine Goodale Eastman, 1885-91, 22, 214

Sitting Bull: Champion of His People, 4, 202

Sitting Bull: Champion of the Sioux, 4, 237

Sitting Bull: War Chief of the Sioux, 194

Sitting on the Blue-Eyed Bear: Navajo Myths and Legends, 92

Six Days from Sunday, 116

Sky Clears: Poetry of the American Indians, The, 98

Sky Man on the Totem Pole?, 145
Small Wolf, 115
Smoke from Their Fires: The Life of
a Kwakiutl Chief, 214
Snow Walker, The, 177
Some People Are Indians, 139
Son of Old Man Hat: A Navaho Au-
tobiography, 221
Song from the Earth: American In-
dian Painting, 23, 350
Songs of the Chippewa, 338
Songs of the Dream People, 84
Soul Catcher, 170
Soul of an Indian, The, 15, 49, 73,
29, 299
Sound of Flutes and Other Indian
Legends, The, 82
Southwestern Weaving, 352
Speaking of Indians, 300
Spider, the Cave and the Pottery
Bowl, The, 119
Spin a Silver Dollar: The Story of a
Desert Trading-Post, 216
Spotted Flower and the Ponokomita,
8, 47, 119
Spotted Tail's Folk: A History of the
Brulé Sioux, 262
Stay Away, Joe, 70, 165
Stephannie and the Coyote, 321
Story Catcher, The, 7, 155
Story of Hiawatha, The, 80
Story of the Totem Pole, The, 284
Storytelling Stone: Myths and Tales
of the American Indians, The, 12,
91
Stranger and Afraid, A, 114
Studies in Southeastern Indian Lan-
guages, 307
Summer Maker: An Ojibway Indian
Myth, The, 79
Sun Chief: Autobiography of a Hopi,
234
Sun Dance People: The Plains In-
dians, Their Past and Present, The,
244
Sun in the Sky: The Hopi Indians of
the Arizona Mesa Lands, 300
Surrounded, The, 54, 70, 176
Susette La Flesche: Voice of the O-
maha Indians, 8, 199
Sword of the Wilderness, 10, 140

Tales from the Igloo, 93
Tales of Power, 304
Tales of the North American Indians,
12, 111
Tanaina Tales from Alaska, 62, 95
Taos Indians and Their Sacred Blue
Lake, The, 74, 322

Tapestries in Sand: The Spirit of In-
dian Sandpainting, 353
Teachings from the American Earth:
Indian Religion and Philosophy,
316
Teachings of Don Juan, The, 305
Tecumseh and His Times, 57, 229
Tecumseh and the Indian Confedera-
tion, 1811–1813: The Indian Na-
tions East of the Mississippi Are
Defeated, 247
Tecumseh: Destiny's Warrior, 199
Tell Them They Lie: The Sequoyah
Myth, 236
Tell Them Willie Boy Is Here, 220
Temptations of Big Bear, The, 20,
70, 186
Ten Grandmothers, The, 16, 313
Tendoy: Chief of the Lemhis, 213
Textbooks and the American Indian,
26, 28, 68
There Is My People Sleeping, 61, 94
These Were the Sioux, 301
They Came Here First: The Epic of
the American Indian, 54, 265
They Put on Masks, 337
This Country Was Ours: A Documen-
tary History of the American In-
dian, 276
This Land Was Theirs: A Study of
the North American Indian, 17,
267
Three Perspectives on Ethnicity:
Blacks, Chicanos, and Native A-
mericans, 255
Three Years among the Comanches:
The Narrative of Nelson Lee, the
Texas Ranger, 220
Tinker and the Medicine Men: The
Story of a Navajo Boy of Monu-
ment Valley, 323
Tisha: The Story of a Young Teacher
in the Alaskan Wilderness, 235
To Make My Name Good: A Re-
Examination of the Southern
Kwakiutl Potlatch, 308
To Serve the Devil, 262
To Spoil the Sun, 20, 21, 154
Top of the World, 180
Touch the Earth: A Self-Portrait of
Indian Existence, 104
Towappu: A Puritan Renegade, 156
Tragedy Strikes at Wounded Knee
and Other Essays on Indian Life
in South Dakota and Nebraska,
272
Trail of Tears: The Story of the
American Indian Removals, 1813–
1855, The, 264

Trees Stand Shining: Poetry of the North American Indians, The, 86
Tribal Scenes and Ceremonies, 327
Tribes of California, 315
Trickster: A Study in American Indian Mythology, The, 109
Truth about Geronimo, The, 256
Truth of a Hopi, 108
Tsali, 209
Twilight of the Sioux: The Song of the Indian Wars; The Song of the Messiah, The, 107
Two Great Scouts and Their Pawnee Battalion, 23, 215
Two Leggings: The Making of a Crow Warrior, 226

Uncle Sam's Stepchildren: The Reformation of United States Indian Policy, 1865-1887, 268
Uses of Plants by the Indians of the Missouri River Region, 310

Valley of the Shadow, The, 125
Vanishing American, The, 17
Vanishing Race: Selections from Edward S. Curtis' *The North American Indian*, The, 309
Vanishing White Man, The, 334
Vengeance Trail of Josey Wales, The, 162
Very Small Remnant, A, 4, 183
Village Indians of the Upper Missouri: The Mandans, Hidatsas, and Arikaras, The, 266
Voices from Wah'Kon-Tah: Contemporary Poetry of Native Americans, 99
Voices from Wounded Knee, 1973, 323
Voices of Earth and Sky: Vision Search of the Native Americans, 297
Voices of the Plains Cree, 45, 296

Wah'Kon-Tah: The Osage and the White Man's Road, 55, 224
Walk in Beauty: The Navajo and Their Blankets, 343
Walk in My Moccasins, 136
Walk in the Sky, 146
Walks Far Woman, 183
Wampum, 293
War Chief Joseph, 203
War Drums at Eden Prairie, 129
War with the Seminoles: 1835-1842, 248
Warrior Who Killed Custer, The, 216

Warriors of the Rainbow: Strange and Prophetic Dreams of the Indian Peoples, 238
Waterless Mountain, 138
Way: An Indian Anthology of American Indian Literature, The, 18, 113
Way of Our People, The, 123
Way to Rainy Mountain, The, 57, 93
We Have Not Vanished: Eastern Indians of the United States, 323
We Rode the Wind: Recollections of Nineteenth-Century Tribal Life, 191
We Talk, You Listen: New Tribes, New Turf, 48, 74, 330
West with the White Chiefs, 145
Whale People, The, 143
What They Used to Tell About: Indian Legends from Labrador, 99
When Clay Sings, 338
When Shall They Rest? The Cherokees' Long Struggle with America, 243
When the Corn Is Red, 88
When the Legends Die, 5, 8, 9, 70, 160
When the Tree Flowered: A Fictional Autobiography of Eagle Voice, a Sioux Indian, 5, 178
When Thunders Spoke, 60, 134
Whirling Rainbows, 135
Whirlwind Is a Ghost Dancing, 77
Whispering Trees, 10, 126
Whispering Wind: Poetry by Young American Indians, The, 50, 90
White Captives, 22, 149
White Falcon, 11
White Falcon: An Indian Boy in Early America, 21, 156
White Man's Road, The, 140
White on Red, 27
White Shadows among the Mighty Sioux, 161
Who Discovered America? Settlers and Explorers of the New World before the Time of Columbus, 73, 291
Why Gone Those Times? Blackfoot Tales, 94
Why the Beaver Has a Broad Tail, 82
Wild Runners, The, 142
William Beltz, 197
William Warren: The Story of an American Indian, 45, 187
Wind over Wisconsin, 165
Windigo and Other Tales of the Ojibways, 94
Windsinger, 169

Winged Moccasins: The Story of
Sacajawea, 201
Winter in the Blood, 20, 63, 70, 185
Winter-Telling Stories, 87
Winter Wife: An Abenaki Folktale,
The, 81
Without Reserve, 212
Wizards and Wampum: Legends of
the Iroquois, 89
Wolf and the Raven: Totem Poles of
Southeastern Alaska, The, 344
Wolf Brother, 147
Wolf That I Am: In Search of the
Red Earth People, 104
Woman Chief, 8, 134
Woman of the People, A, 10, 161
Women of the West, 292
Wooden Leg: A Warrior Who Fought
Custer, 224
Wordarrows: Indians and Whites in
the New Fur Trade, 63, 335
Worlds between Two Rivers: Per-

spectives on American Indians in
Iowa, The, 252
World's Rim: Great Mysteries of the
North American Indians, The, 302
Wounded Knee: An Indian History
of the American West, 243
Wrath of Coyote, The, 152
Writer and the Shaman: A Morphol-
ogy of the American Indian, The,
26, 34

Yaqui Life, A, 225
Year of Small Shadow, The, 127
Year of the Three-Legged Deer, The,
119
Yellow Leaf, 118
Yemassee: A Romance of Carolina,
182
Yes is Better Than No, 20, 159
Yurok Myths, 103

Zia, 130
Zunis: Self-Portrayals, The, 113

# Authors

Anna Lee Stensland is Professor of English and Chair of the English Department, University of Minnesota, Duluth. She received her doctorate in English Education from the University of Wisconsin at Madison and has taught at Dakota Wesleyan College and Stout State College, Wisconsin. Stensland is currently the editor of *Minnesota English Journal* and is the author of a number of journal articles on American Indian literature and culture.

Aune M. Fadum, Assistant Professor of Elementary Education at the University of Minnesota, Duluth, received her masters degree from that institution in 1969. From 1965-1968 she taught elementary school on the Nett Lake Reservation, Minnesota. In 1975 Fadum served as a reading consultant for the Duluth Indian Education Advisory Committee which developed the *Anishinabe Reading Materials*. She has also worked with the Grand Portage Indian Project to develop bilingual reading materials based on oral legends of the Chippewa Indians.